*A Gust for Paradise*

Jan Theodore de Bry, after Maerten de Vos. God Speaking to Adam and Eve.
Photo © Museum Plantin-Moretus and Print Room, Antwerp.

# A
# GUST FOR
# Paradise

## MILTON'S EDEN
## AND THE
## VISUAL ARTS

DIANE KELSEY MCCOLLEY

UNIVERSITY OF ILLINOIS PRESS
URBANA AND CHICAGO

Publication of this work has been supported in part by grants from the Research Council of Rutgers, the State University of New Jersey.

*The book is printed on acid-free paper.*

Library of Congress Cataloging-in-Publication Data
McColley, Diane Kelsey, 1934–
  A gust for paradise : Milton's Eden and the visual arts / Diane Kelsey McColley.
      p.   cm.
  Includes bibliographical references and index.
  ISBN 0-252-01828-1 (cl)
    1. Milton, John, 1608–1674. Paradise lost.   2. Adam (Biblical figure) in fiction, drama, poetry, etc.   3. Eve (Biblical figure) in fiction, drama, poetry, etc.   4. Bible. O.T. Genesis II, 4–III, 24—Illustrations.   5. Art and literature—England—History—17th century.   6. Milton, John, 1608–1674—Knowledge—Art.   7. Paradise in literature.   8. Eden in literature.   9. Paradise in art. 10. Eden in art.   I. Title.
PR3562.M19   1993
821' .4—dc20                 #25747851                  92-13654
                                                          CIP

Permissions to incorporate previously published matter have been granted by the editors and publishers of the following: " 'Tongues of Men and Angels': *Ad Leonoram Romae Canentem*," in *Urbane Milton: The Latin Poetry,* ed. James A. Freeman and Anthony Low (*Milton Studies* 19 [1984]); "The Iconography of Eden," in *Milton Studies* 24 (1988): 107–21; "Eve and the Arts of Eden," in *Milton and the Idea of Woman,* ed. Julia M. Walker (Urbana: University of Illinois Press, 1988); and "Edenic Iconography: *Paradise Lost* and the Mosaics of San Marco," in *Milton in Italy: Contexts, Images, Contradictions,* ed. Mario A. Di Cesare, Medieval & Renaissance Texts & Studies, vol. 90 (Binghamton, N.Y., 1991), pp. 197–214. Copyright, Center for Medieval and Early Renaissance Studies, SUNY Binghamton.

# Contents

# Illustrations

# Notes on Editions and Abbreviations

All parenthetical citations are to John Milton, *Paradise Lost: A Poem in Twelve Books,* ed. Merritt Y. Hughes (New York: Odessey Press, 1962).

AV    The Holy Bible: Authorized ("King James") Version, first published 1611. Quotations not otherwise cited are from this version.

BCP    Church of England: Book of Common Prayer. I have used the Folger edition of the 1559 prayer book, ed. John C. Booty (Washington: Folger Books, 1976) conferred with the 1604 and 1626 editions. For the psalter, which the Folger edition omits, I have used the modern spelling of the 1928 American edition, as revised in 1953. Psalms are numbered as in AV and BCP, with Vulgate numbering in parentheses as needed.

CM    *The Works of John Milton,* general editor Frank Allen Patterson, 18 vols. plus index (New York: Columbia University Press, 1931–40); esp. vol. 17, ed. James Holly Hanford and Waldo Hilary Dunn, and vol. 18, ed. Thomas Ollive Mabbott and J. Milton French.

EETS    Early English Text Society

MQ    *Milton Quarterly*

MS    *Milton Studies*

SM    *The Student's Milton,* ed. Frank Allen Patterson (New York: Appleton-Century-Crofts, rev. ed., 1933, rpt. 1961). Apart from *Paradise Lost,* quotations from Milton's works not otherwise cited are from this edition.

YP    *Complete Prose Works of John Milton,* general editor Don M. Wolfe, 8 vols. (New Haven: Yale University Press, 1953–82), esp.:

Vol. 1 (1624–42), ed. Don M. Wolfe (1953)
Vol. 2 (1643–48), ed. Ernest Sirluck (1959)
Vol. 6 (c. 1658–60) ed. Maurice Kelley (1973)
Vol. 7 (1659–60), ed. Robert W. Ayers (rev. ed., 1980)

Note on orthography: I have retained the spellings of editions cited but altered forms of letters no longer used in English print.

# Preface

This multidisciplinary study addresses interpretations of the first three chapters of Genesis in *Paradise Lost* and other seventeenth-century English poems and in their cultural contexts from the Middle Ages through the Reformation. It considers the arts of Eden in two ways. The first is topical: it discusses poems, visual images, and music concerned with divine and human creativity. The second is ethical: it interprets these works as patterns for the creation of the arts and the preservation of the earth. The central topos is the "daily work of body or mind" of Adam and Eve in *Paradise Lost* as primal artists and care-takers of nature, engaged in creative activities that knit communities, communicate joy, and could be done forever without harming the earth or the least of its lodgers. The arts it considers cultivate aware-ness of the concinnity of creation: a consciousness not only linear and binary but radiant and multiple; not only monodic but also choral. Seventeenth-century English poetry allied to Genesis nourishes this Edenic awareness, not only by its topics but also by the nature of its language, which weaves sound, image, metaphor, and concept as closely as nature weaves life, and so exercises our sense of connections. Its visual and musical contexts interconnect with it.

As a reader of the manuscript remarked, the volume is really two books in one: an account of the iconography of Eden in the visual arts and an account of prelapsarian life, rather than the lapse of conscience called the Fall, as the beginning of civilized arts, especially in *Paradise Lost*. I have combined them in order to suggest multiple connections, a process which, apart from being necessary to contextual criticism, is essential to the topic of Edenic thought. Both visual artists and poets of the seventeenth-century reimagine Eden, and so re-Edenize the imagination. For readers primarily interested in Milton, I hope to supply new or extended interpretations of *Paradise Lost,* and also ex-amples of a lively and varied visual environment that provide clues to his charitable choices and iconoclasms and enrich one's many-leveled engagement with his epic. For those interested primarily in the visual arts, I hope to provide examples and interpretations of insufficiently recognized topics and motifs, and also to show what became of them in the imagination of a master poet whose work energizes our responses to other arts and experiences and who makes the prototypical man and woman not only products of art and consumers of natural abundance but producers of both. A corollary purpose is to expose popular slanders against religious art that result from theory rather than observation.

The research recorded here grew out of love for Milton's depiction of an energetic "state of innocence" and a desire to know whether the topos of original righteousness also appeared in the visual arts of his time. A survey of reference books and direct questions to art historians produced a short answer: no. Delvings in rare book and print collections produced a more complicated one. A few artists in the seventeenth century, and even fewer before that, did depict Adam and Eve in felicity before the Fall. Unlike Milton, they did not show them tending trees, making love, or singing, but they did show them conversing, joining hands, or praying. In addition, many who adhered to the biblical events did so in such loving detail, with such brightness, tenderness, and strength, as to constitute a celebration of creation, and some included motifs clearly pointing to the possibilities of regenerate life on a damaged but reparable planet. These commendations of primal life suggest not an escape from difficulty, as so many unimaginative minds have supposed paradise to be, but a re-creation of the possibilities of Edenic consciousness and conduct, not without labor and pain but with hope for earth as well as heaven. They are engaging in themselves and interesting in relation to Milton: among the throngs of artists and poets who treated the Genesis story, many saw it as an occasion for rejoicing in creation, some saw it as a pattern for rehabilitation, and one saw in it an opportunity to show a man and a woman living spirited, productive, and imitable lives in harmony with God, each other, and the animal and vegetable creation in their charge.

Having found that the topic exists in the visual arts after all, I turned to music and collected psalms, canticles, and anthems that celebrate creation imagery by mimetic re-creation of what Milton in "At a Solemn Musick" called "the fair musick that all creatures made." This part of the project outgrew the bounds of one book, but I have included observations on the interillumination of words and music that resonates in seventeenth-century poetry and especially in the morning hymn of Milton's Adam and Eve.

In poetry and drama, one can find in treatments of "Our First Parents" some glowing abstractions and occasional interesting details about life before the Fall, but apart from Milton most prove rhapsodic, rather than usefully mimetic, and are marred by misogynous implications about original vanity in the Mother of Us All that Milton was careful to question or remove. However, the creation imagery of seventeenth-century lyrics and hexameral commentaries, especially by Browne, Donne, Herbert, Marvell, and Traherne, respects God's work and the capacity of human beings to respond to grace and salvage the wreckage called the Fall.

These chapters gather connections among poetry, iconography, music, natural history, theology, and government. The first chapter addresses ethical perspectives and current issues in literary criticism. It is, I confess, sometimes tendentious and occasionally irked. Chapters 2 and 3 trace themes of the Genesis creation story in the visual arts from the monuments and manuscripts of the Middle Ages to Bible illustrations and engravings of the sixteenth and seventeenth centuries, and consider their moral and ecological implications. This section has two primary purposes, one Miltonic and the other more general. It uses visual analogues to support Milton's account of the prelapsarian and regenerate experience of Adam and Eve, as well as to show how far beyond other representations he goes; and it also addresses the Genesis story in the arts more generally in order, I hope, to show what the attacks on it in current criticism are missing. I have therefore included a few motifs not directly pertinent to Milton, but within the regenerative treatment of Genesis that culminates in *Paradise Lost*. Chapters 4 through 6 concern Milton's work and, to a small extent, other creation poetry. The fourth chapter shows how the Genesis tradition in the arts flows into *Paradise Lost* and is transformed by it, with special attention to the creation of the arts of language and music by Adam and Eve. The fifth questions recent versions of the "fortunate fall" as the beginning of human maturity and moral understanding or of civilized arts and pleasures, and discusses the arts of government and the development of conscience in the unfallen colloquies of Milton's Adam and Eve. The sixth concerns human work, the possibilities of Edenic technology, the care of the earth—another topic exceeding the bounds of one book—and the relations of the sexes within a resplendent cosmos.

My purpose in using visual contexts is not to prove the "influence" of particular examples, but to provide a gallery of works that share with Milton and other English poets a positive attitude toward the whole creation, including Eve; a clear rejection of any notion of the

fortunateness of the sin itself; and a hopeful opinion of divinely renewed opportunities not only for redemption in the long run but also
for reparation in present experience. This tradition is embodied in images of the first man and the first woman and the Garden they were
given to till and keep that encourage the work of renewal in the whole
race they represent. Seeing how Milton culminated this confluence
does not diminish his originality, but shows by many contrasts how
innovative he was.

Relating poetry and the visual arts is a risky undertaking, especially
with regard to a time of fervent iconoclasm and a poet of the Word
who, both before and during his blindness, wrote by inward light. The
images reproduced here are not intended to interfere with the reader's
imagining of *Paradise Lost* or any other poem. That kind of "influence"
would violate the principle on which Milton objected to fixed forms of
prayer or merely customary opinions. Milton did not favor icons, but
he crafted images and verbal music that open perceptual and spiritual
eyes and ears. The imagination needs to be free to create images in
response to the poem, and to enhance them at each re-reading. But this
freedom is already hampered by current prejudices, which favor some
artistic representations of Genesis and neglect others. Awareness of a
poem's visual environment affects the tones we hear in it, and the more
we recognize the variety within that environment, the more nuanced
our reading can be. It is with the hope, not of nominating particular
images to illustrate paradise, but of freeing the imagination by suggesting their diversity, with special attention to kinds that seem little
noticed now, that I have collected the pictures in this volume.

The matter of Genesis touches mythic depths. At the same time, it
is most striking in the arts when treated most literally. Although many
critics and feminist readers prefer the "priestly" account of Genesis,
with its magnificent creation hymn and its simultaneous creation of
male and female, visual artists work in wood, stone, glass, metal, and
paint, and love the miracle of an earnest and compassionate Creator
molding a beautiful human being from earth or bone. The poetry of
re-creation rejoices in pure light, but the light also falls on faces, feet,
fingers, feathers, and fins. Hymns and psalms "know the way to heav-
en's door," as Herbert says, but they are made of pitch, pulse, breath,
and infinite fresh ways of setting familiar words.

Three approaches to Genesis that have received much attention are
not included here. First, I have not used the language of biblical textual
criticism, because that was not the approach to Scripture taken by
those artists and poets with whose work I am concerned. Most
seventeenth-century readers believed that Genesis was written down

by Moses, under the guidance of the Holy Ghost, helped by a carefully cherished oral tradition that went back to Adam himself. Milton acknowledged problems of transmission of biblical texts, but believed the texts perspicuous to every reader who is guided by the Spirit. Second, I have not much engaged in comparative mythology. Apart from certain symbols derived from Egyptian hieroglyphs and a few motifs from classical myth, nonbiblical creation stories do not appear to have greatly affected the work of the artists and writers with whom I am primarily concerned. Apocryphal and pseudepigraphal works occasionally pertain, especially those apocryphal books retained in the English Bible and lectionary as wisdom, not dogma. But most were subordinated by the artists and English poets represented here for the same reasons that they were excluded from the canonical Scriptures: inauthenticity of language or eccentricity of doctrine. In the establishment of the biblical canon, the most misogynous candidates were omitted, as were Gnostic interpretations of the origins of evil and the meaning of "forbidden knowledge." Third, I have not psychologized the Genesis story. Bible readers in Milton's time were eager to alter their lives in the light of the Word, but very circumspect about reversing that application.

Part of the motive for this study is a set of recurrent catchphrases I hear among students, colleagues, and the population at large. One is that there is no good without evil. This assumption, I felt, ought to be examined. It may have some truth as an observation of the way things are, but as a philosophical shrug it can be mischievous, and as an assertion that evil is necessary for goodness to function, it can be dangerous. Good, as represented in the arts considered here, increases by combating evil, and the benefits of a creation that admits the rebellious and chaotic are part of the justification of God's ways. But goodness would have plenty else to do if evil did not keep getting in the way, as it is likely to do to excess if one depends on enmity as the spur of virtue rather than choosing good for its own sake.

Another such dubious premise in popular commentary is that Western religion radically separates the human from the divine. I hope that the verbal and visual images in this study will help to modify this concept.

Yet another is the common saying that we cannot return to Eden, and the literary critical one that any recovery of innocence we might experience through art is illusory. That we have to live with evil within us and round us Milton certainly affirmed. He called regenerate life "sharp tribulation" and had no patience with people who imagined themselves perfect already. But the poetry and art collected here

dispute the idea that innocence—that is, not-nocence, harmlessness toward other creatures—is impossible at all. Its reparation is part of humanity's primary work. Not-nocence is the opposite of naiveté. It
requires a sufficiently complex grasp of a complex world of interconnected lives, and of the reverberations of each action and inaction, to
render us responsible toward them. It is partly because that level of
consciousness, or Edenic conscience, is so difficult to maintain that
"fallen" humanity cannot live Edenically. Despite the deservedly famous demonstration of Stanley Fish that *Paradise Lost* is designed to
expose the reader's guiltiness, its further, fuller effect is to increase the
reader's fund, however wanting, of that complex awareness that enables right action. Certainly, we cannot go *back* to Eden, but Milton
and like-minded artists can help form in the mind a patch of innocence
in which to labor to restore such a complex consciousness, both for the
sake of present justice and, in their view, to go *forward* toward the time
when a purged and renewed earth—the Archangel Michael says to
Milton's Adam—"Shall all be Paradise." In this view, humane civilization is not founded on conflict, in the sense of Marx or Foucault,
but on what is basically and recoverably human in humanity.

But the principal object of my iconoclasm is the cliché that life in
paradise would be dull. That assertion seems to me patently untrue of
Milton's paradise, where the forms of goodness are endlessly diverse
and expansible, and of any other well-imagined scene of well-doing.
It is Satan's hate that flattens variegated vitality into trifling banality.
Yet there appears to be a curious lack of faith in, or even desire
for, undefiled joy in the modern world, a sense that a life of rampant
blessedness would be less interesting than one providing warfare
against, or tolerance of, or opportunity for, every vice. These assumptions—that virtue depends on the failures of others (and righteousness is therefore uncompassionate and unattractive), that Western
spirituality divides humanity and divinity, and that goodness and
blessedness are impossible or, worse, uninteresting—are chimeras I
nominate for disposal.

This study is the result of much wandering in realms of paper, pig-
ment, stone, and song, and many people gave help and friendship
along the way. The Research Council of Rutgers, the State University
of New Jersey, provided two one-semester leaves, grants-in-aid for research expenses, photographs, and copyright fees, and partial subven-
tion of publication. Kathleen Swaim made useful recommendations
on the first three chapters while they were still in a state of chaos.
Debra Ollikkalla both amended the musical sections and provided
musical exierence. Winifred Hodge, an environmental scientist,

commented helpfully on portions of an early draft. Librarians who gave special aid include Mervin Janetta of the British Library, Mr. A. F. Jesson of the Bible House Collection in the Cambridge University Library, Adelaide Bennett of the Index of Christian Art at Princeton University, and the staffs of the Rare Book and Special Collections Library and the Ricker Architecture and Art Library at the University of Illinois at Urbana-Champaign and the Print Room of the Museum Plantin-Moretus, Antwerp. Permissions to incorporate previously published matter have been granted by the editors and publishers of *Milton Studies, Milton and the Idea of Woman,* and *Milton in Italy.* Some points in the last section of the last chapter were anticipated in "Milton and the Sexes," in *The Cambridge Companion to Milton.* Ann Lowry midwifed the manuscript through the acceptance process at the University of Illinois Press, and Patricia Hollahan's superb editing nursed it to presentability. Students whose observations have been particularly helpful include Elaine Perez Zickler, Liz Klem, Steven Patterson, Susan Lyndell, Helen Bolt, and Robert Miller, whose paper on "This Pendant World" called my attention to the richness of that suspenseful phrase. Among those who gave hospitality during my travels are Nicola and Cedric Brown, Sue and Hans-Peter Dürr, Pamela and John Newton, Vince and Tessa Bowen, Don and Marilyn Queller, Philipp and Raina Fehl, Olivann and John Hobbie, Hubert and Patricia White, Mileva and Christopher Brown, Mindele, Cecil, and Elizabeth Treip, Walter and Charlotte Arnstein, and my father, Lauren Kelsey. Walter Arnstein's remark on my title, "How curious that we retain the negative form 'disgust' but not the positive 'gust,'" epitomizes the approach I have meant to take. I wish to acknowledge my gratitude, as ever, for the published work and private encouragement of the late Arthur E. Barker, without whose illuminations I might never have searched through Milton's Garden. I thank my husband Robert for innumerable kindnesses, our son Rob for his instinctive sympathy with wild creatures, and our far-flung children and children-in-law, Rebecca and David, Susanna and Russell, Teresa, Margaret, and Carolyn, who have shared accommodations and keen eyes on many art and nature treks. Carolyn A. McColley, Marguerite Pease, John and Eva Frayne, David Fletcher, Flavio Giacomantonio, Florence Steinert, Irene Bergal, Barbara Bowen, Edward Davidson, William Shullenberger, Jean and Robert Clarkson, Carole and John Buckler, and Kathleen Swaim gave books and references. Alan Herbst, rector of Emmanuel Church, Champaign, read the manuscript for theological coherence and also provided a useful metaphor: if he were to choose one architectural feature by which to characterize the church, it would not be the windows, the carvings, or the gothic arches. Instead, he would take visitors down to the crypt and through the crawl space under the choir and show them the stone pillar that anchors the altar to bedrock. The poems and pictures proffered here are similarly founded. The source of their matter and the destination of their praise is in the heavens, and they are rooted deep in earth.

This book is dedicated to Kelsey Sara Amanda Wilk and other heirs of this pendant world.

*A Gust for Paradise*

# 1

# In the Beginning

Where wast thou when I laid the foundations of the earth?
Job 38:4

他he people have a general sense of the loss of Paradise," Milton is reported to have said, "but not an equal gust for the regaining of it."[1] The comment addresses an attitude that Milton challenged whenever he set pen to paper. "Gust" suggests appetite, taste, foretaste, trial, relish, zest. It recalls the "gusto de vera beatitudina" of Bembo's prayer to Love in *Il Cortegiano,* which Hoby translates "a smacke of the ryghte blysse."[2] It suggests, too, both the savor of poetry[3] and a rush of wind, and so the inspiring Spirit whose province is "th'upright heart and pure" (1.8). Even though he called his longest poem *Paradise Lost,* the far larger portion of its earthly scenes devoted to keeping paradise than to losing it creates a taste for blessedness and reactivates paradisal choices for life not only beyond this world but in it. The "Recover'd Paradise" of *Paradise Regained,* restored "to all mankind . . . and *Eden* rais'd in the wast Wilderness" (1.3-7), depends on an inward connection to eternity, but it is not only an inward and transcendent place;[4] is also cosmic, global, and local. The choices of the poem's hero re-create the consciences and guide the labors of those who choose to be farmers of Eden.

Milton's early plan for a tragedy called "Paradise Lost" foresaw Adam and Eve only "with the serpent" and "fallen" because, he then thought, people "cannot se[e] Adam in the state of innocence by reason of thire sin."[5] In the event, however, he wrote an epic instead, devoted much of it to the state of original righteousness, and contrived a style to "purge with sovereign eyesalve that intellectual ray which God hath planted in us"[6] so that readers might learn to see and love "the state of innocence" and, though no longer innocent, work toward healing the wounds of hate and recovering blessedness by "Light after light well us'd" (3.196). In this enterprise he joined and was joined by artists, musicians and other poets who looked to the creation story

attributed to Moses, the "Shepherd, who first taught the chosen Seed"
(1.8) and "principal Secretary to the holy Ghost,"[7] as a wellspring of
regenerative art.

Nevertheless, the topos of the good creation is still one that people
often "cannot see." Twentieth-century audiences reminded of the Genesis story are more likely to think of the Fall of Man and the Fault of
Woman than hear "fair musick" worth rejoining. Pictures of innocent
or repentant Adam and Eve are less often reproduced than images of
their fall that seem to imply erotic seduction and blame Eve. Images
that affirm the possibility of regeneration receive scant comment.[8] The
seventeenth-century outpouring of liturgical and domestic sacred part
music, with its celebratory creation imagery and multivocal harmony,
gets less attention in literary studies than secular solo song. Curricula
and anthologies oftener include Dante's *Inferno* than his *Purgatorio* or
*Paradiso,* as if only the damned truly spoke to our condition, and give
more room to Satan and the Fall in *Paradise Lost* than to its alluring
details of creative activity. Some otherwise careful readers, in spite of
Milton's powerful and richly textured presentation of primal life, suppose Paradise unexciting and innocence bland, assume (like Molière's
Philinthe) that virtue needs evil to feed on,[9] or think angels—those
hair-raising ardent energies—tedious, and Satan—the great archvan-
dal, the crusher of all that dares be beautiful—the liveliest character in
the poem.[10]

Many reasons suggest themselves for this lack of empathy with innocence. One is the cultural despair—wrought by technologically per-
fected monstrosities of warfare and genocide and the poisoning of air,
water, and earth—that has made so much twentieth-century art a cry
of rage or an unbandaging of wounds. Many artists and critics, rightly
moved by the holocausts, tortures, starvations, pollutions, and tyrannies manifested in such magnitude, find evil and suffering more appropriate subjects than gladness and beauty. A less humane cause may
be that as a culture we are not so alert to, or so easily entertained by,
celestial ardor as by devilish glee; perhaps the visual rays of our imaginations are paralyzed by a kind of spiritual repression that numbs the
receptors of "ryghte blysse." Under the influence of reductive psychol-
ogies or theories of power and patronage, many critics suppose that
the "real" motives even of the most complex artists or the most virtuous characters are impelled by the basest instincts, and when faced
with representations of blessedness so thoroughly drain them of significance as to seem biased against joy. The result privileges fallenness.

According to the Articles of Religion, "man is very farre gone from
originall righteousnes, and is of his owne nature enclined to evill."[11]

The point is not that "man" is entirely evil, but that "he" is inclined "by his own nature" to be so: that is, by unregenerated egoism unless free will is restored by grace. The whole of Genesis can be read, as can the whole of Scripture, as a call to repair the lapse by which the human race, despite all its obvious promise, acquires its propensity for destruction: a propensity named the "Fall" to signify a description of reality combined with a belief that humanity was not originally or inevitably corrupt. "Original righteousness" or "original justice," as it was also called, is a natural interest in the welfare of all lives.

Cosmology, as S. K. Heninger shows, shapes poetics.[12] Similarly, our conceptions of our beginnings, as a species and as a human family, radically affect human relationships, purposes, and arts. One interpretation of evolution assumes biological determinism and competition among species and emphasizes our likeness to other primates,[13] over whom we have achieved some problematic technical superiority which may be in the process of destroying them and us. It tells us that we are bipeds, somewhat less hairy than our ancestors, with manipulative intellects and opposing thumbs, who throve through competitive outwitting of other creatures, on whose continued existence we nevertheless depend. This conception might have made us respect our fellow animals, but it provides no model of a peaceable kingdom and no explanation of arts that tap the wellsprings of beauty and creativity in the human breast. An alternative hypothesis emphasizes symbiosis and the advantages of cooperation.[14] A current account of beginnings traces our dust to a primal and continuing explosion, begun at what some see as a moment of supreme beauty whose elegant unity, the womb of diversity, may some day be discerned; we are conscious starstuff fed on stored-up sunlight, and like the universe, consciousness is capable of infinite expansion. The arts of the twentieth century may be emerging into a new recognition of the immeasurable beauty of creation, of language, and of each life. This view of evolution has much in common with the Genesis creation story.

Myths of origins are the soil from which poetry springs. Hesiod, Homer, and Vergil present numinous embodiments of primal processes and a sense of the place and work of human beings within a generative world. Milton and his contemporaries gave precedence to the Hebrew apprehension of a Creator free of the nature-gods' fickleness and both benevolent and just, though sometimes inscrutable and unsettling, who produces cosmic glory, a nurturing earth, intricate, odd, and terrifying beasts, and man and woman gifted with their Maker's likeness yet free to participate in their own soul-making, all of which he declares good. When in 1572 Tycho Brahe discovered a star where none had been before, a new perception also came into view: creation is still in progress. Milton contemplated the implications of two cosmologies, the harmonious mathematics of Pythagorus, christened by reference to Scripture, and the infinite universe posited by Giordano Bruno; and in response to both he found harmonious language for a complexly processive cosmos and consciousness. Whether in the seventeenth century or the twentieth, the regenerative poetry, art, and music of creation affirm in conception and confirm in artistry our ability to be more than dust and offer a cordial to lack of appetite for joy.

Language, images, and music help shape consciousness and its ethical form, conscience. Seventeenth-century English poetry rooted in Genesis—as most serious art of that time was, in some sense, rooted—combines all three arts in language that is intrinsically what we would now call ecological: that is, concerned with the knowledge of the *oikos,* the house living creatures share. It is a poetry of multiple connection, designed to promote awareness of an interwoven creation, and to weave that awareness into the language we use. It holds that humanity is one family whose diverse members are called to purposeful employments, synchronically bound together through place and time, allied to other beings both like and different from them, and therefore capable of love. The primal employments given to Adam and Eve are the establishment of the human family and the dressing and keeping of a Garden that is an epitome of creation. "Dressing" is georgic, and implies all useful arts. "Keeping" is ecological, and implies respect for the way the world is made. The "dominion" given them is a kind of government that preserves the well-being of the planetary house and its diverse inhabitants.

The Book of Genesis presents a powerfully beautiful creation full of unpredictable oddities; human dignity spoiled by distrust, acquisitiveness, and violence; and the development of means of reconciliation through the calling and saving of the just, the conversion of the unjust—such as the trickster Jacob and the brothers of Joseph—and the reconciliation of warring brethren. Jacob and Esau lay down their arms, fall upon each other's necks, and weep. Joseph finds a way to let his betrayers recognize their guilt and repent. Judah offers himself to shield his brother from servitude and his father from sorrow, and Joseph not only forgives his betrayers but tells them not to grieve, for God has brought good out of the evil they have done, and made it a means to save their people. Again and again in scriptural history, grace makes the powerless healers, for divine strength "is made perfect in weakness" (2 Cor. 12:9).

The topos of the good creation, with its corollaries, "original righteousness" and regenerate righteousness modeled upon it, furnished seventeenth-century poets, artists, and musicians a nexus of imagery of primal blessedness and pristine choice and a theory of art as a means, in Donne's words, "to keep the world in reparation."[15] Paintings, engravings, anthems, psalms, meditations, and poems proliferated and interacted to encourage quotidian repairs in an age urgently aware of the interdependence between the arts and an ethically alert civilization. Milton, the primary poet of primal things, preeminently expresses this Edenic conscience, but it also irradiates the work of others who use images of the first creation to re-create a paradisal attentiveness even in "the field of this World" where "good and evil . . . grow up together almost inseparably."[16] Northern European artists, especially, depicted an exuberant creation; the original delightfulness of man, woman, and all the animals; and the mutuality of male and female in blessedness, in their lapse into violence and greed, and in the beginnings of recovery. And zest for re-creation animates the other arts as well. Poets acknowledged the strain between heaven and earth under the pressure of worldly politics and sciences and sought to reunite them. Part music wove diverse voices into the "Song of pure concent"[17]—that is, the right tuning that makes complex harmony possible—from which humanity so often withdraws. The motive of rejoining earth to the fuller harmony from which it fell connects the arts of the seventeenth century.

At present, so many people think that faith is opposed to reality, or a sense of the eternal opposed to a sense of present human and environmental needs, that it is difficult even to talk about their relations; a dualism that presupposes conflict colors the expectations we bring to language.[18] "Paradise," therefore, is a dangerous word. It has come to mean a utopian dream of safety and ease into which we can withdraw from the incessant and sometimes ugly demands of what people (with equal partiality) call "reality."[19] The artists who take the state of innocence as their domain do not, in Elizabeth Bowen's words, "attempt a picnic in Eden,"[20] but portray the prime Garden as a primer for action in the present world of potentiality which might come nearer to being "this other Eden, demi-Paradise."[21]

Milton's Adam and Eve—portraits of the primal artists—represent an innocence that is the seedbed of moral, intellectual, erotic, and spiritual growth. To be in-nocent—not poisonous—is, etymologically, to be harmless: a good start at moral consciousness but only a start. To be awake in the way that Milton depicts Edenic and redeemed consciousness is to discern and abet goodness wherever it may be found.

If no one can be as pure of heart as unfallen Eve and Adam, anyone can, as George Herbert admonishes those who enter through the porch of poetry, groan to be so—labor to give goodness birth.[22] The arts of Eden replenish imaginations and aid re-creation by reuniting matter and spirit in the numinous substances of language, image, and music.

Lately the Book of Genesis and the arts it has inspired have been under attack from those who believe that religion is the servant of politics and monotheism the apotheosis of monarchy, promoting the combativeness and injustices of the patriarchal phase of civilization and of human "dominion" over other creatures. Some critics hold that monotheism is intrinsically imperial and its god coldly detached from his creatures, or Genesis a Levite plot to suppress Goddess-worship and subject women,[23] and argue that the mischief wrought by religious and cultural imperialism can be cured by dimissing all religions that have ever made hierarchical distinctions of sex or caste, even those that have unsettled or discarded these distinctions in opposition to secular pressures to retain them.

Merlin Stone, in her speculative reconstruction of the origins of Genesis, *When God Was a Woman,* argues that the story of Adam and Eve was constructed by the Jewish clergy in reaction to the ancient and widespread worship of the Goddess, or Queen of Heaven, known by various names such as Astaroth, Astarte, and Isis, whose religion, originating from reverence for women's capacity to produce life, was repeatedly repressed, but still active in Canaan and surrounding countries when Genesis was composed. The features of Goddess-worship that made it unacceptable to the Israelites included female sexual autonomy, control over reproduction, and lack of concern for the paternity of children; unlimited sexual relations between the priestess, as incarnation of the Goddess, and her worshippers; a yearly marriage between the priestess and a young man, often called her son, who may subsequently be killed; and prophecy induced by hallucinogenic snake venom. Believing that all religion is a reflection of politics or a tool of power, Stone argues that if we interpret the misogyny in Jewish and Christian thought as a reaction to a woman-dominated religion and culture, we can desacralize the scriptures in which it is inscribed. She sees the story of Adam and Eve, in which Eve listens to a snake and eats of a forbidden tree, as an effort to suppress the religion of the Snake Goddess, and in the bargain to suppress all women.

The Hebrew creation myth, which blamed the female of the species for initial sexual consciousness in order to suppress the worship of the Queen of Heaven, her sacred women and matrilineal customs, from that time on assigned to women the role of sexual temptress. . . . perhaps most significant was the fact that the story also stated that it was the will of the male deity that Eve would henceforth desire only her husband, redundantly reminding us that this whole fable was designed and propagated to provide "divine" sanction for male supremecy and a male kinship system, possible only with a certain knowledge of paternity.

"With these facts," Stone concludes, we can "clear away the centuries of confusion, misunderstanding, and suppression of information, so that we may gain the vantage point necessary for examining the image, status, and roles still assigned to women today." If we expose the world's major religions as expressions of archaic social systems and give women unlimited sexual autonomy without regard for paternity—the implication seems to be—"the myth of the Garden of Eden will no longer be able to haunt us."[24]

That is not, of course, the way Milton tells the story. The Fall and an awareness of nudity were not for him or for the Bible commentators of the Reformation the discovery of sexuality. Calvin and most other Reformation writers directly refuted that interpretation. Whereas Stone insists that Eve had to eat the forbidden fruit first—that is, in Stone's view, become conscious of sexuality—Calvin insists that she did not, and that sexuality is not the point: Adam ate first, and Eve snared him by repeating Satan's lie that there was knowledge and power in the fruit itself.[25] Milton dismisses the identification of sin with sex differently, by showing Adam and Eve fully enjoying "connubial Love" (4.743), the fountain of "all the Charities" (756),[26] before the Fall. Adam's love-longing and sense of oneness with Eve figure in his fall, but the chief cause, as for Calvin, is "th' infernal Serpent" (1.34) who is not the source and symbol of female power but the instrument of the evil inscribed in the thoroughly masculine Satan. It is not sexual desire that motivates Adam's and Eve's separation from the "fair musick that all creatures made," but the desire, with which Satan infects them, for excessive, autonomous power.

In *Eve: The History of an Idea,* John A. Phillips is disturbed that Genesis implies a male God different and separate from his creation and thus "undercuts the presupposition of earlier myths of the interpenetration of human and divine." Phillips writes,

The creation language of Genesis is not the language of nature . . . it is the language of *technology*. . . .Even humanity is not of God's body, but rather is fashioned by the divine potter from

a clod of earth. . . . The more sophisticated account of creation in
Chapter 1 of Genesis . . . carries out its masculinizing of the relationship between God and his world on another level. God
does not even handle his raw material; instead, he "speaks" his
creation into being. . . . Creation, unlike procreation, depends on
conceptualizing. There thus appears to be a more than coinciden-
tal relationship between the beginning of history . . . and the notably antifeminine plot of such myths. The beginning of
civilization seems to require a seizure of religious power by male
gods, in order to break the ties of humanity to blood, soil, and
nature.[27]

Phillips, then, links conceptualizing to maleness, and blood, soil, and
nature to femaleness, as do a surprising number of feminist critics.
Milton, whom Phillips lumps among the misogynists, declines to ad-
here to that stereotype. His Eve, as well as his Adam, thinks and
prays; his Adam, as well as his Eve, takes care of the Garden. Phillips's
view that monotheism alienates God from his creatures challenges the
very stuff of Christian poetry: incarnation, divine immanence as well
as transcendence, and nature as the visible speech of God producing
and sustaining all the variegated beauties of the natural world that
"He fathers-forth whose beauty is past change."[28] Centuries of iconography represent a God intimately concerned with humankind and
the rest of nature who breathes the divine spirit into Adam, draws
forth and blesses Eve with profound tenderness, promotes erotic love
and procreation, replenishes the earth with a boundless paternal-
maternal providence, and dwells within whose who invite him.

Phillips's conclusion dismisses attempts "to resuscitate" the Goddess
as well as biblical religions. In the "Death of God movement in the
1960s," he believes, "radical theology proposed that the reality to
which the Bible directed humanity in worship and praise, and which
addressed humanity in its successes and failures, was somehow gone.
God is dead, and positive new religious possibilities, rather than ca-
tastrophe, follow this event."[29] Jonathan Culler has gone farther and
recommended an attack on "respect for religious discourse." He finds
that "religion provides an ideological legitimation for many reaction-
ary or repressive forces in America today," and that "instead of leading
the critiques of superstition, comparative literature is contributing to
the legitimation of religious discourse." Belief in a sacred book is
"untenable in intellectual circles" and religion "a curious, irrelevant
survival"; the job of criticism is "to keep alive the critical, demythol-

ogizing force of contemporary theory."[30] The premise of Culler's stance is that literary study should "situate" nationalism and religion in order to overcome "exclusions of other texts, other discourses, other peoples." But he seems to believe that disparaging the beliefs of "other peoples" will produce mutual respect, and that intellectualizing and secularizing texts will draw the West nearer the rest of the world.

In contrast, a prominent Islamic scholar doubts the efficacy of disbelief for furthering global amity, as Culler seems to believe it can do. Seyyed Hossein Nasr fears that Christianity is becoming so compromised by secularism that dialogue with other religions will no longer be possible. He argues that all believers, whatever their traditions, have more in common with each other than with secularism, and that "the time has come for serious theology in the West to take cognizance of the religious and metaphysical significance of other religions" that can "offset the withering effect of secularism and pseudo-religious ideologies."[31] The scheme of rallying the world under the flag of secularity does not seem likely bring the nations closer together, since many of our global neighbors believe that materialism and the loss of spirituality are exactly what is wrong with the Western world.

Milton—the epic poet who departed from the epic tradition by taking not national origins but human origins, not military heroes but heroes of faith as his subject—is an obvious target for critics who hold Jewish and Christian thought responsible for the world's injustices. Sandra Gilbert asserts that "Milton's myth of origins" summarized "a long misogynistic tradition," and that both his poem and "his inferior and Satanically inspired Eve" have "intimidated women and blocked their view of possibilities both real and literary." Jacqueline DiSalvo finds that "the exaltation of a transcendent God established a hierarchy between heaven and earth which easily might buttress social inequalities," and that Eve's fall "far from being a mere weakness of the flesh . . . is a political and ideological affirmation of the rights of the flesh." Christine Froula believes that Milton promotes "hierarchical dualism" and makes Eve "the image of the idealized and objectified woman whose belief in her role underwrites patriarchal power." Since biological paternity, unlike maternity, is invisible, men invented the worship of an invisible God to gain ascendency over women. Eve's fall is "gnostic": the "serpent tempts Eve . . . to cease respecting the authority fetish of an invisible power and to see the world for herself." We must undo the "patriarchal economy" by "using interpretive strategies that mark a shift from a sacred to a secular interpretive model, from an economy of invisible transactions to one of visible exchange," situating *Paradise Lost* in history as a "cultural artifact" and using it as "a powerful instrument for the undoing of the cultural economy inscribed in it."[32] Richard Corum maintains that "Milton's God depends on an imperial technology of power which reached Milton through Tudor bureaucracy and monastic Catholicism from imperial Rome and the Ottoman empire." Supposing that this God requires absolute submission, and aligning the feminine with the chaotic and rebellious, Corum believes that Milton tried obediently to repress the feminine in his epic but partly failed, leaving a residue of unspoken fragments of himself which constitute the interest of the poem. He holds that *Paradise Lost* is "a vast confusion of eternal, conceptualized spirit and temporal, narrative matter," omitting as Phillips does the incarnational fusion of spirit and matter that is the essence of Milton's language. In order to join "those who have struggled to reduce this patriarchal structure of imperial signification to a concept in the minds, and in the practice, of one's predecessors, however brilliant or influential" we must "acknowledge the injustices and damages to self and alien societies, to women and children caused by the orthodoxy of Milton's God."[33] Corum attributes patriarchal repression to an "orthodox" religion he thinks Milton shares, which he believes denies materiality and underpins tyranny; he associates the feminine with the irrational and makes the patriarchal strand of biblical societies into an idol of the whole.[34]

Although these critiques mean well toward women and global consciousness, they oppose the feminine to both faith and reason and throw out the twin babies of centuries of spiritual discovery and civilized arts with the bathwater of misogyny and imperialism. The assumption that spiritual experience in biblical religions is intrinsically alien from matter and maternity (based on selected sources and not shared by religious feminists) has seeped into a good deal of current criticism. But it does not correspond with the ways centuries of artists, poets, and composers have understood the God of Genesis or treated the creation in their works.

Critical modes whose purposes are ethical or political seek social justice, partly by exposing unjust habits of thought and language, partly by the dissolution of old certainties to make way for new speculations. But criticism is unjust itself when, rather than working to amend inequities, it reduces whole civilizations to a few idols and attempts to smash them, "situates" poems in ways that detach them from our souls, reduces the motives of art to power, profit, and appetite, or sets intellect against faith, present against past, women against men, and politics against art—as if the cooperation of these pairs were not needed against violence and the poisoning of the earth. Justice includes respect for the multiple concerns of those who have enriched human culture, and whose works are now subjected to new iconoclasms. Artists allied to beauty work for the love of living things, not just of themselves, and their gifts can enlarge and activate our sympathies. If we are unjust to a civilization cultivated by artists of many times, places, and resources of spirit, we lose their winnings and harden our minds in the forms of the old injustices.[35] If we deprive poetry not only of certainty, which it almost never claims, but of verity, so that it loses its life within us, we lose part of the complex wisdom on which political and economic justice depend; and these, though basic, are only the beginnings of equity. In its fullest sense, justice opens opportunities for creativity, a clean and beautiful earth, moral wisdom, spiritual joy. Such things cannot be rooted in a thin layer of ideas. They require a rich, deep soil.

In his discussion of duties toward our neighbors in *Christian Doctrine*, Milton lists "CANDOR; whereby we cheerfully acknowledge the gifts of God in our neighbor, and interpret all his words and actions in a favorable sense." Among the vices opposed to this virtue are "unmerited praise or blame," "evil surmising," "precipitancy in passing judgment," and "calumny, which consists in a malicious construction of the motives of others." The allies of candor include "the spirit of admonition ... by which we freely warn sinners of their danger."[36] Calumny characterizes both the misogyny and misanthropy that speckle some products of the Genesis tradition and the criticism that crowds the whole of it under these labels. Candid criticism freely admonishes the arts and cheerfully acknowledges their gifts.

What place do the arts of Eden have in a world where so many evils cry to be cured?

Civility requires an ability to imagine other people's lives. When a Greek singer known as Thespis stepped out of the choir and became, for the moment, someone else, art taught dramatically that we can lay ourselves aside and enter empathetically into the lives of others. When inspired gatherers we call Moses and Homer produced epics of the roots and uprootings of civilizations, their many voices[37] let us become, as we read, many people in turn. Homer, singer of a world havocked by moral shortsightedness and of a stalwart wanderer's quest for home, roots civilization in homefelt loyalties stretched to embrace a sorrowing enemy. Moses, a man of few words called to be God's scribe, became a conduit of goodness and holiness to imaginations that without such physic could be "evil continually" (Gen. 6:5). From

such "texts" or weavings come interwoven understandings that form
the fabric of any civilization.

Tyranny and cruelty lack imagination, not only for suffering but
also for the diverse and surprising shapes goodness can take. And the
obvious forms of brutality and despotism are not the only ones. Those
who exploit and pollute nature and human bodies reach similar results
more slowly. All of us, when we consume the products of the earth and
human labor without thought for the cost to the environment, to
other species, and to other people commit slow violence. When we
trivialize spiritual experience and shred the fabric of civilization because of its flaws, we rob human beings of dignity and richness of soul.
Part of the work of the arts is to alert us to the delicate microcosms of
other lives and to our responsibility for our effects on them. Along
with the mind's endeavors and the body's pains, the arts contribute to
ethical societies, not only by exposing evil but also by revealing whatever is hopeful, holy, growing, courageous, and capable—however
humbly—of light.

Edenic poetry, imagery, and music has at heart the purpose of re-
creating a paradisal consciousness; that is, responsiveness to the whole
of creation and to each life. The artists of regeneration do not ignore
evil but show that goodness is its best solvent.[38] They encourage reparation of the world by stocking the imagination with images and
sounds of the "fair musick that all creatures made" at the world's birth
and can learn to make again, inviting us to become, like Dante emerging from the Garden of Eden on the Mount of Purgatory, "rifatto si
come pianta novelle / rinovellate di novella fronda,"[39] remade like new
plants renewed with new leaves. They work to re-create a paradisal or
Edenic imagination, consciousness, and conscience, a kind of thought
and language that is not only linear, binary, dialectical, or vertical/hor-
izontal, but also radiant, global, multispherical, synchronic, aware of
all creatures on earth or in the heavens, or possible creatures in those
places, whose being or well-being may be affected by each of one's actions, and a consideration of them whenever one chooses to act.
Paradisal consciousness does not impose ideal order or homogeneity,
but has a caring eye for particulars. It assumes that each human being
and each of whatever other spiritual beings inhabit the cosmos is a mi-
crocosmos at least as richly complicated as oneself, values other species
for their own sake, and practices a strict regard for the long-term
health of earth and of each life. It listens delightedly to all the voices in
a complex harmony and joins in, likes thanksgiving and praise, and is
concerned with confronting evil without doing evil, but bringing
what good one can out of it. When joined to faith, which Kathleen

Swaim calls "that other way of knowing" that can "serve some of the same positive ends as innocence before the fall,"[40] it affirms a providential creation, suitable for growing souls, in which one's choices have cosmic reverberations, engaging the spiritual powers of good and evil, as well as affecting the immediate well-being of one's neighbor, including each living thing in one's neighborhood. The arts of Eden encourage such consciousness by letting us relish "a smacke of the ryght blisse" and stirring up a gust to find and care for "Recover'd Paradise." In this way they commit the energies of the arts to enriching souls and renewing the face of the earth.


## NOTES

1. Parker, *Milton*, 1:615; French, *Life Records*, 5:32; Todd, *Some Account*, 1:210 n. Part of this paragraph is from my essay, " 'Tongues of Men and Angels': *Ad Leonoram Romae Canentem*," which appeared in *Urbane Milton: The Latin Poetry*, ed. James A. Freeman and Anthony Low (*MS* 19 [1984]) and is reprinted by permission.

2. Castiglione, *Il Libro del Cortegiano*, sig. Piv; *The Courtyer*, sig. Yi.

3. Richard Baxter speaks of "so sweet a gust, and fervent ascendent holy LOVE, as breatheth in Mr. G. Herbert's Poems": *More Reasons*, quoted in Ray, *Herbert Allusion Book*, 109.

4. On the "paradise within" see Martz, *Paradise Within*; on the transcendent Paradise see Swaim, *Before and After the Fall*, and Kaufmann, *Paradise in the Age of Milton*. Joseph Duncan gathers the history of thought about the Garden of Eden, including views of paradise as regenerate life, in *Milton's Earthly Paradise* and James Grantham Turner collects views of it as erotic fulfillment in *One Flesh*. Dustin Griffin discusses eighteenth-century responses in *Regaining Paradise*. Milton unifies all three "paradises"—inward, ethical, and heavenly; the present study is particularly concerned with earthly work as participating in immortal and providential processes.

5. "Subjects for Poems and Plays from the Cambridge Manuscript," in *SM*, 1129.

6. *Of Reformation*, in *SM*, 452.

7. Donne, *Essayes in Divinity*, 11.

8. J. B. Trapp places the topos of the Fall in the context of redemption in "Iconography of the Fall," and Roland M. Frye compares Milton's depiction of the Fall with visual artists' in chapter 16 of *Milton's Imagery*, noting the rarity of attributing separate falls to Adam and Eve. What has been underrepresented is the treatment of the Fall as a violation of a good creation whose repair is part of the process of regeneration.

9. Molière, *Misanthrope*, 5.1: "If every heart were frank and kind and just, / what could our virtues do but gather dust?"

10. Thomas Greene, for example, judges that "although the anatomy of evil in [*Paradise Lost*] is so brilliant as to be unsurpassed in its kind, the dramatization of goodness fails" (*Descent from Heaven*, 409), and Harold Bloom states, "It is Milton's Satan that we must think upon when the Western literary sublime demands to be exemplified and defined" (*Ruin*, 111). Duncan quotes critics who find Milton's prelapsarian imagery intentionally dubious (*Milton's Earthly Paradise*, 229-31).

11. *Articles agreed upon by the . . . whole cleargie* (London, 1629), article 9, sig. B4r. The point that free will requires grace is made in article 10, "Of free-will": "The condition of man after the fall of *Adam* is such, that he cannot turne and prepare himself by his owne naturall strength and good works to faith and calling vpon God: Wherfore we haue no power to do good workes pleasant and acceptable to God, without the grace of God by Christ preuenting [that is, preceding] vs, that we may haue a good will, and working with vs, when we haue that good will" (sig. B4r).

12. Heninger, *Touches of Sweet Harmony*, 3-18.

13. Compare for example Michelangelo's *Creation of Adam* with Jay H. Matternes's careful reconstruction for *National Geographic* of the evolution of a modern human male from skeletal remains of *Australopithecus afarensis*, with stance, facial expression, body hair, and other details chosen to stress resemblence.

14. Lewis Thomas's Elihu Root lectures make this point. "The biosphere, for all its wild complexity, seems to rely more on symbiotic arrangements than we used to believe, and there is a generally amiable aspect to nature that needs more acknowledgment than we have given it in the past. . . . The long-term winners in evolution seem to me to behave this way, with the conspicuous exception of ourselves. We have tended to exploit and to cheat whenever the occasion seemed to provide a short-term advantage." I am grateful to Fay Porter Nowell for calling my attention to these articles.

15. Donne, *Essayes in Divinity*, 70. Donne adds that "we have here two employments, one to conserve this world, another to increase Gods Kingdome," an echo of the two employments enjoined in Genesis, to dress and keep the Garden and to increase and multiply.

16. Milton, *Areopagitica*, in *SM*, 738. Milton's "almost" is often ignored.

17. Milton, "At a Solemn Musick," in *SM*, 19, l. 6.

18. Richard Shoaf makes useful distinctions between dualism and duality in *Milton, Poet of Duality*: dualism polarizes, duality is two-in-one; as in language, ambiguity, where two or more meanings "contend for the same semantic space," is to be distinguished from polysemy, where multiple meanings join and choice is possible (viii-ix).

19. Kaufmann identifies three strategies for "relating fallen reality to ideal reality." "The Paradisal Enclave," by "subtracting from present reality everything regarded as evil," sacrifices openness and has little practical application.

"The Paradisal Way," or regenerate life, involves openness and process and is the stage of salvation Milton called "INCOMPLETE GLORIFICATION" in which "WE ARE JUSTIFIED AND ADOPTED BY GOD THE FATHER AND ARE FILLED WITH A CERTAIN AWARENESS BOTH OF PRESENT GRACE AND DIGNITY AND OF FUTURE GLORY, SO THAT WE HAVE ALREADY BEGUN TO BE BLESSED" (*YP* 6:502). "The Final Marriage of Heaven and Earth" is "that consummated union of earth and heaven which means beatitude not only for individuals but for nature and the entire community of man" (*Paradise*, 11-23).

20. Bowen, *Collected Impressions*, 264-69. Bowen's point is that we cannot live forever in the childhood Eden of uncritical reading, when the brain is not yet "posted between [the reader's] self and the story." Yet "the imagination, which may appear to bear such individual fruit, is rooted in a compost of forgotten books" read in that state of literary innocence when "fact and fiction were the same." My thanks to Professor William Alfred for this reference.

21. Shakespeare, *Richard II*, 2.1.42.

22. Herbert, "Superliminare," *Works*, 25.

23. Harold Bloom, in *The Book of J*, pries off these imputations from the Yahwistic writer of Genesis, whom he imagines as a woman of unsurpassed sophistication and irony.

24. Stone, *When God Was a Woman*, 222 and 240-41. I applaud Stone's hope that women and men can "learn to consider each other's ideas and opinions with respect, and regard the world and its riches as a place that belongs to every living being on it" (241).

25. Calvin, *A commentarie vpon Genesis*, 92.

26. Milton uses the language of patriarchal kinship systems to persuade an audience some of whom were indeed skeptical of sexuality: from pure sexual relations "all the Charities / Of Father, Son, and Brother first were known." That is, without "connubial Love" there would be no such relations, a state Stone also acknowledges but prefers.

27. Phillips, *Eve*, xiv, 6, 12-13.

28. Hopkins, "Pied Beauty," in *Poems*, 69-70.

29. Phillips, *Eve*, 176.

30. Culler, "Comparative Literature and the Pieties," 30-32.

31. Nasr, "A Muslim Reflection," 115. On the validity of religious discourse see Steiner, *Real Presences*; Alston, *Divine Nature and Human Language*; Otto, *Idea of the Holy*; and Smith, *Beyond the Post-Modern Mind*. For modern definitions and analyses of religion see Alston, *Religious Belief and Philosophical Thought*; on the epistemology of religious and scientific understanding, Gerhart and Russell, *Metaphoric Process*; for the centrality of religion in the Renaissance mind, Shuger, *Habits of Thought*; for the possibilities of a "post-critical" reading of the Bible, the importance of discourse between belief and other disciplines, and the need for rigorous hermeneutics, Ricoeur,

*Essays on Biblical Interpretation;* Mudge's introduction trenchantly analyzes modern fear of Scripture (4).

32. Gilbert, "Patriarchal Poetry," 368-82; Di Salvo, *War of Titans*, 267-68; Froula, "When Eve Reads Milton" 329, 335-36. Froula's "gnostic" should not be confused with early Christian Gnosticism, which denied freedom of the will: see Pagels, *Adam, Eve, and the Serpent* and *Gnostic Gospels*.

33. Corum, "In White Ink," 127-28 and 140-41.

34. Recent responses to attacks on Milton include Shullenberger, "Wrestling with the Angel"; Gallagher, *Milton, the Bible, and Misogyny;* and Wittreich, *Feminist Milton,* which surveys the responses of women readers in the eighteenth and early nineteenth centuries and concludes that Milton's supposed misogyny is really the creation of patriarchal critics whose assumptions recent feminist critics have adopted. Essays in *Milton and the Idea of Woman,* edited by Julia M. Walker, take feminist critiques and methods into account while applying them to Milton in diverse ways, many of them sympathetic to Milton within the "spirit of admonition."

35. I want to distinguish here between cultural tradition as static, customary ways of thinking and cultural tradition as the handing down of hard-won understanding from which to carry on new work. Achsah Guibbory, in *The Map of Time,* makes the important point that Milton was "radically committed to change" (180) and that the Jewish and Christian conception of linear history links "the repetitive, cyclical pattern with error, custom, and tradition" by which people "impede progress, and succumb to a cyclical pattern of decline." The structures and endings of Milton's poems are "characteristically forward-looking" (175), and *Paradise Regained,* in particular, "clearly illustrates the crucial difference between the view of history that emphasizes parallels and that which stresses a typological, progressive relationship between historical persons or events" (188). Regina Schwartz, in *Remembering and Repeating,* points out that the pattern of Milton's poems is not creation leading to decay but chaos leading to perpetual creation (chapter 1), and that ritual repetition "signals both the renewal of human memory—to acknowledge contingency is to defeat the chaos of presumption—and the renewal of divine initiative—to praise the creation is ritually to reenact it. Such repeatings are the touchstones of a theodicy in which to remember is to redeem and to be redeemed" (91). Remembering allows us to amend the errors of the past; commemoration promotes the renewal of creativity.

36. *De Doctrina Christiana,* trans. Charles Sumner, in *CM* 17:310-27. I have preferred Sumner's translation for stylistic reasons, while recognizing that Milton's Latin or John Carey's *YP* translation should be consulted in matters of theology and doctrine. "Precipitancy in passing judgment" is what Milton most complains of from his critics in his prose tracts and his sonnet "A Book was writ of late call'd *Tetrachordon.*"

37. Homer speaks of the poet "with his many voices" in *Odyssey* 22.393.

38. In a recent article on postmodernist critical theories, Anthony Low writes that a Christian aesthetics, while rightly dealing with sin and salvation, "must allow . . . some place for harmony and radiance, for immanence and transcendence, and, in brief, for wholeness and glory as well as absence, discontinuity, *kenosis,* and suffering" ("Idolatry, Iconoclasm, and Beauty of Form," 10-11).

39. Dante, *Purgatorio* 33.143-44.

40. Swaim, *Before and After the Fall,* 16-17. She continues, "After the fall, if faith can be activated, it . . . will open up future possibilities and make love, affirmation, growth, and joy accessible. It will teach the believer to transcend the experiential and the self" (16-17). See also Knedlik's discussion of the effects of faith both before and after the Fall on the ability to imagine creative futures in "Fancy, Faith, and Generative Mimesis." Georgia Christopher carefully defines the hermeneutics of Protestant faith in God's word in *Milton and the Science of the Saints.*

# 2
# The Iconography of Eden

Witness this new-made World, another Heav'n
From Heaven Gate not far.
*Paradise Lost* 7.617-18

**M**an is a lumpe," John Donne wrote to Edward Herbert, "where all beasts kneaded bee, / Wisdome makes him an Arke where all agree; / ... our businesse is, to rectifie / Nature to what she was."[1] Seventeenth-century poets and artists held that our business in the world, and God's business in us, is to rectify Nature—both the little arks we are and the larger ark of earth—to what she was "till disproportion'd sin," as Milton has it, "Broke the fair musick that all creatures made." The purpose of the arts is to raise our imaginations so that "we on Earth" may "renew that Song, / And keep in tune with Heav'n."[2] Milton stands alone as provider of a copious dramatic rendering of "what she was" on which to model the work of rectification and so rejoin the song. But other writers and artists also furnished diverse images of the world's making and its ruin pertinent to its repair and filled with choices and implications that exercise those faculties of the beholder needed for the work.

If we are to read the poetry of genesis with a view to regenesis, we need a just idea of the world it aims to regenerate. Although Genesis is often treated as the story of human, and especially female, frailty, an alternative tradition rejoices in the whole creation with its "two great Sexes" (8.151) and works for its recovery from the propensity toward malice called the Fall by re-creation of the imagination.

Because Genesis 1-4 assigns dominion over living things to Adam and Eve and dominion over Eve to Adam, visual and literary creation images have often been interpreted, either complacently or critically, from a patriarchal point of view; and the misapprehension rubs off even on Milton, who took the best of what can be found in previous and contemporary iconography and incomparably enhanced it. This chapter draws together depictions of Genesis in the visual arts that are innocent of exploitative and misogynist implications or consciously oppose them. They concern a creator deeply concerned for the welfare of an exuberant natural world filled with fish, fowl, cattle, and creeping things; and a man and a woman whom other sentient creatures love and who are mutually and equally responsible for the care and the loss of this harmony and for its recovery.[3]

Images of the Creation and Fall proliferated in many media and spread by means of engravings during the sixteenth and seventeenth centuries. The story was an inviting one for Renaissance artists in love with beauty and newly educated in anatomy; it let them celebrate the naked human body unconfined to pagan fable, revel in drawing and painting lush landscapes and winsome beasts, including newly discovered exotic ones, and represent a major religious subject without offending iconoclasts. Moreover, in an age of violent controversy, the original goodness of creation was a topic on which Catholics and Protestants could sometimes agree, and engravings of it by artists of both kinds circulated freely. It especially appealed to the Reformation instinct to return to earliest roots, as found in Scripture. The first man and the first woman formed the first church and prefigured the apostolic one that the Reformation sought to re-form.

As Ernest Gilman's salutary study makes clear, the iconoclasm of the English Reformation "and the body of controversy it provoked . . . pose a crucial dilemma for the literary imagination of the sixteenth and seventeenth centuries." The Edwardian Injunctions prohibited icon-worship but permitted images as aids to remembering the Scriptures. Although in Renaissance aesthetics "*pictura* and *poesis* were companionable sisters in the service of the poet's art," for zealous reformers not only images in churches but "the very imagining power of the mind was tainted by the pride and sensuality of fallen humanity and open to the perils of worship misdirected from the Creator to the creation." Both in churches and in minds, "the word was the bulwark of the spirit against the carnal enticements of the image." The challenge to poets was to reform the very image-making processes of the imagination.[4]

Since the Hebrew creation story teaches exactly that distinction between the Creator and the creation and founds their true relation on it, pictorial treatments of Genesis have a built-in antidote to any impulse to use them as icons rather than aids to recollection. Their variety guards against petrification of the imagination.

An artist setting about to draw Adam and Eve had many choices. Which event in their lives should be central? Should the principal subject be their creation, their lives in innocence, their fall, or its effects?

If the creation, what part, by what kind of Creator, with what implications about the book of creatures and about Edenic marriage? If
their fall, as Milton asks, "What cause?" Should their bodies and the
emblematic plants and animals around them suggest pride, weakness,
vainglory, recklessness, stupidity, lust, understandable hubris, irresis-
tably distracting erotic beauty?[5] Should their stances and gestures imply complacency, collusion, dispute, a fearsome risk, a frivolous frolic,
a defection by savages, a mistake by essentially good and happy beings,
a fated compliance, a free choice? What kind of serpent, if any, should
tempt? A woman-headed one, often resembling Eve, was popular in
the fifteenth century and retained by High Renaissance artists;[6] a
male, a charming putto, a bristling monster were all occasionally used;
a literal snake was increasingly popular in the sixteenth century, especially in the Protestant north.[7] What should Eve's part be: rational
persuasion, sexual enticement, emotional blackmail, overwhelming
glamour, overweening ambition, childish sensuality? Or Adam's: eager
acceptance, pained acquiescence, feeble resistance, uxorious collapse?
Which of the two was more to blame, or was the act entirely mutual?
What effects should be suggested: a *felix culpa,* a poisoning of the
whole creation, a trivialization of life, a merely "human" or even "hu-
manizing" frailty, a costly but correctable wrong? What symbols—every shape, gesture, plant, animal, stone, and star having multiple
emblematic meanings—should have prominence? What commentaries, iconological handbooks, iconographic traditions, and iconoclasms
need heeding?

All of these choices bore upon each image of the state of innocence
and the primal choice between good and evil; and often the artist embedded images of choice itself, sometimes by depicting Adam and Eve
in the moment of choosing, before the fatal act, and often by surrounding them with plants and animals whose multiple symbolic associations make us conscious that the benignity or depravity of
everything in nature depends on moral choice. This polysemousness—
sometimes miscalled ambiguity—brings home to viewers the perti-
nence of that primal image to all choice and exercises their powers to
make both vital and fine distinctions. The choices available to both artist and audience produce great variety, and small variations can mean
large differences of interpretation on the part of the artist and the
viewer.[8]

The treatments most poets and their readers in the age of Milton
knew best are not what we might expect. A respected modern dictionary of symbolism states that in the Temptation (conflated with the
Fall) "Adam and Eve stand by the tree, Eve holding the fruit or in the

act of plucking it, or, having taken a bite, offering it to Adam."[9] But such versions depart, both iconographically and theologically, from the main tradition. More often, either Adam is actively reaching for the fruit or both hold it equally, and indications that Eve has eaten first are rare. The definition privileges an iconography favored by Renaissance artists who modeled figures after classical sculpture, sometimes with attitudes suggested by "pagan" subjects, and by their increasingly sensuous successors, whose memorable paintings dominate our imagination of the Fall.[10] By appearing (at least to modern viewers) to associate Eve with sensuality and subordinate Adam's fall to hers, these works have suggested three related conceptions of Genesis that other images do not support: that the choice is between voluptuous earthly pleasure, leading to woe, and austere spiritual discipline, leading to heaven; that Forbidden Knowledge is sexual knowledge;[11] and that Woman is the villain of the piece.

The following account will surprise readers who have formed an impression from paintings such as those of Raphael, Michelangelo, Titian, Tintoretto, and Rubens that the Fall is the most important event in the story or that representations of Genesis force a choice between a doctrine of sin and a celebration of humanity. It begins with a brief catalogue of subjects; continues with examples from the Middle Ages, divided into monuments and manuscripts—that is, church decoration and manuscript illumination, which were often closely related—and concludes with sixteenth- and seventeenth-century Bible illustrations. Both this and the ensuing chapter include discussion of the iconology (that is, interpretation of symbols) that informs the iconography (that is, depiction of images) of the Garden of Eden.

### Genesis Cycles

With some noteworthy exceptions, most artists depicted only those events actually narrated in Genesis. Which events they chose tells much about their interpretation. The accompanying illustrations provide a variety of treatments, beginning with an unusually complete series (figs. 1-12) by Jacob Floris van Langeren published in England by William Slatyer during the 1630s. The standard topics are these:

*The Creation of the World,* or the Six Days' Work, contained in one scene or several. Some are preceded or accompanied by the Fall of the Rebel Angels. The Creator is sometimes represented as the Father; sometimes as the Son, either as Christ-Logos with cruciform aureole or else as a young bearded man; sometimes as the Tetragrammaton or four-letter name of God (or, occasionally, a radiance) in circular, elliptical, or triangular form. During the sixteenth and seventeenth centuries God as Father is often the choice of Catholic artists. Protestant artists, unable or reluctant to break the commandment against graven images and portray an invisible God in visible form, chose the Christ-Logos, justified by the Incarnation, or, increasingly, the Tetragrammaton.

Two engravings by Jan Collaert after Maerten de Vos illustrate the first and third of the these choices, the figure of God the Father (fig. 15) and, replacing it, the Hebrew Name and Latin "Father" (fig. 16). Throughout the Middle Ages, however, and sometimes in the sixteenth century, the Christ-Logos was depicted, in response to the first chapter of John: "In the beginning was the Word. . . . All things were made by him. . . . And the Word was made flesh, and dwelt among us" (John 1:1-14). Milton, though distinctly Reformed, uses language suggestive of all three ways of representing the Creator, including the "Almighty Father" (3.56), the Son in whom "all his Father shone / Substantially express'd" (3.139-40), a "voice" (4.467), and "Omnipresence" (11.336).

The parts of this topic are the Creation of Light; the Separation of Light from Darkness, or in some cases the Creation of Day and Night; the Creation of the Firmament and the Separation of the Firmament from the Waters; the Separation of Water and Dry Land; the Creation of Vegetation; the Creation of the Sun, Moon, and Stars; the Creation of the Animals; the Creation of Adam and Eve; and the Blessing of Creation, or of the personified Days.

The one of these scenes aptest to confuse is the Creation of the Firmament and its separation from the waters (fig. 13). In the Pythagorean system the firmament is either the *primum mobile* or the sphere of the fixed stars.[12] But Thomas Traherne defines it as "that vast extended Space between the upper and the lower Waters"—that is, the region of air between "the terrestial Waters" and "the Clouds we see, which water and refresh the dry Earth in convenient Seasons."[13] For Milton it is a globose "partition" of "Elemental Air" separating "The Waters underneath from those above": the amniotic waters surrounding the universe that protect it from Chaos, "For as Earth, so [God] the World / Built on circumfluous Waters calm, in wide / Chrystalline Ocean, and the loud misrule / Of *Chaos* far remov'd," and this "Heav'n he nam'd the Firmament"; into this Firmament God set "Lights . . . to give Light on the Earth" (7.269-72, 343-45).

Some series end with God Resting on the Seventh Day (fig. 34, lower right). This topic is fairly common in the Middle Ages, usually with the Christ-Logos on a cushioned seat holding a closed book. In

the Egerton Genesis (British Library MS. Egerton 1894) he is reclin-
ing in a flowery meadow.

The story of Adam and Eve includes the Creation of Adam, the
Naming of the Animals, the Creation of Eve, the Presentation of Eve
to Adam and the Naming of Eve, the Admonition, the Institution of
the Sabbath, the Temptation and Fall, the Hiding from the Voice of
God, the Judgment, the Clothing of Adam and Eve, the Expulsion,
Labor, the Sacrifices of Cain and Abel, the Murder of Abel, the
Mourning over the Body of Abel, and, occasionally, the Death of
Adam.

*The Creation of Adam* shows God molding him, or breathing the
breath of life into him, or both: Jan Wierix provides an example of the
first (fig. 22); Collaert (fig. 15, right side) and Jan Sadeler after Crispijn van den Broeck (fig. 17) provide two versions of the second. Milton uses both:

> he form'd thee, *Adam,* thee O Man
> Dust of the ground, and in thy nostrils breath'd
> The breath of Life; in his own Image hee
> Created thee, in the Image of God
> Express, and thou becam'st a living Soul.
>                                         (7.524-28)

"Express" is a multiple pun, for God molds or "presses out" Adam
from dust, he creates him specially and rapidly, and he makes him to
express his manifest image. When Michael speaks of the "respiration to
the just" in 12.540 his verb brings to mind the original "inspiration"
of the breath of life into Adam's nostrils made so explicit in the
engravings.

In the *Naming of the Animals* the birds and beasts come to Adam,
sometimes in pairs, to receive their names (figs. 5, top, and 27, left).
Sometimes Eve is already present, in spite of her subsequent creation
according to Genesis 2. Milton, however, as John Leonard points
out, treats the naming of paired animals as the experience that moves
Adam to perceive his need for a mate like himself, and request one
(8.337-68).[14]

*The Creation of Eve* is probably the most popular topic apart from
the Fall and usually serves as the Creation of Man. A separate Creation
of Adam is comparatively rare. The Creator blesses her as she emerges
from Adam's side (fig. 5), perhaps to emphasize that they are "one
flesh" and to reinforce the typology that associates the Creation of Eve
with the emergence of the Church from Christ's side at the Crucifixion; or else he raises her from behind him, fully formed (fig. 18).

Much more rarely, he extracts a rib and fashions her with his hands (fig. 28), as he does in *Paradise Lost*. The commoner version, showing Eve bodily separated from Adam, refers both to Genesis 1:27, "male and female created he them," and to Genesis 2:24, identifying husband and wife as "one flesh." Those in which Eve is "born" directly from Adam's side may also allude to the emergence of the sacraments from the side of Christ at the Crucifixion, or to 1 Cor. 11:8, "For the man is not of the woman but the woman of the man," which as many feminists point out reverses the natural birth process. The images of the "birth" of Eve show God receiving her with great solicitude, however, while images in which God "edifies" her from the foundation of Adam's rib suggest a more direct creative act. Both imagine the creation of Eve on the basis of a literal reading of Genesis.

Many series go directly from the Creation of Eve to the Fall, giving a strong impression of cause and effect.

*The Presentation of Eve to Adam, or the Marriage of Adam and Eve, and the Naming of Eve*. God gives Eve to Adam, who may gesture toward her as he names her (fig. 27, bottom); or God takes the part of a priest and joins their hands (fig. 24).[15]

*The Admonition, or God Speaking to Adam and Eve*. God invites Adam and Eve to eat freely of the trees in the Garden, but commands them to eschew the forbidden fruit (fig. 26). Eve is nearly always present. Often the Creator holds Adam's hand, but in the sculpture in the Chapter House at Salisbury Cathedral, he holds Eve's.

*The Fall*. Usually the Temptation of Eve by the Serpent and the Temptation of Adam by Eve are contained in one scene constituting the Fall, with the actual eating of the forbidden fruit implied. Occasionally the two temptations are divided. When more than one image of the fruit is visible, they may be regarded as one fruit in a narrative: Eve takes the fruit and gives it to Adam, and both of them eat it at unspecified times. However, versions in which Eve holds two unbitten fruits (fig. 45) or Adam and Eve each hold one imply, as Calvin taught, that Eve did not eat the fruit before Adam.[16] In the simplest and probably most common motif, the Fall is mutual and simultaneous, Adam and Eve standing on either side of the forbidden tree, each with fruit in their hands or both holding one fruit together.[17] Usually in English Bibles Adam and Eve grasp one fruit together, or Adam takes it from Eve (fig. 44), or only Adam holds it (fig. 42).

*The Hiding from the Voice of God*. Adam and Eve crouch "amongst the trees of the Garden," illustrating Genesis 3:8 (fig. 7, top).

*The Judgment.* Adam and Eve may hang their heads (fig. 7, bottom) or kneel together repentantly (figs. 23 and 29). In some versions Adam points toward Eve, laying the blame on her (fig. 29, lower left); Eve may point to the Serpent.

*The Clothing of Adam and Eve.* God or an angel clothes them either with animal skins (as implied in Gen. 3:21) or with woven cloth (fig. 19, left). Although clothing denotes fallenness it is also regenerative, representing the "Robe of righteousness" (10.222).

*The Expulsion,* often by an angel with a sword (fig. 8) but sometimes by God or the angel with a hand on Adam's shoulder (fig. 29, lower right).[18]

*Labor.* Adam digging the now recalcitrant soil and Eve spinning or nursing her children (fig. 51). Sometimes Adam rests beside his family (fig. 20) in an image of the Family of Adam; more rarely, Adam and Eve are shown with the infant Seth. Some series include an angel giving them their tools, usually mattock or spade and distaff or spindle (fig. 35).

The division of labor participates in what readers may consider a too-rigid distinction between men's work and women's work,[19] but, apart from the fact that at the subsistence level Adam's work needs broad shoulders and Eve's agile fingers, they are also regenerative images. Adam's work is the source of nurture and of the elements of the sacrament; Eve's work of clothing recalls the first gift of God to fallen Adam and Eve. Together, Adam's agriculture and Eve's craft form the institution of the peaceful arts. Images of Adam with his spade and Eve spinning or suckling her child are further dignified by association with Christ, as Second Adam, and Mary, as Second Eve.[20]

*The Sacrifices of Cain and Abel, the Slaying of Abel, and the Mourning over the Body of Abel* (figs. 9-11 and 21). Many series pass directly from the Fall or Expulsion to the murder of Abel, showing the fratricidal effects of the mortal fruit. Occasionally a series concludes with the Death of Adam.

In depictions of the Passion of Christ, Adam and Eve appear in a further topos, called either the Harrowing of Hell or the Delivery of Souls from Limbo, in which Christ having "descended into hell" (as in the Apostles' Creed) leads forth the elect beginning with Adam and Eve, a subject that affirms their redemption (fig. 36). This topic is not strictly scriptural, though it may be deduced from Ephesians 4:8-9.[21] Milton, who believes that body and soul die and are resurrected together, does not include this image; Adam understands that "to the faithful Death [is] the Gate of Life" (12.571).

Sometimes in depictions of the Last Judgment, Adam and Eve are present among the elect, as in the mosaic in the cathedral at Torcello, Signorelli's frescoes at Orvieto, and, more ambiguously, Michelangelo's in the Sistine Chapel.

The major events of Genesis 1-4, the Creation of Light to the Murder of Abel, or selections from them, appear in many forms: early Christian wall-paintings and reliefs on sarcophagi;[22] church windows, sculptures, carvings, mosaics, altar paintings, and frescoes; illuminated manuscripts,[23] printed Bibles, and sets of engravings; narrative paintings and reliefs; glass and pottery, fabrics and furniture, and renderings in other media and contexts. They may present events sequentially or contain several in one frame, one in the foreground and others in the background. Two forms were clearly available to seventeenth-century English poets: church decoration and other public monuments (prints of which may have come to poets who did not travel to them), and numerous engravings, especially book and Bible illustrations but also separate prints or series designed to be bound into Bibles (which purchasers could buy unbound from the publisher and take to the binder) or made into separate books.

These treatments display variegated images of our first parents. Among them we can (if not too inflexibly) sort out two general interpretations compatible with various teachings of the church. The first is that creation, and especially human senses and sexuality, and more especially woman, were primordially flawed, but in a way made fortunate by redemption, provided one firmly rejected the enticements of the flesh. The second is that creation, including both man and woman, was primordially excellent, wounded by the Fall, but redeemed, and that human beings can be regenerated by God as naturally incarnate beings in a material world whose beauty and limitations can help, rather than hinder, the gradual growth of the spirit. Italian Renaissance paintings, by their gorgeous rendering of the human body and the depths and nuances of erotic feeling, give many viewers an impression that Eve herself—for better or worse—was the forbidden fruit. Medieval church and manuscript decorations, seventeenth-century engravings, and many Bible illustrations, on the other hand, may comparatively neglect erotic beauty but express a warm affection of the Creator for humanity, and of the artist for both. These works concern the abundance of creation and make Adam and Eve equally responsible for the Fall and equal partners in regeneration; although the process of renewal may be long, arduous, and painful, work and sexuality are not curses but means of regenerate life. It is this second interpretation of the Genesis story, which delights in an exuberant creation and depicts models and means of regeneration, that I wish primarily to explore. Such differences help us distinguish the attitudes toward creation and human nature found in English poetry and, especially, what various implications Milton chose, cast aside, or integrated in his living fabric of words made flesh and song.

Many cycles, whether book illustrations or monumental series, include only a few of even the standard topics, proceeding from Creation to Fall and Expulsion with no hint of original righteousness or repentance. The major biblical episodes are swiftly linked in a visual story that implies, especially to viewers unfamiliar with redemptive and regenerative interpretations, that as soon as woman was made, man sinned, and labor and death entered the world: an undignified and potentially misogynous summary, though often beautifully and compassionately rendered. Among the best known versions of this basic series are, in Florence, Ghiberti's east doors of the Baptistry, its dome mosaics, and the reliefs at the base of Giotto's bell tower; in Rome, Raphael's series for the Logge in the Vatican and Michelangelo's for the Sistine Chapel. Raphael's is typical in representing the six days' work of a paternal God who presents Eve to Adam; immediately afterwards (visually speaking) she tempts him, standing in a dominant and erotically suggestive attitude while Adam reaches willingly for the fruit. The next scene is the Expulsion. But even some of these contain arguably regenerative motifs. In the creation scene at the beginning of the Baptistry series, innocent Adam and Eve appear, along with four smiling fish, and in Ghiberti's relief new-made Eve is borne up by angels.

As J. B. Trapp has shown, most Genesis cycles appear in redemptive contexts, as parts of programs that conclude with the Crucifixion and Resurrection of Christ or the Last Judgment. Some are parts of typological series paralleling events in the Hebrew Testament with those in the Christian Testament.[24] Some chronological series continue with stories in which the theme of the "one just man" predominates, as in Milton's account of the prophecies to Adam (Books 11 and 12): Noah, Abraham, Joseph, and Moses particularly carry forward the theme of salvation and are understood as types of Christ.

Church windows and "Picture Bibles" often follow typological programs juxtaposing the story of Adam and Eve to events in the life of Christ. For example, the early sixteenth-century windows for King's College Chapel, Cambridge, put the Temptation of Eve (by a Serpent whose face and bosom mirror hers) between the Annunciation and the Nativity. But the typological explanation for this juxtaposition in the fifteenth-century blockbook *Biblia Pauperum* does more than contrast Eve to Mary and sin to salvation: God (from the midst of a tree) says to the Serpent, "She shall crush your head, and you will lie in wait for her heel," words fulfilled, the commentary explains, by the Annunciation. On the same page appears the prophecy of Jeremiah, "The Lord has created a new order of things on earth: woman is to be the protectress of man" (Jer. 31:22).[25] The focus of the commentary is not the judgment of Eve but the judgment of the Serpent, in a prophecy of the Incarnation whose language is redemptive of woman.

Although typological treatments usually contrast Adam to Christ and Eve to Mary, some stress their similarities.[26] In others, the Creation of Eve is the type of the birth of the Church when the side of Christ is pierced, and the sacramental water and blood flow forth, at the Crucifixion. In a *Bible Moralisée* in the Bodleian Library the Creator (as Christ-Logos) leads Adam, with a hand on his shoulder, into Paradise, interpreted as *ecclesia,* and the Creation of Eve, in which the Creator raises her by the wrist, is matched with a Crucifixion: not with water and blood, but with an actual child being extracted from Christ's side as Eve is from Adam's, to reinforce the analogy between Eve and the Church.[27] The *Biblia Pauperum* places the Temptation of Adam and Eve (each holding up fruit) next to the Temptation of Christ, the pairing Milton chose for his epics. (One of the types of the Harrowing of Hell, with Christ leading Adam and Eve out of Hellmouth, is Samson overpowering the lion by forcing open its jaws.)[28]

Typological treatments may present a "fortunate fall": Eve's disobedience appears as a necessary forerunner of the Annunciation and the Nativity. However, the possible suggestion that grace is dependent on sin, and that sin is therefore necessary or desirable, was rejected from Reformation iconography. It was also removed from the English liturgy by the compilers of the Book of Common Prayer. The Exultet with its *felix culpa* is not included, and the typological statement that begins the Almanack does not make the Annunciation parallel to the Fall of Eve, but links it to the Creation as the moment of the Incarnation, with no mention of the Fall nor implication that the Incarnation was dependent on it: "Note that the supputation of the yeere of our Lord in the Church of England, beginneth the xxv. day of March, the same day supposed to be the first day vpon which the world was created, and the day when Christ was conceiued in the wombe of the Virgine Mary."[29]

With regard to creation itself, the impression most short creation series and most typological parallels are likely to give is that creation, especially the creation of woman, led directly to the Fall and a world of woe not to be mended until the Last Judgment, except in the transcendent realm of the spirit. In contrast, some series include motifs that are not only redemptive but also regenerative: that is, they suggest the possibility not only of salvation in the next world but also of the rebirth of human hearts and wills in, and the renewal of, the green and pendent earth on which we live. Such versions include abundant plants and animals and regenerative motifs immediately concerning Adam and Eve themselves: affirmations of their original goodness and, after the Fall, of their repentance and their rehabilitation by a compassionate Christ as Creator who clothes them with his own hands, an act figuring the "garments of salvation" and the "robe of righteousness" of Isaiah 62:10. These motifs were especially favored by northern artists, both Catholic and (in the sixteenth and seventeenth centuries) Protestant; and both the teeming creation and the mutuality of man and woman in both fall and recovery were distinctly preferred for illustrations to Genesis in the vernacular Bibles of the Reformation. What most differentiates artists' approaches to these topics (apart from representing God or his name) is not whether they are Catholic or Protestant but whether they belong to a literal and typological or an allegorical tradition.

Among works by Flemish artists, Nicholaes de Bruÿn's elegant engravings after Maerten de Vos contain the usual scenes but also some regenerative motifs. An energetic Father-God, deeply engaged in his work (as in figs. 13 and 14), accomplishes the six days' creation, breathes life into Adam, raises Eve from his side by the hand, and, in the background, presents Eve to Adam, who gestures his response: "This is now bone of my bones, and flesh of my flesh" (Gen. 2:23). Between these last two scenes is, disconcertingly, a goat, the symbol of lust (though also a favorite Netherlandish animal), but also a unicorn, symbol of purity. This double symbolism, giving viewers multiple connotations and opportunities for choice, is common in seventeenth-century creation pictures. At the same time, the many kinds of animals that surround Adam and Eve are simply themselves, enjoying their Edenic lives. The Admonition follows, with Adam and Eve kneeling prayerfully. Next comes the Fall, with both Adam and Eve leaning voluptuously against the forbidden tree. Adam has already accepted the fruit, while the Serpent, with a woman's face and torso, reaches it or another down, not to Eve but to him. Whatever the chronology of these two gestures, they stress Adam's responsibility for the Fall. The scene includes animals with entirely benign attributes (the hart and the elephant) as well as mainly cautionary ones (goat, boar, and fox). The dog and the rabbits are symbols of fidelity and procreation, the

porcupine of domestic nurture. Next, God finds Adam and Eve at-
tempting to hide, watched by a fox (symbol of deception), while the
hart (symbol of desire for God, from Psalm 42)[30] turns away. In the
final engraving, an angel expels Adam and Eve with a fiery sword. But
behind, God clothes Eve, having already clothed Adam, who kneels.
The narrative engraving by Jan Collaert after Maerten de Vos (fig. 15)
also shows a vigorous and fatherly God thoroughly entwined with a
responsive creation, filling the skies, the waters, and the land with
lively creatures, breathing life into Adam, and blessing Eve, whose
making is the center of a wholly beneficent scene. The series by Wierix
and Sadeler show Adam and Eve (fig. 23) or Eve especially (fig. 19)
kneeling in repentance. These examples of a benign creation and a mutual fall, repentance and clothing are part of a renovative interpretation of Genesis of which Milton's epic is the fullest flowering.

Whether serial or placed together in one frame, Genesis cycles differ
as to what parts of the story predominate. Many Renaissance and Reformation versions make central not the Fall but the Creation of Eve,
perhaps representing the Creation of Man in Genesis 1:27. It serves as
the frontispiece or the headpiece to Genesis in several early Reformation Bibles, and although there may be foreshadowings of the Fall included, the most notable features are the tenderness and attentiveness
of the Creator and the presence of sympathetic animals and sometimes
angels.[31] Ghiberti's bronze relief for the Baptistry doors—the *Gate of
Paradise*—makes the Creation of Eve the central event, with Fall in the
background, in which the two participants are entirely mutual. It is
also architecturally central in Michelangelo's ceiling painting for the
Sistine Chapel. His particular contribution to the iconography of Eve
is his depiction of her held protectively in God's arm, and peering
warily from under it, in the Creation of Adam. "I, ere thou spak'st, /
Knew it not good for Man to be alone," Milton writes; "What next I
bring shall please thee, be assur'd" (8.444-49). Michelangelo's linear
program, however, makes Eve's creation from Adam's side seem to
lead directly to the Fall; and the Serpent, with its woman's face and
torso, resembles his coarsened fallen Eve. Yet Adam, not dominated by
his wife, is the more forceful figure, thrusting his muscular arm into
the tree or toward the Serpent with perhaps what Roland Frye calls
"an avaricious grasping gesture," or perhaps one of repudiation.[32]

Many viewers have the impression that artists allied with Renaissance humanism endow the humans in the creation story with greater
dignity and centrality than earlier versions do, and in one way that is
true: the human body and human emotions become dominant and
sometimes magnificent. At the same time, many Renaissance paintings

give greater prominence to the Fall, appear to ascribe more fault to woman and the passions of the flesh, and allot less space to the rest of creation than earlier ones had done, and than seventeenth-century northern versions less influenced by classicism would do. Often the southern masters condense the whole story into one powerfully erotic and psychologically shattering dramatic moment that associates Eve with brief pleasure and immeasurable woe. When interpreted allegorically, they imply a dualistic opposition between spirit and flesh[33] that has roots in patristic commentary and especially in early efforts to syncretize Scripture and myth. Perhaps because of the artists' sheer skill and the sensuous gorgeousness of their figures, this impression of the creation story seems to have gained ascendancy. "Forbidden knowledge" is confounded with sexual knowledge,[34] with the implication that human beings must choose between erotic and spiritual fulfillment. In much modern interpretation, sympathy shifts from the spiritual side of the dualism, favored by the church fathers, to the sensual side, tempting the view—emotionally, if not intellectually—that the Fall was "fortunate" in initiating sexual passion and making humanity, in secular terms, more "human." This kind of "fortunate fall" splits humanity and divinity, rather than integrating them as Milton and other English poets thought it was the purpose of art to do.

Charles Trinkaus cautions against applying the term "humanist" to the visual arts unless a documented humanist literary program is present; the "style *all'antica*" developed in parallel with the "*studia humanitatis*," but visual artists and humanist literati were essentially independent. However, "possible connections between humanism and art" may be found in the work of "artists who showed classical, rhetorical, or allegorical elements in their work." It is the application of allegorical thought to Scripture that I find problematic, because it deepens the potentiality for misogyny in interpretations of Eve at the same time that the beauty of Renaissance figure-painting heightens her power as temptress.

Trinkaus points out that Leon Battista Alberti developed "a fully humanist theory of art," defining in *Della pittura* (1435-36) "three necessary elements in painting: the evocation of spatial and historical actuality by a combination of artificial perspective and a system of proportion and scale based on the human figure; the invention of an *istoria* (theme, dramatic situation, or historical episode to be depicted); and its elaboration through the use of appropriate color, light, proportion, composition, and affective movement to communicate a living, moving visual drama that would edify, terrify, instruct, or please the viewer." Raphael's Stanza della Segnatura "made the full statement of the Albertian program for a rhetorical and humanist art . . . providing a complete concordance of pagan antiquity, Christian spirituality, and Roman history."[35] These specifications also apply in literary terms—*ut pictura poesis*—to Milton's poem,[36] but distinctions need to be made as well.

Raphael's fresco of the Fall on the ceiling of the Stanza della Segnatura represents an erotically compelling Eve, with an Eve-faced Serpent and an Adam "overcome with Female charm" (9.1009) reaching for the minute fruit, perhaps a fig, Eve offers; she herself appears to be the delicious prize he craves. When we turn from the Temptation to the other ceiling paintings connected to it and the great frescoes below, we find a regenerative program representing learning, justice, the arts, and the Sacrament, above which is a segment of a Dantean heaven—though unlike Dante, whose *Paradiso* is well populated with women and includes a redeemed Eve at Mary's feet, Raphael admits only Mary.[37]

If one is thinking allegorically, the ceiling painting in the Stanza that "provides a concordance" between classical antiquity and *The Fall* is the *Apollo and Marsyas*. The defeat of the satyr in a music contest by Apollo (who is the patron god of *Parnassus* and the sculptured companion of Minerva in *The School of Athens*) is usually interpreted as "Divine Harmony victorious over Earthly Passions,"[38] or of reason over appetite, or of enlightened art over sensual art. Both Old Testament ceiling scenes, *The Judgment of Solomon* and *The Fall,* relate to this scene, suggesting a victory of reason in *The Judgment of Solomon* but of passion in *The Fall:* an event introducing discord to be restored to harmony by the combination of wisdom, art, and divine grace depicted in *The School of Athens, Parnassus,* and the heavenly and earthly Eucharist traditionally called the *Disputà.*

Since beauty and the senses are good gifts, perverted by the Fall but restorable by grace, wisdom, and good art, one may say that Raphael's beautiful and sensuous Eve represents good, but corruptible, but also redeemable, human qualities, as does Adam. By patristic tradition, however, Eve's are of the senses and passions, Adam's of the mind. Whether or not Raphael intended such an allegory, it is easy to see Eve's elegant sensuousness as a danger to the rational mind unless firmly subordinated; and it is difficult to separate this quality from her womanhood. That is, instead of seeing rational and passionate humanity letting passion disastrously overrule reason—as I would like to think Raphael suggests—we are apt to see sensuous woman overruling rational man. When Milton takes pains to assert Eve's rational and spiritual graces, he mitigates against this common allegory.

In Tintoretto's painting of the Fall at the Scuola Grande de San Rocco (fig. 30) and in his similar brilliant painting for Santa Maria della Trinità now at the Galleria dell'Accademia (Frye, fig. 173), the tension between Adam's hunched and shadowy disobedience and Eve's light-bathed, assured sensuality is devastating. The San Rocco program, however, places the Fall near a Nativity and a Temptation of Christ, connecting the topics of Milton's three major poems about the Son of God. When reproduced outside their redemptive or regenerative contexts, such paintings as Raphael's and Tintoretto's may seem to present a more divisive view of the creation story than they do in context.

When patristic interpreters who adapted the allegorical exegesis of myth promoted an interpretation of Eve as sinful flesh overcoming Adam as reason,[39] their intention was to convert pagans by showing that the Scriptures could be interpreted philosophically. But the accommodation ran the risk of hybridizing the Genesis tradition. The allegorization of Genesis is almost inevitably misogynous, inviting into the Hebrew creation story the far more damaging associations of Greek myth.[40]

In Hesiod's *Theogony* Zeus creates woman in revenge for man's acquisition of fire, or divine knowledge; and his *Works and Days* calls her "this plague for men . . . this sheer inescapable snare."[41] Pandora is designed to bring woe into the world, while Eve is designed as "meet help," and so is capable of redemption and regeneration even though she falls. The Renaissance painting that most explicitly identifies Eve with Pandora is Jean Cousin's *Eva prima Pandora* (Trapp, fig. 26; Frye, fig. 209). But whenever a sensuous, enticing Eve holds out fruit to an Adam weakened by sexual desire, the allegory that opposes man, soul, reason, and virtue to woman, flesh, passion, and corruption is apt to cling to the Genesis story, which by itself does not imply those oppositions. Milton carefully sorts out, while comparing, scriptural and mythical implications when he writes that unfallen Eve is "more lovely" than Pandora. He adds that she is "too like / In sad event," but the context of these lines stresses her difference from Pandora before that sequel. Brought to Adam by the punfully "genial" angel, Eve "deckt . . . her Nuptial Bed" while "heav'nly Choirs the Hymenaen sung"; Pandora was "brought by *Hermes*" and "ensnar'd Mankind . . . to be aveng'd" on Prometheus for his theft (4.709-19). God makes Eve to be Adam's "fit help, thy other self, / Thy wish, exactly to thy heart's desire" (8.450-51) and until the "sad event" she and Adam have lived in "Simplicity and spotless innocence" and "thought no ill . . . the loveliest pair / That ever since in love's imbraces met" (4.318-22). Even

if "help" and "wish" seem unduly patriarchal to modern readers, both
Milton's Eve and the Eve of celebratory iconography are far different
from the "sheer inescapable snare" of Hesiod and the painful dualism
of allegorical interpretations. Similarly, when Milton compares Eve
with Venus, as visual artists sometimes did by imitating the stance of
classical representations of Venus when painting or sculpting Eve
(Cranach or Rizzo, for example), or with other classical figures, he always subordinates the classical analogue, making unfallen Eve more
beautiful and more virtuous or "too like" after the Fall. In this way
Milton clears unfallen Eve of dubious attributes.[42]

An erotic fall, I suspect, is the one most people now think of when
imagining Adam and Eve. But it departs from the iconographic tradition of medieval churches and manuscripts and was increasingly rejected from Reformation Bible illustrations. From the Protestant point
of view, it errs by making Eve's primary function the temptation of
Adam or by implying that the Fall was emotionally fortunate. Milton
does neither.

In contrast to allegorical renderings, the more literally an artist
reads the Genesis story, the more cheerful the rendition is apt to be.
The anonymous early thirteenth-century stone carvers and mosaicists
who decorated Chartres and San Marco, though in very different
styles, loved goodness and holiness, delighted in the creation, sor-
rowed for its hurt, and rejoiced in repentance and deliverance. Milton
and many artists, composers, and other poets of the sixteenth and seventeenth centuries also refused the simple and destructive false dilemma of opposing matter to spirit and developed the literal and
typological mode to give prominence to the blessedness of the creation
and the regeneration—however laborious—of its human tillers and
keepers. This literalism is not opposed to spiritual and moral interpretation, but attaches it firmly to the possibilities of regeneration in daily
experience.[43]

Although treatments of Genesis in the visual arts differ in many
ways, and often include hopeful motifs, they are alike in omitting to
do what Milton did superbly: representing Adam and Eve in innocence, not only enjoying each other and the Garden but learning,
growing, founding the human community, creating the arts, and caring for the earth. With a few exceptions, the dominant pattern even in
regenerative versions in the visual arts is creation, disobedience, loss,
repentance, and rehabilitation, with little notion of an active virtuous
life before the Fall to model a regenerate life upon. Their difference
from less happy versions is in their love of the creation and their inclusion of regenerative motifs. During the Middle Ages, this celebratory view of Genesis appeared in engagingly detailed creation scenes.

At the beginning of the Reformation it appeared in Bible illustrations of the blessing of creation. Around the beginning of the seventeenth century, building on the medieval topos of the marriage of Adam and Eve, it emerged as a celebration, as well, of their nuptial greeting and domestic conversation. Occasionally, as in the Middle Ages, it dwelt upon their repentance and symbolic clothing.

There are, then two positive ways of looking at the Genesis story. One makes the Fall central and even necessary, but deems it fortunate. The other also rejoices in redemption, but not in sin; it celebrates a good creation blighted by human greed, ambition, and forgetfulness, but has faith both in ultimate redemption and in the possibility of repairing both the ark of earth and the inner arks of our souls. The examples that follow exhibit the latter kind.

## Monuments and Manuscripts

Any reasonably well preserved cathedral church and its library offer a lifetime's study. A cathedral's sculptures, glass, and frescoes and the illuminations of its Bibles, missals, breviaries, lectionaries, psalters, antiphonals, and other service books, along with other manuscripts written within its precincts, form an immensely rich and multiply interconnected Bible commentary in which, as Herbert says of the Bible itself, "This verse marks that." For those who accept visual commentary on the Word, his description might fit a cathedral as well, with a happy pun on its storied windows:

> Oh that I knew how all thy lights combine,
> And the configurations of their glorie!
> Seeing not onely how each verse doth shine,
> But all the constellations of the storie.[44]

Most cathedrals include the Creation story in mosaic, sculpture or glass, and many include regenerative motifs as well as redemptive contexts.

That church art survives at all must be part miracle. Wars, iconoclasms, revolutions, weather, pollution, traffic, collectors, and inexpert restorers have taken heavy tolls. Nevertheless, the deep love of Creator and creation expressed in carved and sculpted figures, the vibrant window "lights" and the faithfully detailed illuminations and luminous frescoes that remain form configurations of glory. England, however, was among the places especially hard hit by iconoclasm. Though measures could be taken to preserve its treasures through two world wars, nothing can bring back windows smashed by the pikes of furious revolutionaries, faces slashed off the intricate woodcarvings of choir screens and finials, or statues considered idols, lassoed, and pulled down. Nevertheless, enough remains to assure us that English cathedrals shared an iconography, splendidly confirmed by English manuscripts, in which the Creator (and the artist) expresses delight in all creatures and both sexes. In the creation series on the west front of Wells Cathedral, the Creator has his arm around both Adam and Eve as he shows them the garden and the forbidden tree, and in the same scene in the Chapter House at Salisbury, the Creator holds Eve's hand. English psalters, with their wealth of natural detail, give evidence of a profoundly creation-affirming tradition that may be partly lost from church decoration.

English illuminations, Byzantine mosaics, and the cathedrals of northern France—all connected through an international exchange of artists and manuscripts—present striking examples of Edenic iconography. Because of its amplitude and Milton's probable familiarity with it, I begin the following examples with the Creation Dome of San Marco.[45]

## The Mosaics of San Marco

Italian art affected Milton's imagery, as Roland Frye has generously shown. But it is easy to suppose that what Milton liked best is what modern viewers like: its sensuous humanity and technical excellence. I suspect he was responsive, as well, to qualities we praise less often. Of the public, monumental Creation cycles that he saw on his Italian journey, one that is particularly close to *Paradise Lost* iconographically is the Creation Dome of the Basilica of San Marco in Venice, where during the spring of 1639 he "spent a month's time," Edward Philips tells us, "in viewing of that stately city."[46]

Like *Paradise Lost,* and like medieval creation series in many forms, the San Marco mosaics typologically encompass the whole Bible. The stories in the west atrium favor Noah, Abraham, and Joseph as prefiguring Christian redemption and prepare for the interior, with its empathetic depictions of the life of Christ and its great domes of the Ascension and the gift of the Spirit at Pentecost. Like Milton's poem, the mosaics treat the creation story amply and literally. In the dubious context of a city prone to "gay religions full of Pomp and Gold" (2.372), the Creation mosaics offered the English traveler a breath of more familiar air.

Seventeenth-century Venice—a city "stately" in both senses of the word—had the loveliness we can still see, a civic myth of virgin virtue, and a long-standing reputation for vice. Boccaccio had described it three hundred years earlier as "vinegia dogni bructura ricevitrice,"[47] which a seventeenth-century translator renders "the receptacle of all foule sinne and abhomination."[48] The city carried on then, as now, a tourist industry that permitted access to many public buildings, and descriptions of San Marco and its Treasury[49] catalogue precious ornaments with an admiration of sheer wealth reminiscent of Milton's Mammon,

> the least erected Spirit that fell
> From Heav'n, for ev'n in Heav'n his looks and thoughts
> Were always downward bent, admiring more
> The riches of Heav'n's pavement, trodd'n Gold,
> Then aught divine or holy else enjoy'd
> In vision beatific.

(1.679-84)

Entering San Marco in 1644 had a similar effect on John Evelyn, who says little of the marvelously crafted scriptural subjects of the great domes and storied walls, but remarks that "the floor is all inlaid with agates, lazulis, calcedons, jaspers, porphyries, and other rich marbles, admirable also for the work; the walls sumptuously encrusted, and presenting to the imagination the shapes of men, birds, houses, flowers, and a thousand varieties."[50] He notes much else as well of the preciousness of marbles, gold, and other riches for which Milton's bard says men have "Rifl'd the bowels of thir mother Earth / For Treasures better hid" (1.687-88).

The decorations of the Palazzo Ducale (of which the Basilica was the chapel) represent qualities of Venetian politics both compatible with and antithetical to Milton's Reformed and parliamentarian views. On the one hand they celebrate a republican spirit and a resistence to the hegemony of papal Rome that Milton applauded. On the other, their glorification of Venice and her doges as deified conquerors is incompatible with the thought of the poet who a decade later would support the assassination of overweening monarchs.[51] For all these reasons, the morally earnest John Milton no doubt had occasion to employ the advice of Henry Wotton, who had been King James's ambassador to Venice, that "i pensieri stretti, & il viso sciolto"—confined thoughts and an open countenance—would keep his conscience and his person safe,[52] and to cultivate that capacity for seeing and knowing and yet abstaining that Venice, with its infinite airy charm, is especially suited to exercise.

Within this context, the Creation mosaics of the Basilica (figs. 27-29) offer a spirit closer to that of the English Reformation. The devisers of the San Marco program read Genesis, in part, as Milton did:

not confining the story to crime and punishment but affirming the original goodness of God's works, including Eve, and the repentance and rehabilitation of both Eve and Adam. The fullness of the San Marco program may be seen by comparison with three other versions available to Milton: the mosaic dome of the Baptistry in Florence, the paintings of Tintoretto, and the illustrations to English Bibles.

The thirteenth-century mosaics of the Baptistry[53] begin with an unusual scene that shows the Christ-Logos, in the heavens, blessing a creation to which the dove of the Holy Spirit descends; it includes earth, water, sun, moon, six single representative animals (ox, goat, hart, ram, lion, and horse), four large smiling fish, and Adam and Eve. Then, as in Genesis, the narrative starts over and presents the Creation of Adam and the Blessing of Adam and Eve, who rises from Adam's side, the Christ-Logos sitting apart on concentric spheres in both. These scenes are followed directly by the Fall in which Adam reaches for a fig Eve holds, while the snake speaks to her; then the Judgment, the stern Christ-figure pointing accusingly at Adam and Eve, while a scowling Adam points at Eve, who looks more repentant; the Expulsion by a six-winged seraph with a sword; and Labor, Eve drawing wool from a distaff and Adam hoeing very rocky ground. However, Adam and Eve both emerge from the Garden repentant and already carrying their tools, and the Christ-Logos leans from his spheres far above to bless their labor. The next scenes are the story of Cain and Abel (who gives God a live lamb). Apart from the first panel, no birds or animals (except the Serpent) appear with Adam and Eve, and the Creator sits apart and does not touch them.[54] In this typical progression, though it is sympathetically done, the creation of woman leads directly to the Fall, and the postlapsarian scenes proceed directly to its terrible effects. Milton and the San Marco mosaics sweeten this story with details of creation and renewal.

As already noted, paintings like Tintoretto's (fig. 30) at the Scuola di San Rocco, an easy walk from San Marco, may arouse disconcertingly mixed feelings and morally murky interpretations. Illustrations in English Bibles, by contrast, lack erotic beauty but show the abundance of creation and place responsibility for the Fall either squarely on Adam or on Adam and Eve together. In the Speed genealogies (fig. 44)[55] Adam and Eve visually participate equally in the Fall surrounded by various beasts, some emblematic of the Fall but others simply present: lions, squirrel, fox, cat, a handsome ox, a herd of sheep, birds on the wing, a dog, a cow, and a pair of camels. These attributes—visual equality of the sexes and the presence of diverse other creatures—may also be found in frontispieces or headpieces to Genesis in English Bibles and in series of engravings published for insertion by the binder. These and the designs of the San Marco mosaics are like-minded.

Because of their vivid color contrasts and their location just inside the south door of the west façade, the San Marco Creation mosaics, flooded with afternoon sunlight, are easily visible and richly beautiful, and although the anatomically naive figures lack the rounded, tactile verisimilitude of Renaissance paintings, their unpretentious humanity is appealing. The scenes praise the diversity of being and a Creator compassionately engaged in the making, blessing, and renewing of life. Their iconographic program has been traced to the fifth-century Greek manuscript known as the Cotton Genesis,[56] which belongs to a tradition that according to Trapp "was known in England by the end of the first quarter of the twelfth century."[57] The program is composed of twenty-six images arranged in three concentric circles, always beginning on the east.[58] Around the whole composition runs an inscription describing ardent cherubim praising with serene voices in the flaming radiance of Christ[59] (recalling the flowering of polyphony during the twelfth and thirteenth centuries), and four angels with flamelike wings fill the pendentives beneath the dome. The Son issuing from the heavenly gates "on the wings of Cherubim" with numberless angels to create the world in *Paradise Lost* (7.218) has light and power beyond color and line, but both works express his radiance and the angelic anthems that accompany his acts of creation.

The dome series (fig. 27) starts with the dove of the Holy Spirit brooding upon the waters: "on the wat'ry calm," as Raphael tells Adam, "His brooding wings the Spirit of God outspread, / And vital virtue infus'd, and vital warmth / Throughout the fluid Mass" (7.234-37). Next comes the separation of light from darkness "by the Hemisphere / Divided" (250-51)—so Milton graphically divides his lines—represented as two spheres from each of which pour six rays of light. In *Paradise Lost* morn goes forth "array'd in Gold / Empyreal" while "from before her vanisht Night, / Shot through with orient Beams" (6.12-15). Milton celebrates both day and "ambrosial Night with clouds exhal'd / From that high mount of God, whence light and shade / Spring both" (5.642-44): one of many "boths" in *Paradise Lost* that affirm the varied goodness of the whole creation, including things that archetypal critics align with the feminine and with evil.

The San Marco Creator is represented as the Logos "by whom all things were made"[60] in incarnate form, with cruciform aureole and cross-tipped staff. He is accompanied by tunic-clad angels or personifications of the six Days. At the blessing of the first five, an affirmation of the goodness of nature, they become clothed in white robes, while at their feet a river runs, complete with crocodile (sometimes but not

necessarily a symbol of chaos); and beside them pairs of birds appear
to be preparing to obey the command to increase and multiply.[61] In
the next panel, the animals appear in pairs; like Milton, the mosaicist
values reproductivity. Then, conflating Genesis 1 and 2, come the
shaping of Adam "out of the dust of the ground" and the sanctification
of the seventh Day, who kneels to be blessed before the Lord resting
(Gen. 2:2) on his throne. The Creator animates Adam, giving him a
winged soul, and leads him by the hand into Paradise, where two trees
and the personifications of the four rivers—two with mustaches—
await him. Next (in the outer circle) Adam names the animals (fig. 27,
left) "Approaching two and two" (8.350); "they rejoice / Each with
thir kind," as Milton's Adam says while pleading for a fit mate, "Lion
with Lioness, / So fitly them in pairs thou hast combin'd" (392-94).
Here, Adam's hand appears to rest on the lioness's head.

This affirmation of creativity and procreativity continues in the mosaics' treatment of Eve. Apart from the inescapable fact of the biblical
narrative that she fell first for the Serpent's fable and tempted Adam,
they give her equal dignity. While most versions show God delivering
her whole from Adam's side or raising her up from behind him, the
San Marco creation of Eve (fig. 28) follows Genesis 2 literally.[62] The
Creator extracts a rib from Adam, skin still attached, and molds, or
sculpts, Eve with the loving care of an artist; the Vulgate rendering of
the "edification" or building of Eve is clearly figured. This motif appears also in a painting by Paolo Veronese (fig. 31), who worked in
Venice and so knew the San Marco interpretation.

It is this rarer but more scriptural image, not the predominant one,
that Milton chooses. The Creator appears, Adam says, in a glorious
shape,

> Who stooping op'n'd my left side, and took
> From thence a Rib, with cordial spirits warm,
> But suddenly with flesh fill'd up and heal'd;
> The Rib he formed and fashion'd with his hands;
> Under his forming hands a Creature grew,
> Manlike but different sex.
>
> (8.465-71)

The emphasis on the Creator's hands suggests that Milton consciously
chose and stressed the forming of Eve as a separate work of art attentively made.

Having thus made Eve, the San Marco Creator presents her to
Adam (fig. 27, bottom), his hand on her shoulder. Here Milton differs,

since Eve comes "Led by her Heav'nly Maker, though unseen, / And guided by his voice" (8.485-86), a scene the mosaicist could not very well represent. Nevertheless, both declare her "divinely brought" (500) and Adam's gesture expresses his response in Genesis as Milton's words do: "I now see / Bone of my bone, Flesh of my Flesh, my Self / Before me; Woman is her Name, of Man / Extracted" (494-97). This motif was favored by seventeenth-century engravers and appears in de Bry's illustration after Maerten de Vos for the Mainz Latin Bible of 1609.

The mosaics render the Fall literally and refrain from blaming the nature of woman or sexuality. As in *Paradise Lost,* Eve is tempted separately, though Adam appears nearby, gazing absentmindedly away. She then plucks the fruit and gives it to Adam. There is no representation of Eve eating the fruit; as in many Reformation Bibles, Adam's eating is the Fall. The separation of temptations is much increased both spatially and psychologically in *Paradise Lost,* giving Adam and Eve greater individual moral responsibility (however misused) than conflated versions.

After the covering with fig leaves, hiding, and denial of guilt, the San Marco series continues with two motifs crucial to *Paradise Lost*. At the Judgment, Adam and Eve kneel repentantly (fig. 29); in *Paradise Lost,* after Adam's recriminations, their reconciliation initiated by Eve, and Adam's understanding of the Judge's prophecy, both "forthwith to the place / Repairing where he judg'd them prostrate fell" (10.1098-99).[63] Milton's "both," and the equal posture and expression of Adam and Eve in San Marco, are significant: some works, including the Ghent Altarpiece and Antonio Rizzo's sculptures in the Palazzo Ducale (Frye, figs. 187-88), show falling or fallen Adam in an agony of indecision or remorse, but Eve wearing a more ambiguous, perhaps sly, expression.[64] The spectacle of Adam and Eve kneeling together in repentant prayer is also central to another Venetian work, the eleventh-century Last Judgment in the cathedral at Torcello, in which Adam and Eve are treated with great and equal dignity. Milton too, as if to refute a conventional assumption, pointedly affirms the view that Eve is equally, soberly sorry:

> nor *Eve*
> Felt less remorse: they forthwith to the place
> Repairing where he judg'd them prostrate fell
> Before him reverent, and both confess'd
> Humbly their faults, and pardon begg'd.
> (10.1097-1101)

To complete the regenerative emphasis, the Christ-Logos clothes each of them (fig. 29); but we actually see him clothing Eve, not with skins but with cloth, as carefully as we have seen him creating her. Robing is a scriptural symbol of regeneration: "he hath clothed me with the garments of salvation, he hath covered me with the robe of righteousness, as a bridegroom decketh himself with ornaments, and as a bride adorneth herself with her jewels" (Isa. 62:10).[65] Fra Angelico, in his *Annunciation with the Expulsion,* shows Adam and Eve clothed in the "fine linen, clean and white" which is "the righteousness of the saints" (Rev. 19:8). In *Paradise Lost* the Judge turns servant and clothes them, both physically and spiritually, with similar compassion; he

> then pitying how they stood
> Before him naked to the air, that now
> Must suffer change, disdain'd not to begin
> Thenceforth the form of servant to assume,
> As when he wash'd his servants' feet, so now
> As Father of his Family he clad
> Their nakedness with Skins of Beasts, or slain,
> Or as the Snake with youthful Coat repaid;
> And thought not much to clothe his Enemies:
> Nor hee thir outward only with the Skins
> Of Beasts, but inward nakedess, much more
> Opprobrious, with his Robe of righteousness,
> Arraying cover'd from his Father's sight.
>
> (10.211-23)

Within this passage of physical and spiritual care, Milton considers also the "coats of skins" of Genesis 3:21 and suggests a nonviolent explanation. The Argument to Book Ten also underscores the Son's compassion and Eve's inclusion in regeneration: he "in pity clothes them both."

The San Marco Expulsion differs markedly from the familiar motif of angel with flaming sword chasing a terrified pair; instead the Christ-Logos, with his hand on Adam's shoulder, guides them through the gate of Paradise. Milton also depicts a swift but gentle Expulsion, with Michael their guide, who takes them by the hands. In the scene depicting labor, as Kurt Weitzmann points out, Eve seated with her distaff resembles images of the Virgin Enthroned.[66]

Finally, the postlapsarian sequence includes, in the tympanum of the southwest entry to the nave, the unusual motif of the begetting of Cain—Adam and Eve in bed together—surmounted by the injunction to "increase and multiply." Although one is inevitably aware of the transmission of original sin and its violent result, the commendation itself completes the approbation of human love and procreation that begins with the presentation of Eve to Adam. Milton, however, removes the ambiguity by celebrating the marriage bed *before* the Fall: one of many motifs he startlingly sanctifies in this way.

Although both the mosaics and the poem also depict sin and loss, the emphasis in both is on creation and regeneration; and this affirmation assumes the original goodness and the capacity for rebirth of Eve as well as Adam. The mosaics correspond to Milton's moral sense better than lusher but morally ambivalent versions do; yet the beauty of those Renaissance paintings that seem so marvelously to live and breathe gleams in the innocent sensuousness and radiant awareness of Milton's unfallen Adam and Eve.

Milton, of course, treats the story in a far more amplified way than a visual artist can: he has the expansiveness and music of a language receptive to many languages and a dramatic epic form open to reverberations. The Creation as Raphael recounts it in Book Seven combines the medieval artist's delight in detail with an Ovidian exuberance and the fearful power and awesome processes of the Book of Job. Milton incorporates into his Paradise the visual delight, the erotic power, and the nuances of human emotion that the Renaissance painters used to adorn our great progenitors. But he does so while Adam and Eve are still in a state of innocence, with "Sanctitude severe and pure . . . in true filial freedom plac't" (4.293-94) enjoying "Love unlibidinous" (5.449), trusting and free of suspicion, jealousy, possessiveness, pettiness, inchastity, or duplicity. He achieves a combination in the scenes *before* the Fall, but applicable to regeneration, of the physical beauty, the psychological complexity, and the drama of Renaissance painting with the love of innocence, the pleasure in the diversity of living things, and the sense of deep involvement of the Creator with the creation found in the medieval tradition represented by the mosaics, and so integrates the human and the divine.

When Milton describes the roof and floor of the nuptial bower of Adam and Eve, he both acknowledges the art form of the mosaicist and reverses the relation of art to nature in it: artists wrought flowers in stone, but the flowers of Paradise themselves "wrought / Mosaic" (4.699-700). *Paradise Lost* is wrought of the living word with its capacity for severe sanctity and limitless freedom, joy and gaiety, probing drama and infinite music. But the mosaicist shares with Milton an ability to call forth a pleasure in living things that is durably fresh, to evoke love of innocence, and to stir up hope of the renewal of blessedness.

## Chartres

The thirteenth century produced many benign creation scenes, not only in the Byzantine style of San Marco but for Gothic churches as well. A beautiful sculptured series of eighteen scenes adorns the central bay of the north porch at Chartres Cathedral. Each scene encompasses a section of the outer and the inner side of the archivolt; in most of the creation scenes, the Christ-Logos is seated, while beside him on the inner surface are the beings he is creating. First, with earnest, gentle face and raised hands, he makes earth and sky. Then, apparently with Moses rather than the Creator on the outer side, come Day and Night, shown as two young figures holding hands. The Creation of the Angels follows; then the Creation of the Plants, the Creation of the Sun and Moon (held by angels), and the Creation of the Birds and Fish: this scene has a human figure cheek-to-cheek with the Creator identified as "Adam in God's mind."[67] After the Creation of the Animals comes a special scene for the creation of the Earthly Paradise, in which verdant trees rise from a mount surrounded by a turreted and battlemented wall. In this series, Adam and Eve are made separately. In the Creation of Adam—on the outer edge, with more charming animals on the inner one—God molds the man; Adam's head is on his Maker's lap, being gently shaped, and his hand is on his Maker's knee. At this point the figures reverse, as they start down the other side of the arch, Adam and Eve being the two topmost Makings. The sculpture of the Creation of Eve (fig. 32) has, like that of Adam, remarkable tenderness; she stands close against her Maker's side and he holds her hand as with parted lips he speaks the blessing. The four rivers then appear, as smiling youths with urns, and then scenes of Adam giving thanks to God[68] and perhaps "Adam and Eve happy in Eden."[69] The Temptation is mutilated, but the arm positions make it apparent that Adam is reaching for a fruit Eve holds out to him; he holds his other hand to his throat. In the next scene, Adam hides under a shrub, half-kneeling and holding his head in misery, and in the Judgment, he points accusingly at Eve, who hangs her head in sorrow behind him. They are chased from Paradise by an angel with a flaming sword, and finally Adam labors, digging the rock with his spade, while Eve spins, and the Creator beside them on the outer side of the arch looks toward them and again holds up two fingers in blessing. The separate, solicitous making of Adam and Eve, their attitudes in the Judgment, and the blessing on labor are analogous to *Paradise Lost*.

The face and hands of the Creator in these sculptures combine a deliberation and potency one might call paternal with a gentleness and deep compassion one might call motherly. The images concur with the representation of the Creator as the compassionate Son during several centuries of Christian art, and with Julian of Norwich's conception of God when she exclaims, "We owe our being to him—and this is the essence of motherhood!—and all the delightful, loving protection that ever follows. God is as really our Mother as he is our Father."[70]

The "Old Testament" portal contains also the stories of Balaam, Job, Gideon, Samson, Solomon, Esther, Judith, and Tobias, read as types of redemption. Samson kills the lion and finds honey in its mouth, representing the conquest of evil (though lions are not always symbolic of evil) and the sweetness of salvation; his carrying off the gates of Gaza prefigures Christ's Resurrection, as he bursts the door of his tomb, and his breaking open the gates of hell.[71]

One may see a connection with Eve's labor of spinning in the north porch, where the contemplative life is represented by women reading and praying, and the active life by women preparing and spinning wool: a particularly significant symbol in the cathedral to which pilgrims came to do homage to the garment of the Virgin, women touching the reliquary with tunics they would wear to give them strength during the pangs of childbearing.

## Strasbourg

The west portals of Strasbourg Cathedral were heavily damaged during the French Revolution, and much of their sculpture was redone in the nineteenth century. The iconographic scheme, however, retains a medieval unity that juxtaposes Old and New Testament stories in a traditional way, but with unusual emphasis on ethical teachings traced to the influence of the thirteenth-century Dominican monk, Albertus Magnus.[72] The creation series, with its crucial moment of choice, is thus placed in a context not only of salvation but also of the moral degeneration or regeneration between which people have constantly to choose. The Wise and Foolish Virgins epitomize this theme, the foolish ones dangling their empty lamps while flirting with a jolly tempter whose true nature is seen through a split in his garment revealing toads and vipers clinging to his flesh. Both the west front and the windows of the nave represent personifications of Virtues slaying Vices, a topos based on the *Psychomachia* of Prudentius. Because virtues are traditionally represented as elegant ladies, often crowned, and vices as commoners, such representations were often defaced by revolutionaries for whom the image overrode the implicit teaching, reiterated by Chaucer's Wife of Bath, that true nobility dwells in "gentil dedes," not birth or "old richesse."[73] The west front also represents the labors of the twelve months.

The museum of Notre Dame de Strasbourg preserves a charming fragment of the thirteenth-century creation sculptures, titled "Adam Put by God into the Garden of Eden," sharing the warm intimacy expressed by the sculptures at Chartres; Adam stands close against the right side of his Maker, who holds his right hand. The present series of eighteen scenes on the west façade includes a creation of Eve with the Creator's hand held firmly and gently on her head, an Expulsion with the sad faces held close together, and a family group in which Adam, Eve, and the child Cain all touch the infant Abel on Eve's lap. Next to the Admonition and Fall, on an inner arch, is the Temptation of Christ, and next to the Family of Adam and the Labors of Adam and Eve, Samson wrestles with the lion. Milton reconfigures these typological connections in his three major poems, with their shared concern for moral choice.

These figured arches enclose the late thirteenth- or early fourteenth-century tympanum of the Passion, including Christ leading a repentant Adam and Eve out of Hellmouth. Eve stands at the right side of Adam, who holds her right hand in his, and a naked child—Abel or Seth or the Seed of Woman, standing on the back of a demon who squats on the fallen gate of hell—leans against Eve with his hand on her head.

## Rheims

The rare image of Adam and Eve in Eden before the Fall appears in the thirteenth-century creation sculptures of Rheims Cathedral, rimming the arch of the north rose window and contemporary with it: high, but visible to the naked eye if one is familiar with the motifs. The graceful figures look classical, a fact that has been attributed to contact with Greece during the Fourth Crusade.[74] The series begins with Adam alone, brooding. Eve emerges from his left side, and the two then sit side by side conversing, almost cheek to cheek. Eve speaks, with her hand on Adam's upper arm, possibly gesturing toward a small tree growing between Adam's knees and held against his shoulder. The scene just above shows the Creator seated, holding a closed book, resting and looking down on his finished work: the implication is that "God saw every thing that he had made, and, behold, it was very good" (Gen. 1:31). The ensuing scenes declare the equality of man and woman in both sin and regeneration, with an unusual emphasis on good labor. At the Fall, Adam takes the fruit and holds his right hand to his throat, as at Chartres; both sit, with the forbidden tree between them. At the Expulsion Adam and Eve, side by side, cover their nakedness with their hands. In separate sculptures, Adam digs with a mattock and Eve spins, both now clothed in cloth. More labors follow which are probably also symbols of redemption: carrying a lamb, pruning a vine, forging at an anvil or brick-making.[75] The story of Cain and Abel contains another unusual and optimistic motif, an angel bearing to heaven the soul of Abel, who in *Paradise Lost,* too, will "Lose no reward, though here thou see him die" (11.458-59). Just after it, the Christ-Logos, seated, holds up his hand in blessing, perhaps on the scenes of prophecy and labor that follow: two prophets or patriarchs, a thresher winnowing grain, a baker putting a loaf into an oven, a woman perhaps kneading loaves, and (perhaps) a musician.[76]

The rose window these sculptures arch is similarly of the regenerative mode. Above the rose, Mary suckles her Child. In the middle God creates sun, moon, and angels. The surrounding corolla pictures the Creation of Adam, a Creation of Eve in which the Christ-Logos extracts a rib from Adam, and, notably, Adam and Eve conversing in Paradise.[77] At the Fall, Eve speaks with the Snake while Adam takes a fruit from her hand; then they hide in shame and God reproaches Adam alone. After the Expulsion, Adam digs and Eve spins; but in a separate scene, Eve suckles her child, like Mary above. Other scenes show Cain tilling, Abel's sacrifice, and the Murder of Abel. Smaller sections in the outer ring contain angels and animals, including birds, fish, ass, ram, dog, hart, hounds, and an ostrich. The celebratory iconography of this Church of St. Mary also glows from the west rose, in which Mary is surrounded by twenty-four angel musicians playing different instruments, including double flute, tambourines, a gittern, a lyra or hurdy-gurdy, and a great curved horn.

### Manuscript Illustration

In spite of their comparative fragility, works on vellum provide a durable record of iconographic traditions. They are widespread, concealable from iconoclasts, and numerous, having been made not only for monastical and liturgical but also private devotional use. Manuscript creation series show that the regenerative tradition was very much alive in England during the thirteenth through fifteenth centuries. I begin however with an earlier manuscript that is eccentric in relation to motifs that were to become traditional, yet shows a spirit common to later English manuscript illustration.

### The Anglo-Saxon Genesis

Many versions of the creation story, by both northern and southern European artists, depict a Creator who is close to his creatures, typically touching Adam and Eve with his hands as he makes, blesses, or leads them. The Anglo-Saxon Genesis of the Junius manuscript and its illustrations represent an attentive God and express a cordial sympathy with Eve in her innocence and repentance. As Trapp observes, this manuscript is unusual because it "makes no explicit reference to Redemption or to Judgment."[78] In compensation, however, it expresses a respect for the creativity of God and the initial excellence of Adam and Eve that portends regeneration.

In *Genesis A* of the eleventh-century Junius manuscript,[79] the Life-giver and Savior (contrasted with the "braggart wreckers") shapes, names, and divides day and night, which have "performed the will of the Lord unceasingly upon the earth."[80] That night and darkness are separate shapings, with God-given names, is a feature of Genesis picked up by those who wish to stress that the whole creation was originally good. Unfortunately the creation of Eve is missing from the text of the Junius manuscript, but the ensuing passages establish two important matters, that Eve received her soul directly from God and that she was present for the admonition.

> It did not seem apt then to the Guardian of the skies that Adam should long remain the lonely tender and keeper of Paradise, the new creation. Therefore . . . the Author of Light and of life brought the woman into being and bestowed this helpmate upon the cherished man. . . . He instilled in her life and an immortal soul. They were comparable with the angels once Eve, bride of Adam, was furnished with a spirit. In youthfulness they both were born, radiantly beautiful, into the world by the ordaining lord's might. They knew nothing of committing or practising evil but in the bosoms of them both was a burning love of the Lord.
>
> Then the benign-hearted King, the ordaining Lord of all his creatures, blessed those first two of humankind, the father and the mother, the female and the male.

The Creator encourages the pair to increase and multiply, gives the whole creation—including the salt seas—into their joint dominion, using the dual pronoun to include them both, and asks them among this abundance to leave untouched one tree: "Then they bowed their heads devoutly to the heaven-King and spoke their thanks for all, for his skills and for those precepts." This gratitude remained a slender part of the iconography of Genesis until Milton picked it up and let it bloom. Gratitude, especially for precepts, is one of the components of blessedness hardest for Milton's Satan to find joy in.

The illustrations to the Junius manuscript, apparently derived from earlier Scandinavian models,[81] contain several unusual but not egregious features. The Creation of Adam and Eve shows the Christ-Logos blessing Eve while holding her hand (Frye, fig. 35);[82] the blessing of Adam and Eve together, who stand and hold up their hands in reverence; yet another blessing among trees and lively beasts, including a peacock, a lion, goats, and the ever-present hart; and Adam and Eve in earnest conversation, gesturing toward two trees as frankly sexual as the flora of Georgia O'Keeffe, with fantastic animals cavorting below. Several versions of the Temptation and Fall appear: Eve listening to the Serpent, Eve tempted by Satan in angelic form, Adam and Eve each receiving fruit from the fallen angel while Eve bites a third, Adam receiving fruit from Eve while the fallen angel eggs her on. In the text of *Genesis B* (interpolated into *Genesis A*) a secret messenger from Satan takes the form of a snake and cleverly tells Adam that he brings a message from God commanding him to eat of the once forbidden tree, now that his obedience has been tried, and obtain its supposed benefits. Adam withstands him, but he persuades Eve, whom God had given "a frailer resolution," partly by promising to protect Adam by not reporting Adam's hostility when he goes back to heaven. Even after she succumbs, Eve is "the most beautiful of wives that might come into the world, because she was the work of the hand of the heavenking." Calling her tempter "God's good angel," she claims to be able to see, now that she has eaten, the throne of God with multitudes of angels, and offers gladly to share the source of her enlightenment with Adam, eventually wearing him down. "Yet she did it out of loyal intent. She did not know that there were to follow so many hurts and terrible torments for humankind."

Illustrations follow of the shame and hiding (apart and sulking) of Adam and Eve, the Judgment (with the Serpent upright on the end of his tail, Adam partially and Eve fully kneeling), the Expulsion, and the Birth of (apparently) Abel. The text emphasizes remorse, especially Eve's. The repentant pair converse sorrowfully and often fall on their knees together, and Eve freely confesses and laments her fault. They are judged, dressed, and expelled, but God does not repay their defection by withdrawing his providence: he leaves them "the dome of the sky adorned with holy stars" and "the spacious bounty of earth," commanding each species to provide their fruits.

The God of this manuscript is capable of great severity, crushing the rebel angels like a Nordic warlord for their arrogant rejection of "God's loving friendship"; and the aftermath of the fall issuing out of the murder of Abel is grim. But Adam and Eve receive respect along with suitable grief. Later medieval versions of the Genesis story do not share the idiosyncracies (as they came to be) of its Anglo-Saxon illustrators, but many share delight in the Life-giver's inventions and give dignity to Adam and Eve as the work of his hands.

### English Psalters

Some of the most affirmative among the innumerable images of Adam and Eve in illuminated manuscripts are found in English psalters, a genre that had both liturgical and private devotional use. Some psalters begin with a creation series; some incorporate one into the initial *B* at the beginning of Psalm 1, *Beatus Vir:*

> Blessed is the man that hath not walked in the counsel of the ungodly, nor stood in the way of sinners, and hath not sat in the seat of the scornful.
> But his delight is in the law of the Lord; and in his law will he exercise himself day and night.
> And he shall be like a tree planted by the water-side, that will bring forth his fruit in due season.
>
> (Ps. 1:1-3)

Others include Adam and Eve in illustrations to other psalms, including Psalm 53 (Vulgate 52), and to the Apostle's Creed. At least two English psalters use Old Testament scenes chronologically, starting with Genesis, to illustrate each psalm, regardless of their content.[83] Many include images pertinent to blessedness or regeneration, such as happy birds and animals, the touch of the Creator's hand as Eve emerges from Adam's side, and Eve at the Admonition standing by Adam with her hand on his shoulder. Several less usual motifs occur as well.

In the thirteenth-century Windmill Psalter,[84] made in East Anglia or Canterbury, the historiated initial *B* of Psalm 1 (fig. 33) is fundamentally a Tree of Jesse, but the rim of the initial contains a wholly benign series of the seven days of creation. On the sixth day, at the lower right edge of the *B,* the Christ-Logos creates Eve by modeling her from Adam's bone: the rib is in the Creator's left hand, while on its tip he forms her head—still apparently asleep, but eye-to-eye with him. His expression, here as throughout, is attentive and loving, and animals watch with a wild but benign intensity. At the top of the *B,* the Creator blesses the creation, holding a book inscribed "ego sum pa[stor bonum]," the providential Good Shepherd even in the act of creation, who will return in the Incarnation for which the seed of Jesse provides the human substance.

In the fourteenth-century Tickhill Psalter, made in Worksop Priory, Nottingham, perhaps by Prior Tickhill,[85] the Christ-Logos draws Adam from the earth by the hand and, after the creation of Eve, presents her to Adam, who names her.[86] At the Admonition, he holds Adam's hand; both Adam and Eve raise theirs in a gesture of attention to his words inviting them to eat of every herb and tree but one, and warning them that eating of that one will bring death into the world.

In the late fourteenth-century psalter and Book of Hours made for the Bohun family,[87] along the bottom of the *Beatus* page, the Christ-Logos separates Eve from Adam's flesh, and God rests and pronounces his work good. Between these two miniatures comes a rare sample of life in the Garden, Eve among the fruit trees "Likest . . . *Pomona*" (9.394) and Adam among the animals (fig. 34). On a later page, at the Fall, Adam holds fruit Eve has just given him; repentant, both kneel; the Creator gives fur tunics to both Adam and Eve; Adam digs and Eve spins, still wearing the same well-cut clothes.[88]

A thirteenth-century English *Psalterium et Horae* that belonged to the nuns of Carrow, near Norwich, depicts the Creation of Eve, the Admonition (with Adam and Eve, oddly, clothed), the Fall (with Eve literally de-faced—as Milton's Adam calls her—by a misogynous vandal), and a gentle Expulsion. But in addition (fig. 35), an angel gives spade and distaff to Adam and Eve, an idea Milton uses, but transfers, as he does many others, to their life before the Fall when he suggests that angels may have brought their "Gard'ning Tools" (9.391-92), thus making work, like procreation, originally innocent. In several other English psalters as well—the Psalter of St. Swithin's Priory, the Winchester Psalter, and the Psalter of Queen Mary for example—angels give Adam and Eve the implements necessary for life outside the Garden.[89] A similar motif appears in the rose window of the north transept of Lincoln Cathedral, identified as "The angel instructing Adam and Eve in the arts of digging and spinning."[90] The motif seems to be a speciality of English artists. Milton's speculative use of it not after but before the Fall confirms and expands the impression that labor is a regenerative opportunity rather than a curse; and he treats it that way in Book 10 when Adam says "My labor will sustain me" and assures Eve that whatever may be "remedy or cure / To evils which our own misdeeds have wrought, / Hee will instruct us praying, and of Grace / Beseeching him" (10.1056, 1079-82).

In the early fourteenth-century Psalter of Queen Mary,[91] the Christ-Logos creates the world with compasses, and the creation

series ends with the Creator in a mandorla holding the globe and raising his hand in blessing, surrounded by angels with musical instruments, symbolizing harmony. After the Expulsion, with Adam and
Eve arm in arm, an angel gives them garments and a spade. An angel
also instructs Noah, who has an ax in his hand and begins building an
ark with it, continuing the theme of angelic aid to human labor.

The other redemptive image of Adam and Eve regularly found in
psalters is the Harrowing of Hell, a topic not pertinent to Milton except as part of a tradition that treats Eve with respect. In the Utrecht
Psalter (produced in Rheims in the eighth or ninth century and
brought to Canterbury, where it had considerable influence on English psalters) and in the Canterbury Psalter (derived from the Utrecht
Psalter and located at Trinity College, Cambridge, in Milton's time)
Christ stoops solicitously and raises Adam and Eve from the pit of hell,
to illustrate Psalm 16 (Vulgate 15), verse 10: "For thou wilt not leave
my soul in Hell"; the second half of the verse is illustrated by the Three
Marys at the empty tomb. A similar image of the Harrowing illustrates the Apostles' Creed in the psalters as well as in other genres.
This widespread topic was also a favorite subject of Byzantine artists
and often used in Italy. Adam and Eve emerge from hell with great
dignity in the Last Judgment mosaic at Torcello, and in a fresco in the
Spanish Chapel at Santa Maria Novella in Florence a slightly aged and
very beautiful, deep-eyed Eve accompanies Adam out of hell, followed
by Abel and a throng of the elect that includes both men and women.
A fine fifteenth-century relief in alabaster from Nottingham shows
Christ firmly grasping Adam's wrist while he and Eve prayerfully issue
forth, followed by others, from a gaping, tooth-rimmed Hellmouth.[92]
In the Winchester Psalter, while an angel keeps demons at bay, Adam
leaps forward as Christ raises him by the hand, and Eve kneels grasping the staff of the Cross of the Resurrection Christ holds.[93] Although
in most images Christ leads forth Adam closely followed by Eve, in the
Canterbury Psalter and others related to it, Christ draws them forth
firmly grasping Eve, as well as Adam, by the wrist. And in a psalter at
Trinity College (fig. 36),[94] although Eve is behind Adam, it is her
hand the Savior holds.

Imagery usually associated with the Creation appears in illustrations to other psalms and canticles as well: notably Psalm 148, *Laudate
Dominum,* and the *Canticum Trium Puerum,* or *Benedicite Omnia Opera,* the Song of the Three Children in the fiery furnace from the apocryphal part of Daniel, which would continue to be appointed for
morning prayer in the English rite; Milton models the morning prayer
of Adam and Eve on these two poems and included "The three chil-

dren" in his list of possible topics for poems and plays.[95] In the Utrecht and Canterbury psalters, the *Canticum* is illustrated by an image of the Creator in a circle representing the heavens, with sun and moon (both with faces, as in creation scenes) and stars within it and three angels on each side; beneath him, trees with birds and two groups of "the children of men," and in the center a figure with raised hands between showers of rain and snow; below, the three children in the furnace between streams flowing from wells, and many animals in pairs, including the hart and others familiar from creation scenes. Psalm 148 is decorated with a similar image. In the Bromholm Psalter, made in East Anglia in the early fourteenth century, Psalm 97, *Cantate Domino,* has its initial *C* adorned with two scenes: in the upper half, a Creation, with the Christ-Logos drawing (on the ground) with large compasses, while on one side many kinds of birds, and on the other of many kinds of animals, watch attentively. In the lower half, David (seated, crowned) serves as choirmaster to five tonsured clerks singing from a music book: an appropriate pairing for psalms that re-create "the fair musick that all creatures made."[96]

## The Hague Bible

Medieval Bible illuminations are of course ample and varied.[97] Sometimes the Six Days and God's Rest on the Seventh are all included in the initial *I* of *In principio;* sometimes one or two events cover a whole page; some are in separate series, inset illustrations, or illuminated small initials. Like the psalters, they portray the intense, lively, loving attention of the Creator to his creatures and of them to him. Often he holds or touches them, as in the Lambeth Bible; in a Bible made for the Cathedral at Rheims, the Creator blesses several fish while holding one of them—with his hand, considerately, under water.[98]

An especially attractive and, I think, representative example of Bible illumination that may have influenced Renaissance and Reformation Genesis engravings is the Hague Bible, written in Paris by Raoulet D'Orleans and given to Charles V in 1372. The relation of Creator to creation is, again, one of affectionate intimacy. In the illustration for the fifth day, the Creator holds a bird and a fish in his hands. In the Creation of Adam he blesses the new-made man while holding one arm under his head, their faces close together. He also holds Eve's wrist as she emerges from Adam's side. The Fall is dramatic: Adam holds the fruit in one hand and clutches his throat with the other, as if howling or choking (a motif also found in cathedral sculptures and windows and engraved illustrations), while Eve has fruit in each hand

and reaches one toward Adam. In the next image God clothes Adam and Eve with skins of beasts—heads and tails still attached, in contrast to Milton's doubt about the slaying of animals (10.217-18). The expelling angel has a hand on Adam's shoulder and points a raised sword at him. The murder of Abel contains an inset in which the soul of Cain appears to plead before God. The artist paints a clear message: creation and repentance are good things, the fall a misery.

## Illustrations to English Printed Bibles, 1535-1640

The images of Eden best known to English poets and their audiences were of course illustrations in English printed Bibles: surely eagerly viewed after the hard-won battle for vernacular Scriptures.[99] These abounded in this period both as intrinsic parts of printed Bibles and as separate publications to be inserted by the binder. Since, in the former case especially, they had to be theologically acceptable, every implication is significant. The version of the Fall described as "Eve holding the fruit or in the act of plucking it, or, having taken a bite, offering it to Adam"[100] appears only rarely in the vernacular Bibles of the Reformation, and often the habit of blaming Woman is deliberately foiled. Usually, either Adam holds the fruit, or Eve and Adam grasp it together, implying mutual culpability. If Eve holds the fruit, usually she has not taken a bite, and her gesture implies not sexual seduction but verbal persuasion. During the first century of English Bibles, illustrations specifically and progressively combat all inclination to blame Eve more than Adam for the Fall; and this reform is part of a grander program that, refusing the notion that God made anything defective, proclaims original blessedness, woe for its loss, and hope of regaining what Milton called "our beginning, regeneration, and happiest end, likeness to God."[101]

Creation images, as we have seen, depict God in three principal ways, as benevolent Father, or as Christ-Logos, or as a "glory" or radiance, sometimes in triple or triangular form, usually around a Tetragrammaton, the four-letter Hebrew name vocalized as Yahweh or Jehovah and translated in English Bibles as "the Lord God." Only the earliest English Bibles contain the first two; authorized Bibles use the third. Reformation artists (and some Catholic ones) increasingly used the nonanthropomorphic Tetragrammaton and sometimes reworked engravings to remove the paternal image. At present, some literary critics argue that both the paternity and the invisibility of God are inventions designed to promote male authority. It is important to recognize that patriarchal figures of God were rarely used in English Bibles.[102] When Milton or others do use them, it could be argued that

since a coherent civilization depends on the voluntary acknowledgment of fatherhood—a condition, unlike motherhood, not obvious in
nature—figures of beneficent paternity are a useful "likeness to God"
to promote. Symbols of invisibility, on the other hand, are relatively
gender-free.

The first Bible printed in English, Coverdale's translation of
1535,[103] has four images of Adam and Eve. On the title page by Hans
Holbein (fig. 37, upper left), the serpent speaks to Eve, but Adam, not
Eve, holds the forbidden fruit. At the beginning of Genesis (fig. 38),
six images show Christ as Creator performing the six days' work, in
the sixth stooping to raise Eve by the hand from Adam's side and
kindly blessing them. In the inset illustration to Genesis 2 the Christ-
Logos again blesses them as Eve rises from Adam's side with joined
hands. The fact that these images continued in illustrations to Reformation Bibles makes Milton's more literal version of Genesis 2 the
more remarkable. Although most feminist interpretation sees Genesis
2 as more misogynous than Genesis 1, Milton, like the San Marco mosaicist, prefers it as an opportunity to portray Eve as a particular work
of God's art.

At the beginning of Genesis 3 in the Coverdale Bible comes another
Fall (fig. 41). Here Eve does hold the fruit, and Adam reaches toward
it, distressed but open-palmed. Both are seated (unlike the uxorious
versions where Eve dominates a collapsing Adam), and Eve's gesture is
one of persuasion, not seduction.

The Matthew Bible of 1537 has three pictures of Adam and Eve. On
the title page[104] (fig. 39) Adam's hand grasps fruit in Eve's. This is the
position of his hand in the most frequent image of the Fall; Adam does
not simply receive fruit from Eve, much less eye it with apprehension
or revulsion as he does in versions by Rubens and Tintoretto (Frye,
figs. 171 and 173), but deliberately seizes it. The inset Fall is the same
as in the 1535 Bible (fig. 41). The large frontispiece to Genesis (fig.
40) does not depict the Fall itself, but a moment of choice for the
viewer as well as the protagonists. Again, Eve's persuasive words are
the subject. Her gesture, the goat behind it, and the monkeys above
may prefigure the Fall, but nothing makes it certain to occur. There is
no Serpent visible and no fruit in Eve's hand. She is not beautiful:
erotic passion is not what is happening. They are not upright, and
Adam may be too comfortably seated for comfort, but Eve does not
dominate him and his choice is still open. The animals, conspicuous
among them the hart of Psalm 42, are abundant and benign, and on
high God holds up two fingers—not the one finger of the Admonition—in blessing.

The Great Bible of 1539 is especially important because it went rapidly through six editions and was, as its title pages proclaim, first
"apoynted to the vse of churches" (1540) and then "to be frequented
and vsed in euery church w'in this . . . realme" (1541). All six have the
same illustration to Genesis 3 (fig. 42): Adam, not Eve, holds the forbidden fruit, and this time a Serpent with a human head offers the
fruit to him. This image contrasts to the more common one in which
Adam holds the fruit while the Serpent offers fruit to Eve. Here, Eve
holds no fruit, but faces us and points accusingly toward Adam.

These illustrations concur with Calvin's interpretation of Genesis
and his analysis of the apostle Paul as teaching "not that sinne came by
the woman, but by Adam him selfe," citing Romans 5:12: "by one
man sin entered into the world." Calvin refutes the "common opinion" that Adam "was deceiued by her alluring entisements" rather than
the deceptions of Satan, and holds that "before such time as the
woman had tasted of the fruite of the tree, she told the communication
which she had with the serpent, and insnared her husband with the
same baites wherewith she herself was deceiued . . . he did not transgresse the lawe which was giuen vnto him onely to obey his wife: but
being also drawne by her pestilent ambition . . . he did giue more
credit to the flattering speaches of the deuell, then to the holy word of
God."[105] The gloss on Genesis 3:6 in the Geneva Bible (1578) agrees:
Adam ate "Not so much to please his wife, as moved by ambition at
her persuasion." These comments do not exonerate Eve, but they insist
that the Fall was Adam's choice of the fruit or pestilent pride, not Eve
or erotic love, and that the chief responsibility for the entrance of sin
into the world was his.

Many artists, even before Calvin, indicated that Eve had not yet
eaten by showing her with the fruit (unbitten) in each hand, which is
to say taking it and, usually, offering it to Adam, while Adam and the
Serpent may each hold fruit as well. This interpretation renders the
English words of Genesis 3:6, "she took of the fruit thereof, and did
eat, and gave also unto her husband with her; and he did eat" as parallelism rather than chronology. In the commonest image the act is
completely mutual.[106] In any case the image indicates that Eve had not
yet eaten when Adam accepted the fruit. Lucas van Leyden, preceding
Calvin, drew every conceivable variation on this topic, including several in which Adam apparently receives the fruit before Eve eats.[107]
When Eve both holds and gives Adam unbitten fruit, as is also the case
in the pre-Calvin Hague Bible, the implication of a simultaneous fall,
with Adam making the crucial choice, seems inescapable.

English Bible illustrations either place blame squarely on Adam—a
practice that is androcentric, perhaps, but not antifeminine—or else

represent an entirely mutual fall. And they blame it on persuasion lead-ing to free choice of deceptive ambition, not on passion or any weak-ness intrinsically linked with the feminine. They do not usually connect the Fall with sexual pleasure or imply that it was fortunate in any other way. The theological purposes of these choices are, I believe, ones that Milton saw clearly but treated differently: to show that noth-ing God made was inevitably doomed, to repair the breach between the sexes caused by misogynous assumptions, to encourage families to share a sense of responsibility toward the creation of which they are a part, and to give hope that a creation not intrinsically flawed, but poi-soned by human pride and sloth, could be restored to "what she was."

The sixteenth century produced two more important English Bi-bles, the Geneva Bible translated by Protestant exiles from the reign of Mary Tudor, and the Bishops' Bible, the official Bible of Elizabeth I. The first large Bishops' Bible (1568) has an illustration of the Fall in which Adam reaches for fruit held by a tempting Eve, as does the first large 1611 Authorized Version, but in both cases these were removed from subsequent editions. The first Bishops' Bible also has illustrations of the Creation of the World and the Creation of Eve from Virgil So-lis's *Biblische Figuren,* but with the benevolent Creator replaced by the Tetragrammaton; in the Creation of Eve new arms have been awk-wardly attached to Eve to fill the gap. In subsequent editions, the Creation series (including Cain and Abel) was removed and a head-piece to Genesis substituted with Adam seated under a tree naming or exhorting the animals. These changes form a part of a long-term pat-tern in Protestant Bibles that focuses on the Word of God (literalized in the Name), on the mutual responsibility of man and woman for the Fall, and on the events *before* the Fall that call attention to human potentiality.

Both the Geneva and the Bishops' Bibles sometimes had genealo-gies bound in, headed by a medallion of Adam and Eve, seen as equal parents of the chosen seed, engaged in a thoroughly mutual Fall. Those printed by Christopher Barker, the queen's printer, as well as some authorized versions printed by Robert Barker and his assigns, printers to James I and Charles I, often contain a frontispiece with Adam and Eve each holding fruit and each holding banners proclaim-ing their equal participation in both sin and regeneration (fig. 43). The forbidden tree itself is labeled "Created good and faire, by breach of lawe a snare," and so becomes an emblem of the whole creation. Scrolls from the two fruits in the hands of Adam and Eve explain that "desire to knowe hath wrought ovr woe. By tasting this th'exile of blisse." But the scrolls from their two free hands declare "By promise made restord we be to pleasures of eternitye." Although "desire to know" needs a careful gloss to avoid the impression that ignorance is bliss, and although pun-hunters will give it a prurient one, the main impression is of a regenerative typology in which both Adam and Eve share in both the loss and the recovery. Around Adam and Eve, diverse pleasant beasts in pairs roaming the well-watered Garden include numerous birds and fish, the hart symbolic of the soul's thirst for God, monkey, tortoise, crocodile, and pairs of bears, lions, tigers, horses, elephants, camels, goats, pigs, rhinoceroses, unicorns, foxes, sheep, cattle, dogs, and others: the engraver, it seems, was loath to leave anyone out. The snake who is disturbing this peace bears his comeuppance: "Dvste for to eate mvst be my meate." Again, the whole creation is primordially good, the Fall unfortunate, the Serpent most blamed, and Adam and Eve mutual partners in both sin and regeneration.

Probably the most familiar image of Adam and Eve in the early seventeenth century was that in the Speed Genealogies (fig. 44) regularly bound into Authorized Bibles (and some Geneva Bibles as well) from 1610 to 1640,[108] probably including the 1612 quarto Milton owned.[109] With the exception of the 1611 folio, which reverts to an Italianate image, much like Dürer's 1504 engraving (Frye, fig. 164), of Eve taking the fruit from the Serpent's mouth while Adam reaches out his open hand, the inset picture at the beginning of the genealogies perpetuates the theme of a mutual and unfortunate Fall, though its inscription attributes the disobedience, in the redemptive Pauline text (Rom. 5:19, 21), to "one man."

In the frontispiece (fig. 45) to the Edinburgh Bibles printed by Robert Young in the 1630s, of which Mary Milton is thought to have owned a copy now lost,[110] both Adam and Eve grasp one fruit while Eve takes it or another, implying that they will eat the mortal feast together. This is the common image from which Milton most pointedly departs. But he does not depart from another iconographic implication: at the feet of Adam and Eve, a pair of turtledoves symbolizes the wedded love that is the "happier Eden" (4.507) of the Paradise being lost, and behind them numerous other animals prance or repose. This benign iconography, hinted at in the frontispiece to the Bishops' and Geneva Bibles (fig. 43), is radically different from the convention of incorporating beasts emblematic of the passions the artist thinks caused the Fall. But such confirmation of the original goodness of creation and of wedded love is a subject found increasingly in early seventeenth-century visual interpretations of Genesis.

Title-page design for the first century of English Bibles also moves toward a typology of regeneration. In early Bibles, the left side of the title page represents scenes from the Old Testament and the right side from the New, often connected at the top by the Tetragrammaton, suggesting the unity of purpose of the two dispensations. The 1535 title page (fig. 37) has, on the left, Adam and Eve, with Adam holding the fruit; then Moses receiving the Law and the Reading of the Law. Opposite and antitypical to these—that is, showing a New Testament fulfillment of an Old Testament type—are, across from the Fall, the resurrected Christ trampling serpent, demon, and skull; then his last charge to his apostles, and St. Peter preaching the Gospel. From the Name of God, Adam and Eve are addressed by a scroll (upside down to the reader): "In what daye so ever thou eatest thereof, thou shalt dye," while Christ is acknowledged, "This is my deare sonne, in whom I delyte, heare him." At the bottom of the page, Henry VIII gives a Bible to his bishops, flanked by David and St. Paul. But the title page to the Matthew Bible of 1537 (fig. 39), taken from the Van Liesvelt Dutch Bible (Antwerp, 1526, when Antwerp was a haven for Protestants) parallels the Giving of the Law with the Annunciation, a mutual Fall with the Crucifixion, and Death with the Resurrection. By pairing the Fall not with the Resurrection but with the Crucifixion, this program preserves a theme of salvation by grace without suggesting a kind of *felix culpa* that would make grace dependent on sin or allow too cheerful an attitute toward sin itself. That is, instead of a Fall-and-Resurrection typology, it aligns the sin of Adam and Eve with Death and makes the Fall a type of the Crucifixion: both trees are instruments of pain, though the trespass of one brings death and the redemptive use of the other brings health.

This rejection of a fortunate fall and its replacement by a deplorable one requiring salvation wrought by great pain, but ultimately joyous, is confirmed in verbal front-matter and annotations of English Bibles: in the Bishops' version, "The Summe of the whole Scripture," the prayer following the preface, and the note to the map showing "the situation of Gods garden"; and in the Geneva version, the annotations to Genesis.

The typology of a good creation ill lost but well regained increases in the seventeenth century. Title pages to the Authorized Version usually integrate Old and New Testament figures to suggest that the Law and the Gospel form a coherent and progressive regenerative process. The title page (fig. 46)[111] of a Bible first issued by the University printer at Cambridge in 1629, while Milton was at Christ's College there, shows a small Fall overpowered by imagery of the good creation and its repair in the present world: a proportion observed, quantitatively speaking and without undervaluing the dire results of "Mans

First Disobedience," in the earthly parts of *Paradise Lost*. Other small
medallions show the Sacrifice of Isaac halted by an angel; the Nativity
or Incarnation; and the Resurrection. At the top, the Tetragrammaton
sheds light on a shining world of the present, complete with sailboat
(a symbol, according to Valerian, of the success of the Christian
religion)[112] flanked by sun, moon, and stars as they typically appear in
creation imagery. On either side, cherubs proclaim "God saw everything that was made, and behold it was very good" (Gen. 1:31). Beneath the globe, Justice and Peace embrace each other (as in Psalm
85:10). Beside the title, Moses, with both the Law and the rod that
struck water out of rock, faces David—in the position where Aaron
stood on 1611 titles—playing his harp: the image embodies the great
psalm-singing movement that united all classes in this period, and was
perhaps more pleasing to Milton, and more representative of his Protestant college, than the figure of ecclesiastical authority it replaced. Below the title, Christ feeds his disciples, the symbolic sacrificial lamb
before him, framed by the four evangelists; and at the bottom of the
page, the hart of Psalm 42, a major figure in Edenic imagery, completes the hopeful program: "Like as the hart desireth the waterbrooks, so longeth my soul after thee, O God."[113]

This regenerative movement was not confined to England, but may
be found on the Continent and in Catholic Bibles as well. The title
page of the Douai Bible for English-speaking Catholics (Rheims,
1635) has Moses and David on either side, and above them a creation
and blessing of the animals. A four-language *Biblia Sacra* published in
Antwerp in 1637 has on its title page animals from the peaceable kingdom of Isaiah, where "the wolf also shall dwell with the lamb . . . and
the lion shall eat straw like the ox" (Isa. 11:6-7). The phoenix looks
down from above, and an emblem below, "constantia et labor"—akin
to Donne's conceit of the "stiff twin compasses"—shows the hand of
God designing with golden compasses the world which might be
peaceful if all heeded the georgic motto.

## NOTES

1. Donne, "To Sr. *Edward Herbert*. At *Julyers*," *Complete Poetry*, 233-34,
ll. 1-2 and 33-34. Anthony Low points out in *The Georgic Revolution* that although Donne's poems "touch on georgic subjects fairly often," these references "almost invariably . . . are negative." The "nature" to be repaired here is
primarily human nature. But Donne did show interest in stewardship of the
earth in his *Essayes in Divinity* and his sermon to the Virginia Company of
1622 (*Sermons* 4, Sermon 10). Insofar as man is a microcosm in his metaphors, the state of the rest of nature gives evidence of the state of humanity.

Donne's first line may allude to 1 Cor. 5:6-7, "Know ye not that a little leaven leaveneth the whole lump? Purge out therefore the old leaven, that ye may be a new lump, as ye are unleavened." Watts's translation of Augustine's *Confessions* (880) uses the expression "wee are all of the same lump" in connection with Moses' presumed authorship of the Pentateuch (2:353). Augustine's words are "ex eadem namque massa omnes venimus" (352).

Portions of this chapter and the next were published in "The Iconography of Eden" (*MS* 24 [1988]: 107-21) and are reprinted by permission.

2. "At a Solemn Musick," in *SM*, 19, ll. 17-26.

3. R. M. Frye, J. B. Trapp, Murray Roston, and others have applied visual images to the interpretation of Milton's poetry. The present study differs from these in its choice of images and its interpretation of their significance. I do not wish to argue that particular works of art influenced Milton or other poets, unless the analogies are explicitly made in their work. For Protestant writers, images are subordinate to words, and any use of them that might limit response to scriptural language is to be avoided. But awareness of visual contexts can help us interpret poems by seeing both comparisons and distinctions. Milton chose and rejected various strands of interpretation of which the visual arts provide us clear evidence.

4. Gilman, *Iconoclasm*, 1, 35, and passim. Gilman recounts the critical controversy over Milton's "visual imagination" on pages 149-50.

5. The suggestion that the Fall was an act of Promethean heroism seems not to have been considered until the Romantic era.

6. Nona Flores traces this motif in "*Virgineum Vultum Habens,*" and John K. Bonnell discusses it in "The Serpent with a Human Head."

7. In contrast, an illustration in a Vulgate Bible published in Venice in 1615 shows a female Satan tempting Christ.

8. In *Surprised by Sin* Stanley Fish shows how multiple meanings catch us out and make us aware of our sinfulness. But that is only the beginning of choice; Milton and the visual artists allied to him provide surprise by goodness, making their audiences aware of misplaced but reparable capacities.

9. Hall, *Dictionary*, 5.

10. Explicit allusions appear in Antonio Rizzo's sculpture of Eve at the Ducal Palace in Venice, modeled on the Capitoline Venus, Jean Cousin's *Eva Prima Pandora* (Frye, fig. 209), and Saenredam's similar engravings of Adam and Eve and Vertumnus and Pomona (Frye, fig. 207). Cranach's *Eve* at the Art Institute of Chicago (among others) resembles his Venus in *Venus and Cupid* at the National Gallery, London (Frye, fig. 208). Frye mentions other examples (276-80). The less explicit analogies that sensuous figures of Adam and Eve suggest may, of course, be in the eye of the beholder.

11. See Stone, *When God Was a Woman,* and Phillips, *Eve.* Schorsch and Greif trace (and perhaps overemphasize) this motif in popular art in *The Morning Stars Sang,* remarking, "Even 19th-century Americans knew that an aspect of Eve's sin was sexual knowledge" (37). Literal interpreters of Genesis did not see Eve's sin as sexual initiation.

12. Heninger, *Touches of Sweet Harmony,* 120-21.

13. Traherne, *Meditations,* 16-17. Gladys I. Wade presents the evidence for assigning this work to Traherne in her preface (1932) to Traherne's *Poetical Works,* xii-xx; it was previously attributed to Susanna Hopton. See also Day, *Thomas Traherne,* chap. 3.

14. John Leonard sensitively explicates this scene in *Naming in Paradise,* 23-35.

15. Leonard points out the rarity of Adam's naming his consort "Eve" before the Fall in *Paradise Lost,* interpreting the scene of her naming (4.449-91) with graceful good humor and pointing out the fit praise in this name (35-50); usually expositors and inscribers use some form of the generic "Woman" of Genesis 2:23.

16. Calvin, *A commentarie vpon Genesis,* 92. This image appears in art before Calvin's statement, which is quoted in the section on English Bibles later in this chapter.

17. Avril Henry points out that strong vertical lines can either divide or join them. The tree visually dividing Adam and Eve is "divisive. Their personal unity, and that of the world they stand surrogate for, is broken by the serpent and the tree" (*Biblia Pauperum,* 19). At the same time, "the central tree points to an ominous similarity between Adam and Eve: both lose their 'birthright'—a privileged relation to God" (67); in the image described, the Fall parallels Esau's selling his birthright, both as types of the Temptation of Christ.

18. Jessica Prinz Pecorino provides commentary, bibliography, and illustrations in "Eve Unparadised."

19. An exception to this tradition may be found in the frescoes at Solaro, where Adam and Eve work the soil side by side, and in a series of tenth-through twelfth-century ivory caskets in which Eve holds a bellows while Adam works at an anvil (Cologne, Mus. Kunstgewerke; Cleveland Mus. 24.747). By showing Adam and Eve working together as gardeners before the Fall, Milton regenerates a motif usually reserved until after the Fall.

20. In pictures of the *Noli me tangere* the risen Christ appears to Mary Magdalen with spade in hand after his resurrection: she "knew not that it was Jesus . . . supposing him to be the gardener" (John 20:14-15). Examples include a sixteenth-century window in King's College Chapel, a woodcut in Dürer's *Small Passion* of 1511, and a painting by Rubens and J. Brueghel the Elder (San Francisco, de Young Mus.). John Thornton's East Window of York Minster (1405-8) depicts Christ as Reaper of Souls. Pictures of Mary, the Second Eve, sometimes include a sewing basket and often show two children, Jesus and John, who becomes the Baptist, at her side. Eve's labor also participates in a long-standing association between weaving and all civilized arts. The Greeks held it to be the gift of Athena, goddess of wisdom, and in the ideal family of Homer's Alkinoös it is the occupation of the wise Arete and her work a symbol of civility.

21. Article 3 of the Articles of Religion, "Of the going downe of Christ into Hell," states, "As Christ died for vs, and was buried: so also is it to be beleeued that he went downe into hell" (sig. B2v). Compare, however, Andrew Willett, *Limbo-mastix . . . shewing . . . that Christ descended not in soule to hell to deliver the Fathers from thence*. On the literature of the Harrowing of Hell (from the fourth-century apocryphal Gospel of Nicodemus) see Lewalski, *Milton's Brief Epic*, 50-52 and 374. In typological iconography, as the Temptation of Adam and Eve is the type of which the Temptation of Christ is the reverse antitype, so the Harrowing of Hell is the antitype of which Samson is the type, so that the topics of Milton's three major poems are typologically joined through Adam and Eve.

22. For examples see Trapp, "Iconography of the Fall," 226-33.

23. Creation series, or portions of them, appear not only in Bibles or biblical books (Genesis, the Pentateuch, and the Octateuch were often published separately) but also in liturgical service and choir books, psalters, devotional manuals, and other works. The iconographic traditions in illuminated manuscripts are sufficiently widespread, and sufficiently connected to other genres, that some of them seem worth mentioning whether or not any particular poet may have seen any particular (or indeed any) manuscript.

24. "Reference to the Redemption in picturings of the Fall . . . may be taken to be always present" (Trapp, "Iconography of the Fall," 226).

25. Henry, *Biblia Pauperum*, 48 and 50. Henry (using Ronald Knox's translation of the Bible) points out the link between the scheme of the blockbook and the scheme of the King's College Chapel windows (37).

26. On these types in Milton see Pecheux, "Concept of the Second Eve" and "Second Adam." Avril Henry calls Eve the "earthly mother of the Church" (*Biblia Pauperum*, 99).

27. Bodleian MS. 270b, fol. 6. The gesture of holding someone by the wrist rather than the hand is ancient and not authoritarian. In the *Iliad* it is used in dancing and for reassurance (Books 18 and 24).

28. Henry, *Biblia Pauperum*, 65 and 101-3.

29. BCP 1604, "The Hampton Court Book."

30. Psalm numbers are those of the AV and the BCP.

31. Trapp assumes that a version in which the creation of Eve is central "insist[s] on the responsibility of Eve by having as its centrepiece her emergence from Adam's side" and that series with no major intervening image between it and the Fall emphasize "the Creation of Eve as the preliminary to the Fall; that is, wherever Eve is prominent, stress is being laid on her guilt" (255). This assumption needs to be made with caution. In some cases it participates in what Wittreich, in *Feminist Milton*, has called a patriarchal tradition in criticism rather than in the art it interprets.

32. Frye, *Milton's Imagery*, 246; see also Trapp, "Iconography of the Fall," 252 and n. 111. Michael Ayerton comments that Michelangelo "was the one human being capable of representing at least a convincing shadow of the

dynamic force, the energy and splendour which went into the creation of Man. This led him deeply into the dread of hubris . . . [and] to regard his total commitment to the human form as a sculptor as no more than a mere track from corporeal beauty to spiritual beauty which is invisible." The dark side of his Christian Platonism is that the sensual, and so "the very act and material of art," is an obstacle to the intellect "which, left to itself, would inevitably reach God." The implicit iconoclasm is "restrained only by the conviction . . . that visible, human beauty at least demonstrates the presence of God" (*Rudiments of Paradise*, 148).

33. Dualism, as a belief that matter is opposed to spirit, has roots in Pythagorean and Platonic thought. Milton was a monist, believing that all things proceed from God and return to him "if not deprav'd from good . . . one first matter all" (5.469-72). In *De Doctrina Christiana* Milton contrasts terrestrial and celestial life but not body and soul, death and resurrection being "for the perfecting of both" (*SM*, 1004-5).

34. Phillips gathers earlier examples of this confusion, as well, especially in apocryphal and pseudepigraphal writings, in *Eve*. We should be aware of the strength of this basically misogynous view, and also that the more extreme expressions of it were excluded from the canonical Bible.

35. Trinkaus, *Scope of Renaissance Humanism*, 32-43.

36. For an interesting interpretation of this cycle, and especially Raphael's Urania, in connection with Milton see Treip, *Descend from Heav'n Urania*.

37. *Paradiso* 32.1-15. One may compare a northern Catholic image, Goltzius's "Benedicta tv in mulieribvs," in which Mary is surrounded by Eve, Sarah, Leah, Rachel, Elizabeth, Anna, and the mother of Samson; Eve's inscription is "Benedixitque illis Deus, et ait: crescite, et multiplicamini, et replete terram, et subiicite eam" (Gen. 1:28): in *Hendrik Goltzius*, 1:357. Raphael's amazingly beautiful paintings have many and profound meanings, but they are less resistant to feminist and materialist critics' attributions of misogyny and transcendence than Milton or most of the art with which this chapter is concerned.

38. Cuzin, *Raphael*, 104.

39. Sister Mary Irma Corcoran sorts out literal and allegorical hexameral commentary in *Milton's Paradise*, chap. 1. For further information on patristic sources see Robbins, *Hexameral Literature*. Evans discusses allegorical readings in *"Paradise Lost" and the Genesis Tradition*, 69-77.

40. A. M. Cinquemani traces the allegorizing of Eve back to Origen, citing Seznec's comment that the "hybrid doctrine" of conflating Scripture and myth was "inherited from the last defenders of paganism" (Seznec, *Survival of the Pagan Gods*, 104). Cinquemani notes that in *Mythomystes* (1632), Henry Reynolds asks, "What other can *Hesiods Pandora, the first and beautifullest of all women, by whom all euils were dispersed and spred vpon the earth,* meane then

*Moses* his *Eve?*" and "goes further than Origen in this direction, identifying Eve with Homer's Ate, the daughter of Jupiter, 'and a woman pernicious and harmefull to all vs mortalls' (74)" ("Henry Reynold's *Mythomystes*," 1044). Origen claimed the right to allegorize Scripture from the tradition of allegorizing Hesiod in order to defend the bare story from sophisticated ridicule; but the effect is to bring into interpretation of Scripture the irreverencies of the myth, which is far more denigrating toward women, as well as God, than the Genesis narrative.

41. Hesiod, *Poems*, 65-66 and 99.

42. On Milton's use of Ovidian myth see Du Rocher, *Milton and Ovid*.

43. Jean Hagstrum comments in *The Sister Arts* that "for Milton, as for Dante but not for poets standing in the central tradition of antiquity and the Renaissance, the pictorial was a gate that opened not primarily upon visible nature but upon transcendent and invisible reality" (128). I agree with Hagstrom's distinction between the "classical pictorialism" of antiquity and the Renaissance and the "sacramental pictorialism" of the Middle Ages revived by Milton and baroque art, but I would stress that visible and transcendent reality are numinously locked together in both Milton and the medieval and Reformation art to which his work is most comparable.

44. "The H. Scriptures. II," in Herbert, *Works*, 58.

45. A version of the following section appeared as "Edenic Iconography: *Paradise Lost* and the Mosaics of San Marco," in *Milton in Italy.* I concur with Michael O'Connell's caveats about Milton and Italian art in the same volume but wish to distinguish between iconographies more and less compatible with *Paradise Lost.*

46. Philips, "The Life of Mr. John Milton," in *SM*, xxxv.

47. Boccaccio, *Decameron*, ll. 31-32.

48. Boccaccio, *Modell of Wit*, 130.

49. Bardi, *Della Cose Notabili*; Sansovino, *Venetia Citta Nobilissima.* Protestant Englishmen such as Thomas Coryat and John Evelyn had access to the Basilica, its treasury, and the Palazzo Ducale.

50. Evelyn, *Diary,* 197.

51. Milton's references to Venice in his political prose approve its "immovable" Senate but warn against instituting the "fond conceit of something like a duke of Venice"; see *Proposalls of certaine expedients* (1659) in *YP,* 7:336, and *The Readie & Easie Way to Establish a Free Commonwealth* (1660) in *YP,* 7:436 and 446. Milton recommends that members of Parliament sit for life, using the Venetian Senate as an example, and expresses high praise for Pietro Sarpi, "the great and learned *Padre Paolo*" who was the "great Venetian Antagonist of the *Pope*" and "the great unmasker of the *Trentine* Councel," in *Of Reformation,* in *YP,* 1:595 and 581, and *Areopagitica,* in *YP,* 2:501.

52. Wotton, in a letter to Milton of 13 April, 1638, in *SM,* 45.

53. Reproduced in de Witt, *I Mosaici del Battistero,* 4, pls. I-VII.

54. However, in a subsequent image, numerous attractive animals enter Noah's ark in pairs, led by leopards, lions, and wolves, the symbolic animals Dante—who was baptized there—must overcome in Canto 1 of *Inferno*.

55. In 1610 John Speed obtained the right for ten years to insert his genealogies into every edition of the AV, a practice which continued until at least 1640 (Pollard and Redgrave, *Short-Title Catalogue*, 536, no. 23039). The genealogies appear in copies of earlier Bibles, as well.

56. British Library MS. Cotton Otho B.vi. In his introduction to Cockerell, *Book of Old Testament Illustrations*, M. R. James notes that the Cotton Genesis was given by Greek bishops to Henry VIII and belonged successively to Elizabeth I, her Greek tutor, Sir John Fortescue, and Sir Robert Cotton; it was largely destroyed by the Cotton Library fire of 1731. See Weitzmann, "Genesis Mosaics"; Weitzmann cites J. J. Tikkanen, who identified the relation between the miniatures and the mosaics. In the same article Weitzmann notes that he and Herbert Kessler have since made a close study of the manuscript and of the relations between other manuscripts and monumental forms and concluded that the Cotton manuscript is indeed the chief source of the mosaics, with a few iconographic changes increasing Christological elements.

57. Trapp, "Iconography of the Fall," 241; he lists manuscripts of this group on 234-35.

58. Although the mosaics were repaired in the nineteenth century in what some critics deem ruinous ways, the iconography remains intact (Demus, *Mosaics of San Marco*, 2:76). Demus provides a full photographic record of the mosaics of the Basilica, most of the photographs newly made by Ekkehard Ritter, and extensive historical and iconographic scholarship.

59. HIC ARDENT CHERVBIM CHRISTE FLAMATA CALORE / SEMPER ET ETERNI SOLIS RADIATA NITORE / MISTICA STANT CHERVBIM ALAS MONSTRANCIA SENAS / AVE DOMINVM LAVDANT VOCES PROMENDO SERENAS.

60. The formulation of the Nicene Creed (BCP 1559).

61. Weitzmann's suggestion ("Genesis Mosaics," 111).

62. Although some feminists prefer the version in the text of Genesis 1 (a preference Bloom unsettles in *The Book of J*), the more graphic version in Genesis 2 produces more sympathy for Eve in the arts. Fannie Peczenic illuminates Milton's use of it and his antimisogynist revisions of exegetical commentaries, notably Augustine's, in "Milton on the Creation of Eve."

63. This scene is one of the "Christological" additions Weitzmann mentions, taken as he points out from Middle Byzantine Last Judgments such as the one at Torcello ("Genesis Mosaics," 107).

64. An unusual sculpture by Michelangelo Naccherino (1550-1622) near the southwest gate to the Boboli Gardens in Florence shows Adam and Eve, not kneeling, but equally sharing human distress and consolation, Adam (standing with the crossed legs of fallenness) with his fingers touching Eve's hair as she leans sorrowfully on his shoulder. A curly haired pubescent Satan crouches smiling by Adam's knee (Frye, figs. 193-94).

65. See also Psalm 32:1; the parable of the wedding guest, Matt. 22:2-14; 2 Cor. 5:3; Rev. 3:18, 7:9-14, and 16:15; and Dante's interpretation in *Paradiso* 25.91-96. The Isaiah passage concludes, "For as the earth bringeth forth her bud, and as the garden causeth the things that are sown in it to spring forth; so the Lord God will cause righteousness and praise to spring forth before all nations" (Isa. 61:11).

66. Weitzmann, "Genesis Mosaics," 116.

67. Houvet, *Chartres Cathedral*, 49.

68. "Adam rendant grace à Dieu" is the caption to this scene in Houvet, *Cathedrale de Chartres*, 2:44.

69. This is the identification in Miller's revision of Houvet's guidebook, cited above, though in Houvet's photograph in the 1919 volume both figures appear to be male, and the caption is "Adam dans le Paradis Terrestre."

70. Julian, *Revelations*, 107.

71. Katzenellenbogen, *Sculptural Programs*, 70; Mâle, *Chartres*, 114.

72. Kleine-Ehrminger, *Our Lady of Strasbourg*, 63.

73. Chaucer, *The Wife of Bath's Tale*, in *Poetical Works*, 104.

74. Demouay, *Rheims Cathedral*, 43-44.

75. Images of the vine and of the grape harvest recur in this wine-country cathedral, connected both with the sacrament and the scriptural imagery of salvation and with the daily work of the community.

76. My description has been aided by Hans Reinhardt, *La Cathédrale de Reims*, and Peter Kurmann, *La Façade de la Cathédrale de Reims*, vol. 2, pl. 576, "Adam et Eve au Paradise." Étienne Morceau-Nélaton (*La Cathédrale de Reims*, 95) reads the image of Adam and Eve seated side by side as an Admonition with the Creator, as in the previous two images; but Eve appears to be speaking.

77. These scenes are not placed in order in the window. I cannot guarantee that this one does not represent Eve persuading Adam to eat the fruit, but the presence of Adam and Eve conversing in the contemporaneous sculptures outside the window suggests that the scene precedes the Fall.

78. Trapp, "Iconography of the Fall," 240.

79. Bodleian Library MS. Junius 11; it includes an eleventh-century copy of earlier Genesis poems. It is available in fascimile, *The Caedmon Manuscript*. A. N. Doane provides a thorough scholarly introduction and notes in *Genesis A: A New Edition*. The manuscript was first published by Francis Junius in Amsterdam in 1655; for speculations whether Milton knew the poem(s) see note in Masson, *Life of John Milton*, 6:557.

80. These and the ensuing translations are from Bradley, *Anglo-Saxon Poetry*, 15-19, 29-32, 38, and 13.

81. Doane discusses the illustrations in *Genesis A*, 16-24.

82. Apart from this one, Frye reproduces only the illustrations of the falls of Lucifer and the rebel angels, the falls of Adam and Eve, and postlapsarian events, including remorse and recrimination.

83. Exeter College MS. 47 and Bodleian MS. Auct. D.4.4., in James's facsimile, with description, *The Bohun Manuscripts*.

84. Pierpont Morgan Lib. MS. M.102. This manuscript is also decorated throughout with lively line drawings of animals and outlandish humans, who for example seem to be made partly of vegetation or shade themselves with one huge foot.

85. New York Public Library MS. Spencer 26. See Sandler, *Gothic Manuscripts*, 2:32, cat. 26.

86. In the fourteenth-century Psalter of St. Omer the Creation of Eve has two billing doves over it; Eve leaps or runs from behind Adam toward the bare-headed Creator. At the Judgment, Adam and Eve both kneel in repentance.

87. Oxford, Bodleian MS. Auct. D.4.4., fols. 1r and 24v. In James, *Bohun Manuscripts*. See also Sandler, *Gothic Manuscripts*, 2:157-59, cat. 138.

88. Similarly, in the thirteenth-century French Psalter of William de Brailes in the Fitzwilliam Museum, God (as Christ) clothes Adam and Eve simultaneously, drawing garments over their heads, one with each hand. Fitzwilliam MS. 330, #2.

89. Carrow Psalter, Walters Art Gallery MS. 34; Psalter of St. Swithin's Priory, British Library MS. Cotton Nero C.14. For locations of other psalters see subsequent notes.

90. Morgan, *Medieval Painted Glass*, 16-17. Morgan cites as other examples the Leyden Psalter and paintings by the Winchester artists who worked at Sigena.

91. British Library MS. Royal 2.B.vii, fols. 1-5. According to Sandler this psalter was probably in London c. 1310-20 and seized for Queen Mary Tudor in 1553 (*Gothic Manuscripts*, 2:66). For the beautiful creation of the birds and animals from this psalter see vol. 2, fig. 138.

92. Barraclough, ed., *Christian World*, 9, fig. 1. This relief is now in the Victoria and Albert Museum.

93. Wormald, *Winchester Psalter*, pl. 27.

94. Trinity MS. O.4.16, fol. 114; Sandler, *Gothic Manuscripts*, 2, cat. 14. The complete opening, illustrating the Passion from Judas's Kiss to the Ascension and ending with Pentecost, is reproduced in vol. 1, fig. 33-34.

95. Milton, Trinity Manuscript, in *SM*, 1130.

96. Facsimile or illustrated editions: DeWald, *Illustrations of the Utrecht Psalter*; James, *Canterbury Psalter*; Wormald, *Winchester Psalter*; Lindner, *Queen Mary's Psalter*; for the Bromholm Psalter, Cockerell and James, *Two East Anglian Psalters*.

97. For influential early Genesis and Bible manuscripts see Trapp, "Iconography of the Fall," 234-57.

98. Lambeth Bible (Lambeth Palace Library MS. 3), frontispiece to Dodwell, *Canterbury School*; Rheims Bible, Bibliothèque Municipale, MS. 34, fol. 9v.

99. For a history of illustrations in printed Bibles, both English and continental, of the fifteenth and sixteenth centuries see Strachan, *Early Bible Illustrations*. Other important studies include Hindman, *Text and Image*, and Lane, "Genesis Woodcuts." All three studies show similarities among illustrations by the European pool of artists. Several title pages to English Bibles are reproduced in McKerrow and Ferguson, *Title-Page Borders*.

100. Hall, *Dictionary*, 5. The only images I can recall in which Eve has clearly already taken a bite are Lucas Cranach's paintings (c. 1530) in the Uffizi Gallery in Florence and the Art Institute of Chicago, which show a tidy row of toothmarks in the fruit she holds, and Jan Gossaert's in the British Royal Collection.

101. Milton, *Of Reformation*, in *SM*, 454.

102. The bearded figure on high in the frontispiece to the 1537 Bible (fig. 40) and delivering the Ten Commandments to Moses on its title page (fig. 39) are exceptions.

103. Brief histories of early English Bibles include Thompson, *Bible in English*, and Greenslade, "English Versions of the Bible" in *Cambridge History of the Bible*. See also Strachan, *Early Bible Illustrations*.

104. From the Lübeck Lutheran Bible of 1533 (Strachan, *Early Bible Illustrations*, 77).

105. Calvin, *A commentarie vpon Genesis*, 92. The marginal gloss in the 1578 edition miscites the reference as Rom. 15:12. In the same paragraph, Calvin explains 2 Tim. 2:14, "Adam was not deceiued, but the woman" as comparative, to show that Adam was not merely uxorious, but instead consciously chose "pestilent ambition."

106. Cocklereas, in "Much Deceiv'd, Much Failing, Hapless Eve," finds that Adam and Eve are equally culpable in early Christian art, but that in the Romanesque period (1000-1150) Eve becomes the means of transgression. It would be interesting to correlate the histories of these two motifs with historical or philosophical changes. My own research suggests that the motif of mutual culpability was by far the commonest during the Middle Ages and the Reformation, though a separate Temptation of Eve is part of the illustrations to the typological series and the *Speculum Humanae Salvationis* popular in the fourteenth and fifteenth centuries.

107. Many of these are reproduced in Vos, *Lucas van Leyden*.

108. On Speed's right to insert his Genealogies into every edition of the Authorized (or "King James") Version see note 55 above.

109. "Notes on Milton's Bibles," in *CM*, 18:559-61. The Adam and Eve page of the Speed genealogies is missing from Milton's copy of the 1612 Bible in the British Library, but the subsequent pages are there in the standard format. In any case, Milton was surely acquainted with so widespread a publication as well as with Speed, who is buried next to the Miltons, father and son, in St. Giles, Cripplegate.

110. "Notes on Milton's Bibles," in *CM*, 18:561.

111. A similarly cheerful title page appears on a Vulgate Bible published in Antwerp in 1624; Moses and David flank the title, and at the top God creates numerous animals, including hart, elephant, and a pair of unicorns, while beside this image two cherubs hold banners declaring "VIDET DEVS CVNCTA QVE FECERAT ET ERANT VALDE BONA. Gen. 1." See also McMullin, "The 1629 Cambridge Bible."

112. Valerian, *Hieroglyphiques,* 602.

113. Coverdale's translation, spelling modernized. It is Psalm 41 in the 1535 Bible, and begins "Like as the hert desyreth the water brokes, so longeth my soule after the, O God." Coverdale's psalter, also in the Great Bible, continued to be bound into Bibles after the AV appeared and was the psalter of the BCP, and so the text of musical settings.

# 3
# Original Blessedness

And God saw everything that he had made, and,
behold, it was very good.
Genesis 1:31

During the late sixteenth and early seventeenth centuries,
prints illustrating scriptural stories flowed out of the art cen-
ters of the Low Countries either as loose sets or bound as
separate books, with or without commentary. Many of these include
regenerative motifs while recognizing the painful side of life in the
fallen world. The iconographic part of this study concludes with a
look at three such series and some individual images and at invitations
to choice in them.

### Sadeler after van den Broeck
A set engraved by Jan Sadeler after Crispijn van den Broeck was
published both by Gerard de Jode in Antwerp and, with the paternal
figure of God replaced by the Tetragrammaton, by the Dutch publisher C. J. Visscher (figs. 17-20).[1] The human figures in these engravings are particularly beautiful, and the animals lively and abundant.
The de Jode series begins with God the Father creating a great flash of
light, followed by a Creation of the Animals that includes fox, boar,
elephant, sheep, cattle, rabbits, turkey, and (in the foreground) snail,
tortoise, a monkey with his paw on a gourd, and a smiling monkey
under a tree with a peacock and a parrot: the two monkeys and their
companions prefigure the Fall. In the de Jode Creation of Adam, the
Creator helps Adam stand up and introduces him to the animals. The
hart, a lion, and a very nice ram and ewe are prominent, and in the
foreground are a snake, a grasshopper or locust, and a lizard or sala-
mander. All of these have multiple implications: the locust, for example, was a plague to Pharoah, but food to John the Baptist. In the
Visscher version (fig. 17), God represented by his Name in a radiance
breathes his Spirit into Adam, and enjoins him to name all living

things. The Creation of Eve in the Visscher series replaces God (seen in de Jode, fig. 18) in the same fashion, with added scriptural inscriptions, and in the gap left by the removal of the paternal figure adds more animals: a browsing goat, a turkey who regards Eve with interest, and an amazed stag (or hart), the symbol of contemplation, who gazes raptly at the radiance of God. The plantain or waybread perhaps represents humility, and the as yet unblooming columbine (from columba, dove) the Holy Spirit.[2] The Fall in these series is in the classical style, with Eve taking the fruit from the snake and giving it to Adam, who is seated and reaches out his hand: in this case the artist's love of beauty brings with it a Renaissance iconography. But the next plate, illustrating Genesis 3:9 and 3:21, shame and clothing (fig. 19), is in the regenerative mode. God the Father (despite the caption) speaks to them more in sorrow than in anger, and clothes them; Adam looks thoroughly woebegone, and Eve kneels in mournful penitence at his feet as Milton's Eve does after the Judgment. The bear is a symbol of gluttony and (because of the legend that she shapes her cubs with her tongue) of conversion.[3] The Expulsion features a vigorous angel, from whom Adam and Eve fearfully flee. In the next scene (fig. 20) a handsome bearded Adam rests with his mattock by him, a still beautiful Eve suckles the infant Abel, with carrots and turnips on the ground before her, and Cain beside them feeds and caresses a lamb. Behind, Adam plows with the help of an ox, and Eve cooks beside a rough shelter, Adam with her holding a slingshot. The inscription tells that fallen man endures misery with conjugal life, and all parts begin to decay with heavy pain. The series ends with an engraving after Michael de Coxcij (fig. 21) of Eve lamenting over the body of Abel and Adam grieving.

## Slatyer and van Langeren

Although Bible illustrations were not encouraged in England during the iconoclastic 1640s and 1650s, some Authorized Versions printed by or for the Company of Stationers headed Genesis with a mutual Fall surrounded by happy animals in pairs, and lavish sets of engravings continued to be bound into private copies of the Bible.

A particularly interesting set, published in England around 1636,[4] is the series of forty plates engraved, apparently after Maerten de Vos, by Jacob Floris van Langeren,[5] with perfunctory verses in four languages by William Slatyer, former chaplain to Queen Anne, the wife of James I. The first twelve illustrate Genesis from the beginning to the Rapture of Enoch (figs. 1-12). These are not the "Popish pictures" published, like these, by Robert Peake,[6] and nothing in their iconography would be likely to offend any Protestant who could countenance Bible illustrations at all. The Tetragrammaton in a glory represents the Creator bringing forth light and teeming populations, breathing life into Adam and presenting the animals for him to name, and calling forth Eve from Adam's side. The engravings are more elegant than photographs convey, but have an unclassical northern earthiness that distinguishes their figures from the sublime though also earthly beauty of Milton's protagonists. The images of Adam and Eve have five unusual features that come close to the spirit of *Paradise Lost*.

First, the title page (for some reason never completed, but still used) shows roped-together ovals that include the Fall and Expulsion, but makes central, instead, the Creation of Adam and a significant new topos: the first meeting of Adam and Eve, who run toward each other with open arms. This motif recurs in the background of the Creation of Eve, while the Voice of God declares "It is not good for man to be alone," a point reaffirmed by the four-language commendation of woman as meet help. The print strikingly represents Eve, rising from Adam's body, as flesh of his flesh.

The motif of the eager nuptial greeting illustrates the change in attitude toward marriage and the goodness of creation and procreation that Milton brought to consummation. It is allied to the quieter meeting in the fifteenth-century *Seven Ages of the World* (fig. 54), to illustrations in works of Fletcher and Cats (figs. 55 and 56), and to images of Adam and Eve with their arms around each other as God speaks to them, found in the background of the beautiful painting of the Fall (1592) by Cornelis Cornelisz. van Haarlem (Frye, fig. 167) and in many other versions of the Admonition (such as fig. 26). In the Slatyer and van Langeren series, its recurrence and its complete separation from the Fall imply both divine approval and human possibilities.

Second, between the Creation of Eve and the Fall comes an even rarer image: the Institution of the Sabbath, with Adam and Eve kneeling in prayer. In most series, the only event, if any, to come between the presentation of Eve to Adam and the Fall is the Admonition, a series of events that does not speak well for human virtue or God's gift of woman. The image Slatyer interprets as the first sabbath does apparently derive from de Vos's Admonition, which de Bruÿn engraved. But another engraver working after de Vos, Jan Theodore de Bry, produced a similar image (frontispiece) with an inscription in French from Psalm 117, "Praise the Lord all ye people"—all people being incipient in Adam and Eve.[7] De Bry's version includes two groups of animals: monkey, goat, and fox, emblematic of the Fall, and more benign ones, especially the drinking hart, close to the prayerful pair. A similar print in the Kitto Bible,[8] also identified by its inscription as the Sanctification of the Sabbath, portrays God the Father blessing and speaking to Adam and Eve, who kneel among sympathetic "Creatures wanting voice" (9.199), while a thistle pointedly located in front of Adam's groin foreshadows the thorns and thistles the ground will bring forth after the Fall (Gen. 3:18). Slatyer's identification of van Langeren's version (which has a gourd, symbol of transience and of resurrection, but no thistles) as a sabbath participates in this slender tradition. The publication in England of an engraving of Adam and Eve praying together before the Fall is a telling event. Like the nuptial greeting and the cheerful title page of the Cambridge Bible, it affirms the original blessedness of Adam and Eve and the happy possibilities of "our business" of rectification.

Third, in the image of the Fall, as in de Bruÿn's and in some English Bibles, Adam, not Eve, holds the forbidden fruit; and the fruit-dangling Serpent faces him, not her. The caption stresses Eve's fault, but the image assigns final responsibility to Adam.[9]

Fourth, the attempt of Adam and Eve to hide from God and his discovery of them (with animals bounding away) is followed by a Judgment which includes the clothing of Adam and Eve with "skin-coats" of animals, probably not with "youthful coat repaid" (10.216-18) as Milton suggests. Again, the image contributes to a rehabilitative view of Genesis and Milton improves on it.

Fifth, the series does not stop with the mourning over Abel, but goes on to illustrate the invention of the arts (cf. 11.556-80); the establishment of the City of Enoch, of the line of Seth; and, to show the difficult but possible renewal of righteousness, the Rapture of Enoch,

> The only righteous in a World perverse,
> And therefore hated, therefore so beset
> With Foes for daring single to be just,
> And utter odious Truth, that God would come
> To judge them with his Saints: him the most High
> Rapt in a balmy Cloud with winged Steeds
> Did, as thou saw'st, receive, to walk with God.
>
> (11.701-7)

The unusual emphasis on the marriage and the rarely imagined prelapsarian prayers of Adam and Eve, along with hints at the possibility of renewed righteousness, provide a "smacke of the ryghte blisse" of which Milton's epic offers a full feast.

## Saenredam: A Moment of Choice

Many seventeenth-century engravings contain invitations to interpretive choice.[10] Among these are the Genesis engravings of 1604 by
Jan Saenredam after Abraham Bloemart (figs. 47-52), northern artists
influenced by Renaissance classicism. God is not depicted; after the
iconoclasm of 1572, works of art showing divine beings were not safe
in the Protestant Netherlands, and these artists prefer realism to symbols of God. Adam appears in the first engraving as the Lord of Creation among adoring animals drawn with a typically northern
empathy. But the rest of the series uses animals emblematically. In the
Fall Eve is decidedly dominant, though she turns her shapely back as
she reaches to take a fruit from the Serpent's mouth and offer one to
Adam, who also holds one. The postlapsarian scenes evoke pathos by
the shame, labor, and grief of the still beautiful figures.

The second engraving in the series (fig. 48) is not a Fall, but a colloquy that may be a temptation of Adam by Eve, whose gesture and
stance suggest persuasion with erotic overtones, yet remains a moment
of choice for Adam and Eve and for the viewer. God is emblematically
represented by the columbine, with its tripartite leaves, whose name
and blossoms "of the shape of little birds"[11] associate it, especially the
white one, with the Holy Spirit.[12] Gestures and attributes are ominous; yet each contains the possibility of good as well as evil and so
exposes the viewers' predilections. The beautiful bodies and clasped
hands signify perfect health and marital union as well as warning
against amorous excess. Eve gestures toward a tree, Adam carries a
broken branch, and their posture and exchange of glances suggest
erotic absorbtion and ingratiation. Yet neither discussions of trees nor
erotic attentiveness necessitate a fall.

The gourd is also ambivalent. In Whitney's emblem[13] it signifies
worldly pride or transitory happiness. Whitney's has climbed a tree,
and Saenredam's lies meekly (if umbilically) on the ground; but its fallenness suggests the transitoriness of its strength. On the other hand,
the gourd is a symbol of resurrection and emblematically opposed to
the apple.[14] God caused one to grow and shade the dejected Jonah,
which gladdened him, and then smote it, to teach Jonah the value of
life. Although Jonah's gourd withered, his prophecy was heeded and
therefore abrogated, and Nineveh and all her cattle were spared. In
Saenredam's engraving, too, the gourd may be seen as warning, not
prediction, or as a prefiguration of regeneration as well as of the Fall.
The gourd is also an attribute of pilgrims, who used it as a water jar;
it is included in paintings of Christ at Emmaus and of Tobias accompanied by the Archangel Raphael, who according to legend planted

the melon family in the Garden of Eden.[15] However, Milton calls attention to it twice as food, the "smelling Gourd" of 7.321. When Eve says she will pluck choice food from "Each Plant & juiciest Gourd" (clearly not the bottle-gourd) "To entertain our Angel guest" (5.326-27) she is offering Raphael his own correct attribute.

The dominant animal, of course, is the vulture, unclean in Jewish dietary laws and predicted to possess the land after the Lord's vengeance in Isaiah 34:15. Its identity as a vulture is suggested by the turn of its head, the standard stance in iconologies. Normally a vulture portends death. Milton compares Satan to one (3.431) and Death to carrion-fowl "lur'd / With scent of living Carcasses design'd / For death" (10.276-78). It gnaws the vital organs of those who, like Prometheus, steal forbidden knowledge, and since it lives on carrion one supposes that it is waiting for Eve to persuade Adam to eat the fruit so that death will enter the Garden and it can eat, too. But before the Fall all animals were presumed vegetarians; the lion ate straw, like the ox. Sir Thomas Browne explains that "if (as most conceive) there were but two created of every kind, they could not at that time destroy either man or themselves; for this had frustrated the command of multiplication, destroyed a species, and imperfected the Creation"[16] (as man has not refrained from doing since). Only after the Fall do they—"to graze the Herb all leaving"—begin to devour each other (10.711-12).

In sixteenth- and seventeenth-century iconologies, the vulture is a symbol of providence and an attribute of Nature, as in Cesare Ripa's *Iconologia;* but in Ripa the warning note sounds, for whereas Natura, with her dripping, milk-filled breasts, represents nurture, the vulture, whom Ripa believes to be an avid bird of prey, represents the contrasting principle of change that gradually devours all corruptible things ("l'altro principio dimandato materia, la quale per l'appetito della Forma, mouendosi, & alterandosi, strugge à poco à poco tutte le cose corruttibili").[17] In *Horus Apollo,* it is also a bird of prey, and is a symbol of compassion either "by its contrary, because this bird pities no other beast," or because it devotes itself to its young and (by a common confusion with the legend of the pelican) in famine feeds them with blood from its own breast.[18]

However, in the *Hieroglyphics* of Valerian (1556), the vulture, the sacred bird of Egypt, is "a symbol of justice because of its innocence," since it does not kill or mistreat any living creature:

for the vulture meddles with nothing that lives, nor kills anything that moves, as the Sparrowhawk and the Eagle do: but content-

ing itself with corpses, has never been seen polluting itself by eating any birds, as the Egyptians have observed. It never trespasses
against nor damages fruits, nor brings any harm to domestic animals. . . . [T]hey even protect humans against the animals that
are of a harmful and injurious disposition. And in fact they say
that the Vulture is the first among the birds to protect man
against Serpents; and that whoever carries with him the heart of
one of them, will be not only protected from the violence of Serpents, but also the dangers of all beasts and thieves [or whatever
flies]: in a word, exempts himself even from the indignation of
Princes.[19]

The vulture also stands for maternity, prescience, clarity of vision, and
Urania, the celestial muse.[20] These attributes[21] are peculiarly relevant
to the scene in the engraving, in which Adam and Eve are deciding
which use of nature—for good or for evil—to choose. Simultaneously
sinister and sacred, the vulture is a perfect hieroglyph of the choice still
open to them in this engraving and open again to those who would
rectify Nature to what she still might be.

## *Before the Fall: The Iconography of Original Innocence*

The choices that manifest themselves in Saenredam's engraving are
present in all Edenic imagery that includes animals and identifiable
plants. Many have multiple connotations, derived from the Bible, classical literature, bestiaries, herbals, and iconological handbooks. Allegorical significance often derives from observation, and in the
sixteenth and seventeenth centuries artists were increasingly able to
draw from life as menageries arrived from newly explored exotic
places. At the same time, some continued to copy animals or their
stances out of bestiaries going as far back as the fifth-century *Physiologus,* with their built-in allegorical explanations; in the *Physiologus,*
most of the animals represent either Christ or the devil, along with
various virtues and vices.[22]

These images are complex, since symbols can signify different and
even opposite things at once. In his well-known warning against in-
flexible interpretation of scriptural signs, Augustine points out that
the same similitude may be used both *in bono* and *in malo;* "in a good
sense" in one place and "in an evil sense" in another: "Thus the serpent
appears in a good sense in 'wise as serpents,' but in a bad sense in 'the
serpent seduced Eve by his subtlety.' " Similitudes may also mean not
contrary but diverse or multiple things, according to their contexts.[23]

If we oversimplify, it is easy to suppose that the occupants of Eden always represent either lost good (like the hart) or, more often, chosen evil (like the goat), and to see prefigurations of the Fall rather than configurations of delight.

In order to perceive the state of innocence, we need to be aware of two things: that each creature may have benign or regenerate connotations as well as fallen ones, and that each is originally good.[24] These principles apply signally to the forbidden tree, which is itself an emblem of choice.[25] That is, Adam and Eve may exercise their wills and understandings by refraining from eating its fruit, thus using it to acquire "knowledge of good and evil" by constancy and a small but significant exercise in self-restraint; or they may use it destructively by engorging the evil of faithlessness into their own natures. Used well, the tree provides opportunity for faith even before the Fall; used ill, it brings the pain of evil into human experience. In different ways, all things in nature are instrumental for good or evil. By this instrumentality, God's Garden manifests the "radical openness"[26] that makes room for growth, even through awareness of evil, without evil-doing. Nature and art in the postlapsarian world are also, in Donne's words, "Poysonous, or purgative, or cordiall,"[27] depending on our responses.

## The Beasts of Eden

For the seventeenth-century iconologist, as well as the twentieth-century ecologist—to pick up the pun in Donne's doughy metaphor—all beasts needed be. Northern versions of the Garden of Eden are crowded with life, more in the medieval tradition than the classicizing Renaissance one, and even artists who used classical figures for Adam and Eve often produced a revel of winsome animals,[28] which make their way into poems as well. The creation of the birds, fish, and beasts (including southern paintings such as Tintoretto's) shows great warmth, energy, and tenderness in the Creator at work and a responsive adoring attention from his creatures. A real interest in their natures is already visible in thirteenth-century bestiaries; by the late fifteenth century artists had begun placing them in natural land-scapes,[29] and representations became more diversified and accurate in the sixteenth century through the discoveries of explorers and world travelers. Artists in the early seventeenth century represented them with growing realism—one German woodcut pasted into Genesis in a 1615 English Bible includes a horse in the act of manuring the soil and a bull mounting a cow.[30] This interest in animals is especially manifest in the paintings of Jan Brueghel the Elder and Roelandt Savery, who repeatedly painted the Garden full of devotedly detailed and vigorous birds and beasts who are their real subject, while a minute Adam and Eve, whether receiving instructions from God, or falling, or just discussing trees, nearly disappear among fauna and foliage.

At the same time, for the seventeenth-century mind, everything in the visible world provides signs of things invisible, from the creativity of God to the complexities of our own psyches. The mind, as Andrew Marvell says, is "that ocean where each kind / Does straight its own resemblance find."[31] The animals of Eden represent both the visible creation to be restored to health and the internal workings of nature in each person. When in harmony, they speak also of the eternal. The caption to the Creation scene engraved by Adrian Collaert after a drawing by Hans Bol (fig. 53) makes this point: "For the invisible things of [God] from the creation of the world are clearly seen, being understood by the things that are made, even his eternal power and Godhead" (Rom. 1:20). Other inscriptions[32] carry out the Trinitarian theme of this image, in which Adam and Eve and the animals, especially the hart, respond to the descent of the Spirit, poured out by the Lord God through his Word.

The idea that invisible things are understood by the things that are made is one Milton favored. "Cuncta quidem Deus est, per cunctaque fusus [For God is all, and diffused through all]," he wrote in "Ad Leonoram." "In contemplation of created things / By steps we may ascend to God," Adam says in *Paradise Lost* (5.511-12). In *Of Education* we attain "knowledge of God and things invisible" by "orderly conning over the visible and inferior creature." And the concinnity of the sensible with the intelligible extends to ways of seeing, because the mind itself is designed to be a receptor of the meaning that the visible world is designed to signify, and of the truth it only imperfectly represents: "The wisdom of God created understanding, fit and proportionable to truth, the object and end of it, as the eye to the thing visible."[33]

The common assumption that the animals and plants in the Garden are prefigurations of the Fall[34] derives from the use of animals to represent fallen human passions: the lion as wrath, the pig as sloth, the fox as deception; and many artists did use them this way, putting in the foreground an animal suggesting a cause or result of the Fall. Saenredam, for example, puts a large goat, representing lust, in front of a voluptuous Adam and Eve (Frye, fig. 207). Burkmair (Frye, fig. 216) blames the Fall on concupiscence (the monkey) and fraud (the fox), and Dürer (Frye, fig. 218) on liberty (that is, license), or possibly "female lubricity," in the shape of a cat watching a mouse (a common motif), combined with the phlegmatic temperament, in the shape of a badger:[35] a notion agreeable to Milton's sense that sin is "not properly an action, for in reality it implies defect."[36] Jan Brueghel, collaborating with Rubens, gives the peacock pride of place (Frye, plate vii). Even in scenes before the Fall, animals may be prolepses of it. In many a Creation of Eve the cat scrutinizes the mouse with unsettling intensity.

But, as in the case of the vulture, these emblems do not define the animal kingdom before the Fall set it in disarray. Since all things were "created good and fair" and became "By breache of lawe a snare" (fig. 43), all of nature is instrumental, not intrinsically dangerous, and any creature can be an emblem of both good and evil. The beasts of Eden each represent, according to the iconologists, a multitude of virtues, vices, opportunities, and vulnerabilities, so that each representation engages the viewer in interpretive choices that either reenact the primal choice of Adam and Eve or redress it. Almost everything in the Garden has potentiality for good or ill, and everything can be either well used or abused in the fallen but redeemed and potentially regenerate world.

To add to this complexity, in seventeenth-century versions especially, the Earthly Paradise teems with animals that will become poisonous pests or dangerous carnivores, and also with snakes, snails, toads, frogs, beetles, and other creatures that squeamish humans regard with revulsion. Since man as microcosm was thought to contain the natures of all created things, we need to interpret these hieroglyphs with care, lest we assume that the artists mean to tell us that God embedded repellent characteristics in humankind.

On the scale of nature, in seventeenth-century (and earlier) thought, man-the-microcosm is placed between angels and beasts and partakes of the nature of both. By means of moral choices, a human being is always growing more like the angels or more like the animals. To be increasingly bestial is, for a human soul, degrading, because she forgets her celestial nature, but there is nothing degrading about being an animal to start with. Having no moral accountability, and being obedient to the natures God has given them and—more fully before the Fall—to human leadership, beasts are innocent. "Why brook'st thou, ignorant horse, subjection? / Why dost thou bull, and bore . . . by'one mans stroke die[?]" Donne asks; "You have not sinned."[37] But when a human being, a microcosm containing the whole scale of nature, lets the instinctual parts rule the rational and spiritual, the ark of the self is in mutiny. Donne interprets Genesis 1:26 to mean, on the figurative level, dominion over the beasts within. The preacher's job is to "make that ravening Wolfe a Man, that licentious Goate a man, that

insinuating Serpent a man." In the well-tuned soul, the beasts or passions regain innocence. "I am as well content to be a sheep, as a Lion,
so God will be my shepherd." Meanwhile, our animal nature should
cure pride; "in being earth, we are equall."[38]

When human potentialities for good became depraved in fallenness,
all of nature fell from its original goodness, but both retain the capacity to return to their original harmony. Meanwhile, we can learn from
all the animals: "from the labouring Beast," Traherne specifies, " . . . to
be profitable and useful to all, as they are; from the Innocent, let me
learn to be such; from the Wise to be so; from the Couragious to be
so in thy Service." Equally, animals that became voracious and dangerous by Adam's default can warn and discipline us: "Deliver me, O
Lord, from all brutish Appetites and beastly Affections; deliver me
from their Ignorance and Insatiableness, their Fury, their Rage, their
Madness; in all of which, without thy Aid, Mercy, and Grace, I should
be as very a Beast as they."[39]

Those animals in the Garden that have been allegorized as fallen appetites, though they may be prolepses of the Fall, also represent the
virtues, passions, and pleasures that are the stuff of regeneration.
"Happy is hee," as Donne continues to Edward Herbert, who "Can
use his horse, goate, wolfe, and every beast / And is not Asse himselfe
to all the rest." It will enrich our understanding of paradisal imagery
if we ask how one can use the goat, wolf, vulture, snake, and crocodile
within.

As Donne's poem implies, in seventeenth-century thought each human contains protoplastically all the capacities the various animals display severally: skills, virtues, passions, and evil inclinations all have
their traditional animal analogues. In the Garden of Eden, all creatures
near and (now) far lived together in a complex harmony just as all affections were "rightly tempered" in the human soul. When "disproportion'd sin" broke their harmony, the affections went to war with
each other, as the animals themselves did, becoming what Tennyson
would call "Nature, red in tooth and claw."[40] In Milton's lines, where
once "About them frisking play'd / All Beasts of th'Earth, since wilde"
(4.340-41), now

> Discord first
> Daughter of Sin, among th'irrational,
> Death introduc'd through fierce antipathy:
> Beast now with Beast gan war, and Fowl with Fowl,
> And Fish with Fish; to graze the Herb all leaving,
> Devour'd each other; nor stood much in awe

Of Man, but fled him, or with count'nance grim
Glar'd on him passing.

(10.707-14)

The paradise within undergoes a similar change, and Adam is "in a
troubl'd Sea of passion tost" (10.718). But "Wisdome," as Donne's
poem says, can sort out these warring inward beasts, making a person
not a chaotic lump but an ark, a regenerate peaceable kingdom.

The best opportunities for painting diverse animals together in
peace were the Garden of Eden, Noah's Ark, and the myth of Orpheus. Painters disposed the animals about Orpheus in ways that make
a clear analogy between the harmony of the animals (allegorized as the
passions) charmed by his music and the harmony of the Garden of
Eden.[41] Both the Garden of Eden and Orpheus playing to the animals
allegorically represent the passions in a state of temperance, and some
groupings specifically represent the four temperaments; in Goltzius's
engraving of Adam and Eve after Spranger, they are the dog (the mel-
ancholic), the lion (the choleric), the stag (the sanguine), and the
hedgehog (the phlegmatic); but in Dürer's 1504 engraving (Frye, fig.
164) the same humors are represented by the elk, the cat, the rabbit,
and the ox.[42] Donne's "ark" is a rich type, and George Herbert gathers
many resonances, including scriptural ones, when he writes,

My soul's a shepherd too; a flock it feeds
    Of thoughts, and words, and deeds.
The pasture is thy word: the streams, thy grace
    Enriching all the place.
Shepherd and flock shall sing, and all my powers
    Out-sing the day-light houres.[43]

The tradition that associates the beasts with merely harmful passions derives (like disabling allegorizations of Eve) more from the
moralizing of myth than from Scripture. In the Psalms and the Book
of Job, the wildest animals demonstrate the awesome inventiveness
and providence of their Creator, and the analogies of recalcitrant goats
or unclean swine come from the practical experience of a pastoral people rather than a systematic sense that animals resemble degraded humans. Some Scriptures compare humans unfavorably with other
creatures: "Yea, the stork in the heaven knoweth her appointed times;
and the the turtle and the crane and the swallow observe the time of
their coming; but my people know not the judgment of the Lord"
(Jer. 8:7). More often, the animals illustrate God's providence,
whether in life or death, as Hamlet remembers: "There's special prov-

idence in the fall of a sparrow."[44] "Consider the ravens: for they neither sow nor reap; which have neither storehouse nor barn; and God feedeth them" (Luke 12:24). "He sendeth the springs into the valleys, which run among the hills. / They give drink to every beast of the field: the wild asses quench their thirst. / By them shall the fowls of the heaven have their habitation, which sing among the branches" (Ps. 104.10-14).

However, the association of beasts with sinful passions has deep classical roots. Circe, or sensuality, turns men into animals who, in medieval and Renaissance interpretations, represent the seven deadly sins. To use Spenser's identifications in Lucifera's procession in *The Faerie Queene* (1.4.17-36), the peacock is an emblem of pride, the lion of wrath, the wolf of envy, the camel of avarice, the goat of lechery, the swine of drunkenness and gluttony, and the ass of sloth. But most animals participate in the long tradition of multiple significance. According to Renaissance iconologists, the dog represents both envy and domestic fidelity; the monkey impudence, but also the cure of pride, perhaps by aping our affectations. The horse embodies both war and constancy, the lion courage and magnanimity as well as wrath. The goat usually suggests lust, but Ripa calls it an emblem of the sanguine humor,[45] and the mountain goat poised on the cliff in Dürer's 1504 engraving (Frye, fig. 164) represents Christ, who according to Physiologus sees all things as from the mountain peaks.[46] The ostrich, curiously prominent in many pictures of Paradise, is a symbol of forgetfulness, surely an attribute of man's lapse, derived from the observation in Job that she "leaveth her eggs in the sand, and warmeth them in dust, And forgetteth that the foot may crush them, or that the wild beast may break them" (Job 39:14-15). But the ostrich also "raises its eyes to heaven" and waits for the rising of the Pleides to lay its eggs, so that they will be warm enough on their own, and is a symbol of those who forget "those things which are behind" in order to strive "for the prize of a heavenly vocation."[47] The cock not only recalls the betrayal of Christ by Peter and his remorse, but is also a symbol of vigilance, and is the "bird of dawning" that at Christmas "singeth all night long."[48] The serpent, created "Not noxious but obedient" to unfallen Adam and Eve (7.498), has redemptive and regenerative meanings opposed to the evil purposes for which Satan misused one. The brazen serpent that cures snakebite, raised on a pole in Numbers 21:8, is a type of Christ, and snakes, because they renew their skins, are classical symbols of rebirth, especially in Vergil. Animals in Valerian often represent opposites: the crocodile perdition, but also God; the crow concord and battle; the pelican piety and folly;

the wolf pestilence and prosperity. Those animals and the human passions or actions they represent show their good sides in Paradise and also warn of what will happen when Adam and Eve break "the fair musick that all creatures made." All beasts that are not purely good (as a few seem to be even in the fallen world) have such multiple connotations, and these make them capable of representing the virtues that result from regeneration and overcome their obverse vices.

In scenes before the Fall, all animals are innocent; their fallen attributes are in our minds, not them. Sir Thomas Browne explains that Eve need not fly the Serpent (nor need it have a human face to allay fear) because

> it was not agreeable unto the condition of Paradise and the state of innocency therin; if in that place as most determine, no creature was hurtful or terrible unto man, and those destructive effects they now discover succeeded the curse, and came in with thorns and briars. . . . For noxious animals could offend them no more in the Garden, than Noah in the Ark: as they peaceably received their names, so they friendly possessed their natures: and were their conditions destructive unto each other, they were not so unto man, whose constitutions were then antidotes, and needed not fear poysons.[49]

That is, even if the animals had been naturally constituted capable of doing harm, the perfectly tempered and sustained bodies of Adam and Eve were immune and their pure minds kept potential violence in check. Traherne concurs: "It's observable, that when God reviewed his Works, and saw the Serpents, and savage Beasts, yet he said they were very good. . . . had not Man sinned, these could not have hurt him."[50] Milton chooses to make this point through Eve; "every Beast" is naturally "more duteous at her call" than the enslaved "Herd disguis'd" to Circe's (9.521-22).

## Vegetable Gold

Interpretive choices also reside in herb, flower, fruit, and tree. The strawberry, for example, symbolizes lasciviousness (as Bosch uses it); the sweet flower under which snakes hide, in Vergil's third Eclogue; and, as a berry without thorns, "perfect righteousness."[51] The "Platan" or plane tree (Platanus orientalis) under which Adam stands when Eve first sees him in *Paradise Lost* (4.478) offers shade in noonday Eden; it may suggest the wisdom under whose branches the wise man lodges, covered from the heat, in Ecclesiasticus 14. According to

Mirella Levi D'Ancona it is "a bachelor, because unlike the elm, it did not support the vine" (Horace, *Carmina,* 2.15.4), a "steriles platani" (Vergil, *Georgics,* 2.70)—appropriate for Adam before Eve consents to join him—and also a symbol of "charity, firmness, and moral superiority," "good against all evil," and, like the columbine, the seven gifts of the Holy Ghost.[52] Bartholomeus reports that a broth of its leaves and rind "helpeth against venime" and that a *"Platanus...of* another sorte, whereof some grow in *England,"* bears a woolly fruit the size of a filbert that "helpeth them that are bitten of Serpents."[53]

Herbals and horticultural handbooks treat plants as "physic" in the fallen world: medicinal for the body, as in John Gerard's *Herball or Generall Historie of Plantes* (London, 1597) or the *Theatrum Botanicum: The Theater of Plants,* by the king's herbarist, John Parkinson (London, 1640); and edifying to the soul, as in Levinus Lemnius's *An Herbal for the Bible,* Englished by Thomas Newton (London, 1587) or Ralph Austen's *The Spirituall Use of an Orchard, or Garden of Fruit-Trees* (Oxford, 1657). Typically, gardening books begin with the Garden of Eden and suggest that good husbandry can return the earth to something nearer its original condition. "The great Husbandman . . . made Man to Husbandize the fruits of the Earth," Walter Blith observes, "and dress, and keep them for the use of the whole Creation." God gave man pattern and precedent, as well as precept, by bringing "that old Masse and Chaos into so vast an Improvement, as all the world admires, and subsists from," and "made him Lord of all untill the fall; And after that . . . Adam is sent forth to till the Earth, and improve it." Austen, urging enclosure in his *Treatise of Fruit-Trees,* asks, "Are not these the times of the Gospell prophesied of Esay 49.19,20. when the Wast and desolate places shall be inhabited [?]" and urges those making divisions, "let the Poore be first provided for."[54]

Scholars who relate Milton primarily to classical tradition, though recognizing the rebirth symbolism of, for example, Ovid's lovers changed to trees and flowers, are apt to stress their fallen implications, since metamorphoses so often transform victims of their own or others' sensuality and offer only figurative cures. Who would not rather be Daphne than a laurel tree, Hyacinth than hyacinth? The plants of God's Garden, however, are not emblems of sensuality. As nurture, beauty, and metaphor they are not nocent, for the reasons Browne explains, nor tamed into uninteresting symmetry nor vainglorious show: "not nice Art / In Beds and curious Knots, but Nature boon / Pour'd forth profuse" the flowers of Paradise (4.241-43). Privileging fallen implications not only deprives the Garden of innocence but invests its imagery with misogyny, since Eve is particularly associated with flowers.[55] In *Paradise Lost,* flowers are associated with innocent sexuality before the Fall[56] and also with spiritual graces and creative art.

The beneficent properties and allegorical attributes of plants figure in the iconography of Eden, but the innocently joyful and regenerative potentialities of labor are not usually part of paradisal iconography until artists begin to illustrate Milton's georgic poem.[57] Agricultural scenes sometimes follow Genesis series in cathedral decorations, but the link between the Garden of Eden itself and the art of gardening receives only slight hints in a few seventeenth-century illustrations to gardening books, such as the title page of John Parkinson's *Paradisi in Sole Paradisus* showing Adam and Eve picking, not nursing, fruit in a botanical garden (Frye, fig. 168).

In illuminations and paintings, it is vegetation that most clearly allies the earthly to the heavenly paradise. Giovanni de Paolo's predella for the church of San Dominico in Siena garnishes Eden and Heaven with similar trees bearing "vegetable Gold" (4.220) and with carnations (love), violets (humility), lilies (purity), and roses (joy). The meadow in the Ghent Altarpiece through which the multitudes come to worship the Lamb is full of flowers—forty recognizable varieties—like those that in other paintings pave the garden of Eden. The "gay enamell'd colors" of fruits and flowers (4.149) and the "vegetable Gold" of the Tree of Life in Milton's paradise link it with medieval heaven-gardens like the one in *Pearl,* and thence with the jewel imagery of Revelation; but they are still "vegetable" and both give and need organic human nurture.

The relation between the flourishing of nature and prelapsarian or restored righteousness is marked for special attention in Milton's Bible:[58]

> Let the field be joyful, and all that is therein:
>     then shall all the trees of the woods rejoice
> Before the Lord: for he cometh, for he cometh to judge the
>     earth: he shall judge the world with righteousness,
>     and the people with his truth.
>
> (Ps. 96:12-13)

Milton acknowledges the connection in *Paradise Lost* when nature blossoms at the approaches of the Son (6.781-84) and of Eve (8.40-47). And the encouraging relation between man and herb is reciprocal. At the end of *Il Penseroso,* the speaker plans to retire to a "Mossy Cell, / Where I may sit and rightly spell, / Of . . . every Herb that sips the dew." Herbert rejoices that "Herbs gladly cure our flesh; because that they / Finde their acquaintance there."[59] And flowering figures the relation between a right spirit and art: in "The Flower" his Lord's returns cause him to "bud again." In the fallen world, flowers, like leaves of grass, provide a salutary emblem of both mortality and regeneration: not *carpe diem,* but *carpe aeternitatem,* which for Herbert applies both to the refreshments within mortal life and the ultimate paradise to which mortals pass:

> These are thy wonders, Lord of love,
> To make us see we are but flowers that glide:
> Which when we once can finde and prove,
> Thou hast a garden for us, where to bide.
>> Who would be more,
>> Swelling through store,
> Forfeit their Paradise by their pride.[60]

In fact, those who "swell through store" forfeit three paradises: the temporal spiritual orchard of "Paradise"; the earthly life of "Providence," where God "tempr'st all," but human beings who swell through store can make the earthly cupboard bare; and the heavenly paradise to which "The Flower" flows: "O that I once past changing were, / Fast in thy Paradise, where no flower can wither!" But this flower can "bud again" in posies whose "odour will ascend" as long as people read poems, and those poems can make us careful of flower-works of all kinds.[61]

### *Beatus Vir* and *Beata Mulier:*
### Adam and Eve before the Fall

We have seen depictions of the original innocence of nature and of the parents of humankind, God's particular blessings of Adam and Eve, together and apart, and a few medieval instances of Adam and Eve in the state of innocence apart from the scriptural events: the Junius manuscript, the creation series at Rheims, Adam's thanksgiving in the north porch at Chartres, the Bohun Psalter and Hours (fig. 34). During the fifteenth century this theme was increased by the popularity of the Marriage of Adam and Eve, in which God joins their hands, and in the late sixteenth and early seventeenth centuries in representations by northern artists of an Admonition in which God speaks benevolently to Adam and Eve, as to his own family, while they stand encircled in each other's arms, and occasionally by a Sanctification of the Sabbath in which Adam and Eve kneel in prayer. These topics seem to have grown largely out of the work of Maerten de Vos, a wellspring of biblical imagery who "invented" the designs used by many Antwerp

engravers; his version of the Admonition may have become the Sabbath in the work of van Langeren and de Bry. Also at the end of the
sixteenth century came a new topic, the nuptial greeting of Adam and
Eve seen twice in van Langeren's series and also in illustrations to Jacob Cats's Edenic epithalamion, which does not illustrate a specific
verse of Genesis or derive from subtle alteration of a traditional topic.
The image seems to be as spontaneous as the embrace it records. Once
one is aware of the topos of original righteousness, one sees in
sixteenth- and early seventeenth-century Genesis series a new wave of
gratitude for the beauty of creation and the delight of innocent love.

In addition, during the seventeenth century a few illustrations to
poems and plays in the Genesis tradition showed Adam and Eve walking or conversing in the Garden in concord with each other and the
beasts of Eden. After the publication of *Paradise Lost,* this celebration
of original innocence greatly increased—partly because of the temper
of the times and partly because of Milton's poem and its illustrations.
The following examples trace this theme from the fifteenth to the early
eighteenth century.

## The Blessing of Creation

A beautiful illumination attributed to Simon Marmion serves as the
frontispiece to *Les Sept Ages du Monde* (fig. 54), a manuscript probably
made at Mons around 1460.[62] God enthroned in glory (and triple
crowned), surrounded by seraphim, cherubim, and other angels,
blesses a world composed of the starry sphere, the spheres of the six
moving heavenly bodies, and earth with its moon. In a tranquil landscape, seabirds rest on calm waves, while other birds wing the air. A
river with more birds winds luminously through a pleasant grove.
Near Adam and Eve are the rabbit of fecundity, the swan (which in
Valerian represents a pure heart), the hart drinking at the waterbrooks, and the lion of magnanimity. Adam's gesture beckons; Eve
steps forward with perhaps a touch of "modest pride, / And sweet reluctant amorous delay" (4.310-11).

A formally similar image of the Blessing of Creation was used as the
frontispiece in Luther's translation of the Bible (Frye, fig. 88). Here
again God (without the triple crown) blesses the whole creation while
Adam speaks earnestly to a modest Eve in a well-watered grove. The
print is less elegant than the illumination, and less serene. A large fish
opens shark-toothed jaws to devour a small one, most of the animals
have turned their backs on the Lords of Creation, and the foremost
fowl is the cock, associated both with betrayal by the story of Peter's
denial (Luke 22:34, 54-62), and with the vigilance Adam and Eve

need and will forget. Nevertheless, the main theme of this widely known Reformation image is the blessing of the plenteous world. The dog barks, the donkey brays, the serpent goes upright on its coils, and the fecund rabbit and contemplative stag share central space near the harmless human pair.

## The Marriage of Adam and Eve

After the blessing, perhaps the medieval topic that leads most directly to images of original righteousness in the age of Milton is God's joining of the hands of Adam and Eve, which became especially popular in the early fifteenth century, as in the many versions of the *Speculum Humanae Salvationis,* Jean Corbechon's *Des Proprietez des Choses* (c. 1415)—with angels as wedding guests—and the French manuscript illustrated in figure 24. Here, as often, the witnesses include animals who look pleased with the proceedings. They are varied, solid, and full of alacrity. The toad scoots plumply, the fish energetically ply the waves, animals arrive with eager paws and noses, the cock stands well awake on his spiky toes. Their well-being resides in this human pair, the harmony of the world in their faithfulness to the commandments to leave one tree inviolable and to govern the animals and dress and keep the Garden, in which tasks Eve is Adam's meet help. Duvet's engraving of the marriage (Frye, fig. 211), crowded with descendants, manifests their other calling, to increase God's kingdom, as does a cut by H. S. Beham in which a young, unmitered Creator joins their hands, inscribed "Seyt fruchtbar vnd ineret euch vnd erfet das Erdtrich" (Gen. 1:28 and 9:1). This version is clearly a defense of marriage, with a caption explaining that it is blessed by God and forbidden to none.

## God Speaking to Adam and Eve

Marital concord is also displayed in images of the Admonition of Genesis 2:16-17, found in fifteenth-century Dutch Bibles[63] and later paintings and engravings. Although in Genesis "the Lord God commanded the man," in art Eve is almost always present, and the topic is often called "God Speaking to Adam and Eve." In some seventeenth-century versions, Adam and Eve listen with their arms wound around each other or with clasped hands: in the moment of hearing God's command, they are affectionately united, the state which Milton suggests Satan most envies. Some—whom Milton calls "Hypocrites" (4.744)—may read into these images a sense that the marital bliss of Adam and Eve is a cause of the Fall, especially since they are uncomfortably similar to Dürer's woodcut of the Fall (Frye, fig. 218) and Cranach's illustration for the Luther Bible, in which Adam and Eve stand by the forbidden tree in much the same position as in Saenredam's engraving of the moment of choice (fig. 48)—except that in the Bible illustration Adam holds the forbidden fruit behind him. These imply the sexual motive for falling that other Reformation versions avoid. But the likelier interpretation of images of nuptial unity during the Admonition, rather than the Fall, is that a marriage attentive to God is good bliss, and the Fall will break it. Like Milton's poem, they disentangle sexuality from fallenness by placing Adam and Eve happily entwined under God's unreproving eye while he utters the warning against the forbidden tree; the original innocence of their married happiness, though vulnerable, is affirmed. Sometimes such scenes were domesticated to decorate home furnishings. A seventeenth-century cabinet (figs. 25 and 26), possibly a gift for a bride's boudoir, includes such an Admonition: the first bride and groom stand close together and Adam (who is redder than Eve, as "a man of red clay") has an arm around Eve's shoulders and carefully holds her wrist, like the Creator in medieval creation scenes. In Jacob de Backer's painting, with a Creation of Eve and various benign animals in the background, Eve has her hand on Adam's shoulder.[64]

Cornelis Cornelisz. van Haarlem's monumental painting (1592) in the Rijksmuseum (Frye, fig. 167) features the Fall, with a putto-like Serpent handing fruit toward Eve, while Adam, gazing at Eve, grasps a fruit she holds, and between them a monkey embraces a cat. But in the background, "our first parents" stand calmly with their arms around each other's waists while God speaks to them, apparently, in the form of a descended cloud. The painting contains a fine lion, an owl in the tree, dogs, sheep, turkeys, deer, storks, a porcupine, butterflies, a faint dragon above the lion, a fox, a slug, a leech, frogs, and a hedgehog.

It is important to remember that the verse on which this topic is based has two parts. God tells Adam and Eve that they may eat of all the other trees in the Garden, and that they must refrain from eating the fruit of one. The one restraint, these paintings imply, is meant to preserve the harmony of human love and of all the creatures who in marriage and admonition scenes alertly watch or innocently play. The knowledge of evil that eating the fruit will impart is the knowledge that deserting this exercise of self-control has opened the way to the ravages of sin and death.

## The Earthly Paradise

In several early seventeenth-century paintings, while Adam and Eve are present, Paradise itself is the principal subject. Poussin's *Spring* is a

well-known example, but like most neoclassical paintings it depicts a
subdued natural world consisting primarily of vegetation. Northern
painters populated the lavish landscape with meticulously painted
fruitful trees, graceful flowers and ferns, and animals that leap, cavort,
graze, ruminate, wing the air, and row "with Oary feet" (7.440) in the
ways of their kinds with amazing animation. A painting at Blessing-
thorne by Abraham Hondius depicts Adam and Eve in the background, very small, conversing under a tree, but the foreground is
occupied by prancing pairs of animals, the pond by swans, and the
trees and sky by perching and fluttering birds. Jan Brueghel the Elder
and Roelandt Savery each painted several such paradises. Brueghel's
paintings reproduced in Frye (plate vii, with figures by Rubens, and
figs. 158 and 159) include the Fall, but in another at the Louvre God
shows Adam and Eve the one sacrosanct tree that makes them a visible
church, again giving the impression that the welfare of all the lively
creatures who fill the Garden depends on their response to this trust.

## Sweet Society

A few artists detach Adam and Eve from the context of the Admonition and allow them to live in the Garden, as their creation in God's
image equips them to do and Milton so engagingly shows them doing,
in that period between the Admonition and the Fall during which
alone "original righteousness" can have been put into practice. The
Reformation, with its biblical literalism and its desire to return to the
purity of an early church of which the Garden was the type, had begun
to change attitudes toward the first creation, women, and marriage so
that some artists represented Paradise not only as a good creation
quickly blighted but as the original model of upright life.

Some illustrations in which Adam and Eve are clearly still sinless
have, nevertheless, Satan or other demons lurking in the foliage. That
is true of the illustration to Act Two of Andreini's *L'Adamo* (Milan,
1617) and of a series after Nicholas van Hoey, court painter (c. 1590-
1609) to Henry IV of France, whose unfallen Adam and Eve display
an unusual degree of amorous frivolity, while putti pick fruit and
weave garlands. In this series, Eve falls while Adam converses with
an angel.[65] When Milton first shows us Adam and Eve as "Lords of
all" among "all kind / Of living Creatures" (4.290, 286-87) walking
hand in hand through the Garden in "Simplicitie and spotless innocence" (318), Satan is also lurking, but Adam and Eve are more
sturdily innocent. Milton defines original righteousness as "Truth,
Wisdom, Sanctitude severe and pure, / Severe, but in true filial
freedom plac't" (293-94). It includes, as he dramatized it and his

contemporaries understood it, justice, honesty, responsibility, trustworthiness, candor, including charitable interpretation of the actions and words of others, and an encouraging respect for, and pleasure in, the lives and doings of all beings. (Sanctitude, though severe, does not prohibit any pure pleasure, including wit and play.) These qualities allow freedom, creativity, and loving-kindness in the human and cosmic communities and are the sources of the "true autority" (295) without which human beings could not justly be "Lords" of the rest of the creation.

Other versions in the visual arts of the topic of Adam and Eve at home in the Garden (with no lurking demon) emerged, without glamour or nostalgia, and without the voluptuous, sometimes disturbing beauty of Renaissance paintings, in quiet ways that engage the viewer's perceptions. These images allow Adam and Eve a few moments, at least, of waking bliss.

One reason for their rarity seems to be the assumption that if Adam and Eve had lived together in the Garden for more than a few hours, they would have discovered sex and conceived someone free of original sin. Such a conception would have divided the human race into two tribes, fallen and unfallen: an eventuality that nothing in Scripture allows us to believe. Milton's ebullient refutation of the whole tradition of prelapsarian virginity by insisting that sexual intercourse occurred in Paradise is one of his bravest elaborations. No visual artist could go so far. However, glimpses of Adam and Eve living at least a few sin-free moments of married amity did appear in advance of Milton's epic, in which Adam and Eve have their feet firmly on the ground, surrounded by carefully detailed plants and animals.

Some depictions of original righteousness are apt to produce a series of impressions: first, that all is well; second, that something is wrong; and third, that with sufficient grace and effort, all might have been well after all, as in the frontispiece to the 1537 Bible (fig. 39) where sin has not yet been irrevocably chosen. Another such instance is the frontispiece (fig. 55) to Joseph Fletcher's *History of the Perfect-Cursed-Blessed Man* (1628). The figures of Adam and Eve are copies of those in earlier engravings by Jan Sadeler I (Turner, fig. 7) and Adrian Collaert after Maerten de Vos. Sadeler's includes the figure of God and is clearly an Admonition, but Collaert's replaces God with a radiance, making the topic less plain. By taking the figures out of the context of the Admonition entirely, like the de Bry and van Langeren engravings, the illustration to Fletcher suggests a time in Paradise when Adam and Eve live in obedience. A Latin caption, "Dum stetis innocuus, stetit Omnipotentis Imaga Viva Dei, prima sorte statuius

Homo," proclaims that while Mankind stood innocent, the living image of almighty God remained, in the first state of creation. Clearly, Adam and Eve have not fallen. They are naked. The Tetragrammaton, in a glory, sheds its light. No Serpent entwines the tree nor apes pluck its fruit. The wolf and the lamb, the dog and the rabbit, lie down together. The lion is at rest. The perching bird on the left is neither owl nor cormorant, those birds of possible ill omen—though it could be a mockingbird; instead, the crane, representing vigilance, and the swan of good augury adorn the river of Paradise, suggesting that all could be well if the humans remained watchful. Behind Adam stands a camel, associated with caravans bringing the riches of the East and signifying strength and wealth: hence, in his fallen aspect, avarice, but here, where there are no possessions, simply abundance. Behind Eve is an elephant, signifying temperance, benevolence, and piety. Flying birds suggest the soul's felicity. Adam and Eve have their arms around each other in a companionable way that does not suggest lust but does imply close concord. Adam makes an explanatory gesture, perhaps toward a tree, perhaps to our eyes toward Eve's doubly fruitful breast. Eve's gesture is ambiguous. According to Bulwer's *Chirologia,* a handbook of gestures published sixteen years later, a finger pointing to one's head means "a close inclination to vice."[66] But that could be an interpretation of, rather than a prescription for, these figures. In the Sadeler and Collaert versions, the gesture is Eve's response to the presence of God, and in other Dutch works it denotes pious wonder.[67] In an image of the Crucifixion in the *Biblia Pauperum,* Longinus points to his healed eyes with a similar gesture.[68] Fletcher's poem itself supports the view that Eve is innately wicked. But the emphasis of the illustration, affirmed by its inscription from Psalm 8, is on creation in God's image and lordship over the peaceable kingdom to be restored according to the prophecy of Isaiah: "The wolf also shall dwell with the lamb . . . and the lion shall eat straw like the ox" (Isa. 11:11).

The inscription may trouble ecologically minded readers: "Lord, thou hast crowned him with glory and worship and hast put all things in subjection to him. Psal. 8.1.5.6." This verse and Genesis 1:28, to which it alludes, need their contexts for just interpretation. The psalm asks "What is man, that thou art mindful of him?" and the dominion in Genesis is clearly protective, immediately followed by the prescription of a vegetarian diet.

Not long after Slatyer published van Langeren's Genesis series, the Dutch statesman Jacob Cats wrote an extended wedding poem for Adam and Eve.[69] The illustrations by Adriaen van de Venne for Cats's *The Marriage of Our first Parents* may be the most innocent

representations of original righteousness before Milton's. One is a
nuptial greeting like that in the Slatyer and van Langeren series, but a
half-page illustration of that topic alone, in which an earnestly devoted
Adam grasps the hand and shoulder of a modest but housewifely Eve,
with a pair of turtledoves and pairs of cats, dogs, monkeys, and rabbits
at their feet and other animals in the background; rays of light shine
on them from a glory signed with the Tetragrammaton above them.[70]
The other (fig. 56) presents Eve and Adam in amicable colloquy. They
are conversing beneath a tree, but showing no undue interest in it; instead they are taking pleasure in the "Innumerous living Creatures"
(7.455). The most prominent animal is the tortoise, an emblem of domestic contentment because, being attached to its house, it is always at
home. It is often found with Adam and Eve but is usually much
smaller. The monkeys, instead of eating fruit, are happily prancing,
and the cat, instead of watching a mouse, is exchanging gazes—albeit
intently—with a rabbit: a pairing of fecundity and that risky opportunity called liberty. Most of the animals represented have, of course,
unfallen, fallen, and regenerate connotations, but the engraving as a
whole subordinates potentially sinister characteristics to beneficent
ones. The peacock, perched over Eve's head, symbolizes the pride that
goes before a fall, but also immortality and, as Juno's bird, the conse-
cration of women. The owl is a portent of death but also, by association with Minerva, a symbol of wisdom. The ass traditionally
represents both stubbornness and humility. Here, it is paired with the
ox in a way reminiscent of many a Nativity scene; the allusion prefigures the Incarnation, which could have taken place without the Fall.[71]
The ox and the ass, Avril Henry points out, "represent recognition of
God," deriving from Isaiah 1:3, "the ox knoweth his owner and the ass
his master's crib, but Israel doth not know, my people doth not
consider."[72] If the inventor of this engraving had the Bible verse in
mind, it too has double application to Adam and Eve, referring both
to their unfallen closeness to God and the lack of consideration that
causes, or is, the Fall. The rhinoceros stands for both ferocity and ro-
bustness, the parrot both eloquence and mockery. The "land frog"
comes from *Physiologus,* according to whom it represents abstinence
from "worldly desires" (XXXV). The snake, a tiny worm behind the
frog, represents the subtlety of both evil and the wisdom that over-
comes evil: one must be gentle as doves and wise as serpents (Matt.
10:16). The hedgehog, according to *Physiologus* XVII, robs the vine
and rolls over the fruit to carry it off to its young—a thief to man, but
a nurturer to hedgehogs—and Physiologus draws the moral "do not
let the devil . . . cut away all your spiritual fruits." But in Caxton's *Mir-*

*rour of the World* it "woloweth" on already fallen apples until well
laden and "goeth his way with them syngyng," in Cats's poem it offers
Eve an innocent picnic, and in Valerian's *Hieroglyphica* it represents
"the man who knows how to take advantage of opportunity" and is
armed against dangers.[73] The horse signifies constancy and sagacity,
but also war; the camel either riches or avarice. The elephant that
"wreath[s] his Lithe Proboscis" to "make them mirth" (4.346-47) is
famous for temperance, benevolence, and courage, and an emblem of
religion. Except that it can be used by men for fighting there seems to
be nothing against it. In Beza's paraphrase of Job, God calls attention
to the elephant, "whose bignes in comparison of thee, thou seest what
it is: & yet he eateth hay like the oxe, neither doth he proudly abuse
that his mightines of lims." He is "a most singular testimonie of my
omnipotent and incomprehensible power . . . yet he is content with his
fodder, which the mountains do yield him, he is gentle and hurteth no
man, neither do other beasts avoid his presence and companie, but
rather desire it."[74]

A particularly interesting feature of this engraving is the grouping
of the horse, the camel, the elephant, and the turkey. Traditionally, the
first three represent Europe, Asia, and Africa. The turkey completes
the group by representing the Indies, which is to say the Americas; his
French name, *dindon*, from "d'Indon," inscribes his New World origin. The grouping represents all peoples, the *omnes gentes* of Psalm 117
and of de Bry's engraving, and suggests that all nations as well as all
creatures could live together in peace as they did in the peaceable
garden.

The crocodile, to the Western mind, seems merely fearful—we expect the lady to wind up inside—and it can be a symbol of perdition
or, as in Spenser, of guile.[75] But in Wither's *Emblemes* it symbolizes
"the armour of true vertue," and in Whitney's it represents "Prouiden-
tia" because it foretells the extent of the Nile's floods.[76] Like the vulture, it was for the Egyptians (as iconologies point out) a symbol of
divinity because it sees when it is not seen and because, Valerian explains, the Egyptians worship God in silence and the crocodile is silent. The psalmist, too, asks all the world to keep silent before God,
and St. Cyprian adduces the moral that God hears not the voice but
the heart.[77] Most wonderfully, it receives a whole chapter of powerful
poetic description from the Voice from the Whirlwind in the Book of
Job: "By his neesings a light doth shine, and his eyes are like the eye-
lids of the dawn. . . . The flakes of his flesh are joined together; they are
firm in themselves. . . . When he raiseth up himself, the mighty are
afraid" (Job 41). But van de Venne's crocodile is not Job's untamable

leviathan, unnerver of power. In Cats's poem it contends with the other animals for the honor of carrying Eve on its back, arguing that only it can go both by land and by water, and Adam resolves the contest by saying that each animal may carry her at the appropriate moment, reserving the safe and careful tortoise for the time when Eve herself will carry tender fruit within.[78]

Van de Venne's solid-looking, unaristocratic, innocently earthy pair enjoying the diverse delightfulness of other creatures offers those who would "repair the ruins of our first parents"[79] an image of accessible blessedness. Their happiness implies right choices among the possibilities the animals embody. Milton, of course, adds incomparable beauty and wisdom through the gift of language. But these visual artists caught glimmers of the Edenic joy that floods his luminous poem. Though vandalized by the Destroyer and painfully to be resought, life in the Garden touched seventeenth-century culture with a grateful persuasion that a world of delight in all that rightly grows is humankind's native home.

## Eden after Milton

It would be hard to assess the extent to which Milton single-handedly changed attitudes toward Paradise, and especially toward Eve and marriage. That there is a change is certain. Some of Milton's literary contemporaries contributed to it, notably Jacob Cats and Joost van den Vondel, along with Bible annotators who affirmed the reality of God's Garden and the blessing on creation and wedlock. But Milton's imagining of the paradise that was lost and his implications about what can be regained are incomparably more complex and profound than others, and these changed people's ways of looking at nature and at human relations, especially the microcosm of marriage.[80] By combining the Reformation view of marriage as a divine institution with the height of sensuous delight, but much more by presenting Eve as a spiritually equal companion capable of graceful, earnest conversation and active accomplishment, Milton contributed hugely to the relations of the sexes, and in the ensuing century this contribution may be seen in literature, art, and music. Haydn's *Creation,* inspired by *Paradise Lost,* musically expresses divine energy bringing to harmonious being an astonishing audible light, glorious heavens of stars, the sun coming forth like a bridegroom, the splash of streams, the opening of buds, the wallowing of great whales, the prance of horses, the jewel falls of birdsong, and the joined and wonder-struck hearts of Adam and Eve.

However, in eighteenth-century pictures of Adam and Eve, including many illustrations to *Paradise Lost*, idealized images replace the more attainable life in the Garden represented in Milton's own time, and illustrators in the Age of Sensibility abstract fairness and tranquility from the complex moral awareness and active virtue, intense beauty and radiant joyfulness in Milton's poem. From the point of view of scriptural faith, images lacking moral complexity tempt in two ways. They may suggest a primeval beauty now wholly lost, a land of dreams rather than an image of the relations among God, nature, men, and women for which we can imperfectly but heartily strive. Or, obversely, they may help wed the viewer to the world, immersing us in a landscape increasingly detached from the eternal "Song of pure concent, / Ay sung before the saphire-colour'd throne / To him that sits thereon," rather than helping us "keep in tune with Heav'n."[81] Hayman's illustrations to Tonson's 1749 edition of *Paradise Lost* present an Adam and Eve who are sweet and gentle, but lacking in moral potency, more in the tradition of van Hoey than of de Vos or van den Broeck. It is hard to imagine them singing exuberant canticles or debating what form of government might best preserve their virtue and freedom from Satan's wiles. Yet his illustration of Eve sustaining her roses suggests Edenic nurture as no one had done before Milton. Other artists continued to expand the topic of Edenic innocence begun a century earlier, some undoubtedly influenced by Milton and his illustrators.

In the engraving by Johann Ulrich Kraus after Georg-Christoph Eimmart (fig. 57) illustrating Genesis 2:2-3, Adam and Eve, standing, as Milton has them do, in joyful prayer, complete the circle of praising angels. In *Figures de la Bible a La Haye*, published by Pierre de Houdt in The Hague in 1728, an illustration drawn by Gerard Hoet and engraved by Joseph Mulder with Genesis 2:25, "Adam and Eve were both naked and were not ashamed," inscribed in six languages (Hebrew, Latin, English, French, German, and Dutch) shows happy, childlike lovers—lacking Miltonic dignity and purposefulness—walking hand in hand among fruitful trees, a handsome pineapple, and plenty of friendly animals. Another, only slightly less sentimental engraving in the Kitto Bible,[82] by Gerard Vander Gucht (who engraved portraits of Milton) and Matthias Scheits (fig. 58) again shows Adam and Eve hand in hand among animals, with what might be a cormorant perched on the tree (4.196) beside them, the light that pours down upon them confirming the inscription's assertion that they were made in God's image.

## Summary: Reading the Iconography of Eden

When considering visual contexts for Edenic poems, it is useful to remember that most visual images of Paradise are in some way redemptive, and many are also regenerative: that is, they depict the repentance and rehabilitation of Adam and Eve themselves, or depict their creation in a way that affirms their original goodness and so their capacity for regeneration. A few are genuinely prelapsarian, providing images of the lives of Adam and Eve before the Fall on which to base ideas of regenerate life.

Pictures of the Fall may direct blame toward Eve, but during the Reformation it was often deliberately transferred to Adam; however, most Bible illustrations and the majority of other forms represent a mutual Fall. Genesis cycles showing the plenitude of creation do not imply a fortunate fall; they distinguish between the effects of sin, which are not happy, and the effects of grace and human responses to it, which bring good out of evil.

While they value visible things for their own sake, these images are not intended to replace contemplation of things unseen; they are one means of seeing the spiritual import of material things. They are fruits of, and perhaps objects for, meditation and study, with multiple symbolic meanings, exercising choice, and with room for new discoveries. Once a proper relation of spirit and matter is established, each living thing can be enjoyed for itself as well, opening eyes to the delights of God's boundless creativity. For the seventeenth-century viewer or reader, the stories in the Bible were both literal and figurative, and representations of the Garden of Eden had, as Marianne Moore once observed of the garden of poetry, "real toads in them."[83]

The creatures in the Garden of Eden, as the God of Genesis made it and other makers painted, printed, sculpted, vitrified, and versified it, are also around us now. They and their moral significations are ethically related, since the better humankind can shepherd its flock of feelings and ideas, the more harmoniously we can live with the rest of creation. "The heart of man," Donne's poem says, "is an epitome of God's great booke / Of creatures"; and everything he made is, depending on how one uses it, "poysonous, or purgative, or cordiall." What is true of nature is also true of art, which goes hand in hand with nature. Seeing nature and human nature as innocent, cursed, and blessed, seventeenth-century visual and literary arts about Eden take us literally, symbolically, and mimetically through those three stages. Their images are hieroglyphs of real and daily choices by which we preserve or spoil or renew the world. We can look at Saenredam's vulture, van de Venne's crocodile, and Milton's lavish garden and see defect and disintegration; or we can use these glyphic tests as purgatives and cordials by which to "rectify / Nature" and those epitomes of nature they help us learn we are.

## NOTES

1. De Jode, *Thesaurus Sacrorvm* (1585). Parts of an excellently preserved copy in the Huntington Library and a single print from the Print Room of the Plantin-Moretus Museum in Antwerp are combined in these figures. The finely engraved Visscher series, with the figure of God replaced by the Name as in figure 17, in the print collection of the Fogg Museum at Harvard University has more complex expressions, especially sorrowing Eve's.

2. Ferguson, *Signs and Symbols,* 36 and 30.

3. Hall, *Dictionary,* 42.

4. The British Library owns two good copies of this set, bound into Bibles published in 1649 (shelfmark 1486.cc.5) and 1663 (shelfmark C.65.d.5), and the Bible House collection now in the Cambridge University Library has one. The *Short-Title Catalogue* 22634.5 cites copies at Glasgow and Harvard.

5. The van Langeren or van Langren family is known primarily for mapmaking. Reference works identify Jacob Floris van Langeren as working in Amsterdam between 1580 and 1608, but this series has dedicatory verse to Charles I of England from both Slatyer and van Langeren. The final emblem in Hawkins's *Parthenia Sacra* (1633) is signed "Jacob van Langeren fecit."

6. See Herbert, *Historical Catalogue,* no. 476. Peake's New Testament series, also bound into the 1663 Bible in the British Library, has an iconic quality absent from the Dutch Protestant style of van Langeren.

7. The de Bry family worked in England. Theodore, father of Jan Theodore, illustrated Heriot's *Virginia.* Psalm 117 (Vulgate 116) is sung twice in the Latin Easter Vigil; the first reading is the creation story from Genesis.

8. The Kitto Bible, Huntington Library call number 49000, vol. 1, fol. 160. The Kitto Bible is a multivolume scrapbook of prints and drawings of scriptural subjects, collected in England during the early nineteenth century. Many of them were cut from Bibles and other books and are not identified.

9. From the visual image alone one would not be sure who is tempting whom, an ambiguity used more pointedly by Marcantonio and Rubens and traceable to Raphael. In Marcantonio's engraving after Raphael, Adam appears to be holding out fruit to Eve (reproduced in Bartsch, *Illustrated Bartsch,* vol. 26, no. 1). In Rubens's similar painting in his house in Antwerp, Eve holds the fruit (which is almost impossible to see) in such a way that Adam seems to be coaxing her to give it to him.

10. Stanley Fish discusses interpretive choice in *Paradise Lost,* and the reader's propensity to misapply "fallen" connotations, throughout *Surprised by Sin.* While Fish stresses the position of the guilty reader, I would like to

emphasize the presence of regenerate, as well as fallen and unfallen, interpretive invitations in the poem and in the visual arts, and the possibility that both Milton and the visual artists are addressing believers in the process of regeneration, who will take delight in discovering them.

11. Gerard, *Herball* (1597); quoted from *Leaves from Gerard's Herball,* 69.

12. Ferguson, *Signs and Symbols,* 30.

13. Whitney, *Emblemes,* no. 24.

14. Levi D'Ancona, *Garden of the Renaissance,* 157; Ferguson, *Signs and Symbols,* 30.

15. This angelic gardening is mentioned in the Slavonic 3 Baruch 4:7, in Charlesworth, *Pseudepigrapha,* 1:666. Paintings of Tobias and Raphael, often with a gourd flask, were popular in this period.

16. Browne, *Pseudodoxia Epidemica,* in *Works,* 2:344.

17. Ripa, *Iconologia,* 176. On Ripa's importance see Gordon, *Renaissance Imagination,* 51-74.

18. *Orus Apollo* (1543), sig. b. Horus Apollo, or Horapollo (named for the Egyptian and Greek gods of the sun), was thought in the Renaissance to have been an Egyptian priest, though both the antiquity and the source[s] of the work have since been questioned. See Horus Apollo, *Hieroglyphics of Horapollo;* Lewalski, *Protestant Poetics,* 179-80 and 465, n. 3.; Dieckmann, "Renaissance Hieroglyphics"; Gombrich, "Icones Symbolicae," 163-92; Johnston, "Heavenly Perspective," chap. 3.

19. Valerian, *Hieroglyphiques,* 227. Valerian's iconology was reprinted in various languages during the sixteenth and seventeenth centuries.

20. *Orus Apollo* (1543) and *Hori Apollonis* (1606); Valerian, *Hieroglyphica* (1610) and *Hieroglyphiques* (1615); Ripa, *Iconologia* (1593), *Nova iconologia* (1618), and *Iconologie* (1636).

21. Not all of the attributes in the iconologies are relevant to English poets, however. Browne points out in *Pseudodoxia Epidemica* that many, including many church fathers, thought that "Vultures all are females, and impregnated by the wind. . . . Wherein notwithstanding what injury is offered unto the Creation in this confinement of sex, and what disturbance unto Philosophy in the concessions of windy conceptions, we shall not here declare" (*Works,* 2:380). The tradition is nonscriptural; in Isaiah 34:15 "there shall the vultures also be gathered, every one with her mate."

22. *Physiologus* ("the Natural Historian") is a fifth-century, or earlier, Greek bestiary with allegorizations perhaps compiled from hexameral commentaries such as those of Basil and Ambrose. This and other early bestiaries are discussed in James's introduction to *The Bestiary.* For the hexameral commentaries see Corcoran, *Milton's Paradise,* and Robbins, *Hexameral Literature.*

23. Augustine, *On Christian Doctrine,* in *Opera,* III.xxv. "Contraria scilicet, cum alius in bono alias in malo res eadem per similitudinem ponitur. . . . Sic et aliae res non singulae, sed unaquaque earum non solum duo aliqua diversa, sed etiam nonnumquam multa significat pro loco sententiae,

sicut posita reperitur" (*De Doctrina Christiana*, 100-101). Milton's definition of "candor" as interpretation "in a favorable sense" echoes Augustine's "in bono."

24. Regina Schwartz, bringing the Hebraic sense of clean and unclean animals to bear on her account of Milton's creation scenes, cites animals who violate "creaturely catagories": "A fish that crawls (shellfish), a bird that walks (stork), an animal that flies (insects)—any creature that violates its category is unclean, for such creatures violate no less than world order" (*Remembering and Repeating*, 14-15). Seventeenth-century Christian commentary does not usually divide animals according to Jewish dietary laws (in any case, Adam and Eve do not eat animals), though they provide one set of connotations; and commentators like Edward Topsell agreed, against the Manichean heresy, that God created nothing evil. Naturally mixed forms—amphibians, for example—were thought emblematic of humanity's twin nature, animal and spiritual. While Satan "understands his own descent into a serpent as a fall from pure to mixed, from holy to unclean," and shudders "This essence to incarnate and imbrute" (*Remembering and Repeating*, 16), the Son, whom Schwartz later calls "the radically innovative God-man" (104), does not so shudder, and Peter's dream of clean and unclean beasts in Acts 10 leads him to the moral insight that there are no clean and unclean groups of people, "But in every nation he that feareth [God] and worketh righteousness, is accepted of him."

25. Corcoran cites various patristic interpretations of the tree in *Milton's Paradise*, including "the generally accepted opinion that it conferred experimental knowledge of good and evil—the good of obedience to the commands of God and the evil of disobedience—as opposed to the theoretical knowledge already possessed by man as necessary to his rational self-government" (25). Ainsworth comments on Genesis 2:15-17 that "the morall law, and worke thereof, was written in [Adam's] heart," and that "Besides the law of nature, graven on *Adams* heart, wherby he was bound to love, honour, and obey his Creator: God here giveth him (for a triall of his love) a significative law, concerning a thing of it selfe indifferent, but at the pleasure of God made unlawfull and evill for man to doe: that by observing this outward rite, he might testifie his willing obedience unto the Lord." The "tree of knowledge of good and evil" was "So named, because Gods law, which forbad man to eat of this tree, should teach what is good and evill . . . shewing mans goodness and righteousnesse, if he did obey . . . or his evill if he did transgresse: for the *knowledge of sin* is *by the Law*, Rom. 3:20. Also, knowledge is used for *sense*, or *experience*" (*Annotations*, 11). Cowley, in "The Tree of Knowledge," writes that "The Phoenix Truth" rested on "That right Porphyrian Tree which did true Logick shew," but not by eating: "The onely Science Man by this did get, / Was but to know he nothing knew" (*Works*, 1:145). Milton called the tree "a pledge, as it were, and memorial of obedience. It was called the tree of knowledge of good and evil from the event; for since Adam tasted it, we not

only know evil, but we know good only by means of evil. For it is by evil that virtue is chiefly exercised, and shines with greater brightness" (*De Doctrina Christiana* 1.10, in *SM*, 986). That definition does not entirely explain the use of the term "Tree of Knowledge" in *Paradise Lost* by unfallen Adam; he understands it as "The only sign of our obedience left / Among so many signs of power and rule" (4.428-29), with the implication that power needs always to be referred to God in order to be kept wholesome. Before the Fall, Adam and Eve exercise virtue by knowing evil without doing evil.

26. Kaufmann sees this openness in the waters of Eden, through the traditional association of "the Deep" with "the Abyss," carrying "the threat as well as the promise of flux" (*Paradise*, 16).

27. Donne, "To Sr. *Edward Herbert*. At *Julyers*," *Complete Poetry*, 233-34, l. 42.

28. The painting of the Fall in which Rubens supplied the figures and Jan Brueghel the Elder the teeming animals and vegetation (Frye, plate vii) is an example of north joining south, Rubens having been in Italy. Sadeler's series (figs. 17-21) is influenced by Renaissance classicism but includes more animals than southern versions, apart from the topics of their creation and naming, usually have.

29. Sandler says of a bestiary (c. 1300) at Canterbury, "Common animals are exceptionally well drawn with an acute sense of proportion, movement, and texture, and sensitive appreciation of animal nature or psychology. . . . [And] the plant forms—oak, grape, ivy, strawberry—are rendered with as fresh a look at nature as the domestic animals" (*Gothic Manuscripts*, 1:28-29). Snyder shows that in a Dutch edition of Bartholomeus published in Haarlem in 1485, "The Bellaert Master discards the convention of displaying [plants, animals, fishes, and birds] as multi-vignettes or single motifs, and instead sprinkles the flora and fauna quite naturally in a panoramic landscape so that they all live harmoniously on one page." His work "has all the naturalism of an open-air zoo" ("Bellaert Master," 43 and 62).

30. British Library shelfmark 1411.e.3.

31. Marvell, "The Garden," *Complete Poems*, 101.

32. Inscriptions are Ps. 33:6 (Vulgate Ps. 32), Matt. 28:19, Rom.11:36, and verses from the Athanasian Creed (required on numerous feast days in the BCP) concerning the uncreated Trinity and the Unity of the Godhead.

33. Milton, *Of Education*, in *SM*, 726, and *Of Reformation*, in *SM*, 453.

34. For example, in *The Morning Stars Sang*, Schorsch and Greif note that "birds [are] almost always present in scenes suggesting sexual sin" (37). But birds are also symbols of the soul (the Christ Child often holds one), and Henry points out that in the thirteenth-century *Bible Moralisée* "the creation of the birds on the sixth day of Creation signifies contemplatives who aspire to ascend to heaven" (*Biblia Pauperum*, 14).

35. Ripa uses the badger in his emblem of sloth, or Accidia: "Donna, uestituta di pelle di Tasso" (*Iconologia*, 3). Although badgers are scarcely

slothful, they are nocturnal, so that they may have seemed slothful to daylight observers.

36. Milton, *De Doctrina Christiana*, in *SM*, 999.

37. Donne, "Why are wee by all creatures waited on?" *Complete Poetry*, 343.

38. Donne, sermon on Genesis 1:26, in *Sermons*, 9:58, 63, and 69.

39. Traherne, *Meditations*, 68-69.

40. Tennyson, *In Memoriam*, LVI, in *Works*, 442.

41. Examples of Orpheus charming the animals in Edenic landscapes include paintings by Jacques Savery I, c. 1600 (Rijksmuseum, Amsterdam), and Frederick van Valckenborch, 1601 (Munich, private collection), and an engraving by Nicholaes de Bruÿn in the Print Room of the Rijksmuseum.

42. Goltzius, *Hendrik Goltzius*, 356-57; Harbison, *Symbols in Transformation*, 16.

43. Herbert, "Christmas," in *Works*, 80-81.

44. *Hamlet* 5.2.230-31; Matt. 10:29.

45. Ripa, *Iconologia*, 89-93.

46. *Physiologus*, emblem XLIII.

47. *Physiologus*, emblem XXXI.

48. *Hamlet* 1.2.157-64. According to Réau, the cock is a symbol of the resurrection: "Son chant matinal rille non seulement du sommeil, mais de la mort" (*Iconographie*, 1:88).

49. Browne, *Pseudodoxia Epidemica*, in *Works*, 2:344.

50. Traherne, *Meditations*, 68.

51. Levi D'Ancona, *Garden of the Renaissance*, 365, and Ferguson, *Signs and Symbols*, 38.

52. Levi D'Ancona, *Garden of the Renaissance*, 307-10.

53. Bartholomaeus Anglicus, *Batman vppon Bartholome*, 310v. Bartholomaeus was a thirteenth-century naturalist.

54. Blith, *The English Improver Improved*, 3-4; Austen, *Treatise*, dedicatory letter to Samuel Hartlib. In *Environ'd with Eternity*, Charlotte Otten calls attention to the writings of the "hortulan saints" (chap. 3), to the healing abilities of "salvific plants" (27), and to "terraculture" as the best way of recapturing "the blessedness of the Edenic pre-lapsarian state" (5). Otten's emphasis on terraculture as regenerate activity is important in itself and as a corrective for the dominance of erotic concerns in recent Milton criticism.

55. For Karl P. Wentersdorf, Milton's "trees—stately and strong, and thus images of masculinity—are also, because of their biblical associations, symbols of holiness. Contrasted with the noble trees are the flowers . . . beautiful and frail, and thus an embodiment of the feminine principle; and for Milton, they symbolize the attractive and seductive aspects of physical love" ("*Paradise Lost* IX," 134). Wentersdorf considers the floral imagery associated with Eve as "usually images of carnal sensuality" (140, n. 2) and adduces these associations to discredit Eve's motives for separate gardening as symbolizing "the

moral dangers implied in her work plan" (135-36). I have discussed the positive attributes of her vegetable imagery in *Milton's Eve* (145-47). A. Bartlett Giamatti also discredits nature and Eve in Milton's paradise in *Earthly Paradise*, chap. 6.

56. Turner links erotic luxuriance to plants in *One Flesh*, 240-42.

57. Anthony Low in *The Georgic Revolution* shows how unusual Milton was in exalting work; labor, especially among aristocratic writers, was a curse, inapplicable to unfallen life.

58. On underlinings and marginal notations in Milton's Bible see *CM*, 18:559-65; notes on the Psalms are on p. 560.

59. Herbert, "Man," in *Works*, 90-92.

60. Herbert, "The Flower," in *Works*, 165-67. Another silken "twist" in floral iconography has brought Herbert's imagery back into the visual arts; the Sarum Group of embroiderers have recently made an altar frontal for Herbert's church at Bemerton inspired by this poem.

61. Herbert, *Works:* "Paradise," 132-33; "The Flower," 165-67; "Providence," 116-21, l. 119.

62. Reproduced with commentary by Delaissé in *Miniatures médiévales*.

63. Several of these are illustrated in Lane, "Genesis Woodcuts."

64. De Backer, *Aards Paradijs*, Groeningemuseum, Bruges.

65. A set of drawings after van Hoey's series may be found in Robels, *Niederlandische Zeichenungen*. Van Hoey's set was engraved by Raphael Custodis.

66. Bulwer, *Chirologia*, 172.

67. In a fragment of Adriaen van Wesel's lovely Nativity with musical angels in the Rijksmuseum, for example, a figure representing either Joseph or one of the shepherds, reverently attentive, makes the identical gesture.

68. Henry, *Biblia Pauperum*, 97 and 99n.

69. Cats, "Gront Houwelick." Geoffrey Bullough provides a summary, a partial translation, and evidence for Milton's possible acquaintance with Cats, in "Milton and Cats."

70. Cats, "Gront Houwelick," 7. The artists seem to be Adriaen van de Venne and C. van den Queboorn, or van Queboren, who did a portrait of Elizabeth of Bohemia in 1625. A romanticized version of this image, made by A. Matham after A. van de Venne, appears in Cats's *Wercken*, where a slimmer and calmer pair are surrounded by clouds of beaming cherubs and animals in pairs nuzzling each other, monkeys embracing, elephants clasping trunks, snakes entwining, lions preparing to mate: an unfallen festival of Venus.

71. Dennis Danielson traces this tradition and applies it to Milton in *Milton's Good God*, 215-44, drawing the analogy between a potential nonlapsarian Incarnation and the proclamation of the Son as Messiah to the angels before any fall had occurred. Peter A. Fiore documents the tradition (but does not think it applies to Milton) in "Account Mee Man," 51-56.

72. Henry, *Biblia Pauperum*, 51.

73. Caxton, *Mirrour,* 101-2; Valerian, *Hieroglyphiques,* 98-99.

74. Beza, *Job expounded,* sig. Z6. Beza takes behemoth for an elephant, and imagines that the "tail" of Job 17 is the elephant's snout. Alter translates behemoth as the hippopotamus and his "tail" as "his member" (*Art of Biblical Poetry,* 108 and 116, n. 5), and Mitchell translates "His penis stiffens like a pine; his testicles bulge with vigor" (*Book of Job,* 85).

75. Spenser, *Faerie Queene,* I.18.

76. Wither, *Emblemes,* 112; Whitney, *Choice of Emblemes,* Emblem 3.

77. Valerian, *Hieroglyphiques,* 361.

78. Bullough, "Milton and Cats," 117. Though Cats domesticates the fiercer beasts, commentaries on Job respect their wildness.

79. Milton, *Of Education,* in *SM,* 726.

80. For eighteenth-century responses to *Paradise Lost* as a model for recovery, see Griffin, *Regaining Paradise;* for eighteenth-century women's responses to the poem as a model for relations between the sexes, see Wittreich, *Feminist Milton.* For iconographic influence see Pointon, *Milton and English Art;* Ravenhall's articles on Hayman, Atterbury, and Aldrich; and Labriola and Sichi, *Milton's Legacy.*

81. Milton, "At a Solemn Musick," in *SM,* 19, l. 27

82. Kitto Bible, vol. 2, fol. 200.

83. Moore, "Poetry" (original version), in *Complete Poems,* 267.

# 4

# The Arts of Eden

What is all this juice and all this joy?
A strain of the earth's sweet being in the beginning
In Eden garden.
                         Gerard Manley Hopkins

In Milton's epic, the visual imagery of Paradise joins many other arts: language, music, government, care of the earth, the preservation in peace of earthly creatures, and marriage as font of civility and friendship. These integrated activities are the work Adam and Eve gladly produce in response to God, nature, and each other. But they are the beginnings of the same work in the present world as well. Adam and Eve share equally in this work, but they also have particular callings, Eve as creative artist and Adam as the just governor who protects the freedom and listens to the voices of those he leads—on one occasion, too compliantly. Their work is also the work of the reader. Just as the details of visual art offer interpretive choices that re-enact the primal choice between good and evil, the poet presents such choices to the reader in symbolic imagery and in the decisions of his characters. Each act of interpretation produces significance *in bono* or *in malo,* or a complex of both.[1]

## Ithuriel's Spear: Candor and the Art of Reading

Near the end of Book 4 of *Paradise Lost,* we come upon a multi-layered image. Innocent Adam and Eve, in the innermost, flower-decked, awe-encircled bower, sleep in each other's arms. Squatting by Eve, Lucifer turned Satan turned toad assays "if, inspiring venom" (that is, breathing poison) into her ear he might raise "Vain hopes, vain aims, inordinate desires / Blown up with high conceits engend'ring pride" (4.804, 808-9). As toad, he recalls the symbolically similar amphibians of Revelation 16:13: "And I saw three unclean spirits like frogs come out of the mouth of the dragon." His shape glyphs the uncleanness that comes out of his mouth. Standing over Satan, the archangel Ithuriel, searcher-out of truth, touches him "lightly" with his spear, causing *him* to be "blown up"—as is fitting for the father of gunpowder—into his true form, an inadvertant frog-prince or reverse Orgoglio, for "no falsehood can endure / Touch of Celestial temper, but returns / Of force to its own likeness" (4.811-13).

The literalness of Satan's exposure by the literalization of conceits; his explosion at the touch of truth; Milton's embellished yet literal reading of Genesis; and his attention everywhere to the letter of language—etymology, metaphoric roots and branches, connotations spelled and dispelled, links of sense (as image) with sense (as significance) and both with sound—all beg us to consider the investigative and connective power of exact words. Ithuriel, with his more vocal companion Zephon, has been instructed to "Search through this Garden, leave unsearcht no nook" (4.789). He is therefore a *figura* of the reader, who is called to read the poem whole and attend to all its details. His searching and disclosing also comment on the reader's calling to search every nook of the poem and, using the tempered spear of interpretation "to [which] must be added industrious and select reading, steady observation, [and] insight into all seemly and generous arts and affairs,"[2] to free the text to do its work.

Satan provides a proleptic parody of Ithuriel's close reading when he plans, "But first with narrow search I must walk round / This Garden and no corner leave unspi'd." A cannibal-critic, he looks only for what he can use as material—as he deconstructively quips—"to build / Thir ruin" (4.528-29, 521-22). *His* spear, though presumably also of celestial temper, props the "uneasy steps" of "unblest feet" (1.295, 238), a figure of limping prosody, and becomes the wand of his disguise (3.644) which like Comus's charming-rod can only disable. It is the staff of death.

For Milton sin is defect, inanition, withering, sterility, and death, and paradise is life without sin.[3] He includes in the unfallen lives of Adam and Eve the buds of all human activities in a state of health. Adam and Eve enjoy a sensuous and erotic life in Milton's Eden/Hedon that is too pure to cloy.[4] They sound the inexhaustible wells of language. They discover the infinite delights of music and "concent" together: the earmark of paradisal life, for "the man that hath not music in himself, / Nor is not moved with concord of sweet sounds, / Is fit for treasons, stratagems, and spoils."[5] Their interests include gardening (good care of the whole earth, and the mother of metaphor); angels (as many kinds as individuals, as Dante says,[6] all artists and absolute lovers); animals (gorgeous, graceful, edifying, funny, fascinating, unexpected, prodding open the imagination); potential children (all different, each a fresh microcosm of beauty, talent, affection, amusement, and unpredictable opinions); ethically considered scientific inquiry; the problem of establishing good government among

free people threatened by a clever and vicious enemy; the glory that
heaven and earth are full of; and conversation of the most felicitous
reciprocity, dense with poetic shoots. And since their health encompasses some difficulty and distress, by which even sinless beings learn
and grow, they have bracing opportunities to work through spiritual
difficulties and dangers and remain whole and joyful. Adam and Eve
have plenty to do and be, without "Vain hopes, vain aims." Yet some
readers have thought Satan—who takes a delighted interest in nothing
and no one, with whom one would be hard put to sustain a conversation at all, and who never creates but devastates—more lively than
Adam and Eve, and paid more attention to what is wrong with Adam
and Eve than to what is right with them.

One of the things that is right with them is that they are splendid
artists, blithely engaged in acts that are pregnant with all the arts that
do not hurt the earth, nor the community, nor the soul, but enhance
them all: poetic speech, music, the rudiments of dance and dramatic
play, and, as part of their vocation of horticulture, both graceful movement and visual art. Their works manifest their creation in God's image. We have seen how artists sometimes depict God as Artifex,
energetically engaged in the work of creation. Veronese's painting of
God sculpting Eve and opening her eyes (fig. 31) and Poussin's *Creation of Adam,* in which God molds Adam's eye sockets with forefinger
and thumb, make explicit the analogy between the Maker as artist who
gives us eyes and the artist as maker who helps us see.[7] In *Paradise Lost,*
God's forming of Adam and Eve, and the jewel tones of his Garden,
wrought with the luminous detail of a Van Eyck painting (4.236-66,
for example, and Raphael's observant description of the creation of the
animals) portray God as Artifex, and Milton portrays God's human
images as creators of Edenic arts. What they make of the matter God
gives them is the model for good arts in a regenerate world. The arts
they enjoy beautify life, edify souls, and could be done forever without
harming any creature. Their language, music, stewardship of the
earth, marriage, friendship, hospitality, study, worship, and praise provide endless pleasure and interest because they are rooted in a diversified and layered world dense with beings and meanings, and because
they lead through infinite pores into eternity.

## *Resplendent Globe: The Arts in Paradise Lost*

Adam and Eve cultivate the firstlings of these integrated arts
within an art form—the poem—whose medium is language full of
imagery and of music: angelic anthems, the songs and canticles of

Adam and Eve, the voices of all nature coursing through Milton's well-tuned phrases, the flexible rhythms of fit locutions drawn from the resources of many languages, the sheer beauty of sound that draws the pleasure and purity of music into the words themselves and, as R. M. Frye pleasantly observes, converts us as we read "into musical instruments and into musicians."[8] This music joins with the visual beauty of the teeming cosmos, earth, and garden, and the energy and delight with which the poet brings all heaven and earth before our senses—angels and nightingales, stars and flowers, ramping lions and gauzy wings of insects with "smallest Lineaments exact / In all the Liveries deckt of Summer's pride / With spots of Gold and Purple, azure and green" (7.477-79); onomatopoetic "Shoals / Of Fish that with their Fins and shining Scales / Glide under the green Wave" and "with quick glance / Show to the Sun thir wav'd coats dropt with Gold" (400-403, 405-6); "umbrageous Grots" and "smell of field and grove" (257, 265); daily work and amorous delight. All are lavishly offered to stir up a gust for paradise and show how beneficent arts can furnish earth and replenish souls.

## The Music of Creation

The arts of Eden form a unified enterprise.[9] When their topic is the creation, visual and verbal images respond both to nature and to the poetry of Genesis, Job, and the Psalms and Canticles. When Psalms and Canticles are set to music, the three arts join, since seventeenth-century music not only beautifies words but also mimes their imagery. When poets write about creation and re-creation they incorporate both imagery and music into their words. In order to read the poetry of creation, we need not only to see its images but also to hear its music.

Renaissance and early baroque musicians composed, in part, mimetically; their music imitates and illuminates the images, concepts, and expressiveness of the words that inspire it. Returning briefly to sixteenth-century Italy, I should like to take as an emblem of this integration that figure of the hart which we have seen in so many creation images, representing the psalm verse, "Like as the hart desireth the waterbrooks, so longeth my soul after thee, O God" (Ps. 42:1). Historically, this psalm was linked to baptism and the waters of regeneration. In the Salisbury and Roman missals it is sung during the Easter Vigil at the beginning of the baptismal rite and its first three verses are used as the last tract following earlier readings. The first reading is Genesis 1-2:2, and the creation story is referred to throughout the service.[10]

The mystical union of nature, image, words, and music occurs in Palestrina's motet on those words: "Sicut cervus desiderat ad fontes aquarum, ita desiderat anima mea ad te Deus."[11] Its combination of pictorial image, verbal rhythm, and musical setting lets the singer, or the attentive listener, experience thirsting and drinking, both physically and spiritually. The image of the hart evokes both that eagerly leaping animal and its picture, with its alert prongs, common to creation scenes in so many books and churches. The rhythm of the words, with their periodic suspension, re-creates the rhythm of desire and of turning toward the source.

Palestrina's setting expresses the yearning of the language, of the hart, and of the heart. It casts the thirsting sounds of "sicut cervus desiderat ad fontes" in ascending imitative melodic phrases rising to "fontes." "Aquarum" liquifies in rippling melisma. "Anima mea" is a cry of longing intensified by musical suspensions, and "ad te deus" comes to rest on long held notes, the tension released by descending runs in the lower voices, creating a figure of deep refreshment and peace. The beauty of Palestrina's imitative melodic lines, each responding to and enhancing the others, re-creates the longing and satisfaction that the visual imagery of the verse also suggests, in a figure that attaches the soul to nature in the very moment that it attaches it to God. Yet this satisfaction does not extinguish the desire. The psalmist, in the ensuing verses, is still "athirst for God," and the music by its beauty creates thirst for the fountain of beauty and beatitude itself, the "well of water springing up into everlasting life" (John 4:14). The motet is a "gusto de vera beatitudina." When one has said the words, heard the music, and seen the image of the hart amid the yet-unspoiled joys of Eden Garden, the three arts charge each other. When one meets a hart, in a poem or in nature, the words of the psalm, the music, the image of the Garden, and the thirst for God all come with it. This concinnity provides experience of paradisal consciousness. For the Renaissance mind, it is a proof of the divine origins of the cosmos and of the responding soul.

The music of beginnings constantly recurs in liturgy. If there is one set of words that has been communally said or sung more often than any other in the Western world, it is probably the conclusion to psalms and canticles in Christian liturgy that hooks time into eternity: "Gloria Patri et Filio et Spiritui Sancto. Sicut erat in principio et nunc et semper et in saecula saeculorum"; in the Book of Common Prayer, "Glory be to the Father, and to the Son: and to the Holy Ghost. As it was in the beginning, is now, and ever shall be: world without end." This *in principio* refers to an "at first" in heaven that precedes the *in principio* of

Genesis 1:1, the "at first" of the creation of the world. The *saecula* are endless ages. The verse tells that the glory of God resplendent in the hallelujahs of his creatures came before and survives through the dust and heat of human history and will continue forever. Whenever these words are sung, the singers and hearers mimetically reenter the harmony out of which humankind and the earth in their charge so frequently fall. Poets, among them Herbert, Donne, and Milton, found in music and the music of poetry ways of rejoining this extemporal song.

Composers setting these words renew them in ever fresh ways, sometimes calling attention to *now*, sometimes to *always*, but always linking now to forever. Thomas Weelkes, for example, brings his Ninth Service to a climax on these words at the end of the Nunc Dimittis, as David Wulstan points out: " '[A]s it was in the beginning' gradually ascends to a brilliantly highlighted top G—appearing for the first time in the whole service."[12] And this G recurs in the highest voice at the instant three of the lower voices are singing "is now."

Monteverdi (whose music Milton admired) set Psalm 117 (Vulgate 116), "Praise the Lord all ye nations"—the psalm used as the tract after the Genesis reading in the Easter Vigil and associated with Genesis in de Bry's engraving—in a way that also exemplifies mimetic music. At the beginning, the music for "omnes gentes" ("all ye peoples") blossoms in dense homophonic chords, representing both the unity and the harmony of many voices. At the end, the setting of "sicut erat in principio" repeats these same striking chords, literally rejoining the music of "as it was in the beginning" to the music as it was at the beginning of the psalm. Mimetically, it joins the music of "all people" to the beginning of beginnings; and it joins the singers and hearers both to "all people" and to eternal choirs. To hear is to be integrated.

For Psalm 113 (Vulgate 112), Laudate Pueri, Monteverdi uses imitative counterpoint for "sicut erat in principio," so that each voice returns to the other voices' beginnings. Thus singers and hearers experience and carry on the continuity of praise through the *saecula*. They are being and doing what the psalm and its *gloria* enjoin.

For Psalm 1, Beatus Vir, tied to Genesis in many psalters, Monteverdi builds from "et nunc" to a longer "et semper" to "lincked sweetnes long drawn out" on "et in saecula saeculorum," interspersing repeated "glorias." The psalm setting takes such sprightly joy in the just person's blessedness that it confers blessing and a thirst for *justitia*. Its beauty seals justice and happiness together as natural partners. Musically as well as verbally, in all these psalms and their glorias, singers and listeners rejoin the "celestial consort," as Milton and his contemporaries thought art should help us do.[13]

In early seventeenth-century English cathedrals, royal chapels, many college chapels, and some large parish churches, liturgy was a musical as well as a verbal experience, as it had always been; the Reformation altered the tradition by supplying a vernacular liturgy and requiring simpler vocal textures to increase verbal clarity. During the 1640s and 1650s, however, radical reformers not only abolished many ceremonies and much church art but also removed organs and destroyed choir books. Music in church distracted attention from the words, they thought, and was a royalist activity; only psalms set to a few simple tunes that everyone could learn were suitable for the people of God. Milton censured the fixed forms of Anglican liturgy along with Anglican politics, and we find no laments for the loss of "the beauty of holiness" in his prose. He had lamented, rather, that "stones, and pillers, and crucifixes, have now the honor and the alms due to Christ's living members" and held that the liturgy ought to be "purged and physicked."[14] But he loved sacred or "solemn" music. In *Paradise Lost* the arts are integrated in the church of Adam and Eve, which is a church of all the people, where ceremony is not separated from spirit nor from the rest of life. Milton's "At a Solemn Musick," written with English sacred choral music ringing in his ears, enjoins an inclusive "us" to keep in tune with heaven's choir. *Paradise Lost* shows what the human family could be if "we" rejoined the universal song. In both, Milton provides mimetic experience of keeping in tune with heaven now and preparing for it by regenerating paradisal concent in the present world, "as it was in the beginning."

Seventeenth-century "solemn musick" is mainly part music. In order to hear the music of paradisal poetry, one needs to know four things about Renaissance and early baroque vocal polyphony, still the music of seventeenth-century English liturgy and much domestic music-making.

First, it was closely linked with words in several ways. The English reformers desired that the vernacular liturgy should be clearly understood, and composers set words intelligibly by matching note lengths to syllables and by using homophonic sections and wide spacing of imitative entries to display the text. But they also went further, and used musical rhetoric and mimesis to illuminate words that, said or sung daily, were already familiar to the hearers. The best known liturgical composers in early seventeenth-century England were the organists of the Chapel Royal for Elizabeth I and James I: William Byrd, who composed both Latin and English service music, and Orlando Gibbons.

They and other English composers applied musical rhetoric to the vernacular liturgy.

Second, the tuning was not the equally tempered scale of the modern keyboard, which compromises natural intervals to allow one instrument with fixed tuning to modulate freely through all keys. Natural tuning preserves the purest possible mathematical ratios of musical consonances, which do not perfectly correspond from octave to octave; to be perfectly in tune with each other, unaccompanied singers adjust to these differences. Organs were tuned for pure thirds in the church modes, to come as close as possible to natural tuning. Pure intonation requires freedom from vibrato, since fluctuating vibrations cannot produce clear consonances. When singers achieve pure intonation, extraordinary things happen. Their voices clasp together, adjusting to each other, in a kind of spontaneous vocal embrace. Their individual vocal lines, however, are all the more distinct, and clarity of line improves audibility of words. Since their intonation corresponds to the mathematical structure of the universe, and since (as philosophers said) numbers are eternal, singers in natural tuning "concent" with physical matter, the tuning of the spheres, and the angels and saints "singing everlastingly," and thus literally "keep in tune with Heav'n."[15]

Third, Renaissance choral music does not have a stressed "beat"; it is measured by a steady pulse, accurately kept, but divided not into metrical units but into rhythmic phrases corresponding with the verbal ones. Over the steady pulse the lines move to correspond with syllable length and word stress, and also flow freely between duple rhythms, often used to express words about earth and its inhabitants, and triple rhythms, often used to express words about heaven and God. Similarly, Renaissance music has few key signatures, because composers did not yet habitually compose a piece around a fixed tonal center; they modulated freely among church modes, as among rhythmic figures, to suit the words and the melodic inventions they invoked.

Fourth, the voicing of Renaissance music is not a matter of solo melody and accompaniment. All voice parts have equal interest, and each is responsive to all the rest. The clarity and pure "concent" of each line depends on each singer's careful listening to the others, and on a reticent singing style: a choir is not a collection of solo voices, but is, as Giovanni De' Bardi of the Florentine Camarata described it, a matter of "joining one's voice with the voices of others and forming one body with these."[16] Like rhythm and mode, the voicing is flexible. Seventeenth-century English choral music uses both polyphony, with several voices singing separate vocal lines (in which they may or may

not "imitate" each other by singing similar melodic phrases but entering at different times), and homophony, with the various voice parts
singing in the same rhythm, as in most congregational hymn-singing.
Polyphony is often used to represent heavenly voices, and homophony
to represent earthly ones; or polyphony to represent diverse voices
and homophony to emphasize their unity. English choirs were usually
arranged antiphonally, with all voice parts represented on both sides
of the chancel aisle; and composers used every possible combination of
voices for expressive purposes. The diverse yet united harmonies of
many voices that all these flexibilities allowed imitate the harmony
of creation before "disproportion'd sin . . . Broke the fair musick that
all creatures made."

The music of creation entered the ears of seventeenth-century English poets through liturgy and psalm-singing, with their constant re-
minders of "the beginning." In the daily offices of morning prayer and
evening prayer the Gloria Patri is said or sung at the end of every
psalm, every canticle except the Te Deum Laudamus, and the invitatory prayers for each service.[17] In the sixteenth and seventeenth centuries, five canticles and from two to twelve psalms were appointed for
each day. The Gloria Patri might, then, be said and sung from eight to
nineteen times on a given day. In practice, the usual service music was
composed of settings of the Preces or antiphonal prayers (including
the Invitatory and the Kyrie) and the canticles called Venite, Te
Deum, Benedictus, Magnificat, and Nunc Dimittis. In addition to the
Gloria Patri, among the verses said or sung daily that remind one of
the creation "as it was in the beginning," the Venite affirms a providential Creator:

> In his hands are all the corners of the earth: and the strength of the
>     hills is his also.
> The sea is his, and he made it: and his hands prepared the dry land.

The Te Deum describes the unified *gloria* of heaven and earth:

> All the earth doth worship thee, the Father everlasting.
> To thee all angels cry aloud: the heavens and all the powers therein.
> To thee Cherubin and Seraphin, continually do cry.
> Holy, holy, holy, lord God of Sabaoth.
> Heaven and earth are full of the majesty of thy glory.

The Jubilate reminds the congregation of their beginnings: "Be ye
sure that the Lord he is God: it is he that hath made us, and not we
ourselves." The Cantate Domino calls on all creation to sing, both "all
peoples" accompanied by harps, trumpets, and shawms, and "the
sea . . . and all that therein is: the round world, and they that dwell

therein. Let the floods clap their hands, and let the hills be joyful together before the Lord: for he is come to judge the earth." The Deus
Misereatur links praise and plenty: "Let the people praise thee . . .
Then shall the earth bring forth her increase"; those who keep cove-
nant and praise God together work together in harmony, and the earth
responds. The Benedicite is a splendid creation poem, and underlies
the morning canticle of Milton's Adam and Eve.

William Byrd's English Te Deum, from his *Great Service* (that is, his
longer setting of the canticles of the daily office in the Book of Common Prayer), illustrates the rhythmic flexibility and the variety of voicing of mimetic music.[18] Over the steady pulse, the phrasing shifts
fluidly between three-pulse and two- or four-pulse configurations.
"All the earth doth worship thee" is for full choir and mainly homophonic, as befits the thought, with long notes emphasizing "all," "worship," and "thee"; and the result is an alternation of threes and twos
that combines heavenly and earthly numbers. The cry of the angels begins homphonically and antiphonally, answering to the description in
Isaiah 6 of angelic song, "one cried to another," and then moves to
polyphony for full choir, expressing the music of heaven as an unbro-
ken, interwoven responsiveness of many voices. In the Benedictus
Byrd brings the polyphonically multiplied voices of "his holy prophets" to a rich harmonic resolution on "which have been since the world
began." The various settings of "As it was in the beginning, is now,
and ever shall be, world without end, Amen" bloom in extraordinarily
different ways to conclude each canticle with a sense of soaring reunion, giving the listener the experience that raised Milton's "phanta-
sie" to "That undisturbed Song of pure concent" and took Herbert to
heaven's door on wings of music.

Milton condensed the themes of creation, fall, and reunion in "At
a Solemn Musick," and *Paradise Lost* epically expands them. It sings
"the fair musick that all creatures made" *in principio*, recounts the
dissonant jar of "disproportion'd sin," and shows ways regenerate human beings, and with them "the Choir / Of Creatures wanting voice"
(9.198-99), can rejoin the song. That music resonates throughout the
paradisal scenes in *Paradise Lost*, in which Adam and Eve join the music Milton urges us to "rejoin." The culminating work of their art is
their morning canticle in Book 5, to which we shall return as the moment that gathers together words, music, and images of many creatures in one resplendent hymn.

## The Language of Eden

The single medium through which all arts are expressed in *Paradise
Lost* is of course language—but language in which sound, image, and

concept fuse. The unity of the three is part of the process of regeneration of the imagination offered to the reader. When all our faculties are working together to perceive concordant images, sounds, and structures of thought, we sense the mystic concinnity of the design of creation and of the mind itself, for "The wisdom of God created understanding, fit and proportionable to truth, the object and end of it, as the eye to the thing visible."[19] When we perceive the connections between language and many levels of perception and thought at once, we become converted to speakers of the language of Eden. Because it is the primary way the biblical God manifests himself and also provides the stuff of ethical concord, language is the root art, the activity on which the well-being of the human family most depends.

It has become customary to discuss "the language of Adam" in ways that miss this quality of paradisal utterance by setting up an absolute division between a divinely given and a humanly created *logos*. Hans Aarsleff perfectly enunciates this division when he states, "The basic problem is simple: language is either a divine gift or a human creation. If it is divine or Adamic, then both our language and [our] knowledge are in ruins, and it is our task to restore the lost order and harmony of the original. This view favors rationalism in philosophy and the imitation doctrine in art. But for seventeenth-century poets, if language is a human creation, then everyone is a little Adam, and we make our own world in the communal language we create. Language is art, poetry is truth, and expression better than imitation."[20] But Edenic language is not dualistic, but monistic and multiple; "divine gift" and "human creation" are reciprocal. When Adam names the animals and Eve the flowers in *Paradise Lost,* God endues their "sudden apprehension" with knowledge that enables right naming (8.352-54) and right nurture—what Eve calls breeding up (11.276-77). At Adam's first consciousness, he says, "To speak I tri'd, and forthwith spake, / My Tongue obey'd and readily could name / What'er I saw" (8.271-73). But like all divine gifts, this one provides the seeds, not the crop, of human culture, to be creatively brought forth by human art. As Ralegh explains in a quintessential statement about the relation between providence and self-fashioning, "God gaue vnto man all kindes of seedes and grafts of life"; whichever of these a person chooses to "plant and cultiue" will "futurely grow in him, and bring forth fruit, agreable to his own choyce and plantation."[21]

The language of Adam is usually defined as that sought in the seventeenth century by the Royal Society: one word, one thing; the only truths reside in a perfectly denotative vocabulary, allowing no error or misunderstanding, no hypocrisy or fraud, only an accurate representation of the nature of the thing itself.[22] This concept has many merits for science and law, but it cannot cope either with spiritual experience or with the complexity of multiply related details that constitutes life being lived, and it is inadequate for paradise. The language of Adam and Eve and regenerate humankind, as English Renaissance poets worked to restore it, is free of deception, but not by means of homogeneity of thought or absence of resonance. Rather, it has a quality analogous to music. Musical pitches, with their mixture of fundamental and overtones, are by nature complex. When people sing exactly on pitch (as angels always do), with the fundamental and the overtones in tune, that phenomenon has remarkable effects. Since the components of pitch are a physical property of matter, it puts the whole body physically in tune with the rest of the universe. It resonates in the objects around the singers, so that, as George Herbert put it, even stones respond to music.[23]

The language of Edenic consciousness has similar properties. Herbert was the first to make these musical qualities of language a principal feature of English poetry, with Milton and Marvell close behind. All use concenting overtones to show us the connectedness of significances and sounds and create moments of multiplicity where literality leaps into mystery. Language, for these poets, increases and multiplies its resonances more, the more meet it is.

For many seventeenth-century poets, the paradise within and the paradise without are two regions of the same geography. Heavenliness, while one is on earth, plants in the soul "bright *shootes* of everlastingness,"[24] and these rays or sprouts (or both, since plants are, ultimately, light) bear fruit in moral action. Once one's beasts have taken their "due place" in the ark, one "Can sow, and dares trust corne, where they have bin."[25] In Edenic poems, paradisal music, language, and action form a unity of consciousness.

Marvell's *Upon Appleton House*,[26] for example, shows by multiply concenting words how the gardening of language can create a map of paradise. In the Eden of Appleton, language discovers in nature and in georgic tasks layer upon layer of awareness and delight. By reliteralizing metaphor and remetaphorizing the literal, Marvell's language displays the connections between the topography of words and the topography of our habitats. Only "man unruled" builds "unproportioned dwellings." Other animals "are by their dens expressed," making their dwellings fit metaphors for themselves: birds "contrive an equal [proportioned, right-sized, and tranquil] nest"; "the low-roofed tortoises [that emblem of domesticity] do dwell / In cases fit of tortoise shell": houses that properly belong to them, not to the boudoirs of fine ladies. What we do to our dens, our Edens, Marvell tells us, is an extension of what we are and what we speak. "Maria" (second Eve), speaker of "heaven's dialect," gives the topography her own attributes: beauty to the gardens, straightness to the woods, sweetness to the meadows, purity to the river. Insofar as she is Mary Fairfax, the hyperbole is instructive praise. Insofar as she is Eve-in-innocence, the nurturing conscience in humanity that helps living things prosper, it is a moral truth: we endow or impoverish nature with our inward state. Fitness of language emends that state. The program of the Royal Society was to control language in order to control nature. The program of poets is to explore the inner sap of nature and of language and to see the connections between the book of nature and "heaven's dialect." Both nature and language are so bountiful and so interwoven that one never ceases to find new meanings in them.

George Herbert (named for the patron saint of agriculture and of England)[27] demonstrates the concent of paradisal language and form in "Paradise,"[28] which concerns a verbally mimetic orchard of believers bringing forth fruit within God's providential care. Charlotte Otten calls the poem "a Paradise of words properly pruned" and reminds us that terraculture reflects "the work of Christ the Gardener."[29] If he were a lesser poet, Herbert's playful pruning could be merely clever, but his perfect match of theme and form tropes the farming of Eden.

> I blesse thee, Lord, because I GROW
> Among thy trees, which a ROW
> To thee both fruit and order OW.

Like the "delicious Paradise" that crowns the Edenic mountain "with her enclosure green" (4.131-32) and like the Garden of the Song of Songs (and like Michelangelo's Eve within God's embrace) Herbert's Paradise is a Garden enclosed:

> What open force, or hidden CHARM
> Can blast my fruit, or bring me HARM,
> While the inclosure is thine ARM?

That is almost the argument of Milton's Eve (9.337-41), had she remembered the "Maker wise" and prayed at the beginning of her trial, like the Lady of the *Mask*, and Herbert here:

> Inclose me still for fear I START.
> Be to me rather sharp and TART,
> Th[a]n let me want thy hand & ART.

Like Donne, Herbert prefers the rod of God's mercy to withdrawal from God's arm. And this chastisement takes place even in "Paradise." Like Milton's Garden of Eden, Herbert's orchard of regenerate souls has to be pruned in order to be fruitful. Merciful discipline is part of growth for Adam and Eve and part of the process of regeneration for the redeemed;

> When thou dost greater judgements SPARE,
> And with thy knife but prune and PARE,
> Ev'n fruitful trees more fruitfull ARE.

"Faithful are the wounds of a friend" (Proverbs 27:6), especially God's "cuttings," because they return one to oneself and one's true purposes and destination.

> Such sharpness shows the sweetest FREND:
> Such cuttings rather heal th[a]n REND:
> And such beginnings touch their END.

Not only are the paradise within and the outward paradise of believers joined, but also the two paradises, our "beginnings" and "end," that frame human life. "Cuttings," moreover, horticulturally considered, are "ends" that become "beginnings."

In the verbal wit[30] of "Paradise," Herbert cultivates, as always, the garden of language, and by his polyphonic consciousness makes that garden a paradise. Its composition is contrapuntal, in the sense that the words, while proceeding linearly, also reenter in new registers and thus build harmonic chords. The "sharp" of "sharp and tart" modulates to the "sharpness" of the "sweetest friend," and these form a movingly dissonant chord[31] with "knife" and "cuttings." "Tart" and "sweet" are appropriate to a poem about fruit, and "art" connects the garden and the poem, the Maker and the maker. The visual and verbal mimesis of pruning, on the end-rhymes, matches the purposive "end" of a poem that, moreover, ends on "end."

The poem also makes sight and sound completely consonant; word and image are Edenic on the most literal level of the word itself. The rhymes, in addition to being "cuttings," are enclosures; each encloses the subsequent rhymes which the paring discloses. And that disclosure is not limited to the rhymes. A second meaning of "still" is exposed by "start," and a healed form of "start" turns up in "beginnings." "Hand" links to "arm" but gets another meaning at "art." To complete its apt form, the poem's five stanzas suggest the classical advice to "order" trees by rows quincuncially arranged in groups of five, which Browne was to recommend as the practice of the ancients.[32]

In paradisal language, forms, metaphorical roots, prosody, puns, images, connotations, and allusiveness all resonate so that the most exact phrase also has the most power of suggestion. While one word may mean one thing in the sense that it does not evade or deceive, while it is not ambiguous in the slovenly sense of promiscuous openness to whatever meaning the reader wishes to thrust into it, each word in these Edenic poems produces consonant harmonics, so that one can contemplate it over and over and more and more deeply and learn more and more about its apt connections with other words and about the connections among words and things and deeds. Edenic language says many true things at once, awakening conscience to the ecology of meaning, as the beauty of music tunes body and soul to the wholeness of the whole Making. Such language is ever fresh, changing like new leaves, or like music responsive to the challenge of the Psalms to sing a new song.

As in the visual arts, in the verbal arts the fullest resonances come from the most specific figures. In the natural tuning of language, the more precise a word is, the more it keeps touch with its roots (or fundamental), the more overtones are audible, and the more in tune they are. I have mentioned the example of Adam's creation "in the image of God / Express" (7.526-27); Adam is expressed (pressed out) of earth and God expresses his own image in him by breathing life into his nostrils; he makes him expressly, that is, explicitly, in his image, and does so specially and efficiently. Both the word's sounds and its place at the end of a phrase but the beginning of a line reinforce this combination of deliberateness and energy. "Express" is so expressive precisely because it is so precise.

Wordplay shares with music the ability to reveal connections. It leaps agilely between literal and metaphoric meanings and seals them together by means of sound. One of the grounds on which Milton's Adam and Eve are sometimes thought fallen before the Fall is that they indulge in wordplay: a violation of the ideal single-mindedness of words. But—like everything else—all the resources of language may be used *in bono* or *in malo*. Milton understood the difference between either duplicitous or frivolous language and felicitous or even holy puns. Unfallen Adam and Eve, unfallen angels, and God himself (as in his play on Hedon/Eden in 8.401-2, saying Adam wants to "taste / No pleasure . . . solitarie" though he dwells "in pleasure") all use wordplay within the decorum of their characters.

When the Son commends the Father's compassion he says,

> O Father, gracious was that word that clos'd
> Thy sovran sentence, that Man should find grace;

For which both Heav'n and Earth shall high extol
Thy praises, with th'innumerable sound
Of Hymns and sacred Songs, wherewith thy Throne
Encompass'd shall resound thee ever blest.

(3.144-49)

The Son's speech is itself a hymn of praise, full of musical language and multiple connections. It begins with univocal wordplay about God's words: "gracious was that word ... that Man should find grace." "That word" closed a "sovran sentence," both grammatical and judicial. "Sovran" means not only supreme but also efficacious, as in the common phrase "a sovereign remedy." "Clos'd" means concluded, unified, and brought to agreement; "close" is also a musical term, meaning a cadence. "Innumerable" expresses both the countless angels who will sing and the unmetrical[33] "numbers" of their polyphony. "High extol" recalls the root meaning of "lift up" and the high tessitura of voices lifted up in praise; and we may remember by more distant echoes that the Son himself ("qui tollis peccata mundi") will also lift up prayers, and be extolled by "every creature which is in heaven, and on the earth, and under the earth, and such as are in the sea, and all that are in them" (Rev. 6:13). "Encompassed" describes the encircling angel choirs in a way that connects to the golden compasses of creation. "Resound" literally re-sounds as it echoes "sound."

After the Fall, to be sure, Adam's puns on election and sapience trivialize wisdom: "*Eve,* now I see thou art exact of taste, / And elegant, of Sapience no small part" (from *sapere* 'to taste'); and to make matters worse he has the bad taste to relish his own joke: "Since to each meaning savor we apply, / and Palate call judicious" (9.1017-20). Here he parodies justice and foretells Babel. Before the Fall, however, when Eve tells the Serpent that the forbidden fruit is "fruitless" to her she understands the polysemousness of nature's Book. When unfallen Adam calls Earth "this punctual spot" (8.23) he not only conflates time ("punctual" as "on time") and space ("punctual" as being a "point"), as is proper for astronomical thought, but also the local and the cosmic, so as to give us a sudden new perspective. We see Earth from a place in Eden and from a vast galactic distance at once. Now that we have seen it from space on our television screens, perhaps we can learn the interwovenness and conditionality of "this pendant world" (2.1052) as Adam sees it. The precise but polysemous diction that makes us see both specificity and wholeness is the true language of Eden.

As Stanley Fish so acutely shows in *Surprised by Sin,* Miltonic polysemousness is partly composed of false connotations supplied by the "fallen" reader, which Milton's language invites and then rebukes (142–57). I would add that Edenic language, while it does indeed expose whatever guilt the reader may bring to it, does even more to elicit joy by revealing that innocent words are not less but more resonant, fuller of kinds and connections of meaning, after being purged of false associations. We are constantly surprised, not just by sin but by the infinitely expanding quality of sinfree pleasures. Adam and Eve address in their morning hymn, for example, the planet we, not they, call Lucifer, Venus, Hesperus, Vesper, and *stella matutina*, an epithet of Mary, Second Eve. Milton calls Christ "our Morning Star" in *Paradise Regained* (1.294). The fallen Light-bearer and the fallen Venus figure in our responses but not theirs, as do the paradisal and reviving associations of Hesper/Vesper, Mary, and Christ. Adam and Eve sing with pure perceptions what now can be perceived again, through the lens of faith, by the "intellectual ray" undergoing the poem's purgative process that increases its acuity.

> Fairest of Stars, last in the train of Night,
> If better thou belong not to the dawn,
> Sure pledge of day, that crown'st the smiling Morn
> With thy bright Circlet, praise [God] in thy Sphere
> While day arises, that sweet hour of Prime.
>
> (5.166-70)

Adam and Eve express a Pythagorean recognition that the morning star and the evening star are the same, and an instinctive understanding of the circularity of its appearances as, with a complex metaphorical wordplay on crown, circlet, and sphere, they praise the beauty of the planet that looks like a shining crown and see that it crowns both night and dawn. Like the night that lets the heavens declare the glory of God, it is not portentously double; it is twice-beautiful. Their recognition that the last comes first is morally useful and part of a recurrent astronomical economy that questions conventional hierarchies. Like the visual arts, the passage helps us choose significance; we see that both the literal, circular twice-brightness of the heavenly body and the spiritual beauty of first-and-lastness oppose the evil that has come to attach itself to the name of Lucifer, and that both kinds of beauty spread their rays to touch other images throughout the poem. The multeity, as Joseph Summers testifies, is all on the side of glory.

Richard Corum concocts a false dichotomy between literal and spiritual speech when he writes, "As generations of deconstructive critics have observed, with Dr. Johnson foremost among them," what Milton writes is "a vast confusion of eternal, conceptualized spirit and temporal, narrative matter."[34] Corum's example is Milton's metaphor of the ploughman in Book 4, as Ithuriel and Zephon return to the angelic guardians with Satan in his true but faded form. When the angels "begin to hem him round / With ported spears"—like an Uccello battle scene—these spears are

> as thick as when a field
> Of *Ceres* ripe for harvest waving bends
> Her bearded Grove of ears, which way the wind
> Sways them; the careful Plowman doubting stands
> Lest on the threshing floor his hopeful sheaves
> Prove chaff.
>
> (4.980-85)

This moment does for us what Homeric similes do; by a sudden shift in perspective angelic epic battle is connected to homely experience, and our lives to the lives of celestial spirits. But Corum chooses to identify the ploughman as God "doubting his own troops" and then to find that concept ridiculous. If we attend to the sounds of words, we enter the world of the ploughman and for a moment become him. In the lines' consonances and alliterations we hear the "bearded grove of ears" sway in the wind; and, hearing, we are the "ears" as well; if we are reading kinetically, we ourselves sway as the line wavers at "wind / Sways." The georgic metaphor reminds us both of the angels' part and of our part as both gatherers and gathered in the natural and spiritual labor of bringing in sheaves (Luke 10:2), and we become aware that the harvest of souls depends on our responses to the moment of choice that Milton is about to recount. Rather than decreeing battle,

> Th'Eternal to prevent such horrid fray
> Hung forth in Heav'n his golden Scales, yet seen
> Betwixt *Astrea* and the *Scorpion* sign,
> Wherein all things created first he weigh'd
> The pendulous round Earth with balanc't Air
> In counterpoise, now ponders all events,
> Battles and Realms: in these he put two weights
> The sequel each of parting and of fight;
> The latter quick up flew, and kickt the beam.
>
> (4.996-1004)

The kinesis of balance and decision smacks home in "quick . . . kicked," where we hear the clang of an actual pair of scales. The literalizing puns of "ponders," "pendulous," and "balanc't"; the allusion to the Goddess of Justice, whose name means "starry," located in the heavens near the scales that are the attribute of Justice; the stretch of time from creation *in principio,* "at first," to the narrative "now," to the "yet seen" of the reader's present; all these encapsulate the epic of creation and choice in language that itself connects "all things" by the reverberations of its literalities.

Like its resonances, the syntax of *Paradise Lost* represents paradisal consciousness by encompassing many things at once. Along with images and names and nature, the resources of syntax are "seeds" to be used for good or for ill. Satan's orations illustrate syntactic inflation. But the motive of extended cadences in paradisal passages is the reverse of Satan's linguistic manipulations. Edenic syntax embraces many things at once because creation does. The inclusive awareness, receptivity, and sense of connection of the poetic mind acknowledges and enjoys the fullness of the being beyond itself and finds the proportions of its sentences in the proportions of their subjects, and in the mathematical and musical proportions to which the arrangements of matter and of words may correspond.[35] The same multirelational complexity inheres in the structure of the whole poem, and so edifies—with an organic architecture—the resonating soul. Its language is not just the language of Adam but the language of Adam and Eve together.

## Milton's Defense of Poesy

As Barbara Lewalski has observed, Milton portrays Adam and Eve as the inventors of the poetic genres; and "Eve's actual and freely proclaimed hierarchic inferiority to Adam is in some degree counterbalanced by Milton's generic strategy, as he portrays Eve sharing in all the georgic responsibilities and duties of the Garden as well as in the arts of speech and song and dialogue that pertain to humankind. . . . she 'invents,' and anticipates Adam in using, such literary forms as the autobiographical narrative and the love sonnet."[36] The much-labored question of her equality of talent and freedom needs also to be considered in the light of her constant figural alliance with Milton himself, for her questing imagination is vital to the poet who intends his song to soar above the Aonian mount. Although Milton did not write a *Poetics* or an *Apologie for Poetry,* he embodied one in Eve.

While Eve in Book 8, attended by graces and amoretti, visits bud and bloom that "toucht by her fair tendance" (8.47) gladlier grow, Adam attempts to tell a not very sympathetic "Interpreter Spirit" how he feels about her (8.452-611). She is a handmade present from God, his "last, best gift," but God may have subducted "more then enough" from *him.* He is in charge of her, but he is "transported." Her thought is "less exact," yet "Greatness of mind and nobleness thir seat / Build in her loveliest." Yet her powers "subject not"; their marriage is "Harmonie." The patterns of their courtship contain similar transpositions. "She turn'd ... I follow'd her ... she ... approv'd ... I led her." Heaven and earth also approved:

> all Heav'n
> And happy Constellations on that hour
> Shed thir selectest influence; the Earth
> Gave sign of gratulation, and each Hill;
> Joyous the Birds; fresh Gales and gentle Airs
> Whisper'd it to the Woods, and from thir wings
> Flung Rose, flug Odors from the spicy Shrub
> Disporting, till the amorous Bird of Night
> Sung Spousal, and bid haste the Ev'ning Star
> On his Hill top, to light the bridal Lamp.
>                                          (8.511-20)

"O Nightingale," young Milton wrote in his first sonnet, "Whether the Muse, or love call thee his mate, / Both them I serve."

These patterns echo an analogous equivocation and union in *Of Education:* "Logic" (which is also "well-couched") will "open her contracted palm into a graceful and ornate rhetoric ... To which poetry would be made subsequent, or indeed rather precedent, as being less subtile and fine, but more simple, sensuous, and passionate"; genre and decorum teach "what religious, what glorious and magnificent use might be made of poetry, both in divine and humane things."[37] The equivocation and affirmation recall Sidney: "For poesy must not be drawn by the ears; it must be gently led, or rather it must lead; which is partly the cause that made the ancient-learned affirm that it was a divine gift."[38]

Milton may have felt much as Adam did, as he couched his argument in the amazing beauty of his sensuous verse—or hers who brought it nightly to his ear. The relation between the "less winning soft" but "manly" grace and wisdom of his stern story and the delight of verse like Eve "adornd / With what all Earth or Heaven could bestow" (4.479, 490; 8.482-83) is a delicate marriage. The marriage of Adam and Eve tropes its reciprocities. Milton's doctrinal history and his poesie are "one flesh."

Eve embodies and performs a great many properties and processes that Milton elsewhere attibutes to poetry itself, or to himself as poet. These properties and processes belong both to poesy, or the art and craft of making poems, and to poetics, or the gnosis and praxis of interpreting poems, since for Milton one Spirit "who can enrich with all utterance and knowledge"[39] touches both. Eve as exponent of imagination, which is both subsequent and precedent to understanding, figures forth Milton's own art. The images associated with her and her work are commonly understood metaphors for poetry. Her accounts of her creation and of her dream manifest the function of imagination in discerning and choosing good. Her poem in praise of nature and of Adam (4.639-57) allies her to the legendary Arcadian origins of poetry and to Milton's youthful intention to follow those "who never write but honor of them to whom they devote their verse, displaying sublime and pure thoughts, without transgression."[40] Her temptation and fall represent the abuse of poesy by a politic libertine and the divorce of verse from truth: Satan has replaced his limping feet with redundant coils, making intricate seem straight (9.504, 632), and by erecting his argument on this false base debases poetry to propaganda and devises reductive criticism. Eve's final going forth rejoined to Adam and refreshed by propitious dreams mimes the renovation of the imagination that art can provide and its reunion with (re)erected reason, so that humankind may carry seeds of goodness even into a world of woe.

In considering Eve as poesy I do not wish to allegorize her or her work, but to see her as a speaking portrait of the artist. One of the habits of mind that Milton revises in *Paradise Lost* is the allegorizing of Scripture that makes Adam reason, mind, or soul, Eve passion, sense, or flesh, and the Garden abstract moral virtue.[41] Such an interpretation usually divorces kinds of goodness rather than wedding them. Milton selectively retains connotations from such readings, but discards implications that set nature against spirit, myth against history, or man against woman. Adam and Eve are each whole personages, both reasonable and imaginative, both sensuous, passionate and pure. Both are developing in all the ways humans do in relation to each other and to God, nature, angels, art, knowledge, and experience; and the Garden burgeons and beckons as gardens do, needing and repaying real care.[42] However, in those manifold relations, Eve especially figures forth poetic graces and poetic imagination, the work of the faculty of fancy, which shapes the representations of the senses into significant forms (5.104-5). And the relation between her work and the production of poetry is not an arbitrary comparison. Earth is the mother of metaphor; verbal analogies are rooted in the operations of nature, which farming and gardening reveal. It is her work that most startlingly metaphors the poetic process: startlingly, because no other artist or poet had shown Adam and Eve working before the Fall, much less imagined Eve singularly engaged in acts of creative stewardship and design as a regular part of her life, producing—like illuminated texts—"thick-wov'n Arborets and Flours / Imborder'd on each Bank, the hand of *Eve*" (9.437-38).[43]

In the Renaissance, the art of gardening was a habitual metaphor for the art of poesy. Anthology means flowers of knowledge or knowledge of flowers. Titles of collections proliferate plantations, arborets, and flowers: *Poetical Blossoms, The Garden of the Muses, A Hundredth Sundry Flowers, The Arbor of Amity, Underwoods, A Posy of Gilliflowers, Hesperides, A Paradise of Dainty Devices, A Bower of Delights, The Shepherd's Garland, Flosculum Poeticum,* and Milton's own *Sylvae,* to name a few. Puttenham and Shakespeare use the trope of gardening for the relation of art to nature; Spenser describes contrasting bowers that epitomize degenerating and regenerating art; Herbert, Donne, and Marvell wreathe poetical garlands.[44] Sidney says that "Christ vouchsafed to use the flowers" of poetry and later Christopher Smart would say that "flowers are peculiarly the poetry of Christ."[45] Herbert writes, "And so I came to Fancies medow strow'd / With many a flower," and, in "The Flower," "now in age I bud again . . . And relish versing."[46] Milton himself calls his yet-unwritten poems "no bud or blossom" in Sonnet 7, joins other poets to strew the surmised "Laureat Herse" of Lycidas with flowers summoned by the Sicilian muse, offers "some Flowers and some bays" of verse to the marchioness of Winchester, makes his Genius a keeper of groves in *Arcades,* and compares the return of his poetic inspiration, in Elegy V, to the reviving earth in spring who twines her hair with flowers powerful to charm.

Eve is specifically responsible for buds and blossoms in *Paradise Lost.* Seeing Adam enter into thoughts abstruse she

> Rose and went forth among her Fruits and Flow'rs,
> To visit how they prosper'd, bud and bloom,
> Her Nurserie.
>
> (8.45-47)

When Satan finds her she is "stooping to support / Each Flow'r" (9.427-28). She has visited them morning and evening, bred them up "with tender hand / From the first op'ning bud," named, reared, ranked, and watered them, and adorned her nuptial bower with them (11.276-80). Even though Adam and Eve were joined and enjoined by God to dress as well as keep the Garden, it was unheard of before Milton to *show* them gardening, and especially to make Eve a gardener even more committed and original than Adam, and so a *figura* of the poet's own work. Further, in *Paradise Lost,* the Son of God names the Angels "to thir Glory" (5.839-41), Adam names the animals (8.342-54), and Eve names the flowers (11.277). Naming, elsewhere, is Adam's prerogative.[47] It implies knowing the natures of ɔd's creatures—"I nam'd them," Adam says, "and understood / Thir Jature"—and so knowing how to take care of them. And the natures of flowers are of some consequence in *Paradise Lost*. On "the bright consummate flow'r / [that] Spirits odorous breathes" depends all nurture: "flow'rs and thir fruit / Man's nourishment, by gradual scale sublim'd ... give both life and sense, / Fancy and understanding, whence the Soul / Reason receives, and reason is her being, / Discursive, or Intuitive" (5.481-88). Raphael is being quite literal. Flowers work up to fruit, fruit nourishes the bodily senses, senses feed fancy and understanding, and these feed reason. The crossing over from body to spirit, if such a distinction may be made at all, occurs at the bridge of fancy. Fancy is precedent, here, to reason. But flowers are consummate as well as prevenient, their "spirits odorous" a frequent figure of prayer as well as poetry, which is both subsequent and precedent to reason, nourishing the soul and nourished by it.

Just as remarkable as Milton's giving Eve a part in naming is the fact that in their unfallen conversations he gives Eve and Adam almost an equal number of lines. He makes neither Adam the dominant proprietor of Edenic language nor Eve a figure of the "female" vice of loquacity—even in her conversation with the Serpent—nor, conversely, an emblem of the virtue so often commended to women, silence, except during Adam's talk with Raphael. Their verbal conversation is "meet" in innumerable interinanimating ways: hers adventurous, playful, sweet, charming, questioning, but also, especially in the separation scene, ethically acute and probing; his grave, explanatory, and consequential upon hers. Each is sufficient in both reason and spontaneous grace, but in proportion due; together their words resonate like part music, to the enhancement of both.

Anyone who reads and writes may recognize, in Eve's naming, nursing, propping, pruning, watering, selecting, supporting, and adorning, the actions of this work that "under our labor grows" (9.208). One may see also in her plea for freedom and a little solitude a quest for artistic liberty that she shares with Milton in his solitary lucubrations and his independent-minded literary practice. Almost everything she does or says before the Fall allies her to Milton's own craft in some way. Her first speech is about looking into a mirror. When poetry is not a garden it is often a mirror: a *Speculum Humanum*, a *Mirror for Magistrates*, a *Muses's Looking Glass*, a "mirror up to Nature to show Virtue her own feature, scorn her own image."[48] But Milton cautions us against using poetry only as a mirror, or as Narcissus's mirror. Eve, stretched out on the flowery bank of Eden's mirror, at first sees only herself, as we may be prone to do in poetry's, but when she knows that the beautiful reflection is her own image she (not unhesitatingly) joins her fanciful nature (but Milton has exalted fancy to conjunction with understanding) to Adam's wise one.[49]

Janet Knedlik has characterized Satan's mental state on Mount Niphates as a "failure of fancy altogether. He tries and is unable to complete a credible story of how he could be successfully restored to heaven: he fails to include an agent in his story greater than himself. . . . (But how difficult to build any plot around unchanging mind, or to sustain unchanging mind itself . . . in the universe against which Satan strives, a universe of insistent poetic teleology)." Satan bases his plot on his "fixed and frozen necessary: to stage himself as Prime Actor in a drama of divine failure and imperfection. In Book 2, Satan privileges a mimetic projection erected upon the assumption of God's malignity," demanding "a universe in which God is both sovereign and unjust." These premises "unfold themselves into a derivative universe of misery and injustice, as he works the human fall by rereading the world through the text of his own esthetic specifications." Milton's God enters "the mimetic arena with ultimate commitment, however, even allowing his original golden world to become the raw materials of Satan's perversely grounded but splendidly executed fantasy"; God "uses vigorously the discourse of possibility."[50]

Satan's imaginings primarily project his own present states or deconstruct what others imagine. These are the limitations that the renewal of the imaginative faculties offered by poetry and the visual arts can help to overcome. His undelighted broodings over all delight frame Eve's tale of her mirror and of her choice to let herself be enlarged by someone outside herself, the exact opposite of Satan's choice when he "thought himself impair'd" by the anointing of the Son (5.665). In Eve's choice, imagination with its sense of the possibilities of the not yet known is the unfallen analogue of the regenerate imagination piloted by faith.

The virtue of openness to enlargement is also the source of Eve's vulnerability, and of the text's. When she prostitutes her imagination to Satan's deception, she credulously allows someone outside herself to reduce her, as commentators may reduce the text. In the marriage scene, Eve chooses to be enlarged, not to "exist to, for, and from herself" as Christine Froula suggests she ought to do.[51] But she does not think herself impaired, or breached by this expansion, until Satan fathers upon her a poetic of Eve for Eve's sake. Every character in the poem has the choice of being fostered or not by God's "uncontroulable intent,"[52] as does the poet; and the reader has the choice of being nourished or not by the incalculable enlargements the poem offers.

Eve personifies poesy in her work, in the imagery associated with her, and in the method of her vocation. She identifies the voice that calls her from her mirror as simply "a voice" (4.467). Adam says she was "Led by her Heav'nly Maker, though unseen, / And guided by his voice" (8.485-86). But the narrator speaks of the day "the genial Angel to our Sire / Brought her" (4.712-13). Did Milton nod? Or does the equivocation echo Milton's invocation of both the Holy Spirit and the Celestial Muse?

Led by God or his messenger or both, Eve is divinely wrought and brought, but not fixed and finished: God gave man, as Ralegh says, to be his own painter.[53] As a wife she is, like a Muse, or a poem in the making, incalculable, surprising, much beyond expectation, notable for having a will of her own. Adam learns that his image or other half is not just his image, has much to give him that he could not have imagined without her, can enlarge and change him, is not for him (though she becomes for Satan) a text-object to be possessed and bent to his own use but a nigh overwhelming bliss, almost too beautiful to bear, like "amorous delight" or Monteverdi's music or Milton's poem. She needs, as Adam will say fancy does, reason well erect—both hers and his—if harmony, not only solo voice and audience, is to survive, but she is also an erector of reason. She is his but not all his, as Milton says his poetry is his but not all his, but "Hers who brings it nightly to my Ear" (9.47).

Eve's divine origin and calling put her at the crux of present discourse about poetic authority and the nature of inspiration. In an exchange with Edward Pechter, Christine Froula says with asperity, "Mr. Pechter apparently imagines that I take the Holy Spirit to be an actual entity."[54] The exchange delineates a watershed in literary studies between those who treat poems strictly as historical artifacts and those who find art and language synchronic and sometimes numinous. Some, like Pechter, not only respect Milton's reports of interchange with the Holy Spirit but share his acknowledgment of the surprising qualities of that entity's arrivals and choices of conduits.

Milton's position is explicit. His work is guided by "that eternal Spirit, who can enrich with all utterance and knowledge, and send out his seraphim, with the hallowed fire of his altar, to touch and purify the lips of whom he pleases," and whose assistance is obtained only by "devout prayer."[55] If we do not respect the possibility that Milton speaks truly of his experience, we are at liberty to make thorough hash of his poem. If the Spirit whom he asks to "raise and support" (1.23) his poesy (as Eve stoops to raise and support her roses) is a fiction, it pretends to confer a preposterous authority. But if his invocations report experiences tested on his own pulses, they claim no poetical prel-

acy but an access Milton insisted in his reforming prose was available
to all who seek it, however great or humble their tasks: not just meted
to poetic geniuses but poured out in profusion in every calling and
"upon every age and sexe."[56]

Milton again intimately links Eve to his own calling in a love song
to Adam that echoes his invocations by its form and imagery.

> With thee conversing I forget all time,
> All seasons and thir change, all please alike.
> Sweet is the breath of morn, her rising sweet,
> With charm of earliest Birds; pleasant the Sun
> When first on this delightful Land he spreads
> His orient Beams, on herb, tree, fruit, and flow'r,
> Glist'ring with dew; fragrant the fertile earth
> After soft showers; and sweet the coming on
> Of grateful Ev'ning mild, then silent Night
> With this her solemn Bird and this fair Moon,
> And these the Gems of Heav'n, her starry train:
> But neither breath of Morn when she ascends
> With charm of earliest Birds, nor rising Sun
> On this delightful land, nor herb, fruit, flow'r,
> Glist'ring with dew, nor fragrance after showers,
> Nor grateful Ev'ning mild, nor silent Night
> With this her solemn Bird, nor walk by Moon,
> Or glittering Star-light without thee is sweet.
>                                        (4.639-56)

Eve's rondo, with its gracious, dancelike measures,[57] recalls the imagery of Milton's early poems and the Arcadian beginnings of poetry itself in pastoral eclogues, with purer joy. More particularly it repeats
the rhythms and imagery of Milton's invocations—though his state, in
the loss of remembered beauty to his outward eyes, is less happy than
hers except when, like her, he is touched and enlightened from beyond
himself.

> Thus with the Year
> Seasons return, but not to me returns
> Day, or the sweet approach of Ev'n or Morn,
> Or sight of vernal bloom, or Summer's Rose,
> Or flocks, or herds, or human face divine . . .
> So much the rather thou Celestial Light
> Shine inward.
>                                        (3.40-44, 51-52)

Eve's "solemn Bird" is the nightingale, Milton's own poetic emblem
from his first sonnet: doubly appropriate for Eve, since its notes "Por-
tend success in love."[58] In his invocations, Milton wanders night and
morn "where the Muses haunt / Clear Spring, or shady Grove, or
Sunny Hill" (3.27-28),

> Then feed[s] on thoughts, that voluntary move
> Harmonious numbers; as the wakeful Bird
> Sings darkling, and in shadiest Covert hid
> Tunes her nocturnal Note.
>
> (3.37-40)

Eve sings her nocturn as she and Adam move hand in hand toward a
bower whose "thickest covert was inwoven shade" of those most poetical trees, "Laurel and Myrtle"—one furnishing the garland of
Apollo given to poets laureate, the other the emblem of Venus and amorous verse—and whose nuptial bed Eve has decked with "Flowers,
Garlands, and sweet-smelling Herbs" (4.693-94, 709).

Before they enter the bower, Eve and Adam say a prayer (4.724-35)
that begins "Thou also mad'st the Night." The statement participates
in Milton's demolition of Platonic dualism, his rehabilitation of the
original goodness and blessedness of all created things: day and night,
male and female, reason and imagination, wisdom and poetry. Those
archetypal critics who see Eve and femaleness associated with darkness
and the moon and think that Eve must therefore inevitably fall read
differently than I do that prayer, and Milton's relation to the Muse
who brings his poem "nightly" to his ear (9.47).

Eve's song has elements of Milton's own early poems, in addition to
Sonnet 1, that link her poetic development to his. It is especially akin
to L'Allegro and Il Penseroso in its pairing of the pleasures of day and
night and in kindred images, especially from Il Penseroso, in which the
speaker invokes the nightingale, the "Sweet Bird that shunn'st the
noise of folly" (61), beholds the moon, and in the heat of day retires
to "close covert by som Brook" to enjoy "som strange mysterious
dream" (139, 147). Neither poems, nor night, nor dreams are intrinsically bad, but all can be spoiled by those who use them to corrupt
ends.

Eve's question, just after her song, about the stars—"for whom /
This glorious sight, when sleep hath shut all eyes?"—is often alleged
as egocentric questioning of the divine economy, and so a foreshad-
owing of her fall. It does contain a lapse of paradisal consciousness;
she forgets nocturnal creatures and watching angels, and Adam sup-
plies rectification. But an interest in the stars is the province of Urania,

the Muse of astronomy and of Milton, who links "harmonious numbers" to cosmic harmony. Astronomy and other scientific inquiry, Raphael will caution when Adam asks a similar question, can, like poetry, be abused, but also well used. And Eve's question elicits from Adam a brief defense of the arts as he reminds her that "Millions of spiritual Creatures walk the Earth" beholding and praising God's works "Both day and night" and celebrates

> Celestial voices to the midnight air
> Sole, or responsive each to other's note
> Singing thir great Creator: oft in bands
> While they keep watch, or nightly rounding walk,
> With Heav'nly touch of instrumental sounds
> In full harmonic number join'd, thir songs
> Divide the night, and lift our thoughts to Heaven.
> (4.682-88)

When Raphael arrives and Adam requests a feast, Eve's reply (5.321-30) recapitulates Milton's claim of spontaneity in his art and his statements about decorum and "various style." She then considers

> What choice [things] to choose for delicacy best,
> What order, so contriv'd as not to mix
> Tastes, not well join'd, inelegant, but bring
> Taste after taste upheld with kindliest change.
> (5.333-36)

The repetitions of words about choice and taste of course remind readers of the choice "whose mortal tast / Brought Death into the World" (1.2-3), but denote the choice of "all the Trees / In Paradise that bear delicious fruit / So various" (4.421-23) of which they may freely eat. The passage calls attention to its own language and makes Eve's composing of food, as well as her gardening, a trope of poetry. "Inelegant," from *elegere* 'select', means literally "not choice." "Kindliest" alludes to the Prayer Book's "kindly fruits of the earth,"[59] meaning both natural, each in their kind, and pleasant, and hints at the decorum of poetic kinds. Eve proceeds to gather fruit of "all kinds," temper "dulcet creams," and serve a feast fit for an angel. Milton, also long choosing, also gathers, orders, tempers, changes, and disposes kinds in various style.

In her dream, Eve experiences in fancy the operations of evil without doing evil, as the poet must do to depict evil without being corrupted by it: an unsettling task for Milton as for Eve, perhaps, for his depiction of evil lets us feel its power. To forge the dream, Satan plagiarizes images from Eve's waking song, and from *L'Allegro* and *Il Penseroso*. The images are not nocent, but their use is corrupt.

Adam's explanation of the relations of reason and fancy (5.100-121) makes fancy both subsequent (or subordinate) and precedent (or provident) to reason, which is but choosing.[60] When Eve goes off to practice the art of gardening, having persuaded Adam not to let the Foe destroy their artistic liberty, she is much like the poet who continues to sing though "with dangers compast round, / And solitude; yet not alone" (7.27-28) as long as the Spirit whose Temple is the upright heart is with her; and she is much like poetic imagination, whose stay, not free, but shackled by political or spiritual repression, absents it more.

But, as Sidney says, "that which being rightly used doth most good, being abused doth most harm. . . . For I will not deny that a man's wit [or a clever fallen angel's] may make poesy infect the fancy with unworthy objects."[61] Milton echoes these words in reverse with regard to marriage in *Tetrachordon:* "what doth most harm in the abusing, used rightly doth most good."[62] Satan is nearly rapt out of his evil by Eve in naked innocence figuring forth good things, for loveliness has the power to seduce to goodness. But he rejects this final opportunity to choose well, and infects her fancy, and she Adam's, and "so is that honey-flowing matron eloquence apparelled, or rather disguised, in a courtesan-like painted affectation . . . with figures and flowers extremely winter-starved."[63] Satan divorces the signifier from the signified, makes words an autonomous language-game in which he feigns a trivial and tyrannical patriarch, and psychologizes the inclination for forbidden fruit and its alleged power that he has projected into Eve as a "need" (9.731). Language becomes an instrument for deception and exploitation, an implement of rape, rather than an instrument for the pleasure of discovering and nurturing goodness. The line of his argument seems to flow coherently, but the fundamental proposition that he ate the fruit and acquired speech is a lie, and the resonances of his words are not in tune. Eve, thus abused, poisons Adam; Adam, thus diseased, whores Eve; the result is fratricide.

"But what, shall the abuse of a thing make the right use odious?"[64] It is not Eve's imaginative freedom that causes her wild work, but her corruption: a corruption made possible but not inevitable by the receptivity that is, like that of poetic language, a rich virtue when rightly used. As a part of the process of her regeneration, her fancy, seat of dreams, is the faculty that receives separate divine attention, in a healing vision that reconnects fancy to the Word, the Logos for which her bearing will ultimately provide the maternal matrix, when divinity en-

ters humanity through "the Seed of Woman." As Adam and Eve set
forth from the Garden with the task of erecting the infected will and
taking goodness in hand, neither is subsequent or precedent. Unlike
most pictorial versions of the Expulsion, but like Sidney's art and nature, and like Milton's shaping intent and shapely text, Adam and Eve
go forth hand in hand, bearing the seeds of a numerous progeny.

### Pure Concent: The Canticles of Adam and Eve

In the two scenes before and after Ithuriel's spear liberates Eve from
Satan's infiltration, Adam and Eve turn toward each other, in the first
for love and in the second for comfort as well. In the two scenes before
and after those, they turn together toward God to pray. Their evening
and morning prayers unify the arts of Eden: language, music, liturgy,
human love, and bonds with the whole creation. In their luminous
morning hymn they make articulate the voice of nature, incorporating
the images and sounds of many creatures. Their ability to use language
in this way shows their all-embracing perceptions and their sympathy
with each being. Since in the act of prayer Adam and Eve become poets and singers, they are *figurae* of unfallen artists and *exempla* of regenerate ones, inventing and performing the genre that Sidney calls
"that lyrical kind of songs and sonnets: which, Lord, if He gave us
good minds, how well it might be employed, and with how heavenly
fruit, both private and public, in singing the praises of the immortal
beauty, the immortal goodness of that God who giveth us hands to
write and wits to conceive: of which we might well want words, but
never matter; of which we could turn our eyes to nothing but we
should ever have new budding occasions."[65]

Although I have argued lengthily that Eve was right to defend the
exercise of creative freedom even if on her own and at risk,[66] I do not
want to overstress her separate and singular talents. Eve as monody is
a fresh and astonishing creature of her author, but Adam and Eve as
harmony are the core of the world. Two voices, and the promise of
more, make possible boundless delights. The art form in which their
spiritual and musical harmony most fully resounds is their evening
(4.724-35) and especially their morning (5.153-208) prayers. We will
hear more of that resonance the better we know the music Milton
knew.

Milton's warm-toned drawing of Adam and Eve together in prayer
before the Fall is almost without precedent; but glimmers of such a life
appear in literary analogues[67] and, as we have seen, in a few visual depictions. De Bry's engraving, with its inscription of the first half of
Psalm 117, "O praise the Lord all ye peoples, praise him all ye nations"

(frontispiece) suggests that Adam and Eve bear the seed of all nations and of all praise within themselves. Van Langeren's illustration, interpreted by Slatyer as the Institution of the Sabbath (fig. 6), also shows Adam and Eve at prayer. Original righteousness, though not as popular as original sin, is at least acknowledged in these unusual representations, which are part of an early seventeenth-century impulse that Milton's account of richly joyous Edenic activity brings to its fullest consummation. In the engravings, Adam and Eve kneel in awe. Milton, combating fixed forms of worship, varies their stance; in the evening "both stood" (4.720), while before their morning prayer, after their brush with evil, "Lowly they bow'd adoring" (5.144).

Adam and Eve at prayer embody both the culmination of their own paradisal experience and the moments when they are closest to the experience of believing readers. For Adam and Eve liturgy is continuous with all experience. For the faithful in the fallen world it is "the Churches banquet" and "the bird of Paradise" (which, footless in iconography, represents the soul's free flight), and affords "some shoots of blisse, / Heaven once a week; / The next worlds gladnes prepossest in this. . . . The Creatures *Jubile*."[68] The church of Adam and Eve is never far from heaven, meets twice daily, and improvises a new liturgy each time.[69] As Milton's Celestial Patroness "inspires / Easy my unpremeditated verse" (9.23-24), so for Adam and Eve,

> neither various style,
> Nor holy rapture wanted they to praise
> Thir Maker, in fit strains pronounct or sung
> Unmeditated, such prompt eloquence
> Flow'd from their lips, in Prose, or numerous Verse,
> More tuneable than needed Lute or Harp
> To add more sweetness.
>
> (5.146-52)

Mutual spontaneous prayer—two or more people together visibly and audibly opening their souls to "that eternal Spirit, who can enrich with all utterance"—is perhaps the most intimate and risky of human activities. It almost inevitably increases love, and in baring themselves to the Spirit, the participants bare themselves in "holy rapture" to obvious, vulnerable growth of soul. It is not available to hidebound egotists. With the addition of music—and, echoing the rubrics of the Book of Common Prayer, Milton tells us that the prayers of Adam and Eve are either "pronounct or sung"—the opportunity for heavenly interchange is redoubled.

The mutuality of their love and the goodness of the whole creation form the theme of the mutual evening prayer of Adam and Eve, when "both stood, / Both turn'd, and under op'n Sky"—which Raphael will call God's Book—"ador'd / The God that made both Sky, Air, Earth and Heav'n / Which they beheld, the Moon's resplendent Globe / And starry Pole" (4.720-24). The exactness of "resplendent" images their own relation to God as Artist and that of the creation for which they speak. The mutuality of the prayer becomes more poignant when we recall that in Vondel's version of the story, Adam leaves Eve in order to pray, "and in my solitude / Give thanks to [God] for [her] companionship."[70] Here, "both stood, / Both turn'd." The passage parallels the mutuality of their repentant prayers after the Fall, when "both confess'd / Humbly thir faults" (10.1100-1101). In this church, there is no patriarchal priesthood.

The abrupt beginning, "Thou also mad'st the night," suggests that this prayer is linked to a psalm verse that could have begun their previous, unrecorded morning prayer, "This is the day which the Lord hath made; we will rejoice and be glad in it" (Ps. 118:24). Here, Adam and Eve rejoice in each other and in their coming children:

> Thou also mad'st the Night,
> Maker Omnipotent, and thou the Day,
> Which we in our appointed work imploy'd
> Have finisht happy in our mutual help
> And mutual love, the Crown of all our bliss
> Ordain'd by thee, and this delicious place
> For us too large, where thy abundance wants
> Partakers, and uncropt falls to the ground.
> But thou has promis'd from us two a Race
> To fill the Earth, who shall with us extol
> Thy goodness infinite, both when we wake,
> And when we seek, as now, thy gift of sleep.
> (4.725-35)

This prayer, the narrator continues, is "said unanimous": literally, with one soul, proving Adam's claim for "unfeign'd / Union of Mind, or in us both one Soul" (8.603-4). Adam and Eve are so intimately attuned with each other that they can mutually improvise a prayer in "numerous Verse." Immediately, "other Rites / Observing none, but adoration pure / Which God likes best, into thir inmost bower / Handed they went." Their lovemaking there—by which Adam later declares himself "transported" by passion (8.529-30)—is also pure, not "unbefitting holiest place" (4.759) as its close link with their prayer affirms. Milton's yoking together of the act of prayer and the act of love in the evening scenes, "whatever Hypocrites austerely talk," is natural. On those occasions when they sing, the link between "Rites" and "the Rites / Mysterious of connubial Love" (4.742-43) is further reinforced by Renaissance theories of music. For the eternal verities of pitch and measure link music mathematically to the mystic dance of the cosmos and to the divine forms in the mind of God, and so set the affections in right tune. And, for Galileo and Kepler, the pleasure of music was akin to the pleasure of lovemaking. They saw musical proportions as corresponding to the "proportion due" of male and female. Kepler felt that "the progeny of the pentagon, the major third and the minor third, move our souls, images of God, to emotions comparable to the business of generation," and says in a letter explaining the geometry of music, "Non puto me posse clarius et palpabilius rem explicare, quam se dicam te videre imagines illic mentulae, hic vulvae." Galileo reports that the interval of the fifth produces "such a tickling and stimulation of the cartilage of the eardrum that, tempering the sweetness with a dash of sharpness, it seems delightfully to kiss and bite at the same time."[71] These descriptions rely on the perfect consonances of pure intonation, as the beauty of the arts and the lovemaking of Adam and Eve are intensified by their purity.

Their morning prayer is both more liturgical and more explicitly connected with Milton's own work as a poet. It is an "unmeditated" canticle based on Psalm 148, said or sung at evening prayer on the thirtieth and thirty-first of each month, and the Song of the Three Children from the apocryphal portion of the Book of Daniel, which is the morning canticle in the Book of Common Prayer called the Benedicite.[72] Both sources call upon all of nature,[73] from angels to cattle to creeping things, to praise the Lord. They appeared in the metrical psalters set to authorized church tunes, which were bound into sixteenth- and seventeenth-century prayer books and Bibles; in numerous harmonized versions of these printed for home use; and in entirely different translations and settings such as George Wither's *Hymns and Songs of the Church* (1623), set for two voices by Orlando Gibbons, and George Sandys's *Paraphrase vpon the Psalmes of David* and the biblical hymns (1636), set by Henry Lawes "to new Tunes for private Devotion: and a thorow Base, for Voice, or Instrument" and published in 1638, soon after Lawes's publication of *A Mask Presented at Ludlow-Castle* on which he had collaborated with Milton four years earlier. In 1648, Lawes also published *Choice Psalmes* which may be sung "by any three, with a thorow-Base," half of them by his brother William, killed

in the civil war, as a memorial to him, prefaced by commendatory poems including Milton's sonnet to "Harry . . . That with smooth aire
couldst humor best our tongue." In the same year, Milton contributed
to the psalm-singing movement a series of metrical psalms in which he
uncharacteristically confined his muse to the common meter needed
for the common tunes. Lawes's and Gibbons's two-part settings are
performable by anyone and his viol, or his wife or child, or any two or
more people; other settings provide a range of difficulty and musical
interest reaching to the polychoral polyphony of the Chapel Royal.[74]
When Adam and Eve join their voices in prayer, they also join the
voices of pious households all over England and give them a heightened example of domestic hymnody.

Psalm-singing was a major national pastime in Milton's day;[75] his
contemporaries could bring experience of participation in it to their
reading. Adam and Eve, of course, are accomplished artists, but even
the singing of simple harmonies available to the youngest or newest
singer can give a taste of the pleasure and sense of communion that
psalm-singing affords. Milton suggests that sung prayer, spontaneously embellished in various style, is one of the inexhaustible felicities
of unfallen or regenerate life; and here, as in "At a Solemn Musick," he
illustrates its possibilities by incorporating the effects of music into the
words, as Mazzoni observes of Dante,[76] a process that reverses the Renaissance composer's practice of incorporating the effects of words
into music.

Some of the musical treatment of words that informs Milton's verbal treatment of music may be suggested by Adrian Batten's setting of
Psalm 117,[77] the one attributed to Adam and Eve by the inscription of
de Bry's engraving. Batten's word-painting includes the close-weaving
of four vocal lines (which would have required an amicable Cain and
Abel), each voice having a comfortable range, to achieve the serene
harmonies called for by the text: "O praise the Lord all ye heathen,
praise him all ye nations. / For his merciful kindness is ever more and
more towards us: and the truth of the Lord endureth for ever and
ever." The one word unsuitable for Eden, "heathen," from the Coverdale version Batten used, was altered in the Authorized Bible and later
editions of the Book of Common Prayer, where the psalm begins "O
Praise the Lord, all ye nations: praise him, all ye peoples."

Batten uses moderate polyphony to color the diversity of "all ye heathen"; tender and beseeching harmonic changes on "merciful kindness"; strong homophonic unanimity on "for his truth endureth"; and
melisma to prolong "for ever and ever." As is usual in Renaissance music, measure is determined not by bar lines and time signatures but by

the ways the musical line responds to the words. Within the steady pulse of "strictest measure eev'n"[78] the phrasing shifts back and forth between "common" or earthly time, in twos and fours, when the words concern humanity, and triple or "perfect" time on words naming the attributes of God. "His merciful kindness" enters in triple time; "is ever more and more towards us" reverts to common time; "the truth of the Lord" is in triple time; but the two kinds of time, the earthly fours and the heavenly threes, flow together as fluidly as temporal and eternal activities do in Milton's Eden.

Milton's hymn is the proposed archetype of the scriptural hymns it spontaneously elaborates.[79] Adam and Eve are not, like the Three Hebrew Children, in a fiery furnace; but they have just had their first taste of evil in Eve's dream, and we readers have spent two books in hell and more in the hell of Satan's self. The three children in the fiery furnace, refreshed by a wind an angel brings, can still praise fire. And as we are refreshed by the wind of the Spirit that blows through Milton's lines, we are also aware of the misuse the fallen angel makes of the creatures they invoke. Satan has used the sun and a treetop as spying posts, entered the Garden through "Mists and Exhalations," and winged and walked the earth as a bird, a tiger, a lion, and a toad; he will become a snake that lowly creeps: none "nocent yet." And Adam and Eve, like the psalmist, in their closing petition recognize the need for "God's merciful kindness."

The imagery of their song partakes of textural and prosodic as well as thematic musical interest. The recurrent figure denoted by the words "Circle," "Circlet," "Sphere," and "Perpetual Circle" links earth's creatures to the cosmic mystic dance and suggests the "perfect" measure that in Renaissance musical notation is denoted by a circle. But the measure varies, like Batten's, to suit the words. Assuming that, as in well-set words, we stress the most important syllables, within the steady pulse of the decasyllabic lines, the description of God contains three major stresses:

Un*speak*able, who *sitst* above these *Heav*ens.

The passage on angels has varied meters, as angels have varied natures; at the word "angels" the lines break into phrases with shifting stresses, imitating the rhythms of polyphony:

> Speak yee who best can tell, ye Sons of Light,
> Angels, for yee behold him, and with songs
> And choral symphonies, Day without Night,
> Circle his throne rejoicing, yee in Heav'n.
>
> (5.160-63)

At the entry of earthly voices, Milton brings us back to earth in something nearer a regular iambic line, but shifts with a hemiola-like rhythmic figure to three firm accents concerning God:

> On Earth join all ye Creatures to extol
> *Him* first, *him* last, *him* midst, and without end.

The verse is fitly pentametric for "And yee five other wand'ring Fires
that move / In mystic Dance not without Song, resound / His praise,"
but with a stress shifted to "five" and a skipping step after "Dance."
The rhythm again shifts to three main stresses in honor of the Godhead in "His praise who out of Darkness call'd up light." The four elements "that in quaternion run / Perpetual Circle"[80] get four-beat
lines until the exhortation to ceaseless change, when they vary. "Hail
Universal Lord" invites three accents, but with a secondary accent in
"Universal" that connects and barely subordinates the earthly four to
the heavenly three, and the diversity of creatures to the unity of God,
appropriately enough on "vers." The concluding lines similarly incorporate earthly and heavenly time, moving from marching iambs to a
serenely subsiding final cadence that prosodically restores the peace for
which they plead. The prayer is mimetically answered in the tranquil
sounds of the concluding words that reconnect them to "now" and the
rising light of dawn.

Rather than rhyme, the poem weaves close harmony of similar
sounds: dawn, morn, prime; praise, rise, sky, flies; frame, then, seem.
Often this close-weaving is onomatopoetic, providing prosodic word-
painting: "Ye Mists and Exhalations that now rise"; "wet the thirsty
Earth with falling showers"; "Fountains and yee, that warble as ye
flow, / Melodious murmurs." The rhythms provide the arc of the sun,
rising on "climb'st" and falling on "fall'st"; the syncopation of syntax
against line at "mix / And nourish all things, let your ceaseless change /
Vary"; the swoop of "ye Birds, / That singing up to Heaven Gate ascend," incorporating the leap of the heart of Shakespeare's sonnet; the
varied gaits of "Yee that in Waters glide, and yee that walk / The Earth,
and stately tread, or lowly creep." The garland-weaving of repeated
words ("fixt Stars, fixt," "wave ... wave," "warble ... warbling," the
repeated "ye" and the refrain word "praise") suggests the repetitions
heard in contrapuntal imitation; ringing assonance throughout invokes the close harmonies of a setting by Tallis, Byrd, or Monteverdi.

In the act of prayer, Adam and Eve are poets and singers, and so
figures of the poet and exemplars of the inspired invention Milton preferred to a fixed liturgy: both poet and worshiper should be freely responsive to the indwelling Spirit, though they may use established

genres within whose structures spontaneous art can always find new budding occasions.

Imagine doing that. Could anything be more engaging than the mutual, spontaneous production of poetry and song, made possible by shared rapture and established structure? Milton leaves it to our imaginations to (literally) figure out how two people linked in happy nuptial league can unanimously compose "unmeditated" songs, blessed with union of mind "or in [them] both one soul": whether by antiphonal verses or improvised polyphony, aided by mutual infusions of the Celestial Muse. Joseph H. Summers, in an eloquent appreciation of this hymn, has shown how it may be divided into stanzas for antiphonal performance, and Louise Schleiner assigns these stanzas alternately to Adam and Eve with introductory and concluding duets improvised on "tunes they have, with their prelapsarian, unimpaired musical abilities, easily invented and taught to each other, for which they would have a repertoire for twice-daily orisons." Barbara Lewalski challenges us to imagine that "this hymn is the composition of them both, sung *a capella* with sublime beauty and ease . . . by Adam and Eve together."[81] Perhaps we may hear in our minds' ears echoes of the sacred duets of Orlando di Lasso, Monteverdi, Gibbons, and Lawes, sung in exquisitely responsive improvised harmony to words immediately inspired in them both. No doubt Adam and Eve may be imagined creating works of all kinds, "unanimous," antiphonal, and polyphonic; in Paradise, as even in Sidney's Arcadia where improvised poetic exchanges often occur, such compositions, built on a growing collection of structural inventions and remembered tunes, would be endlessly diverse and lovely, and the process of creating them would be an ever-enjoyable literal instance of harmonious interaction.

If the Fall had not interrupted their courses, Adam and Eve, prime artists in a pristine world with God's image and the Holy Ghost fresh within them, might have continued to compose in various style, sometimes speaking, sometimes singing, sometimes—as in Haydn's *Creation*—joined by angels, and increasing voice parts as their tribe increased to something like—on grand occasions—Michael Praetorius's rapturous setting of the Benedicite. This splendid verse anthem, alternating small ensembles with full choirs, divides the canticle into seven verses, one for each day of creation including the sabbath.[82] Each verse, mainly in common time, is followed by one of two alternating refrains in triple time. The first refrain is the first line of the canticle: "O all ye works of the Lord, bless ye the Lord. Praise him and magnify him forever." The second refrain is from the poem preceding the canticle in the apocryphal part of Daniel, known as the Benedictus es, Domine: "Blessed are thou, in the firmament of heaven: and above all to be praised and glorified [and exalted] for ever."[83] Each refrain echoes an ascending "in saecula," forever. The verses begin with two voice parts (Adam and Eve as it were) and increase, by one voice part for each new verse, to eight. The refrains are joyful outbursts for eight-part double choir with organ and instruments. The increasing harmonies gather in all the voices of creation with copious opportunities for word-painting. The blessing invoked from the angels drops from above in two-part polyphony, swelling to homophonic full choir with brass and organ for the "omnia opere domini" of the first refrain. Three high voice parts represent the glow of sun and moon, quickening for the sparkle of stars and the stirring winds. The sound darkens, set for the lower voices, for "night" and "shadows," flashes in polyphonic repetition on "lightening," and suddenly congeals in long homophonic chords on "ice." The "fowls of the air" take soaring flights, the "beasts and cattle" rhythmically prance, the mountains and hills swell in rolling ascending and descending phrases, the grains germinate in distinct homophonic repetitions on "universa germinatia," the fountains, seas, and rivers quickly flow. The voices take a great, slow wallow on "whale" and dart and glide on "all that move in the waters." The invocation to "Israel" separates the two choirs, barely overlapping them, for a clear antiphonal call to sabbath worship expanding through upwardly modulating harmonies on "laudet et superexaltet eum in saecula." "The children of men" are invited in warmly harmonized polyphonic antiphony; "all the servants of the Lord" and the "spirits and souls of the righteous" reunite the two choirs in energetic, mainly homophonic chords. The musical word-painting is not just decorative; it invokes each "kind" as the canticle does, yet the music is structurally and harmonically unified, as the cosmos is. All these voices grow more delicately interwoven as they increase, the refrains evoke vast cosmic resonance, the word "Domino" receives expressive clarity, and each exultant chorus ends with protracted hopeful harmonies on *in saecula*.[84]

In spite of its (ultimately) Venetian style, I see no reason why Adam and Eve should not be imagined making such music: as two voices creating all the possibilities of sacred duets, increasing (if they had not fallen) to multiple choirs as their family grew, sometimes perhaps joining with angels as saints do in many paintings and in "At a Solemn Musick," and as apologists for music habitually said we should prepare to do in heaven. Milton had no objection, in *Il Penseroso*, to letting

the pealing Organ blow
To the full voic'd Quire below,
In Service high, and Anthems cleer,
As may with sweetnes, through mine ear
Dissolve me into extasies,
And bring all Heav'n before mine eyes.

Even though the commonwealth government drove it from the church, Milton represents such music in angelic choirs in both his epics.[85]

Milton incorporates musical effects into the words themselves. If we imagine a life filled with such language, sometimes joined with all the splendors of polyphony and homophony richly illustrating the words in ever varied yet wonderfully fitting and musically gratifying ways, we may have some idea of the endless mutually illuminating pleasures of the arts of Eden. Unfallen or regenerate, the whole human family might join "thir vocal Worship to the Choir / Of Creatures wanting voice" (9.198-99) in any poetic or musical mode as secretaries of God's praise. Surely to do so in the various style, the fluid responsiveness, and the exfoliation of the life of words characteristic of Renaissance music and of Milton's verse proliferates countless joys, and by joining hearts in harmony with each other and with heaven nourishes the life of this fragilely pendant, still resplendent globe.

## NOTES

1. Portions of this chapter appeared in "Eve and the Arts of Eden," published in *Milton and the Idea of Woman,* and in "Subsequent or Precedent? Eve as Milton's Defense of Poesie," *MQ* 20 (1986): 132-36.

2. *The Reason of Church Government Urged,* in *SM,* 526.

3. Milton discusses sin and spiritual death in *De Doctrina Christiana* 1.11-12. Sin has two parts, "evil concupiscence," or the desire of sinning, and the act of sin itself. "Actual Sin . . . may be incurred, not only by actions commonly so called, but also by words and thoughts, and even by omission of good actions." But though it is called actual, sin is not "properly an action, for in reality it implies defect. . . . For every act is in itself good; it is only its irregularity, or deviation from the line of right, which properly speaking is evil. Wherefore the act itself is not the matter of which sin consists, but only the . . . *subject* in which it is committed, by words, by thoughts, and by omission." The punishment of sin is death, which comprehends "all evils whatever." The first degree of death includes guiltiness, "forfeiture of the divine protection and favor; whence results a diminution of the majesty of the human countenance, and a conscious degradation of mind. Hence the whole man becomes

polluted; whence arises shame. . . . The second degree of death is called *spiritual death;* by which is meant the loss of divine grace, and that of innate righteousness, wherein man in the beginning lived unto God. And this death took place not only on the very day, but at the very moment of the fall. They who are delivered from it are said to be *regenerated,* to be *born again,* and to be *created afresh;* which is the work of God alone" (*SM,* 998-99).

4. Summers makes a similar point in *The Muse's Method,* 94.

5. Shakespeare, *Merchant of Venice* 5.1.83-85.

6. "Ciascun distinto de fulgore e d'arte," each distinct in splendor and in art (*Paradiso* 31.132-33).

7. This theme of the opening of eyes is also expressed by seventeenth-century artists through episodes from the apocryphal Book of Tobit, loved for its themes of marriage, angelic protection, and the healing of blindness. Lorna McNeur (in conversation) has pointed out the similarity between Veronese's Adam and the crucified Christ, reinforcing the "edification" of Eve as a type of the church. That type in turn suggests the opening of spiritual eyes.

8. Frye, *Milton's Imagery,* 39.

9. The model for this integration is the liturgy; its secular counterparts are masque and opera.

10. The Easter Vigil was not included in the BCP, but the hart's association with creation and rebirth continued in the arts.

11. Palestrina (1526-94), *Sicut Cervus:* Motet for four voices, in *Le Opere Complete,* 11:42-44. Performance edition by Robert Hufstader. I use this motet as a clear example, not as a particular "influence." Like iconographic resources, musical ones flowed freely between Britain and the Continent, issuing in innovative local variations.

12. Wulstan, *Tudor Music,* 328.

13. Monteverdi, *Selva Morale e Spirituale* (printed 1640). Quotations are from Milton, *L'Allegro,* l. 140, and "At a Solemn Musick," l. 27.

14. *Of Reformation,* in *SM,* 447 and 445. Thomas B. Stroup surveys Milton's objections to Anglican liturgy in *Religious Rite and Ceremony,* 69-70. Gilman recounts the iconoclast cause and Milton's response in *Iconoclasm.*

15. "At a Solemn Musick." On the correspondence of natural or "just" intonation, the tuning of polyphonic music, with Kepler's astronomy see D. P. Walker, *Studies in Musical Science,* chap. 4. David Wulstan discusses the problems of various kinds of temperament in *Tudor Music,* 117.

16. De' Bardi, "Discourse on Ancient Music and Good Singing" (c. 1580), 108.

17. Morning prayer included the Venite Exultamus Domino (Psalm 95), either the Te Deum Laudamus or the Benedicite Omnia Opera Domini Domino, and either the Benedictus (Luke 1:68-79) or the Jubilate Deo (Ps. 100); evening prayer included the Magnificat (Luke 1:46-55) or the Cantate Domino (Ps. 98) and the Nunc Dimittis or the Deus Misereatur (Ps. 67). The Gloria Patri also concluded the Quicunque Vult, a creed said on thirteen major

feast days. For the Communion service composers ordinarily set the Kyrie (responses to the Ten Commandments) and the Creed; they also wrote anthems and settings of the festal psalms. The Invitatory is the set of versicles and responses beginning with the versicle "O Lord open thou our lips" and the response "And our mouth shall show forth thy praise." The full formula for the Gloria Patri concludes the Benedictus (BCP, 57) but the rubric appears in the directions for reading the psalms (52). Attendance at daily services was required at the universities.

18. Byrd, *The Great Service*.

19. *Of Reformation*, in *SM*, 452.

20. I have lifted this statement from Professor Aarsleff's introduction to his seminar in the 1989-90 Program of the Folger Institute. Aarsleff discusses the theory of "Adamic language" and Locke's critique of the problems it causes, in contrast to the principle that human languages are conventional, in *From Locke to Saussure*, 24-31. For a cautionary view of differences between the divine word and human words see also Christopher, *Milton and the Science of the Saints*.

21. Ralegh, *History*, 32.

22. Stanley Fish points out the speciousness of this conception in *Surprised by Sin* (107-30), "Language in Paradise," but states that "Milton need not believe wholeheartedly in the ideal language in order to take advantage of his reader's belief in it. As long as the reader identifies Edenic perfection with a word-thing vocabulary, he must admit his distance from that perfection, whenever he reads into the word more than is literally there, more than the thing," adding that while Satan puns ambiguously, Adam and Eve "pun etymologically, declining a word in its single significance and therefore not punning at all" (128). Although their speech is etymologically rooted and their wordplay often univocal, I would argue that it is also so rich in innocent and regenerate resonances and intimations as to show the impoverishment of the word-thing hypothesis. John Leonard discusses Edenic language, which he does not call the language of Adam in courtesy toward Eve, in *Naming in Paradise*, and shows the richness of Milton's use of it. Russell Fraser reports the history of seventeenth-century distrust of language and projects for its purgation or abolition in *The Language of Adam*, finding that the projectors attempted to reduce phenomena to unassailable abstract principles. Fraser criticizes the reductivism of abstractors and categorizers like Ramus, whom he calls "the philosopher of petrifaction" (52), and finds that "the common denominator which associates the occult with anti-Aristotelianism and new science is hatred of the word made flesh," in contrast to those who *do* number the streaks of the tulip. Leonardo is modern insofar as "he believes in the possibility of boiling down" but "partakes also of the 'Aristotelian' or fact-riveted intelligence—who in more sumptuous ways? 'Write,' he adjures himself . . . 'the tongue of the woodpecker and the jaw of the crocodile. Write the flight of the fourth kind of chewing butterflies, and of the flying ants, and the three

chief positions of the wings of birds in descent' " (61-62). But Fraser finds Milton "modern: cursory, facile," apparently because (besides his redaction of Ramus) Milton believes in divine origins of wisdom (30-31).

In *Divine Word*, Robert L. Entzminger recognizes that in contrast to the Royal Society, "Milton sees Adam as the first poet, expressing his vision through a particular kind of wordplay and spontaneously celebrating his existence with a language that is stylized and opulently redundant" (22). Entzminger discusses seventeenth-century views of language, epistemology, and the limitations of language, along with their sources in Augustine, Luther, and Calvin, and finds in *Paradise Lost* many felicities of Edenic language as well as a sense of the limitations of the human mind even in unfallen speech; see especially chap. 1, " 'Prompt Eloquence': Edenic Speech and the Book of Nature." On Milton's relation to his muse he comments: "Poetry is a divinely appointed vocation, and in order to be 'true' it must first be the product of an author who is pure. . . . Although the epic voice cannot perform his task without divine assistance, the heavenly muse does not reduce her servant to an amanuensis. Rather she permits him access to the principles of God's creation so that he may continue in human words the revelation God accomplishes through the Word" (119). On Milton's muse see also Flinker, "Courting Urania"; Revard, *"L'Allegro* and *Il Penseroso"*; and Treip, "Celestial Patronage."

23. Herbert, "De Musica Sacra," in *Latin Poetry,* 32. In Edmund Blunden's translation, stones "concent to sing" ("Some Seventeenth-Century Latin Poems," 12).

24. Vaughan, "The Retreate," in *Works,* 419. The poem is not about action in the world, however, but about the retreat of the soul to the celestial city from whence it fell. On heavenly mindedness, see Kaufmann, *Paradise.*

25. Donne, "To Sr. *Edward Herbert.* At *Julyers,"* in *Complete Poetry,* 233.

26. Marvell, "Upon Appleton House," in *Complete Poems,* 75-99.

27. St. George was one of two nonbiblical saints retained in the calendar of the seventeenth-century Book of Common Prayer. The other was St. Cecilia, patroness of music.

28. Herbert, "Paradise," in *Works,* 132-33.

29. Otten, *Environ'd with Eternity,* 173-74.

30. Works on Herbert's ways with language include Rosamund Tuve, *A Reading of George Herbert;* Joseph H. Summers, *George Herbert: His Religion and Art;* Helen Vendler, *The Poetry of George Herbert;* Heather A. R. Asals, *Equivocal Predication;* Richard Todd, *The Opacity of Signs;* C. A. Patrides's introduction to his edition of *The English Poems;* M. M. Mahood, "Something Understood"; and Diane McColley, "Herbert's Hierophons."

31. In English Renaissance liturgical music dissonance is often used to express intensity.

32. Browne, *Garden of Cyrus,* in *Works,* 1.178-85.

33. That is, not counted by regular metrical stresses, in contrast to the metrical psalms.

34. Corum, "In White Ink," 128.

35. Lee M. Johnson discusses the structural proportions of verse paragraphs in "Milton's Epic Style."

36. Lewalski, *"Paradise Lost" and the Rhetoric of Literary Forms*, 189. On the invention of the arts by Adam and Eve, see Turner, *One Flesh*, 33-34 and n. 37.

37. *Of Education*, in *SM*, 729.

38. Sidney, *Apology*, 72.

39. *The Reason of Church Government*, in *SM*, 526.

40. *An Apology for Smectymnuus*, in *SM*, 549.

41. Lancetta's *Scena Tragica d'Adamo e d'Eua* (1644) exemplifies such allegorization. J. M. Evans discusses allegorical readings in *"Paradise Lost" and the Genesis Tradition*, 69-99. See also McColley, *Milton's Eve*, 11-12 and 116-17.

42. Otten discusses the abundant significance of literal gardens and gardening in relation to English Renaissance literature, philosophy, and religion in *Environ'd with Eternity*. I have discussed the literal and metaphorical implications of Milton's Garden in *Milton's Eve*, chap. 4.

43. "Hand" as handwork may also be a pun on "hand" as handwriting.

44. Puttenham, *Art of English Poesie*, 308-13; Shakespeare, *Winter's Tale* 4.4; Spenser, *Faerie Queene* 2.12 and 3.6; Herbert, "A Wreath"; Donne, "La Corona"; Marvell, "The Coronet."

45. Sidney, *Apology*, 51; Smart, *Jubilate Agno*, l. 506.

46. Herbert, "The Pilgrimage" and "The Flower" in *Works*, 142 and 166.

47. Both Perkins (*Workes* 2:57) and Donne (*Sermons* 2:346) deny Eve the capacity to name.

48. Shakespeare, *Hamlet* 3.2.22-23.

49. Janet E. Halley argues that Eve's choice is not free but compulsory, because "female heterosexuality is not natural but socially constructed" ("Female Autonomy," 234). In Milton's dramatization, prelapsarian free will chooses an inclination that is no less "natural" because it is composed of multiple considerations.

50. Knedlik, "Fancy, Faith, and Generative Mimesis," 36 and 43.

51. Froula, "When Eve Reads Milton," 328.

52. *Samson Agonistes*, l. 1754.

53. Ralegh, *History*, 35.

54. Froula, "Pechter's Specter," 173, in answer to Edward Pechter, "When Pechter Reads Froula," 163-70. It is unlikely that Mr. Pechter made that mistake. Froula reads *Paradise Lost* from the viewpoint of a feminist sociology of religion that takes Judaism and Christianity to be patriarchal political inventions and asserts, for example, that "Adam fashions a god that is invisible to Eve in order to master her" (173). I also disagree with John Guillory's reductive psychologizing of inspiration in *Poetic Authority*, which assumes that a human relation to God is an archaic idea and reluctance to discard it

"fundamentally a consequence of anxiety about *authority*" (177). In *Prophetic Milton* William Kerrigan astutely observes, "The epic dramatizes a familiar Christian paradox: submitting to the Heavenly Muse, the narrator loses his art to gain his art." Since "the central theological issue of *Paradise Lost* is freedom," Milton has the "aesthetic problem" that characters premeditatedly manipulated solely by "the will of a human author" would make a "puppet master" not only of the human author but of the God whose ways Milton wants to justify. "The genuine artist [according to Augustine] comprehends, through divine illumination, the preexistent principles of harmonious creation. But he cannot, like God, create *ex nihilo* . . . ; he participates with God in the perfecting of nature" (146-47).

55. *The Reason of Church Government*, in *SM*, 526.

56. *Of Reformation*, in *SM*, 452-53: "The wisdom of God created understanding, fit and proportionable to truth, the object and end of it, as the eye to the thing visible. If our understanding have a film of ignorance over it, or be blear with gazing on other false glisterings, what is that to truth? If we will but purge with sovereign eyesalve that intellectual ray which God hath planted in us, then we would believe the scriptures, protesting their own plainness and perspicuity, calling them to be instructed, not only the wise and learned, but the simple, the poor, the babes, foretelling an extraordinary effusion of God's Spirit upon every age and sex, attributing to all men, and requiring from them the ability of searching, trying, examining all things, and by the Spirit discerning that which is good."

57. In a broad sense, not a prosodic one, Eve's poem is a rondeau, which originates in dance; perhaps its form suggests a round dance in which the partners circle in opposite directions, then return to join hands.

58. As lapsarian readers we are aware of Ovid's association of the nightingale with Procne and Philomela and the terrible death of the child Itys (*Metamorphoses*, Book 6), and also of Penelope's poignant "nightingale speech" on the eve of her reunion with Odysseus, and in it the death of the child Itylos (*Odyssey*, Book 19). These analogues of the horrors of the Fall do not stain Eve or Milton's poetic emblem here, but they do add a dimension of sorrow for the loss of innocence to come. Richard Du Rocher interprets Eve's relation to Ovidian myth with extraordinary justice and sensitivity to both analogies and differences in *Milton and Ovid*.

59. From the Litany, prescribed to be used at least three times a week.

60. I have discussed the moral and poetic implications of Eve's dream in *Milton's Eve*, 89-104.

61. Sidney, *Apology*, 59.

62. *Tetrachordon*, in *SM*, 673.

63. Sidney, *Apology*, 81.

64. Sidney, *Apology*, 60.

65. Sidney, *Apology*, 80.

66. McColley, *Milton's Eve*, esp. chap. 5.

67. See for example Salandra, *Adamo Caduto;* Andreini, *L'Adamo;* and Vondel, *Adam in Ballingschap*. Relevant passages are translated in Kirkconnell, *Celestial Cycle*.

68. Herbert, "Prayer," in *Works*, 51; Vaughn, "Son-dayes," in *Works*, 447-48.

69. "The earliest Christian daily public prayer was at dawn and at sunset (*ingressu lucis et noctis*, to use Tertullian's phrase). . . . The office of mattins consisted of specified psalms, hymns, and prayers. The earliest documents mention Pss. 60; 66; 117; and especially Pss. 148-150, called laudes " (C. W. Dugmore, quoted in J. G. Davies, ed., *Dictionary*, 114-15.

70. Vondel, *Adam in Ballingschap*, trans. Kirkconnell, *Celestial Cycle*, 462.

71. Galileo and Kepler are quoted by D. P. Walker in *Studies in Musical Science*, 32 and 53-54. In Pythagorean thought, even numbers are "feminine" and odd numbers "masculine" (Heninger, *Touches of Sweet Harmony*, 86-87), so that the musical proportion 3:2 produces the irreducible combination of the two. Milton's poem never mentions the supposed perfection of masculine numbers and corruptibility (because evenly divisible) of feminine ones, however.

72. The Benedicite was included in the Greek Bible of the Septuagint and also in editions of Luther's translation and the 1611 English version, separated, with the rest of the Apocrypha, from the Old and New Testaments because it was not part of the Hebrew canon. Swaim analyzes the relation of the poem to its sources and to Milton's objections to formulaic liturgy, in "The Morning Hymn of Praise," and points out the appropriateness of the allusion to Daniel, interpreter of dreams, in a passage closely following Eve's dream (14). Regina M. Largent, "A Multilevel Celebration," shows that the hymn is a hexameron, recapitulating the days of creation intuitively, since Adam and Eve have not yet heard Raphael's expansion of Genesis 1 in Book 7. Lieb observes that "Adam and Eve animate apostrophically God's creation to praise their Maker" in "a pattern of symbolic motion equivalent to vocal celebration," in *Dialectics of Creation*, 75. Mary Ann Radzinowicz relates the hymn to Psalms 8, 29, 46, 104, and 114, as well as Psalm 148 and the Benedicite, and to the multivocality of introits, commenting that Milton patterns it "on creation hymns where creation is both subject and audience," and calls it "Milton's purest creation hymn," while "his fullest is the angelic processional at Creation itself" (*Milton's Epics and the Book of Psalms*, 153-54). Schwartz finds the hymn an epitome of the poem, which is itself an extended song of praise, in *Remembering and Repeating*, chap. 3. Francis C. Blessington traces the history of epic hymns and finds that "only Milton inserted the pure hymn and subordinated the epic to it on the ideal level. . . . *Paradise Lost* is the hymn-epic" ("That Undisturbed Song," 494-95).

73. Adam and Eve do not include those features, such as snow and ice, that follow the climatic changes induced by the Fall (10.648-707). Milton's narrator calls destructive storms "outrage from lifeless things" (707). The

psalm and the canticle, and also the great creation poem in Ecclesiasticus 43 (assigned for November 16 in the 1634 BCP), treat storms and cold as God's wondrous works.

74. During the Interregnum chapel and cathedral choirs were silenced, but psalm-singing continued, to simple tunes in church and on many levels of musical complexity at home.

75. For an account of the psalm-singing movement see Temperley, *Music of the English Parish Church*, chap. 3.

76. Mazzoni, *Defense*, 58.

77. Batten (1591-1637?), "O Praise the Lord," from John Barnard's *First Book of Selected Church Musick*.

78. Milton, Sonnet 7, l. 10.

79. Lewalski calls Adam and Eve "the creators (on earth) of the hymn genre, identified in Renaissance criticism as the noblest kind of lyric and perhaps the greatest of all literary genres" (*"Paradise Lost" and the Rhetoric of Literary Forms*, 202).

80. Heninger explains the Pythagorean quaternion or Tetrad of elements in *Touches of Sweet Harmony*, esp. 150-56.

81. Summers, *Muse's Method*, 75-83; Schleiner, *Living Lyre*, 134-36; Lewalski, *"Paradise Lost" and the Rhetoric of Literary Forms*, 202-3. Lewalski further identifies the hymn as having "the three-part structure of a Callimachan literary hymn," a verse form allied to classical lyric hymns, and elements of the Biblical and metrical psalms (204-5). Schleiner's assignment of stanzas resembles Bentley's as noted in Marchant's edition of *Paradise Lost* (London, 1751). Pearce suggests a refutation and reversal of Bentley's divisions, which in Pearce's view give the wrong imagery to each sex; passages on the morning star, the moon, and fountains and rills should "come to Eve's share" as "fitter for her" (Marchant, 377-78). David Wulstan explains how in Milton's time "polyphony, both vocal and instrumental, was frequently improvised" (*Tudor Music*, 260). Such improvisation, though "spontaneous" in being voluntary and occasional, requires skill and a shared *cantus firmus*.

82. Regina Largent divides Milton's anthem this way in "A Multilevel Celebration."

83. This translation is from the AV Apocrypha, slightly conflating the first and last verses. The Latin is "Benedictus es Domine in firmamento coeli et laudabilis et gloriosus et superexaltatus in saecula."

84. Praetorius, "Canticum trium puerorum."

85. Margaret Mather Byard discusses Milton's sources, especially in Roman oratorio, in "Adventrous Song." M. N. K. Mander comments on the relations of monody and polyphony to humanist precepts in "The Music of *L'Allegro* and *Il Penseroso*."

# 5

# Eating Death

The whole creation groaneth and travaileth
in pain together until now.
Romans 8:22

Poore man, thou searchest round
To find out *death,* but misseth *life* at hand.
Herbert, "Vanitie"

L ove, language, music, earth-care, and the invention of the arts
might seem to be Eden enough; but Adam and Eve also have
the founding of the human family and the welfare of the global
menagerie to attend to. These matters require another art, good government; and they bear on the question whether the Fall is, as Stevie
Davies believes, a move from "the closed world of eternal childhood
and spring" to "a world liberated into culture,"[1] or is fortunate in any
other way.

## Thyestean Banquet

Having bought the unlikely proposition that the fruit which God,
who made a world of nurture, had forbidden would "feed at once
both Body and Mind," Eve "pluck'd, she eat":

> Earth felt the wound, and Nature from her seat
> Sighing through all her Works gave signs of woe,
> That all was lost. Back to the Thicket slunk
> The guilty Serpent, and well might, for *Eve*
> Intent now wholly on her taste, naught else
> Regarded, such delight till then, as seem'd,
> In Fruit she never tasted, whether true
> Or fancied so, through expectation high
> Of knowledge, nor was God-head from her thought.
> Greedily she engorg'd without restraint,
> And knew not eating Death.

(9.782-92)

Eve and Adam and their descendants would soon know "eating Death" in a new sense, for her eating when joined to Adam's would release to his dreadful feast that Death who had "Grinn'd horrible" and "blest his maw" when Satan promised all things as his prey (2.846-47). Sensing Satan's triumph, the "meagre Shadow" gloats to his mother-mistress Sin,

> Go whither Fate and inclination strong
> Leads thee, I shall not lag behind, nor err
> The way, thou leading, such a scent I draw
> Of carnage, prey innumerable, and taste
> The savor of Death from all things there that live.
> (10.265-69)

To add olfactory to gustatory narcissism, "with delight he snuff'd the smell / Of mortal change on Earth" (10.272-73). This is not Sister Death from whom saints obtain their peace; she is what grace makes out of dying. This Death gleefully devours the offal into which Sin turns living things, engorges those who die by "violent stroke . . . Fire, Flood, Famine, by Intemperance more" (11.471-72), and brandishes his dart over those whose excesses breed "all maladies / Of ghastly Spasm, or racking torture, qualms / Of heart-sick Agony" (480-82) and a long list of fevers, ulcers, colics, madness, pestilence, and other miseries of those who "serve ungovern'd appetite" and "pervert pure Natures healthful rules . . . since they / God's Image did not reverence in themselves" (517, 523-25). Traherne also identifies sin with physical, mental, and metaphorical illness.

> Mankind is sick, the World distemper'd lies,
>   Opprest with Sins and Miseries.
> Their Sins are Woes; a long corrupted Train
>   Of Poyson, drawn from *Adam's* vein,
>   Stains all his Seed, and all his Kin
>   Are one Disease of Life within
>   They all torment themselves![2]

Modern medicine adds stress and pollution to the list of killers and proves that the effects of ungoverned appetite are not confined to those who indulge it. That is not to say that every misery is either punishment for one's own sin, which was the error of the friends of Job, or the direct result of someone else's, but that human actions or inactions massively increase the pain of the disciplinary toil and mortality that, in the Augustinian view, Adam and Eve by heeding the Serpent brought forth into the world.

In *Paradise Lost,* the Fall initiates global cannibalism. Not only does Earth feel the wound, but

> At that tasted Fruit
> The Sun, as from *Thyestean* Banquet, turn'd
> His course intended;

and the aversion gradually "produc'd / Like change on Sea and Land, sideral blast, / Vapor, and Mist, and Exhalation hot, / Corrupt, and Pestilent"—a sort of natural atmospheric contamination which human activities have since exacerbated. "Thus began / Outrage from lifeless things; but Discord first / Daughter of Sin, among th'irrational / Death introduc'd through fierce antipathy"; the animals begin to kill each other, the "Thyestean banquet" spreads, and Adam recognizes that all he can give his children is "propagated curse" (10.687-89, 692-95, 706-9, 729).

Milton could hardly have chosen a more horrible comparison than the feast of Thyestes, whose brother, in revenge for his adultery, feeds him his own children. That meal is the root horror of the tragedy of the House of Atreus and is analogous to the tragedy of the House of Adam. When the human family follows improvident appetite, it devours its own children with their inheritance. George Herbert speaks in the voice of fallen man who consumes God's stock:

> For what account can thy ill steward make?
> I have abuse'd thy stock, destroy'd thy woods,
> Suckt all thy magazens: my head did ake,
> Till it found out how to consume thy goods.

Adam and Eve depart from the Garden comforted by visions of redemption, but they are still going to suffer the recurrent grief of the global family, the slaying of one brother by another. The family will suffer, as well, the slower slaying of ill stewardship, the rape of nature. Both result from, and summon, "eating Death."

## Felix Culpa?

By now it will be clear that I do not think Milton and other seventeenth-century English writers subscribed to the idea that the Fall was fortunate; and Dennis Danielson has so cogently and learnedly refuted it that it scarcely seems necessary to revive the question. I do so partly in response to the implicit invitation in Danielson's recognition that "it is hard to conceive of a more important question in the study of Milton than whether the Fall is fortunate or unfortunate" and that "the fallacy of the Fortunate Fall" that has "hung like a pall over Milton's epic" is so pervasive that "to be quite rid of its influence is more than one can reasonably hope,"[4] as has indeed proved true in the work of several recent critics. The same may be said of representations in the visual arts: distinctions need to be made between images that explicitly evoke a "fortunate fall" and the "pall" that hangs over images that do not. J. B. Trapp gives examples of the former, stating that in early Christian art "the Fall itself is thrown into highest relief: 'For by one man's disobedience many were made sinners, so by the obedience of one shall many be made righteous.' " He continues, more generally, "contracted representations are only less proleptic in character for stating less explicitly than a full cycle that the Fall is the essential, even the happy, preliminary to salvation and eternal bliss."[5] I have been arguing that this assumption has been overextended, and especially that it does not apply to images acceptable to the Reformation. Since Danielson has represented the theological problem so adequately, this chapter, in league with those before and after it, attacks the "pall" from a cultural point of view.

There are several kinds of *felix culpa* with which to disagree in varying degrees. First, there is the ancient doctrine of the coinherence of opposites,[6] taught by philosophers and mystics from many traditions. Some passages of Scripture, such as the Voice from the whirlwind in Job, present a world made of conflicting natural forces, of whose magnificence normal ethical standards fall short. Those who practice contemplative prayer reach the state in which good and evil are subsumed in the unity of all being. Yet most saints who spend much time in the heaven of contemplation also rush to relieve suffering on earth. Their experience of transcendence does not make them complacent about evil. A binary dialectic[7] that makes opposites interdependent and also plots them along an axis of good and evil can come perilously close to the Manichaean heresy, and it can also make sin seem inevitable, in violation of the doctrine of free will.[8] A subsidiary effect, which I believe Milton consciously opposed, is that in many formulations the opposites include matter and spirit, and female and male; and these get aligned with evil and good. Milton solves the problems of Manichaeism and misogyny, without resorting to transcendence, by not plotting male and female, reason and passion, obedience and freedom, order and fecundity, faith and imagination, or any other pairing of potentially good things along the axis of good and evil. When the Son brings the matter of creation out of the "dark materials" of "Eternal Anarchy" (2.896, 916),

His brooding wings the Spirit of God outspread,
And vital virtue infus'd, and vital warmth
Throughout the fluid Mass, but downward purg'd
The black tartareous cold Infernal dregs
Adverse to Life.

(7.235-59)

He then "conglob'd" and "disparted" (7.239-41) these purged elements in orderly junction and opposition and, when all was done, viewed "all that he had made," and "behold all was entirely good" (548-49). Evil is the perversion of good (1.162-65). The fact that God permits his creatures to choose to become his adversaries, providing a universe open to growth by confronting evil, is potentially good. But being his adversaries or succumbing to them is not.

Second, there is the *necessarium Adae peccatum* and the *felix culpa* of the otherwise splendid typological hymn, the Exultet, sung on Holy Saturday during the Easter Vigil, which in the Sarum Rite exclaims "O truly necessary sin of Adam and of ourselves, which was blotted out by the death of Christ! O happy guilt, the desert of which was to gain such and so great a Redeemer!" Other parts of the Exultet modify this much-quoted sentence.[9] The vigil was omitted from the Book of Common Prayer, and the Epistle for Easter Even seems chosen to revise it, beginning "It is better (if the will of God be so) that ye suffer for well doing than for evil doing" (1 Pet. 3). The gist of the *necessarium Adae peccatum* is summed up in a popular fifteenth-century lyric: "Ne hadde the apple taken ben . . . , Ne hadde never our Lady / A ben Hevene Quen. / Blissed be the time / That apple taken was!"[10] The emotional impulse of this kind of *felix culpa* is generous. The Exultet acknowledges the moving manifestation of divine love in the suffering of Christ, and the lyric gives thanks for the exaltation of Mary. When applied to daily experience, this tradition becomes allied with the observation in a world already fallen that through pain we may come to deeper love and union with God and our neighbors than we had known without it.[11] The difficulty with this doctrine, from a Reformation point of view, is that it allows sentimentality about sin and can be used as an excuse for it; and to visualize the Fall itself as fortunate, as if God's grace depended on human pain or his bounty were increased by sin, is to lack imagination for suffering and for the resources of goodness.

Third, and most attractive to seventeenth-century poets, there is the strong-minded doctrine of the uses of adversity. "Life," John Keats would say later, "is a vale of soul-making."[12] Hardship, which in

Vergil is the cure of natural sloth, is in Christian writers the stuff of rebirth. Because the Fall has weakened virtue and destroyed free will, people need the discipline of necessity and even of affliction: the rod of God's mercy. In some readings, this process leads to higher spiritual states than would have been possible by the path of blessedness. But usually it does not issue from a fortunate fall, but from a fortunate though painful recovery which can raise souls higher than the point from which they fell—"For, if I imp my wing on thine, / Affliction shall advance the flight in me"[13]—though not necessarily higher than they might have risen without falling.

Fourth, there is the idea that Adam and Eve fell upward: instead of a violation of the harmony of creatures the Fall was a beginning of civilization and moral understanding. This idea, so far as I know, does not enter Christian commentary during or before the seventeenth century except in certain (by no means all) Gnostic readings of Genesis that Milton and other major poets did not employ. Disobedience to God could not be a means to moral knowledge or any other achievement; it causes the loss of free will, which can only be restored by the grace of God, received by a willing heart which is itself a gift of grace. Grace does not consist with defiance. Although some poets, such as Vaughan and Traherne, do make Paradise analogous to childhood innocence and wonder, falling into adulthood is for them not an improvement. For most commentators, Adam and Eve fell not from childhood into adulthood but from wisdom and knowledge into moral and intellectual confusion. For Milton, a "perpetual childhood of prescription"[14] was exactly what unfallen Adam and Eve did not have. The one sign of the forbidden tree guaranteed their truly adult, self-governing freedom from prescription until they showed themselves unfit for freedom by violating that one restraint.

Fifth, there is the idea expressed by William Kerrigan and Gordon Braden that "sexual desire, like the appetite for food, becomes capable of heightened satisfaction with the Fall, and this heightening has a name: 'in lust they burn' (9.1015)."[15] This kind of fortunateness may be suggested to some viewers by erotic paintings, and Augustine's theory that innocent sex must be rationally willed may invite it,[16] but it is contrary to both doctrine and poetry in the seventeenth century. For the poets who most thoroughly integrate physical love and the union of souls, especially Milton and sometimes Donne, heightened love and good religion go together. In *Paradise Lost,* Adam and Eve do not rise from the bed of lust satisfied, but "destitute" (9.1062). When Satan's cohorts expect pleasure from repeating the Fall, "they fondly thinking to allay / Thir appetite with gust, instead of Fruit / Chew'd bitter

Ashes" (10.564-66). From the point of view of Arminian Reformers asserting free will and individual conscience, to apply the *felix culpa* to one's own desires would be a dangerous temptation.

Although Milton and his Protestant contemporaries had little sympathy for the first two kinds of "fortunate fall," they would have had even less for the last two. The preceding chapters concerned the goodness of good; this one addresses the evilness of evil. The triple prongs of evil are horror, immensity, and triviality.

## The Fatuous Fall

We have noticed that Milton often moves motifs usually reserved for fallen life to unfallen experience: Eve's dream, prelapsarian lovemaking, gardening tools that angels may have brought, and numerous prelapsarian arts and labors. Everything in human experience that can provide opportunity for love, learning, creative activity, and moral choice, including much that is usually thought "fallen," Milton plants in paradise. In doing so, he detoxifies numerous motifs associated with Eve.[17]

Two other examples are clarified by visual treatments. First, Eve's meeting with her own reflection (4.453-76) also appears in a sixteenth-century painting by Jan Swart van Groningen (fig. 59) that in several ways typifies treatments of the Fall by artists who combined Renaissance style, northern sensibilities, and Reformation doctrine. The beautiful figures and their positions, Eve standing and intent, Adam seated and uneasy, are Renaissance ones. Adam, however, takes the fruit in an exaggerated gesture of deliberate volition, and Eve dangles an unbitten fruit in a way that suggests she has not yet eaten. In the background is the Admonition, with Eve present and God holding Adam's arm. But the left background contains an unusual and nonscriptural event. In the very moment of being expelled by an angel with a threatening sword, Eve has paused to look at her reflection in a pond, and Adam reaches back to grasp her wrist and lead her away. Adam's choice, Swart suggests, constitutes the Fall, but Eve's vanity is incorrigible. When Milton uses or invents the mirror motif, he translates it from the lapsed to the prelapsarian lives of Adam and Eve. That is, he brings Eve's potential vanity into the open at a time when it is still innocent and can be outgrown without sin, a point he makes by assigning the narration and recognition to Eve herself.

Second, in the Genesis series by Nicolas van Hoey, Eve's fall occurs during Adam's conversation with an angel.[18] In *Paradise Lost,* while Adam talks with Raphael, Eve listens until the discourse on astronomy, then innocently departs to look after "Her Nursery" (8.46) and returns still innocent. Milton avoids the implications that Eve fell the first time she was alone and that Adam's attention to someone else gave occasion for her defection, and so supports their prelapsarian freedom, dignity, and activity.

By transferring kinds of experience and increased understanding that could imply a fortunate fall to the perlapsarian scenes, Milton defuses the possibility that the Fall issued in maturity, pleasure, or civilized arts. By moving much that has been considered *unfortunate* from after the Fall to the scenes before it as well, he makes Paradise a place of moral growth in which choice, compassion, and courage take part. All the arts of Eden belong in the former category, for Milton transforms paradise from a statically pastoral to a dynamically georgic realm. Eve's dream and the temptation at the lake are examples of the latter, importing what Milton calls the "good temptation"[19] into prelapsarian life so that Adam and Eve have as grist for spiritual nurture the intellectual, emotional, and imaginative perplexities that others have seen as adversities dependent on the Fall. He converts both kinds of experience into what Irene Samuel calls "the stuff of growth" in paradise.[20]

We have seen that most Bible illustrators rejected an interpretation of the Fall as erotic or fortunate; that many artists infused immediacy and pleasure into the iconography of creation and populated Eden with creatures that combined a medieval delight in profusion with a learned iconological richness of suggestion and increasing anatomical and botanical accuracy; and that they sketched the possibility of a happy unfallen life for Adam and Eve. That cheerful view of the goodness and interest of creation affects depictions of the Fall as well. If earth and its denizens are lovely and lively, engorging death cannot be fortunate. But the idea still insinuates itself that the Fall was a good thing, not only in the complex theological sense but in the secular sense that it represents a liberation, or an intensification, or a creation of "humanity" with all its lovable foibles, or that without sin life would have been sexless or sex lifeless, in spite of Milton's cures for these misapprehensions.

Versions of the Fall in the visual arts sometimes implicate the viewer in this way, giving the act a dense erotic pressure that flattens other considerations. Raphael minimizes the fruit and Tintoretto (fig. 30) the snake in a way that suggests (at least to the "fallen" viewer) that the real forbidden fruit is Eve herself, while Raphael's fruit (apparently a fig) and Tintoretto's snake provide the male symbolism to match the fruitlike lushness of Eve's body. In Titian's version (Trapp, fig. 20) and Ruben's imitation of it (Frye, fig. 171) Adam touches

Eve's breast, or nearly does, in a gesture between remonstrance and caress, and eyes the serpent warily; we see tragic tension in his body and beguiling softness in hers. If one esteems both *eros* and *agape,* the Temptation becomes a tragic dilemma; if one worships only Eros, the Fall seems a good idea. The Reformation taught that its root cause was disbelief,[21] out of which all other sins issue.[22]

An erotic fall was not acceptable as English Bible illustration, probably to avoid several undesirable effects: suggesting that infidelity to God could result in pleasure; debasing God's original creation of sexuality; laying unequal blame on Eve; or extenuating Adam's sin by making woman, rather than a disobedient will, the cause of his fall. Protestant Bible illustrations rarely show the Fall as fortunate even in a teleological sense. Title pages changed to avoid the implication; that of the 1535 English Bible (fig. 37) counterposes the Fall to the Resurrection, but even this hint of a *felix culpa* was absent from the 1537 edition (fig. 39), where the Fall is paired with the Crucifixion and Death with the Resurrection. Either pairing provides a redemptive view, but the latter treats the Fall as the cause of pain to humanity and suffering to Christ.[23] Pre-Reformation northern artists also show by compassionate realism that sin brings suffering and misery. In the Ghent Altarpiece, Adam—whether fallen or about to fall—is not deceived or sexually seduced. His eyes are full of dismal anguish. Hieronymous Bosch's paintings of the mockers of Christ repel the notion that sin humanizes. Around the utterly innocent sufferer, arrogant, sly, and sneering faces representing various sins express a terrifying glee in inflicting agony.

Northern artists also developed the topic of the sexual Fall, but in a way that mocks the participants by rendering it frivolous. In a 1511 woodcut by Hans Baldung Grien (Frye, fig. 191), Adam gazes at the fruit in Eve's hand while himself reaching into the tree behind her for another. But the obvious fruit is the one he already holds in his other hand: her breast. In the inset cut by Lucas Cranach illustrating Genesis 3 in the Luther Bible of 1541, Adam holds the fruit behind him, both gesture toward the Snake, and Eve speaks, her arm slung around Adam's shoulder in a casual, assured way intimating an erotic conspiracy. In Dürer's woodcut from the *Small Passion* (Nuremberg, 1511; Frye, fig. 218) Adam and Eve stand with their arms around each other and their legs crossed, giving an impression of careless arrogance. Adam looks slightly troubled as Eve takes fruit from the mouth of the crested snake, and the badger at their feet, symbol of the phlegmatic temperament, suggests moral sloth. In Lucas van Leyden's engraving of 1519, Adam and Eve hold three fruits—his, hers, and theirs; the serpent holds one as well; and Eve's body seems to be made of fruits—her breasts, her buttocks, her belly, even her heels. Jan Gossaert, known as Mabuse, produced several erotic Falls. One (Frye, fig. 157) is similar to those of Cranach and Dürer, but with Adam taking a fruit directly from the Serpent while Eve holds another; again they have their arms around each other and stand with crossed legs. Another (Frye, fig. 166), shows Adam and Eve seated with crossed legs while Eve reaches for the fruit and Adam reaches for Eve. In a painting in the British Royal Collection, Mabuse makes Adam and Eve spoiled adolescents. Their arms are around each other, the sly-looking Eve stands with crossed legs holding a bitten apple, and Adam has his finger in his mouth.[24] The frivolous fall climaxes in the drawings of Bartholomeus Spranger, where the fruit is a mere snack incidental to grappling limbs. In one, Adam nearly prevents Eve from picking it by his frenzied impetuosity.[25]

The vanity of the Fall is explicitly the topic of Pieter Claesz's *Vanity Still Life,* an example of a popular Dutch genre. Armor, books, an empty glass, a painter's palette, musical instruments, and the classical statue of a boy removing a thorn surround a *memento mori,* the skull and crossed bones; and below, an open sketchbook shows an imitation of Dürer's painting of a jocund Eve stepping blithely toward Adam (or us) with fruit in her hand.[26] For this artist, the *culpa* can render even art vain. In van Hoey's *Expulsion of Adam and Eve* an angel brandishes a flaming sword, but the immediate agent is a grinning skeleton. The infallible eye of Rembrandt in his 1638 etching (Frye, fig. 217) sees through the surface beauty usually granted Adam and Eve in the act of falling and gives them coarse, hunched bodies and closed, ignorant faces by which, in James Turner's perceptive words, "we are drawn into an intimate and disturbing mixture of compassion and revulsion." Rembrandt "has pushed beyond narrative consistency to the psychological core of 'fallenness,' manifested not only in the ugliness of Adam and Eve but in the shock, akin to the first opening of eyes in Genesis, with which we see their nakedness."[27] As Milton's narrator exclaims, "O how unlike / To that first naked Glory" (9.1114-15).

These versions do not suggest that sex is improved by sin. Of course, some viewers will find renderings of fatuous falls like Spranger's rather jolly. But the triflingness of their gestures conveys the message that Adam and Eve debased humanity and sexuality "since they / God's Image did not reverence in themselves." Milton avoids a false opposition of flesh and spirit by presenting pure and sensuous[28] passion and pleasure before the Fall, enjoyed by partners in whom the image shines of a glorious Maker who invented, commended, and blessed a world animated by "two great sexes" and full of beings with seeds within themselves of new life activated by *eros,* and whose very skies are globed and seeded with "male and female light." To suppose that for pleasure to be heightened, the rational and spiritual parts of being human have to be subjected is analogous to Satan's idea that for one person to rise another has to fall. Milton challenges us to imagine a deeper and keener pleasure in lovemaking harmonious with this cosmos than in lust that requires an affected "coyness" and guilt. Like Spranger, he shows Adam and Eve after the Fall in spiritually destitute "disport . . . The solace of their sin" (9.1042-43)—separated from God, love, thought of offspring, and the fructification of the earth—that breeds gross sleep from which they wake weary, angry, and ashamed. They have not found satisfaction, but poisoned the wellspring of life and brought immeasurable suffering into the world.

One may feel the impact of the frivolous fall if one juxtaposes Dürer's woodcut beginning the *Small Passion* with the thorn-crowned *Man of Sorrows* on its title page,[29] or Zacharias Dolendo's engraving of a drawing by Spranger (fig. 60) with Rembrandt's engraving of Christ healing the poor, or with Mathis Grünewald's *Crucifixion.* And one may contemplate the thorn-crowned Christ of the *Ecce Homo* painted with deep compassion by the Italian masters and read Herbert's meditation on Christ's suffering:[30]

> So sits the earths great curse in *Adams* fall
> Upon my head: so I remove it all
> From th' earth unto my brows, and bear the thrall:
> > Was ever grief like mine?

## Milton's Separation Scene, the Unfortunate Fall, and the Critique of Monotheism

By placing in Eden before the Fall scenes and motifs usually placed after it, Milton not only fills Paradise with opportunity but also dramatizes the principles of *Areopagitica* that sin cannot be avoided "by removing the matter of sin" and that to attempt to do so would remove the matter of virtue. "Suppose we could expell sin by this means, look how much we thus expell of sin, so much we expel of virtue: for the matter of them both is the same: remove that, and ye remove them both alike. This justifies the high providence of God, who, though he command us temperance, justice, continence, yet pours out before us even to a profuseness all desirable things, and gives us minds that can wander beyond all limit and satiety."[31]

One of the most misread of Milton's statements, in my teaching experience, is the important principle that the matter of sin and of virtue is the same. The point is not that good and evil coinhere—for Milton evil is "impossible to mix with blessedness"—or that one cannot have virtue without sin. It is, rather, that all created things, all experience, knowledge, and desire, are materials that can be used either for good or for evil. Sin and virtue are different ways of using this "matter." All the prelapsarian experiences sometimes seen as steps toward the Fall provide matter for virtue to work upon.[32] The forbidden tree is the visible emblem of this "matter." A neutral thing in itself (or a slight intoxicant), it acquires moral significance by its use or misuse. By being labeled "forbidden," this one piece of "matter" makes Adam and Eve conscious of the moral profundity of all choices. Unfallen, they have every opportunity to engage in the spiritual warfare of good and evil without doing evil. Their earnest, tender, sprightly, perplexed, honest, ebullient, brave, and vulnerable grapplings with providential profusions that engage them sensuously, imaginatively, emotionally, intellectually, ethically, and prayerfully prove how frivolous, fatuous, and violent evil is.

Just as Adam and Eve do not need a fall to make love or invent civilization, neither do they need one to get to heaven. "Improv'd by tract of time," Raphael tells them, "Your bodies may at last turn all to spirit . . . and wing'd ascend / Ethereal, as wee, or may at choice / Here or in Heav'nly Paradises dwell; / If ye be found obedient" (5.497-501). George Herbert had also expressed the latter belief:

> Before that sinne turn'd flesh to stone,
>     And all our lump to leaven;
> A fervent sigh might well have blown
>     Our innocent earth to heaven.

> For sure when Adam did not know
>     To sinne, or sinne to smother;
> He might to heav'n from Paradise go,
>     As from one room t'another.

What is fortunate is not the loss of this privilege but the fact that "Thou hast restor'd us to this ease / By this thy heav'nly bloud."[33]

That Adam and Eve might have been "improv'd by tract of time" applies especially to the last of Milton's transpositions, which brings into prelapsarian life an activity that only a bold imagination could place there: political controversy. Their discussion of "how that day they best may ply / Thir growing work" (9.201-2) concerns a Garden which God has made really to need their care. Eve's suggestion that they divide their labors "till Noon" (219)—a moderate span—balances individual and communal responsibility. The debate that follows, over the claims of security and freedom, concerns the arts of government and self-government, without which no other arts can prosper.

Whatever readers may think of Eve's departure from Adam, and however many patriarchal critics suppose it a feminine whim, Eve's reasons for it are not frivolous. The balancing of love and work—the two primordial commandments—is crucial stuff, and Eve's concern that their mutual delight should not distract them from taking care of the earth is a paradisal motive. Even if they might better have tempered these ingredients of virtue together, her argument that Satan should not dictate their form of government or hamper their volition and their deployment of creative energies is a paradisal opinion. As Robert Entzminger remarks, Adam and Eve "are as free to make false starts as they are to fall, but the former freedom, as it increases their knowledge of self and God, is actually a safeguard, though of course not an absolute bar, against the latter."[34] The arts of Eden developing in this scene are the arts of government of the self, the family, and the community. By showing Adam and Eve engaged in political debate before the Fall, Milton undercuts yet again the idea that civilization began with the Fall. Instead, the Fall interrupts the peaceful growth of human culture.

The government of a prelapsarian or regenerate community, which protects freedom for the development of virtue, differs from lapsarian law that must assume human beings unable to act responsibly on the basis of conscience. Powerful monarchies or societies whose structure limits mobility and choice are two answers to moral chaos. Milton proposed a kind of republic that made decisions by consultation and enacted as few laws as possible. The commonwealth he envisioned had citizens whose head was their creator, and who were therefore free to follow a rectified conscience.

Milton was well aware of the link between church and monarchy that James I had succinctly characterized: no bishop, no king. He sharply distinguished that link from the relation between godliness and goodness that unites a regenerate community: much faith, much freedom. By means of the separation scene in *Paradise Lost* Milton demonstrates the relation of liberty to monotheism. As long as Adam and Eve trust the "Maker wise" (9.338) they are free because the choices of their paradisal consciences are moved by love. When Eve grants the Serpent more authority than God, she becomes an idolatress, first of the snake and then of the tree. Adam, in turn, becomes an idolator of Eve, the Serpent, and tree. By bowing to lesser authorities than their Creator they lose their inward freedom, become dependent (like Caliban) on an allegedly magical drug for "knowledge," and fall under the power of their archenemy. In the separation scene, Milton forfends the present critique of monotheism.[35]

As founding father and mother of the race, Adam and Eve have to work out the rudiments of everything that will affect it, including government. Their colloquy, in the pattern of a multiple rather than a binary dialectic, recapitulates in prelapsarian form the controversies of the early Christian church and their violent reemergence in the British civil wars.

In *Adam, Eve, and the Serpent* Elaine Pagels presents a narrative history of the related issues of sexuality and freedom in Christianity through the time of Augustine and his opponents. At its center is the question, "Are human beings capable of governing themselves?" Pagels argues that "the majority of Christian converts of the first four centuries regarded the proclamation of moral freedom, grounded in Genesis 1-3, as effectively synonymous with 'the gospel.'" The roots of this freedom are refusal unto death to bow to the idols of imperial Rome, and moral self-government, expressed especially in sexual chastity—privileging celibacy, but also honoring marital fidelity—in contrast to the promiscuity and the sexual exploitation of slaves and children in pagan society. The early church's principles of "sexual self-restraint, sharing one's goods with the destitute, and living with people of all races ... appealed especially ... to those people most vulnerable to sexual abuse, financial exploitation, poverty, and racial hatred." Out of the agonies of Jewish and Christian martyrs came "a new vision of the basis of social and political order" that was to transform the Western world:

> an order no longer founded upon the divine claims of the ruler of the state, but upon qualities that Christians believed were inherent within every man, and, some dared insist, within every woman as well, through our common creation 'in God's image.'
> ... [T]he Christian movement popularized the Hebrew creation story that implicitly asserted the intrinsic value of every human being; and throughout the Roman Empire, despite the Christians' criminal status and the consequent dangers that threatened them, the movement flourished. Tertullian even made the unprecedented claim that every human being has a right to religious liberty:

> It should be considered absurd for one person to compel
> another to honor the gods, when he should voluntarily,
> and in the awareness of his own need, seek their favor *in
> the liberty which is his right.*

In centuries to come, others would infuse into the creation
story even bolder moral visions and insist, for example, that
human creation "in the image of God" not only conveys
"unalienable rights" but also extends to people of every
race, to slaves, to women, and, some would argue, to defective infants, or even to the unborn.

After the conversion of Constantine and the consequent alliance of
church and state, with its perhaps inevitable corruptions, Augustine
came to doubt that baptism washed away sin sufficiently for self-
government to work. Observing these corruptions, his own inability
fully to govern his passionate flesh, and the fact that innocent infants
are sometimes born deformed and subjected to suffering, Augustine
concluded that the fall of Adam had radically altered human nature
and the nature of the whole creation. We are all born with "original
sin," and after baptism this defect of will persists, so that even converts
need external government.[36]

The debate of Adam and Eve in *Paradise Lost* is essentially about
moral self-government, and Eve's position resembles that of the early
church. Milton accepted the doctrine of original sin, and agreed that
"guiltiness is taken away in those who are regenerate, while original
sin remains."[37] But he had a more radical concept of regeneration than
Augustine's: one that includes nothing less than the full renovation of
the will to its prelapsarian liberty, even while "original sin remains,"
because by grace the regenerate are enabled to overcome the thorns in
the flesh and choose good. That effort is laborious. Although "Christ
has redeemed all trangressors, . . . he purifies only such as are zealous
of good works, that is, believers; for no works are good, unless done
in faith."[38] Many people prefer not to make the effort at all, and those
who do need caution against pride and against underestimating the
difficulties; in *An Apology for Smectymnuus* Milton accuses the Remon-
strant of ascribing to himself " 'that temper of the affections,' which
cannot anywhere be but in Paradise."[39] Nevertheless, those who respond to renewal and calling by seeking knowledge of God receive "*supernatural renovation,*" the intent of which is not only to restore the
power of the natural faculties "to form right judgement, and to exercise free will," but also "to create afresh, as it were, the inward man,
and infuse from above new and supernatural faculties into the minds
of the renovated. This is called *regeneration,*" which is

*that change operated by the Word and the Spirit, whereby the old man being destroyed, the inward man is regenerated by God after his own image, in all the faculties of his mind, insomuch that he becomes as it were a new creature, and the whole man is sanctified both in body and soul, for the service of God, and the performance of good works.*

*Is regenerated by God;* namely, the Father; for no one generates, except the Father.

*In all the faculties of his mind;* that is to say, in understanding and will. This renewal can mean nothing, but a restoration to its former liberty.

The ensuing process of repentance and faith has two effects: "the comprehension of spiritual things" and "*love or charity, arising from a sense of the divine love shed abroad in the hearts of the regenerate by the Spirit, whereby those who are ingrafted in Christ being influenced, become dead to sin, and alive again unto God, and bring forth good works spontaneously and freely.* This is also called *holiness.*" Regeneration is accompanied by "spiritual increase," which "unlike physical growth, appears to be to a certain degree in the power of the regenerate themselves," and although perfection is "not to be expected in the present life," yet "it is our duty to strive after it with earnestness." The process continues with justification, adoption, union with Christ and the invisible Church, and "imperfect glorification," in which "we are filled with a *consciousness of present grace and excellency, as well as with an expectation of future glory, insomuch that our blessedness is in a manner already begun.* . . . This assurance of salvation produces a joy unspeakable."[40]

Milton, then, agrees with Augustine that the whole of humankind (as I believe he meant by the word "men") was enslaved to sin by the Fall, but he believes that the wills of regenerate believers can, with their cooperation, be restored and that self-government gives the will the exercise it needs for restoration. For these reasons, he argues in *Areopagitica* that parliament should not enact laws that limit spiritual liberty, even though those who have not responded to renovation and calling will misuse or neglect that freedom. That is, he applies the attitudes of many in the pre-Augustinian church to the state as well.

In the separation debate (9.205-375), Adam and Eve take positions that, in innocent form, delineate the debates over church government in both Augustine's time and Milton's. For Adam, the presence of evil makes necessary external support: "Subtle he needs must be, who could seduce / Angels, nor think superfluous others' aid." For Eve, who is closer to Augustine's opponents, "what is Faith, Love, Virtue unassay'd / Alone, without exterior help sustain'd?" Adam thinks that moral support requires a social structure that operates continuously

to protect members from individual exposure to temptation. Eve
thinks that such a structure would hinder what Milton called "spiritual
increase." Adam agrees that "within [oneself] / The danger lies, yet
lies within his power," for "God left free the will"; but to avert un-
wariness and fraud, "tender love enjoins, / That I should mind thee
oft, and mind thou me." Yet in the end, he subscribes to the principles
of Milton's own arguments for the freedom of the regenerate, of
which Adam and Eve are the unfallen model, lest "trial unsought may
find / Us both securer than thus warn'd thou seem'st."[41]

Both, I think, are right. The problem is one of the *timing* of external
support. To require it continually, as Adam intends at first, puts one in
"a perpetual childhood of prescription." To neglect to give or seek aid
under actual temptation—which defrauds the will—puts the tempted
in mortal danger. Perhaps Adam erred in not setting up a contingency
plan for consultation in case of need; certainly Eve erred in not con-
sulting Adam before she ate the fruit. The debate itself, and its resolution in Eve's moral freedom, is part of the prelapsarian process of
working out the government of the human race. After the Fall, this
gentle, consultative government will be replaced, as Michael predicts,
not just by prescriptive ecclesiastical institutions, not just by corruptible monarchies, but by hideous tyrannies. *Paradise Lost* and its defense
of monotheism do not, as some critics have ahistorically contended,
support monarchy, but an educated and vigilant conscience which no
human power may, and divine power will not, coerce.

The separation scene may have arisen initially out of a theological
problem. Contemplating various interpretations of the Fall, including
Calvin's, Milton like any artist had numerous choices to make. He
agreed with Calvin[42] that for Adam to be present and stand silently by
during the temptation of Eve "is by no manner of meanse credible."
But he disagreed that "before such time as the woman had tasted of
the fruit" she "insnared her husband with the same baites where with
she her selfe was deceived." This concept, displayed in much iconography, was a part of the rejection of an erotic Fall and of a pusillani-
mous shifting of guilt by men onto women in order to shirk
responsibility. But Calvin's scenario impugns as much stupidity and
cowardice to Adam as the one he rejects. If Eve has not eaten when she
tempts Adam, his only motive is disbelief in God and secondhand belief in the Serpent: theologically sound, but dramatically unconvincing
in a poem that had portrayed Adam and Eve as constantly conscious of
God's gifts and worthy of their callings. Instead, Milton invented a
complex of motives that preserves Calvin's sense that Adam did not
frivolously succumb to Eve's "alluring enticements," but to Satan's ar-

guments for disbelief and "pestilent ambition" conveyed through her; and at the same time shows that both Adam and Eve fell not through vanity but by acceding to perverse uses of "matter" they had hitherto used well. To preserve Adam's dignity, Milton needed to contrive a separate fall for Eve; but to preserve Eve's dignity he needed to make that separation a potentially virtuous act. In view of his high opinion of God's image in them, he needed to present separate falls without showing either Adam or Eve to be vain, stupid, cowardly, sexually intemperate, or inordinately ambitious before she or he ate the forbidden fruit, because otherwise the divine image in them would be laughably feeble and their unfallen life could not offer a model for recovering a paradisal conscience. To achieve the motivation of a pair who are genuinely and interestingly good before the Fall and genuinely depraved by it, Milton wrote the separation debate.

I have already argued lengthily that the separation scene does not need to be read as a prologue to an inevitable Fall.[43] Milton gives both Eve and Adam better reasons for Eve's departure than anyone else had; Eve's desire to devote her whole attention to her work for a morning is an obedient impulse that contrasts utterly to motives usually given her; and the scene enacts a confrontation, which all human beings, families, and governments must face, with the problem of how to deal with evil without doing evil or limiting the liberty to do good. Milton turns the theological problem into an opportunity to dramatize within the poem the political problem he had wrestled with in his prose. His handling of it demonstrates Milton's generosity toward human potentialities in both Adam and Eve and shows—to apply to Milton Abdiel's description of the Author of that author—"of our good, and of our dignity / How provident he is" (5.827-28).

Eve's motion to divide their labors does not rest on grounds of efficiency or self-sufficiency. Both are unparadisal ideas—though celerity, alacrity, spontaneity, and exuberance are characteristic of holy activity. It rests on grounds of temperance and sufficiency. Eve and Adam "commune how that day they best [not "most efficiently"] may ply / Thir growing work" and "tend Plant, Herb, and Flow'r" (9.201-2, 206). They have a lavishly diversified creation to take care of. God created it needing their care, for reasons provident of their minds and characters. Eve has observed, as have Adam and Raphael, that their mutual delight, which is one of the best parts of that creation, can usurp their attention from the rest, just as the best angel fell; and to neglect the harmony of creatures, and the individuality of each, would damage their own love too. When the wellspring of "all the Charities" forgets charity it grows stagnant. Eve suggests that they maintain the balance by a morning's concentration on their interesting tasks. When Adam raises his just concern for their safety she poses the question not of self-sufficiency but of carnal dependency—of which self-sufficiency is a branch—as opposed to reliance on God and educated virtue. Eve says that her sufficiency is not derived from herself alone but endowed by her "Maker wise" and strengthened by Adam's "reasoning words." She argues that one should be able to be virtuous "without exterior help sustain'd." She has overheard this entirely Miltonic sentiment being voiced by Raphael and, as Diana Treviño Benet has ably argued,[44] learned it from Raphael's account of Abdiel's singular fidelity (5.803-907). But she does not reject the *interior* help of Adam's education or God's voice. She does not, here, refute God's command or Adam's benevolent authority, but Satan's ability to institute government by fear and dam the flow of charity and truth merely by existing.

What Adam and Eve decide to do about Satan has long-term implications. The immortal evil spirit is not likely to give up because he finds them together on the first try. Supposing they stave off temptation for now, what will happen when their eldest sons conceive their natural but separate interests in plants and animals, or agriculture and husbandry? Will the first parents deny their children all independent exploration, meditation, and mystical, ecological, and artistic leadings of the Spirit into the wilderness, albeit of sweets, lest the Tempter lurk?

Adam and Eve in the separation debate face the same problem we all do: how to live and govern in a world containing powerful evil without letting evil hamper the flow of goodness.[45] Their discussion is uneven, sometimes deflected by vulnerable sensibilities and tentative ideas. They are mature but still growing beings, and new growth is tender. But Milton, granting them that, attributes to both Eve and Adam a serious consideration of their numerous wholesome responsibilities, and so more dignity and burgeoning goodness than anyone else had granted them before or since, including most interpreters of this scene.

With regard to Eve's motives, Milton is not merely not as bad as his predecessors and even his followers. His account is radically rehabilitating. Of the many speculations other writers put forward about Eve's separation from Adam, a common and thoroughly misogynous one was that the forbiddenness of the tree was exactly what attracted her—a variant of the Kerrigan-Braden thesis about lust. Not only pre-Miltonic versions like, for example, Giovanni Francesco Loredano's *Life of Adam*,[46] but a commentary otherwise clearly indebted to Milton holds this view: Eve goes off to the tree because "it is awakening the curiosity of a Woman to forbid her anything."[47] In *Paradise* Eve becomes fascinated with forbiddenness in the process of falli (9.753-55), not before. Just as Milton moves soul-building experience usually thought postlapsarian to the scenes before the Fall, he moves pejorative motifs that elsewhere turn up before the Fall to passages during or after it.

In the "Argument" to Book 9 of *Paradise Lost,* "*Eve* loath to be thought not circumspect or firm enough, urges her going apart, the rather desirous to make trial of her strength." I am not sure how much weight to give Milton's "arguments"; certainly the poetry speedily outgrows these rather impatient summaries. In the poem Eve does not go off on purpose to gaze at the forbidden tree or look for Satan. When he sees her she is tending the Garden, as promised, and, absorbed in her work, she has forgotten all about him: a dangerous omission, but not a case of looking for trouble. She does not tell Adam she wants to try her strength in single combat with Satan; she asks "What is Faith, Love, Virtue unassay'd / Alone, without superior help sustain'd," but that question applies to all her daily "assaying" of these qualities, which by their very nature must continue, in the absence of their object and witness, to be themselves. But even if we are to suppose that Eve desires to make trial of her strength, an Eve loath to be thought not circumspect still looks good by comparison with those who merely want forbidden fruit. If Milton really wanted us to believe that Eve is looking for trouble, however, he need hardly have bothered writing the separation debate; and if he addressed his "Argument" to the expectations of misogynous readers, he defeated those expectations by giving Eve motives more provident of her dignity and of the well-being of the earth.

This providence applies to the fact of the separation as well as the motives. Neither are mere plot devices, but part of a just distribution of worth and blame. If Adam had succumbed to Satan's persuasion, transmitted by Eve, before she had eaten—and on the first day of their lives, as Calvin and most commentators thought—what faith, love, virtue, or intelligence could he ever have had? All he needed to do to save the human race was dissuade her. He would not have the emotional or doctrinal dilemma provided by an Eve already fallen. Milton does not, however, extenuate Adam's sin by this dilemma. On the contrary, his defection deprives both him and Eve of his opportunity to present Eve to God for a cure rather than involve the whole human race in sin.

Adam's fall does not happen until he not only believes or says he believes the Serpent's lies but reconstructs them for himself

(9.926-51), apparently thinking that the snake has actually eaten the fruit and learned logic from it, and expecting "Proportional ascent, which cannot be / But to be Gods, or Angels Demi-gods" (936-37). In this way Milton dramatizes Adam's voluntary "pestilent ambition." Nevertheless, an Eve already fallen makes his fall in part a tragic perversion of his goodness: his love, his loyalty, his sense of union with Eve, which she has broken, not by mere physical separation but by Satan's perversion of her misplaced trust. Milton does not attribute Adam's fall to lust, but to failure to trust God's providence, in spite of considerable experience of it, and to Satanic exploitation of tender, growing goodness. In the course of showing Adam and Eve falling separately, Milton does what artists did by showing them falling together: he gives both of them responsibility and culpability. But the Eve and the Adam who fall in *Paradise Lost* have much lost dignity to regain.

Having so far rehabilitated the man as to give him mixed motives, some of which are perversions of splendid virtues, Milton would have risked making the woman slyer and more presumptuous than Calvin had done, if he had not provided the separation dialogue to show that she did not seek out the tree because of mindless female willfulness, but for two good reasons: to respond to one of her callings and to preserve the foundation of mutual trust and trustworthiness on which any spiritually and culturally thriving community has to be built. The facts that she first underestimates the wiles of the enemy and then breaks trust with God and Adam do not prove that goodness is impossible or freedom wrong. Milton is writing a story for people who want to do the right thing, to keep faith, to follow the vocations God calls them to in a world where evil in disguise keeps its "couchant watch" ready to pounce (4.403-8), and he tells us that if we think it is going to be easy to avoid doing wrong we are much mistaken. But he also teaches that we cannot avoid doing wrong at the cost of prohibitions that impede the perpetual progression of goodness through the whole creation, because that is a wrong in itself.

Adam and Eve do not fall, then, out of petty willfulness or appetite but in the midst of discovery and activity in which the reality of evil is one consideration among others blessedly blissful. Milton shows developing humankind in need of communion and counsel—indeed, Eve begins her suggestion about the day's work with that point. But he had spent his life in defense of the relation between a free and active conscience and the Holy Spirit. He fought all ascendencies of "carnal precedence" over "spiritual dignity."[48] He believed that where the Spirit reigns, government can be light and laws few. He had seen the

government he supported become censorious and legalistic. He knew
how easy it is for good people, in the spirit of righteousness, to sub-
stitute fences, over which evil might lightly leap, for openness to
grace. And he gave these perceptions, in his poem, to a woman.

At the end of the poem, the archangel Michael says of the church—
of which Adam and Eve, and especially Eve, are the type—that "griev-
ous Wolves" will appropriate to themselves "The Spirit of God,
promis'd alike and giv'n / To all Believers" and will force laws not given
by God on "every conscience" by means of "carnal power":

> What will they then
> But force the Spirit of Grace itself, and bind
> His consort Liberty; what, but unbuild
> His living Temples, built by Faith to stand,
> Thir own Faith, not another's.
>
> (12.508-28)

It is not Adam's power over Eve that is in question in the separation
scene but Satan's power to force and bind. Eve does not, unfortunately, live up to her good intentions, but she is wise enough to see
that Satan could subtly unbuild God's living temples from within by
substituting "specious forms" for free faith. How remarkable it is of
Milton to provide her such a grasp of the dilemma of all who want to
be creatively and bravely faithful, how encouraging that he creates an
Eve interested in active faith, love, and virtue. Just as Adam has more
to lose in the Fall than lesser Adams, Eve has more to lose than lesser
Eves. And just as Adam has more to regain, so does Eve. Milton gives
Eve the initiative in responding to the Judgment when she asks Adam's forgiveness, in a scene anticipated by van den Broeck (fig. 19),
and thus contributing to Adam's understanding of their opportunities
and of the generosity of reconciliation.

At the end of the separation scene, Adam addresses Eve's concerns
in his final admonition with its important conditional and subjunctive
clause:[49] "If thou think, trial unsought may find / Us both securer than
thus warn'd thou seem'st, / Go." That is a deft piece of teaching in response to Eve's overconfidence in their safety; she *is* too secure, and by
attributing to her an awareness of that danger, he offers that awareness
to her. He continues: "Go in thy native innocence, rely / On what [that
which] thou hast of virtue, summon all." She is sufficient, "For God
towards thee hath done his part"; but she has to use those gifts: "do
thine" (9.370-75). On that, they agree.

Eve does not summon all. Most unfortunately, she does not
summon Adam. Had she continued her calm correction of Satan's

slanders, and when she became perplexed gone to Adam for counsel, she would have justified her own arguments for uncloistered virtue. Her plea for freedom for spontaneous charitable works is right, but her unilateral decision to take an action that will affect the whole of humanity is wrong. Once Satan had said "Do not believe" (9.684) and misbegotten new conceptions, she should have reopened the dialogue with Adam.

Eve's failure to use what she has of virtue and knowledge—not her desire to preserve for the human family the opportunity to use them—is the beginning of sin, and that includes failure to admit being puzzled and needing consultation, a familiar form of intellectual pride. That failure does not invalidate the motive of keeping an open society, an open church, and an open heart. Until Eve fails, and Adam fails in his turn, Milton provides both with a complexly textured unfallen moral beauty that far surpasses any other granted to them, either penned or limned, and that fosters the recuperation of wisdom and justice in any age or condition. We are a good creation, he tells us, with a frightful capacity to do wrong if we let the forces of destruction trivialize us, but also a larger capacity than we dare acknowledge to be put right.

Whether one interprets the separation scene as the first step toward the Fall, as is so often done,[50] or as an important step in prelapsarian development in which Adam and Eve discuss the art of government, and so establish another major area of mutual creativity, it does not support the idea of a fortunate fall. Either the dream and the separation dialogue show a perfect emotional, ethical, and spiritual union coming apart, or they show a developing emotional, ethical, and spiritual union growing deeper and stronger. In neither case does the breach with God effect an improvement.

## Final Remedy

The highest example of Milton's habit of placing all kinds of useful experience before the Fall is Raphael's account of the Exaltation of the Son. This event, chronologically the first in the epic, suggests by analogy that the Messiah's Incarnation does not depend on the Fall, just as his Begetting does not depend on the fall of the angels, who fall in reaction to it out of grumpy pride. As Dennis Danielson points out, Adam has heard the story of the proclamation of Messiah before he falls;[51] so, I might add, has Eve.

Danielson has thoroughly and percipiently analyzed the so-called paradox of the fortunate fall, surveyed its proponents and opponents in both seventeenth-century religious controversy and twentieth-century criticism, scrutinized its application to Milton, and found it wanting. Adam's supposed *felix culpa* speech (12.469-84), in which A. O. Lovejoy thought he had found the key to the poem,[52] is, like Adam, full of doubts, and Michael's reply and Adam's own modifications caution us against too simple an agreement. As Danielson argues, "If God needed the Fall in order to reveal what Lovejoy calls 'the plenitude of the divine goodness and power' (p. 164), then Milton's careful avoidance of absolute predestination, his assertion of free will and its reflection of the divine image, his defense of free will against different forms of determinism, his exquisite presentation of sinless paradisal human existence—virtually his whole justification of the ways of God—all turn out to be little more than a useless façade over the nightmare abyss of 'divine' intentions." But in fact God's goodness, including the benefits of the Incarnation, is not in any way dependent on sin. "Sin is no *conditio sine qua non* of soul making, and Adam is shown that, too. It may well be that in some sense the Fall occasions more glory to God than there would otherwise be; but as John Goodwin says, even though sin is 'contriveable to [God's] glory,' it is 'no wayes requisite or necessary hereunto.' And likewise for Milton, the Fall was no *felix culpa.*"[53] It certainly is not contrivable to the glory of man.

Milton parodies the fortunate fall when Satan on his gaudy throne in hell utters a forthrightly specious version of it: "From this descent / Celestial Virtues rising, will appear / More glorious and more dread than from no fall" (2.14-16). One passage in *Paradise Lost,* however, raises the question of a fortunate fall more seriously than Adam's doubt-full rejoicing at the end of Book 12. After the repentance of Adam and Eve, when "Prevenient Grace descending had remov'd / The stony from thir hearts, and made new flesh / Regenerate grow instead" (11.3-5), the Son offers their prayers to the Father, saying,

> See Father, what first fruits on Earth are sprung
> From thy implanted Grace in Man, these Sighs
> And Prayers, which in the Golden Censer, mixt
> With Incense, I thy Priest before thee bring,
> Fruits of more pleasing savor from thy seed
> Sown with contrition in his heart, than those
> Which his own hand manuring all the Trees
> Of Paradise could have produc't, ere fall'n
> From innocence.
>
>                                            (11.22-30)

Like his earlier speech on grace (3.144-49), this one contains considerable celestial wordplay, including the etymological pun of "his own hand manuring" and the extended metaphor of fruit, a laden figure. Like Milton's other heavenly scenes, it rehabilitates the liturgy he had found too carnal in its earthly uses. It occurs at the emotional climax of the poem: the offering of repentance on which all else hangs. Its theme is bringing good out of evil, and it seems to suggest a *felix culpa*.

Read literally, of course, its says merely that the spiritual fruit of "Sighs / And Prayers" is better than the material fruit of earthly trees. But read metaphorically, if the Garden represents all the virtues of original righteousness, the passage suggests that repentant prayers are more pleasing to God than innocent good works. Two reasons suggest themselves. One is that to rejoice more for the recovery of the prodigal child than for the quality of not having been lost is part of divine and human compassion; and in this case the whole world's welfare depends on repentance once the Fall has occurred. Another is that God's "implanted Grace" is better than Adam's "own hand." Yet Adam and Eve before the Fall are not just cultivating trees or even virtues; they are already "Reaping immortal fruits of joy and love" (3.67). If they remain upright

> God will deign
> To visit oft the dwellings of just Men
> Delighted, and with frequent intercourse
> Thither will send his winged Messengers
> On errands of supernal Grace.
>                                   (7.569-73)

Nothing before the Fall has impeded influxes of divine grace, and nothing in the Fall makes humans more permeable to it. Grace is part of God's nature, and he gives himself freely. Grace implanted in man bears better fruit than even righteous works alone, with or without a fall.

What Milton does in the Son's speech, it seems to me, is to detach the "felix" from the "culpa" while keeping both. The powerful feelings of gratitude and love expressed in the *felix culpa* tradition are preserved, but the focus is transferred from the fault to the grace that moves Adam and Eve to repent. The point of the passage is not that sin is the cause of redemption, but that grace enables repentance, and repentance is cause for joy. It is because the Fall is so horrible, not because it is in any way happy, that the repentance is so moving. The regenerate prayers of Adam and Eve are "more pleasing" because on them depends the openness to redemption and regeneration of the whole creation. If they had not fallen, God's "implanted Grace" might have produced works "more pleasing" in other ways. Since they did, this moment transforms everything that has gone before, and the whole prelapsarian life of Adam and Eve becomes preparation for regeneration.

The Son's compassionate speech ends with his renewed offer of atonement by his own death, and the Father concurs, but also decrees the Expulsion in words that make no concession to a fortunate fall.

> Those pure immortal Elements that know
> No gross, no unharmonious mixture foul,
> Eject [Man] tainted now, and purge him off
> As a distemper, gross to air as gross,
> And mortal food, as may dispose him best
> For dissolution wrought by Sin, that first
> Distemper'd all things, and of incorrupt
> Corrupted.

Having lost happiness, humankind must also relinquish earthly immortality, which now would serve only "to eternize woe; / Till I provided Death." Death, preveniently laid by and now unleashed, becomes

> His final remedy, and after Life
> Tri'd in sharp tribulation, and refin'd
> By Faith and faithful works, to second Life,
> Wak't in the renovation of the just,
> Resigns him up with Heav'n and Earth renew'd.
> (11.50-66)

Life without justice and purgation would eternize the greed and solipsism of the Fall. But at the last, "eating Death," having done his work, will resign his victims up, now truly awake, in the renovation of both earth and heaven.

We need, then, to make careful distinctions. Evil, Milton says in his invocation before Raphael's great creation poem, is "impossible to mix / With Blessedness" (7.58-59). But after the Fall, the two must be sorted like Psyche's seeds, with the complication that they wear each other's colors. Death comes masked in pleasure, and life wears the fiery coat of affliction. This "sharp tribulation" promotes the process of rebirth. As the world now is, we know good by evil;[54] it takes dialectic to order our intellects and pain to knock open our souls. Although Milton and other poets of his time regarded neither the Fall nor the suffering that results as fortunate, they had much to say about useful ways of responding to adversity.[55] In Herbert's "Love Unknown,"[56] it is medicine to renew, supple, and quicken the sufferer to a state nearer that of Milton's Adam and Eve in Paradise, since God *"fain would have you be new, tender, quick."* But regenerative views of sin and death are not the same as a *felix culpa.* For seventeenth-century writers, the Fall is not the beginning of civilization but the unleashing of death, and death is not, as for Wallace Stevens,[57] "the mother of beauty" but the slave that sweeps up the offal of blight. In the end, death is powerless except to eat up "draff," including itself.

Milton sees everything as matter for love—the *matter* of good and evil is the same—but he does not let us forget the suffering sin causes to guilty and innocent alike. The psalmist's counsel, "fret not thyself because of evildoers" but "trust in the Lord, and do good" (Ps. 37:1-3) is not complacency in the face of evil. The problem Milton broaches, especially in the separation scene, is how to "trust in the Lord, and do good," how to fight evil with faith and goodness rather than with evil, the problem confronted tragically in *Hamlet* and hopefully in *The Tempest,* displayed in *Samson Agonistes,* and resolved by a lucent exemplar in *Paradise Regained,* who raises Eden in the wilderness without "eating Death."

For Milton, Death "to the faithful" is "the Gate of Life" (12.571), but "the Sin-born Monster" Death himself sheds no beauty or paradoxical life on living things, all the plenitude of which "too little seems / To stuff this Maw, this vast unhide-bound Corpse," though his "incestuous Mother" gives him "Herbs, and Fruits, and Flow'rs . . . each Beast . . . and Fish, and Fowl," and begins to infect the Race of Man and "season him thy last and sweetest prey"(10.596-609). The intentionally ugly response of the Almighty lays bare the difference between a fortunate fall and a blessed renewal:

> See with what heat these Dogs of Hell advance
> To waste and havoc yonder World, which I
> So fair and good created, and had still
> Kept in that state, had not the folly of Man
> Let in those wasteful Furies, who . . .
> . . . know not that I call'd and drew them thither
> My hell-hounds, to lick up the draff and filth
> Which man's polluting Sin with taint hath shed
> On what was pure, till cramm'd and gorg'd, nigh burst
> With suckt and glutted offal, at one sling
> Of thy victorious Arm, well-pleasing Son,
> Both *Sin,* and *Death,* and yawning *Grave* at last

Through *Chaos* hurl'd, obstruct the mouth of Hell
For ever, and seal up his ravenous Jaws.
Then Heav'n and Earth renew'd shall be made pure
To sanctity that shall receive no stain:
Till then the Curse pronounc't on both precedes.
(10.616-40)

Milton's God distinguishes between Death's horrible nature and his unwitting service. Just such a distinction divides the infection of evil from the good that can be wrested from it by grace and pain. When that is accomplished, the Judge shall receive the faithful into bliss,

Whether in Heav'n or Earth, for then the Earth
Shall all be Paradise, far happier place
Than this of *Eden,* and far happier days.
(12.463-65)

Sin and Death have not increased this bliss, but have wrought the devastation out of which it must rise. Since grace is boundless, "happier days" would have appeared without them; now it takes the paths it finds.

## NOTES

1. Stevie Davies, *Feminine Reclaimed,* 246-47.
2. Traherne, *Christian Ethicks,* 6.187 in *Thomas Traherne,* 2:187.
3. Herbert, "Sighs and Grones," in *Works,* 83.
4. Danielson, *Milton's Good God,* chap. 7 passim and 226-27.
5. Trapp, "Iconography of the Fall," 230-31.
6. The idea that opposite potentialities are inherent in the material of creation is explored in different ways by Heninger, *Touches of Sweet Harmony;* Lieb, *Dialectics of Creation,* "Prolegomena"; Swaim, *Before and After the Fall,* chap. 2; and Schwartz, *Remembering and Repeating,* chap. 1. Rajan sums it up in *Lofty Rhyme,* chap. 5, esp. 59.
7. Michael Lieb explains Milton's dialectical approach to the postlapsarian search for truth in the introduction to *Dialectics of Creation,* and finds that "the 'systematic oppositions' of conventional dialectics appear as dramatic events in *Paradise Lost.* The argument builds on Kenneth Burke's definition of dialectics as the 'interplay of various factors that mutually modify one another, and may be thought of as voices in a dialogue or roles in a play, with each voice or role in its partiality contributing to the development of the whole" (6-7). The kind of dialectic that takes account of multiple mutually modifying factors is compatible with what I have called paradisal consciousness. Swaim discusses Milton's use of dichotomizing "lapsarian" logic in *Before and After*

*the Fall,* chap. 3, finding binary opposites and a fortunate fall, but adds that Adam and Eve had the opportunity of a "traumaless working of body up to spirit rather than the crisis of the felix culpa" (231).

8. For Milton sin results in spiritual death, which consists first in the obscuring of "that right reason which enabled man to discern the chief good" and second in "that deprivation of righteousness and liberty to do good, and in that slavish subjection to sin and the devil, which constitutes, as it were, the death of the will" (*De Doctrina Christiana,* 12, in *SM,* 999). The tenth of the *Articles of Religion,* "Of free-will," also makes the loss of free will consequent upon sin. Historically, Christians have had varying attitudes toward the degree to which free will is restored by repentance and grace. In *Adam, Eve, and the Serpent* Pagels traces these differences from the apostolic church through Augustine and his opponents.

9. "O certe necessarium ade peccatum et nostrum quod christi morte deletum est. O felix culpa que talem ac tantum meruit habere redemptorem" (Legg, *Sarum Missal*). The translation is from Warren, *Sarum Missal in English,* 1:271. The phrase "and of ourselves [*et nostram*]" was not used in the Roman Missal. The sin of Eve is an "infelix culpa" in the sequence for Easter Day (Legg, 467), and the Exultet rejoices that the "debt of Adam" was "blotted out" by Christ's "holy blood" (Warren, 271).

10. "Adam lay ibounden," in R. T. Davies, *Medieval English Lyrics,* 160-61.

11. Victor Yelverton Haines gives a history and explanation of the *felix culpa* tradition in the first chapter of *The Fortunate Fall of Sir Gawain.*

12. Keats, letter to George and Georgiana Keats (21 April, 1819), in *Letters,* 2:102: "Call the world if you Please 'The vale of Soul-making'. . . . How . . . are these sparks which are God to have identity given them—so as ever to possess a bliss peculiar to each one's individual existence? How, but by the medium of a world like this?"

13. Herbert, "Easter-wings," in *Works,* 43. The "if" is crucial to Herbert's thought.

14. *Areopagitica,* in *SM,* 737.

15. Kerrigan and Braden, "Milton's Coy Eve," 49. The essay promotes the idea that forbiddenness makes a thing more desirable, which Milton ascribes to fallen and, as yet, unregenerate Eve. By making "amorous delay" the purpose of Edenic activity, the article reduces Eve's prelapsarian modesty to an aphrodisiac, and Eve to a perpetual temptress, on the assumption that women's sexual reticence is an offering to male desire. I would argue that when unfallen Adam and Eve are emparadised in one another's arms, their bliss is complete because they also make room in their lives to interact in many other ways, none forbidden, so that sexual temperance—not just "coyness"— enhances sexual love while promoting other kinds of understanding and accomplishment.

Kerrigan and Braden mitigate the impression left by "Milton's Coy Eve" in their expansion of it in *The Idea of the Renaissance,* chap. 10, by adding a passage showing that "sexual pleasure is one of the first victims of guilt" (214).

But their statement that "Miltonic love is ultimately about the determination of female worth" (211) remains.

16. On Augustine's theories of innocent sexuality (which he thought would have been practiced if there had been no fall) and on the pleasure of prelapsarian lovemaking had it occurred, see Turner, *One Flesh*, chap. 2.

17. Richard Du Rocher expertly illuminates this process in Milton's comparisons of Eve with figures of classical myth, in *Milton and Ovid*.

18. Robels, *Niederlandische Zeichenungen*, fig. 21.

19. On the "Good temptation" see *De Doctrina Christiana* 1.8, in *CM*, 15:87-89. Like everything else, temptation "est autem mala vel bona" (cf. Augustine).

20. Samuel, *"Paradise Lost,"* 237-38.

21. J. M. Evans discusses this view in *"Paradise Lost" and the Genesis Tradition*, 278-80. I obviously disagree with his conclusion that "Eve's moral defection took place when she decided to leave Adam" (280).

22. In Milton's famous list of sins in *De Doctrina Christiana* 1.11, the Fall "comprehended at once distrust in the divine veracity . . . unbelief" and numerous others, equally attributed to Adam and Eve (*SM*, 997).

23. The juxtaposition of the Creation of Eve with the Crucifixion is more clearly regenerative, as in the *Biblia Pauperum* (Henry, *Biblia Pauperum*, 97), which expresses deep love both for the Creator and his creation and for the suffering Christ who redeems what he has made.

24. Reproduced in Paul Lambotte, *Flemish Painting*, pl. 53.

25. Paris, Louvre, inv. no. 20461; Harvard, photo collection. Another is reproduced in Trapp, "Iconography of the Fall," fig. 17, and in a less lively engraving here, fig. 60.

26. Claesz, Rijksmuseum Cat. no. A 3930; Dürer, paintings in the Uffizi Gallery and the Prado Museum.

27. Turner, *One Flesh*, 141.

28. Milton apparently invented the word "sensuous" to distinguish innocent enjoyment of the senses from sensuality, in which appetite dominates other faculties.

29. Dürer, *Complete Woodcuts*, figs. 222 and 224; the Fall and the Expulsion have been exchanged in this edition.

30. Herbert, "The Sacrifice," in *Works*, 26-34, ll. 165-68.

31. *Areopagitica*, in *SM*, 741.

32. The classic statements and demonstrations of this principal are found in Arthur Barker's "Structural and Doctrinal Pattern" and *"Paradise Lost:* The Relevance of Regeneration."

33. Herbert, "The H. Communion," *Works*, 52-53, ll. 29-36. The thought is not exclusively Protestant; in Serafino della Salandra's *Adamo Caduto*, Eve asks whether life in the Garden will be eternally sustained by the Tree of Life, and God replies that their life will be eternal, but not there; eventually he will, without parting body and soul, take them to heaven (116).

34. Entzminger, *Divine Word*, 33.

35. In *De Doctrina Christiana* 1.27 Milton defines for regenerate men the liberty that Eve defends for unfallen man and woman: "*Christian liberty* is that whereby *we are loosed as it were by enfranchisement, through Christ our deliverer, from the bondage of sin, and consequently from the rule of law and of man; to the intent that being made sons instead of servants, and perfect men instead of children, we may serve God in love through the guidance of the Spirit of truth*" (*SM*, 1028).

36. Pagels, *Adam, Eve, and the Serpent*, 98, 59, 55-56, and chap. 5, "The Politics of Paradise," which gives a full statement of competing views.

37. *Christian Doctrine* 1.11, in *SM*, 998.

38. *Christian Doctrine* 1.16, in *SM*, 1012.

39. *An Apology for Smectymnuus*, in *SM*, 556.

40. *Christian Doctrine* 1:17-15, in *SM*, 1013-21. This process, made a basic principle of interpretation by the work of Arthur E. Barker, bears repeating here because the distinction between "fallen" and "fallen but regenerate" is so often forgotten.

41. On the meanings of "secure" see Evans, "Mortals' Chiefest Enemy."

42. Calvin, *A commentarie vpon Genesis*, 92.

43. McColley, *Milton's Eve*, chap. 5, which includes a survey of her motives in other works, and passim; and "Free Will and Obedience."

44. Benet, "Abdiel and the Son," and "No Outward Aid Require."

45. "[T]he law must needs be frivolous, which goes to restrain things, uncertainly and yet equally working to good and to evil. And were I the chooser, a dram of well-doing should be preferred before many times as much the forcible hindrance of evil-doing. For God sure esteems the growth and completing of one virtuous person, more than the restraint of ten vicious" (*Areopagitica*, in *SM*, 741).

46. Loredano, *Life of Adam*.

47. An anonymous *History of Adam and Eve* (1753), 2. The writer uses illustrations, an epigraph, and an ecstatic description of Eve out of *Paradise Lost* but does not understand Milton's depiction of her moral responsibility.

48. *Of Reformation*, in *SM*, 445.

49. Joan S. Bennett, in her fine analysis of humanist versus voluntarist antinomianism in " 'Go': Milton's Antinomianism and the Separation Scene" and *Reviving Liberty* (94-118), sees that Adam and Eve have to keep many considerations in balance, but I think undervalues this "if" clause and accepts too readily the premise that Eve lacks "a balanced picture of the work [she] wants to be good at" (113).

50. One early partial exception is the comment by Addison, in *The Spectator*, no. 351: "The Dispute which follows between our two first Parents . . . proceeds from a Difference of Judgment, not of Passion, and is managed with Reason, not Heat: It is such a Dispute as we may suppose might have happened in Paradise, had Man continued happy and innocent. There is a great Delicacy in the Moralities which are interspersed in *Adam's* discourse, and which the most ordinary Reader cannot but take notice of." He does not say

the like for Eve's moralities, however. Quoted from *A Familiar Explanation of the Poetical Works of Milton*, 111.

51. Danielson, *Milton's Good God*, 222. Cf. Mollenkott, "Milton's Rejection of the Fortunate Fall" and Labriola, " 'Thy Humiliation Shall Exalt."

52. Lovejoy, "Milton and the Paradox of the Fortunate Fall." Cf. Miner, "Felix Culpa and the Redemptive Order," and Ferry, "The Bird, the Blind Bard, and the Fortunate Fall."

53. Danielson, *Milton's Good God*, 202 and 224. Danielson points out that the *felix culpa* is "a version of optimism, which denies that there is anything really evil in the world. If the Fall is fortunate, it is hard to conceive of anything to which that adjective does not apply" (205).

54. "Good and evil we know in the field of this world grow up together almost inseparably. . . . And perhaps this is that doom which Adam fell into of knowing good and evil; that is to say, of knowing good by evil" (*Areopagitica*, in *SM*, 738).

55. See, for example, Bacon, "Of Adversity," in *Complete Essays*; Jonson, "A Hymn to God the Father" in *Complete Poetry*; Herbert, "Easter Wings" and the five poems titled "Affliction" in *Works*; Donne, "Hymne to God, my God, in my sicknesse," in *Complete Poetry*; *Devotions*, especially Meditation XVII; and "Sermon preached before the Countess of Bedford" in *Sermons*, 3:187-205.

56. Herbert, "Love Unknown," in *Works*, 129-31.

57. Stevens, "Sunday Morning," in *The Palm at the End of the Mind*, 7.

# 6

# Precincts of Light

La gloria di colui che tutto move
per l'universo penetra e risplende
in una parte più e meno altrove
Dante, *Paradiso*

The art upon which the well-being of all lives depends both springs from and nourishes paradisal consciousness: the art of dressing and keeping the Garden of Earth. "Dressing" is georgic; "keeping" is ecological. Milton incorporates and far surpasses the awakening georgic awareness of his time by creating a language-music designed to promote both specific acknowledgment of the multiplicity of creatures and an ecological *form* of consciousness, to enmesh awareness of connectedness in language itself. His is the poetry of the cosmic house, the eco-verse.

Visual artists contributed to such consciousness by keeping the plenitude of creatures before the eye, in the topics where they could best be kept together and in which their being together is a point of the topic: the Garden of Eden, Noah's Ark, Orpheus Playing to the Animals, the Golden Age, the Peaceable Kingdom. I believe that their increased interest in painting landscapes, often with small biblical or classical figures in bosky and verdant scenes, was in part an acknowledgment of the nonhuman parts of creation and their benefits (or sometimes salutary terrors), not just economic but moral and spiritual, to humanity. Verbal artists—outstandingly Milton, Marvell, Herbert, Browne, and Traherne—developed a language that kept the wholeness of God's providence before the mind and exercised that mind in choices able to replace the ungrateful predations of humankind with a responding providence.

For such artists, what unifies the cosmos is the glory that, Dante says at the beginning of *Paradiso,* pierces the universe and shines in all things according to their receptivity. Whether this light enters visibly (as in images such as the frontispiece, figures 53 and 57, and others that represent God as light) or audibly, as in Milton's poem, full life in

the natural world is as inseparable from the spiritual light that pene-
trates it as the body is from the soul. The universe, "This pendant
world," a jewel hung from heaven "in bigness as a Star / Of smallest
Magnitude close by the Moon" (2.1052-53) is well within "the Precincts of light" (3.88).

At the beginning of his great hexameron in Book 7, Raphael reports a remarkable speech of God, who proposes to create a new
world where a new race will dwell,

> till by degrees of merit rais'd
> They open to themselves at length the way
> Up hither, under long obedience tri'd,
> And Earth be chang'd to Heav'n, and Heav'n to Earth.
> (7.157-60)

The idea that Adam and Eve and their descendants could ascend
through processive merit is fundamental to Milton's rendition of Paradise, but what is most remarkable in this expression of it is the phrase
"and Heav'n to Earth." Earth alone is not the final homeland, but it is
more than a way station on the road to heaven. The Incarnation takes
up humanity into divinity; in this speech heaven and earth will be in-
corporated. The frustration of "merit" by Satan's fraud alters the process but not the end of this interchange. Although Christ will return
"to dissolve / Satan with his perverted World," he will "raise / From
the conflagrant mass, purg'd and refin'd, / New Heav'ns, new Earth,
Ages of endless date / Founded in righteousness and peace and love, /
To bring forth fruits Joy and eternal Bliss" (12.546-51). Before the
Fall, "Reaping immortal fruits of joy and love" (3.67) is what Adam
and Eve are already doing when God beholds them while Satan
"wings his way / Not far off Heav'n, in the Precincts of light" (3.87-
88). After the Fall, even if he expects a conflagration, the honest pil-
grim does not defile the land of his pilgrimage, and the faithful
steward keeps the house garnished for the bridegroom's return. If
earth is ultimately, under both dispensations, meant to merge with
heaven, then earth (as distinct from its corruption) matters,[1] and human care of it is part of both primal and postlapsarian health and of
moral preparation for the merger.

When Michael announces the expulsion, Eve laments the loss of the
Garden and the flowers she has "bred up with tender hand" (11.276).
Adam, more piously though less accurately, laments the loss of God's
presence. Michael's reply comes near to obliterating the wall between
the Garden of Eden and the rest of the world:

> *Adam,* thou know'st Heav'n is his, and all the Earth,
> Not this Rock only; his Omnipresence fills
> Land, Sea, and Air, and every kind that lives,
> Fomented by his virtual power and warm'd:
> All th' Earth he gave thee to possess and rule,
> No despicable gift; surmise not then
> His presence to these narrow bounds confin'd
> Of Paradise or *Eden;* this had been
> Perhaps thy Capital Seat, from whence had spread
> All generations, and had hither come
> From all the ends of th' Earth, to celebrate
> And reverence thee thir great Progenitor.
> But this preëminence thou hast lost, brought down
> To dwell on even ground now with thy Sons:
> Yet doubt not but in Valley and in Plain
> God is as here, and will be found alike
> Present, and of his presence many a sign
> Still following thee, still compassing thee round
> With goodness and paternal Love, his Face
> Express, and of his steps the track Divine.
>
> (11.335-54)

Although Michael's subsequent teaching defines differences between prelapsarian and postlapsarian thought,[2] this passage emphasizes continuities. God manifests himself through all the earth, both before and after the Fall. If there had been no fall, all the earth would have been populated and cared for by the offspring of Adam and Eve. Adam has lost preeminence, but not God's love. Where once the human race might have been "improv'd by tract of time," it must now be regenerated by "supernal Grace contending / With sinfulness of Men" (11.359-60). Adam understands that grace transforms pain and death, the effects of sin, into divine chastisements, and resolves to confront evil regenerately, "to the evil turn / My obvious breast, arming to overcome / By suffering, and earn rest from labor won, / If so I may attain" (373-76).

Human labor after the Fall is spiritual, ethical, and physical, as it was, without suffering and corruption, before the Fall. The arts of regenesis spring, even in grosser air, from a paradisal consciousness—a multiply empathetic, long-term, ecological responsiveness to heaven and earth—which was never confined to one garden. Had there been no fall, Genesis suggests, the human race would still have filled the earth and "subdued" it—keeping temperate order, but also, Milton hints, leaving room for nature to pour forth her "Wilderness of sweets . . . as in her prime" (5.294-95). The wide country of Eden is "pleasant soil" in which God has planted "His far more pleasant Garden" that gathers "In narrow room Nature's whole wealth, yea more" (4.214-15, 207), but the whole earth also shares that wealth, "no despicable gift." Eventually, there would have been traffic throughout the earth and between earth and heaven. With the Expulsion the human family is walled out of Paradise and has to carry it within, in a sphere to which Satan has won access for his demons: "a spacious World, to our native Heaven / Little inferior" (10.467-68). What kind of paradise or inferno we carry with us affects our respect for "Land, Sea, and Air, and every kind that lives."

The civilization "whose goodness is rooted in the fall itself" into which Stevie Davies is so eloquently happy to have fallen—"filled with 'The smell of grain, or tedded grass, or kine, / Or dairy' (IX.450-1)"— is a world she believes has been "liberated into culture." Before the Fall, "Eve has in her hand only primitive garden tools," Davies observes, " 'art yet rude / Guiltless of fire,' yet the suggestion is heavy that this unpromethean satisfaction with childish technology invites and legitimates the natural desire for art which is more than rude."[3] But culture is incompatible only with a static pastoral paradise, and one not only walled *in* (as indeed the word means) but walled *out* from the rest of Eden and its outskirts, the world.[4] Milton's "yet rude" does not necessarily mean "rude until after the Fall," and promethean fire, stolen from a vengeful god, is not the only source of civilization. Insofar as even God's Garden is a place of georgic activity, it suggests the possibility of a civilization not "rooted in the Fall itself," in which art and industry can develop without damaging the earth, and where the rudiments of "art yet rude" do not depend on Sin and Death to grow. God is not Zeus, who "planned in his heart / evil," and Satan is not Prometheus, a suffering friend of humankind "acting in a spirit of kindness."[5] Satan's plot is "all pleasure to destroy, / Save what is in destroying" (9.477-78). Some arts are necessitated by the Fall, but they need not promote its effects. The difference between an unfallen or regenerate civilized life and a fallen one is that the former two do not depend on destruction. The God-filled earth that Michael assures to Adam calls for seeing, hearing, and saving the remnants of Eden in the spiritual battleground of the world.

The world hangs "fast by" Heaven, "in a golden Chain" (2.1051), its interlinked nature linked to the empyrean. Original righteousness is expressed not only in the erect bodies, shining faces, and radiant speech and song of Adam and Eve, but also in their esteeming and care of the earth and their benign relation to its denizens. They are nurturers of the world that nourishes them and join "thir vocal Worship to the Choir / Of Creatures wanting voice" (9.198-99), in harmony with all.

### Fresh Employments

Felicity depends on material simplicity and spiritual riches. For Traherne, the essence of Paradise is praise, rising from Adam's thankful meditation "Upon the Throne in which he sate"—that is, the earth. Upright Man had no need of "vain Inventions"; "No Gold, nor Trade, nor Silver there, / nor Cloaths, no Coin, nor Houses were, / No gaudy Coaches, Feasts, or Palaces." Instead,

> He had an Angel's Ey to see the Price
> Of evry Creature; that made Paradise:
> He had a Tongue, yea more, a Cherub's Sense
> To feel its Worth and Excellence.[6]

If we know the worth of each creature, a paradise of preservation and meditation and a tongue to praise are possession enough.

At the same time, human beings seem made to do work of all kinds. How is it possible to reconcile the desire to make things, endowed as a part of the image of the Maker, with simplicity?

Of the images and propensities usually reserved for postlapsarian life that Milton places in prelapsarian Eden, the two most daring are sex and labor. Sexual activity was by most patristic and mainstream Protestant commentators supposed subsequent to the Fall,[7] and work was for most readers of Genesis a remedy of idleness (even before the Fall) or a curse, not a natural joy. As Anthony Low has pointed out, by making life in paradise not only pastoral but also georgic, Milton "diminishes the distance between Eden and what fallen humanity may still hope to attain, aided by grace."[8] In *Paradise Lost* work is a form of love. It prompts awareness of the needs and natures of other beings and concern for them, exercises mind and body, and provides understanding of the workings of nature and of the mind, limitless conversation, and the abounding interest of cooperating with nature. Eden is profuse; but it needs human work to guard its beauty and keep it fruitful. The same is true of human souls. Work, difficulty, complex problems, spiritual combat, even some distress are available in Milton's Garden.

If Adam and Eve had not fallen, as Milton by his affirmations of free will and his georgic enrichments of paradise, and by Raphael's "tract of time" and Michael's "Capital Seat," invites us to think possible,

would any temperate art or science be closed to them? Obviously, neither acquisition nor elaborate contrivances for physical comfort would
be sought in Eden. Being merely a consumer, rather than a caretaker,
of nature is part of fallenness. But gardening requires tools, and so
raises the question of technology. Would all arts be ephemeral, every
day a new page to be filled with new inventions of poetry, music,
dance, play, and enhancement of the beauty of growing things? Or
would people with perfect memories and skills of improvisation enjoy,
nevertheless, writing poems and setting them to music and adorning
them by means of papyrus and paint? Though they have no need of
buildings, the whole globe being temperate and not yet "turn[ed]
askance" (10.668), when they had children, would they enlarge their
bower, and so develop a moderate architecture? While they are still in
the process of growing sufficiently spiritous for space-travel (5.497-
99), would they and their far-flung young sail to and from the Capital
Seat by wind and water or in "cany Waggons light" (3.439), with all
immortality to do it in? Would they enjoy the decorative arts Eve initiates by decking her nuptial bed "With Flowers, Garlands, and sweet-
smelling Herbs" (4.709)?[9] Though they sing in perfect pitch and have
no need of "Lute or Harp / To add more sweetness" (5.151-52), might
they make instruments to set the air resounding with all the timbres
and harmonies that deepen the pleasure of blending voices in song?
Would they use their gardening tools to carve flutes from pruned
boughs, and twist strings from skins of beasts "as the Snake with
youthful Coat repaid"?[10]

   I raise the speculations for several reasons. First, by including so
much activity and thought in prelapsarian Eden that other poets and
artists leave until after the Fall, Milton proposes that sin does nothing
to promote the arts of civilization except to make them necessary
rather than voluntary, and does a great deal to make them corrupt.
Second, both Raphael's speech on temperate acquisition of knowledge
(7.111-30) and the work and conversation of Adam and Eve correct
Satan's misapprehension that they "only stand / By Ignorance" (4.518-
19). Knowledge itself is not forbidden; only the tree that will give
them knowledge of "Good lost, and Evil got" (9.1072).[11] Science,
then, would proceed at a pace that never outran wisdom, and any application made of scientific knowledge would be both ethical and
beautiful. Third, by placing labor and the beginnings of the arts and
sciences before the Fall, Milton affirms human work and creativity as
both natural and regenerative, not just compensatory.[12] Fourth, and
most important, these momentous changes invite us to apply paradisal
principles to whatever we do in our vocations.[13] Had they not fallen,

Adam and Eve and their offspring would presumably not want to make anything ugly, noisy, noisome, noxious, or hurtful to any creature. We cannot return to Eden, but we can make Edenic choices. If in our arts and techniques we constantly asked ourselves what the consciousness of all lives that fills Edenic language would promote and what it would restrain in whatever we build or fuel, earth would be a healthier planet.

Human souls develop through both contemplation and work, and work is both mutual service and service to nature. Vergil in the *Georgics* suggests that Jove made nature recalcitrant to develop human wit and character:

> The Father himself
> Willed that the path of tillage be not smooth,
> And first ordained that skill should cultivate
> The land, by care sharpening the wits of mortals,
> Nor let his kingdom laze in torpid sloth.

One of the first things men learn from Jove's providential hardships, though, is to "snare wild beasts with nets and birds with lime."[14] In *Paradise Lost* work is essential but innocent before the Fall, "Guiltless of fire" (9.392) and snares. After their morning prayer, Adam and Eve prune "Fruit-trees overwoody" (5.213) to keep them fruitful, and the presence of one forbidden tree prunes *them*. They lead "the Vine / To wed her Elm" and bring "Her dow'r th'adopted Clusters, to adorn / His barren leaves" (215-19)—which is the first task mentioned in the *Georgics*—as Adam's strength might support Eve's fruitfulness. But it is not until after they lose the government of their own appetites, and animals grow fierce as a result (a process we see increasing now as habitats become scarce), that God commands the angels to raise storms and, perhaps, tip the earth on its axis (10.668-71), imposing seasonal and diurnal hardships to sharpen the wits and cure the sloth of a human race for whom work is no longer a joy. For Vergil, civilization depends on these difficulties, but for Milton they are imposed only after Adam and Eve abandon culture in favor of a controlled substance they fancy will give them instant, work-free wisdom.

An epitome of Milton's habit of regenerating motifs usually thought fallen occurs as Eve departs to work alone,

> and like a Wood-Nymph light,
> *Oread* or *Dryad,* or of *Delia's* Train,
> Betook her to the Groves, but *Delia's* self
> In gait surpass'd and Goddess-like deport,

> Though not as shee with Bow and Quiver arm'd,
> But with such Gard'ning Tools as Art yet rude,
> Guiltless of fire had form'd, or Angels brought.
> (9.386-92)

The resonances in this passage are complex. The allusion to Delia, or
Diana of Delos, goddess of chastity, affirms Eve's still unfallen purity.
But Diana is also goddess of the moon, suggesting mutibility. And she
is the goddess to whom Vergil compares Dido when Aeneas first sees
her: a woman who governs her city well, oversees the many kinds of
work going on in it, and distributes the tasks justly, and who is about
to let passion sway her judgment.[15] Eve is not simply like the huntress-
goddess, however, but surpasses her traditionally beautiful walk and
divine dignity; and she is not going to shoot animals but to dress the
garden. She takes with her the rudiments of culture, "such Gard'ning
Tools as Art yet rude, / Guiltless of fire had form'd": Adam and Eve
may have a prepyrotechnic technology, and although "guiltless" may
simply mean inexperienced, there is some suggestion that combustion
would be out of place in Paradise. A temperate technology, then, either would not require fire, or would not develop the metallic arts until the human family had learned enough wisdom to use fire guiltlessly.

But Eve's tools may, instead, be by "Angels brought." This offhand
suggestion opens worlds of possibility, and we ought to remark its
oddity. Is it part of Milton's monism that heaven provides interchange
of commodities as well as food? If angels might bring gardening tools,
might they also bring, for example, "Golden Harps" (7.258)? Though
not needed, such additions are not forbidden. Milton does not imagine music to be purely vocal, much less disembodiedly spiritual, in
heaven, where

> the Harp
> Had work and rested not, the solemn Pipe,
> And Dulcimer, all Organs of sweet stop,
> All sounds on Fret by String or Golden Wire
> Temper'd soft Tunings, intermixt with Voice
> Choral or Unison.
> (7.594-99)

This description also suits musical angels in paintings and carvings
and the rich, varied sonorities of early baroque settings of the Psalms.
Is the materiality of Milton's heaven partly due to the need for matter
in order to make such music? And Milton thinks other arts enjoyed by
angels: architecture, dance, liturgies, parades, conversation; heaven has

portals, chariots, gonfalons, tables, tabernacles, and pavilions, all mys-
teriously meant, "though what if Earth / Be but the shadow of Heav'n,
and things therein / Each to other like, more than on Earth is
thought?" (5.574-76). On earth, such things are burdens and distor-
tions of nature's beauty when they are effects of pride or greed, but
harmless if the artists are careful of the soil from which they spring.

"Milton's heaven," William McClung observes, "is rich in urban
elements."[16] Since the distinction between heaven and earth is always
growing smaller in *Paradise Lost* except when it is growing larger, the
possibility seems implied that as the human race grew, it might gather
in cities—always preserving the Garden as its family seat. And the distinction between the Garden and the rest of the unfallen world, that
the Garden contains nature's "whole wealth," is one of contiguity, not
quality, of riches. Raphael calls the whole earth "with her nether
Ocean circumfus'd" the "pleasant dwelling-place" in which Adam and
Eve will "multiply a Race of Worshippers / Holy and just" if they "per-
severe upright" (7.624-25, 630-31). The possibilities of innocent
urban and chemic arts modeled after heaven's, always careful of landscape and habitat, suggest processes for regenerate arts to follow. The
negative patterns are the building of Pandemonium and Babel. In hell,
demonic developers rip wounds in the infernal landscape to extract
gold, a "precious bane" (1.692), and rapidly erect a showy shrine, as
men taught by Mammon later "with impious hands / Rifl'd the bowels
of thir mother Earth / For Treasures better hid" (1.686-88). Nimrod,
the tyrant who "arrogate[s] Dominion underserv'd," and his ambitious crew "cast" to build their city and vaunting tower mortared with
"black bituminous gurge" (12.27, 41) from Hell. As the world now is,
the cure for technological excesses is an ecologically aware technology.
McClung suggests that "the survival of Eden depends . . . upon whatever accommodation can be reached with the city. To survive, in fact,
Eden must become a garden-city."[17]

Angels bringing gardening tools—and only to Adam—is a motif
other artists put after the Fall (fig. 35). That angels may have brought
to unfallen Eve and Adam tools not guilty of Promethean but forged
in heavenly fire, or that they may have arts "yet rude" but capable of
refinement, makes it possible to think that other arts might develop
innocently without trespassing on the awarenesses and reservations
represented by the forbidden tree. The concept not only dispels the
idea that the Fall is the beginning of civilization but suggests that the
technology of civilization may be measured against the not-nocent
work of Adam and Eve. Insofar as work regards the well-being of all
creatures, it is paradisal. Insofar as it depletes, pollutes, disfigures, and

diseases, it is guilty. After the Fall, inclement seasons make some arts
necessary for survival. The work of Adam and Eve before the Fall, and
the paradisal consciousness of their language and music, show how
this work, too, can nurture rather than spoil.

If Edenic life does not lack beneficent activity, neither does it induce
spiritual indolence. God permits Adam and Eve an enemy who can
test every sort of spiritual valor, and though Satan rejects physical
combat, fearful of Adam's strength "Heroic built . . . exempt from
wound" as he no longer is (9.485-86), he could have stooped to violence if fraud had failed. Eve's dream causes her grief and Adam perplexity; it also instructs both of them in the soul-stretching challenges
of freedom and contingency in a world arranged by a God who permits evil to exist rather than hamper opportunities for goodness by imposing limitations on the will. Adam and Eve disagree about working
separately, and that disagreement gives them both work of mind as
well as body. Even in Paradise, daring children might skin their knees
and need healing herbs; things made could still break; frustrations and
failures that increase spiritual depth and mutual understanding could
occur without the stunting denial called the Fall. Adam and Eve rejoice in "fresh imployments" (5.125) of "body or mind" (4.618) which
not only declare their dignity and heaven's regard but draw them into
communion with each other and with everything that grows.

## All the Creatures

Genesis gives us, Donne recollects, "two employments, one to conserve this world, the other to increase Gods Kingdome." The human
race is called both to increase and multiply and "to keep the world in
reparation, and leave it as well as we found it."[18] Whether from the
point of view of peopling earth or that of peopling heaven, these two
employments need to go hand in hand, since conserving the earth is
much of a piece with justice and spiritual understanding.

Keeping the earth in reparation includes care of those creatures
with which humans share bodily life. Seventeenth-century commentaries and meditations on Genesis point out this kinship of flesh and
commend it as cause for humility and the temperance to preserve these
fellow animals by restraining human greed. In poetry and visual iconography, the unfallen relation between humans and animals is one of
mutual interest and pleasure, the beasts eager observers of the creation of Adam and Eve and happy in their company. In many manuscripts and engravings the animals watch keenly as Eve emerges from
Adam's side. The "Master work" who governs them should be "Magnanimous to correspond with Heav'n," Raphael tells Adam, as well as

"grateful to acknowledge whence his good / Descends" (7.505, 510-13), answerable both to God and to them, and the whole web of being depends on temperate choice. Like language and music, the responsibility to care for the Garden and peaceably govern the animals is agreeable in itself, but also connects Adam and Eve to God and each other. Milton's Eve fully shares with Adam in these activities.[19] Their gardening labors, the sympathetic apostrophes in their morning canticle, and their friendship to the animals show them fit for the work that may prove to be their descendants' most spectacular failure, the care of the earth and all creatures here below.

Milton lavishly subscribes to the sense of stewardship and of delight in the diversity of living beings suggested by the Genesis poem, both in Raphael's empathetic, onomatopoetic creation poem and in descriptions of the life of Adam and Eve among them, as "About them frisking play'd / All Beasts of th' Earth, since wild. . . . Sporting the Lion ramp'd, and in his paw / Dandl'd the Kid; Bears, Tygers, Ounces, Pards / Gamboll'd before them, th' unwieldy Elephant / To make them mirth us'd all his might, and wreath'd / His Lithe Proboscis" (4.340-47). Understanding them, and the differences between them and human beings, is clearly one of the absorbing interests of life in Paradise. Hugh MacCallum includes Adam's naming of the animals in *Paradise Lost* among examples of the "internal operation of grace," but not as a sudden infusion of scientific knowledge; "he knows their 'Nature,'" in contrast to his own, "rather than their natures" and, as in the astronomy lesson, his "understanding of nature develops along normal lines of inquiry and analysis." But Browne thinks the natures of things inscribed in their forms, so that by reading these signs rightly "Adam assigned to every creature a name peculiar to its Nature" as seventeenth-century scientists hoped to learn to do.[20] In either or both cases, Adam's government of the animals should be "magnanimous," and that is a part of a complex education in the acquisition and uses of knowledge and the power it confers. Regina Schwartz acutely proposes "that the ground of the distinction between illicit and laudable knowledge is a deeper opposition, between invasive investigation and appreciation, and that this distinction deepens yet, into the more familiar one of chaos and creation. Knowledge born of a will to dominate an objectified creation 'out there' leads to the return of chaos; knowledge which celebrates creations furthers the continual process of creation."[21] Presumably, like their nurturing of the plants, Adam's and Eve's "dominion" would draw forth the distinct potentialities and protect the natures of all creatures.

At the end of *Paradise Lost,* Adam sees a vision of both city and countryside destroyed by war and marauding bands.

> Where Cattle pastur'd late, now scatter'd lies
> With Carcasses and Arms th'ensanguin'd Field
> Deserted.
>
> (11:653-55)

The echoes of Achilles' shield summon the whole history of human pride and bloodshed and its devastations of the natural and the civilized world. When Enoch, "the only righteous in a World perverse" (11.701), rises in council to speak of right and wrong, "him old and young / Exploded, and had seiz'd with violent hands," had not heaven rapt him home: "so violence / Proceeded, and Oppression, and Sword-Law . . . Adam was all in tears" (11.668-74). When brazen war gives way to "luxury and riot" (715) with equally devastating effects, Adam sees "Peace to corrupt no less than War to waste" (784) and knows that righteousness and peace must embrace each other if each is to live. But when the next just man contrives an ark and lays in provisions,

> lo a wonder strange!
> Of every Beast, and Bird, and Insect small
> Came sevens, and pairs, and enter'd in, as taught
> Thir order.
>
> (11.733-36)

Adam understands the need for the preservation of all species in the world he has made dangerous, and exclaims,

> I revive
> At this last sight, assur'd that Man shall live
> With all the Creatures, and thir seed preserve.
> (11.871-73)

He is too optimistic about the consciences of his offspring. Human greed and carelessness have wiped out the seed—"crack[ed] nature's molds" and spilled the very "germens" (*Lear* 3.3.8)—of many creatures. But Eden Garden is not quite dead, and poets as well as scientists are still at work opening eyes. Milton and Edenic imagery in the visual arts remind us of our responsibilities toward other creatures and show us just how pendant this world is. The urgent work of the present, including the work of language, is to establish peace without an acquisitiveness that, even on a petty scale, can literally consume the earth.

*Male and Female Light*

In *Paradise Lost* the dressing and keeping of language, music, liturgy, government, and earth with all its creatures are given into the hands of two incarnate microcosms descended from primal light, made out of one flesh and rejoined by love to produce new lives. The cultural richness and ecological justice of paradisal life is the work of "male and female light" luminously embodied in Adam and Eve. While, as Janet Halley observes,[22] Milton is partial toward heterosexual monogamy and propagation, much in the relationship of Adam and Eve apart from the "genial bed" applies to other human attachments as well. Their relation is not only erotic but also moral and spiritual, and Milton's careful integration of these splendors makes Edenic marriage "the happier Eden."

Since the classic essay of William and Malleville Haller and Joseph H. Summers's sensitive chapter on the art of love in Milton's Paradise,[23] Edenic marriage has received both hostile and glowing commentary.[24] Feminism sheds both light and umbrage on Milton's place in the history of liberation from under the patriarchal thumb.[25] Edward Le Comte ruminates exuberantly on Milton's sexual imagery, puns, allusions, and attitudes, finding that "a sexual energy is the tension of his greatness."[26] James Turner and Stevie Davies have written elegant and learned rhapsodies upon the raptures of Milton's Eden; Davies places Adam and Eve in a love-embued hermetic cosmos, and Turner brings both Christian-Platonic and radical sectarian views of Genesis to an interpretation of Edenic lovemaking as "the central experience of unfallen life."[27] Much recent criticism detaches erotic experience from spiritual and ethical experience, however, and some paganizes the relation of Adam and Eve by making sexual enjoyment the motive of everything they do. The erotic blessedness of Edenic marriage depends on the relation—even the exaltation by subordination—of sexual bliss to spiritual joy. Because the origin of their consciousness is not Eros but Logos, Adam and Eve are the light of the world, made guardians and conduits of love to the rest of creation.

### Collateral Love

The metatext of Ithuriel's spear, wherein we are invited by kinetic mimesis to stand as angelic interpreters or squat as Aristophanic frog-critics, is surrounded by concentric contexts all of which also touch in some way on the nature and uses of imagination. Most of these spheres around Eve's dream also present to *our* imaginations, with great delicacy and intimacy, the mutuality of paradisal marriage. In the nearest sphere, Eve and Adam make love: festively, before the dream, by connubial rites, and gravely, after it, by honesty and solace. In the next they pray, before their lovemaking and again before their morning's work, imaging forth the whole creation, and ending with a plea that whatever evil caused the dream should be dispersed: a request answered at once by God's dispatching Raphael, not to eliminate the threat but to teach them how to face it. Before their evening prayer, Adam discourses on the nature of their work, and after their morning prayer they set out to do it. In the evening, Eve says or sings a love song to Adam, and in the morning Adam says or sings a love song to Eve. The day of Book 4, they entertain a fallen angel unawares, and the day of Book 5 they entertain an unfallen one awares. And, lest anyone in Milton's audience think any of the arts intrinsically irreligious, *both* Satan and Raphael feign along the way. Satan sits like a cormorant (4.196)[28] and misreads the Garden without delight. Raphael seems "to all the Fowls . . . A *Phenix*" (5.271-72) and reads God's book of creatures with charity and candor. Raphael sails on steady wing, upheld by buxom (obedient) air, in contrast to Satan's pratfalls: one artist hand in hand with nature, the other opposed to her and so subject to fatuous sprawls (2.932-34).

These contexts apply to the variety of experiences that constitute paradisal marriage and contain every sort of imaginative exercise, with Eve's dream and Adam's explanation of what imagination was made for at their center. They demonstrate that no art or pleasure is forbidden that does not deceive, exploit, or enslave, and that imagination can be an antidote against evil as well as a means to apprehend goodness. Ithuriel's action discloses Satan to free Eve, and the poison Satan pours into her ear (which could still have become a mithridate against further nocence) is treated with antidotes of love and prayer. That pattern is an innocent version of the plot of the whole poem. Milton gives us goodness to love in all its rich and various beauty, shows it poisoned, dramatizes the beginning of its restoration in Adam and Eve, sums up the development of regenerative history with all its pains, and hands us the means to continue it: the imaginative stuff of *his* dream, the regenerative poem brought by Urania "nightly" to his ear, that we can use to disperse evil and nourish "fresh imployments."

This central dream, it seems to me, is a crux that distinguishes Milton's version of Edenic human relations by making sorrow and perplexity materials for love and understanding even in prelapsarian life. Critics have often thought that the seeds Satan plants in Eve's imagination sprout in her desire for autonomy in the separation scene and so cause a fatal breach. Readers sometimes feel that Adam's consolation is inadequate, and wonder why Milton gives us no record of a conversation between Adam and Eve reassessing the dream in the light of Raphael's news about Satan's quest.[29] Milton records no conversation between Raphael's departure and the morning of the Fall. Yet much in the dream scene may be traced in unfallen and regenerate achievements. Barbara Lewalski identifies it as a "moral interlude" moving toward "comedic resolution of difficulties through dialogue" and finds that "the fact that they create [their] sublime hymn just after the troubling experience of Eve's dream indicates that their innocence is in no way compromised. Indeed, the successful resolution of that difficulty has elicited their highest achievement in art and divine praise."[30] That ability to bring good out of externally imposed evil by turning trouble into art is a strong argument against a "fortunate fall" into civilization. The pattern of explanation, consolation, creation of a resplendent poem, and turning to "fresh imployments" in the Garden confirms the narrator's statements, "all was clear'd" (5.136) and "So pray'd they innocent, and to thir thoughts / Firm peace recover'd soon and wonted calm" (209-10). The lack of reference to that experience in the separation dialogue may remind us that minds clear of fear and suspicion are vulnerable and need vigilance. Yet the experience itself helps warrant them "sufficient to have stood." It provides imaginative apprehension of evil, and Raphael will introduce them to violence and most pertinently to lies and fraud, giving them the concepts by which to interpret the dream and similar events when need arises. Apart from that, they have unpolluted experience of good on which to base their choices. This experience of good—which Adam says twice (4.411-39; 5.514-18) should be enough to move them to keep "One easy prohibition" (4.433)—is particularly set forth in the spheres surrounding the dream, from the description of the Garden to Raphael's description of universal nurture and spiritual improvement "by tract of time" (5.498).

One of the prelapsarian goods brought out of rejected evil is the emotional and spiritual intimacy of Adam and Eve in the moments after Eve's dream. In a passage Sandra Gilbert thinks representative of "female anxieties" about Milton,[31] Virginia Woolf, confessing to only a cursory reading of *Paradise Lost,* wrote that Milton's poetry "is the essence, of which almost all other poetry is the dilution" but contains "no pity or sympathy or intuition"; Milton "deals in horror & immensity & squalor & sublimity, but never in the passions of the human heart. Has any poem ever let in so little light upon ones own joys & sorrows?"[32] Reading Milton in September of 1918 in the wake of the horrors of the Great War—and one cannot blame her depression after that carnage—Woolf does not find his representations of joy, wonder, spontaneous praise, admiration, gratitude, innocent tenderness, sorrow for having offended, forgiveness, and glad reunion to be among the recognizable "passions of the human heart." Yet who is so unperverse as never to have felt Satan's envy, or too adamant to melt like Adam under beauty's powerful glance? Milton wants to identify the evils that *cause* carnage; and he does that both by confronting evil and by confronting bliss. He especially expresses what human beings feel or would like to feel as inhabitants of the precincts of light, linked to heaven by a spiritual golden chain, and also fully, feelingly human—these are kindred, not contrary, states—and he ties those emotions and intuitions to the rest of the universe and the eternal realms beyond by links of language.

This tying-in to nature and eternity may be seen in a passage that is very human indeed. After her frightening dream, Adam comforts a weeping Eve by assuring her that her Satan-inspired imagining has not tainted her[33] so long as she keeps her will to goodness:

> Be not disheart'n'd then, nor cloud those looks
> That wont to be more cheerful and serene
> Than when fair Morning first smiles on the World,
> And let us to our fresh imployments rise
> Among the Groves, the Fountains, and the Flow'rs
> That open now thir choicest bosom'd smells
> Reserv'd from night, and kept for thee in store.
>    So cheer'd he his fair Spouse, and she was cheer'd,
> But silently a gentle tear let fall
> From either eye, and wip'd them with her hair;
> Two other precious drops that ready stood,
> Each in their crystal sluice, hee ere they fell
> Kiss'd as the gracious signs of sweet remorse
> And pious awe, that fear'd to have offended.
>
>                                    (5.122-35)

The pattern of full telling, attentive listening, sympathetic analysis, and turning to fresh employments is therapeutic, and Adam's words are full of the pity and sympathy and intuition Woolf finds lacking in her provisional reading. In language that is paradisal in its awareness of the natural and spiritual world, he compares his spouse to the fragrant morning landscape with its choicest bosomed smells, by this trope and by his diction reminding us of the beautiful landscape and the beautiful body of the bride that draw such power from each other in the Song of Solomon,[34] and so gathering in resonances from both that lush erotic poem and the allegory attributed to it. The narrator reminds us of Mary Magdalene, the repentant friend of Christ and by some accounts the first woman apostle and preacher. Both allusions suggest that Adam and Eve are a holy people and a type of the marriage of Christ and the Church. Yet the allusions in no way spoil their intimacy, their closeness through vulnerability, or their harmony with nature. Eve's beauty and purity, her grief and relief, and Adam's compassion and healing words are linked to the beauty and balm of the Garden. The musical word-painting of the phrases—the suavity of "more cheerful and serene / Than when fair morning first smiles on the World"; the enjambment of "fell" and the stop at "stood"; the kinetic gesture of "each in their crystal sluice he ere they fell / Kissed"—further ties Adam and Eve to the glories of a creation in which feeling, image, language, and music are woven together, and which is bestowed upon them as the material of their own creations. Milton expresses our joys and sorrows while connecting them to the beauty of all creation and to the fruitful earth, to moral beauty, to music, and to the divine giver and healer, and so gives them new depths and significances.

This scene expresses Edenic consciousness within the language of love, and is a verbal parallel of movements in the visual arts to incorporate fully nuanced human expressiveness with a fully inhabited landscape. Again, Milton has placed before the Fall a scene that others could only place after it: van den Broeck and Sadeler (fig. 19) show an appealing Eve who is remorseful, but not innocent. Milton's Eve is innocent but complex. His scene is as full of human drama and textured emotional depths as a Renaissance or baroque painting. The hymn that follows incorporates all the creatures as a painter like Savery or Brueghel might do, with Adam and Eve not falling but empathetically connected to the creatures they invoke to join, and whose voices they weave into, their harmony.

Adam and Eve before the Fall are emotionally and spiritually free to express a range of human feelings and affections that their descendants often repress. Praise, thankfulness, tenderness, remorse, pious awe, and the longing for moral clarity—though few can achieve it as Adam and Eve can, and for a while do, in *Paradise Lost*—seem to me to be basic passions of the human heart. I don't know where else in art they have been more sturdily expressed than in this short passage and those that frame it: Adam's aubade and his discourse upon good and bad uses of imagination, concluded with a kiss of peace; Milton's epithalamion to Adam and Eve and their morning hymn, embodying those most intimate activities, lovemaking and mutual creative prayer. Milton represents subtleties of emotion felt between two people with hearts and minds of their own who love each other and do not agree about everything. He represents the highest vision and the earthiest savorings of the senses. In case this picture is unlike daily life he gives us ways to be more capable of entering it: exercises in moral conscience and in response to beauty and to the lives of beings as unlike as elephants and archangels.

### Nuptial Rites

When he describes prelapsarian lovemaking, Milton does not indulge in voyeurism, but only "weens" or supposes what happens. But he is perfectly straightforward in his praise of "wedded Love, mysterious Law, true source / Of human offspring, sole propriety / in Paradise" (4.750-52). One reason many commentators thought that Adam and Eve fell on the day they were made (in spite of the Genesis story's sanctification of the Sabbath) was that if Paradise was in good working order, everything including Adam and Eve must be presumed fertile, so that every sexual union would produce issue: those "more hands" that Adam and Eve, artists and gardeners, metonymically look forward to. But conception cannot have occurred before the Fall.[35] According to Genesis, Cain was conceived after the expulsion. Even if we read Genesis 4:1 retrospectively, we are left with the difficulty that if Cain had been conceived before the Fall, he would not participate in "original" sin. The murder of Abel is surely the archetypal effect of the archetypal sin. If it were not, Cain's sin would have stood "in the following of Adam," as the Ninth Article of Religion puts it, rather than "the fault and corruption of the Nature of every man, that naturally is engendered of the off-spring of *Adam;* whereby man is very farre gone from originall righteousness."[36] Milton clearly rejects this Pelagian heresy, which denies the corporate nature of sin.[37] Therefore, Cain was not conceived in the course of the nuptial embraces Milton's Adam and Eve enjoy in their flower-decked, nightingale-serenaded bower (4.736-75).

The either-or dilemma—that either Eve and Adam remained virgins and only embraced partially or allegorically, as the church fathers thought, or Cain was conceived in Paradise—Milton surely regarded a false one.[38] The idea that every divinely sanctioned sexual act produces offspring is classical, not scriptural. Every sacrosanct rape by a pagan god begets a hero or a hapless girl or a troublemaker, but the mothers of biblical heroes—Sarah, Rachel, Manoah's wife, Hannah, Elizabeth—often had to wait through years of married barrenness. If Adam and Eve had not fallen, Eve might have been bloomingly pregnant much of the time, and each child a burgeoning microcosm of beauty, wit, talent, affection, and new ideas. But Milton imagines a time of sheer amorous delight before the first conception, in aid of the other purposes of marriage he lists first in *Tetrachordon*—"a mutual help to piety" and "to civil fellowship of love and amity; then, to generation"[39]—and in preparation for the arrival of new lives.

Milton was not the first or the only writer to affirm that sexual generation was intended by God in the commandment to increase and multiply.[40] Augustine combated allegorists and promoters of married celibacy in this regard: some "hold that this blessing, Increase and multiply, is meant of a spirituall and not corporall faecundity,"

> Bvt wee doubt not at all, that this increase, multiplying, and filling of the earth, was by Gods goodnesse bestowed vpon the marriage which he ordeined in the beginning, ere man sinned, when hee made them male and female; sexes evident in the flesh. [Though these blessings] may not vnfitly be applied spiritually, yet male and female can in no wise be appropriated to any spirituall thing in man: . . . It cannot bee ment of the spirit ruling, and the flesh obeying, of the reason gouerning and the affect working: of the contemplatiue part excelling, and the actiue seruing, nor of the mindes vnderstanding and the bodies sence: but directly, of the band of marriage, combining both sexes in one. . . . [T]he number of Gods cittizens should haue been as great, then, if no man had sinned, as now shalbe gathered by Gods grace out of the multitude of sinners.[41]

Richard Baxter adds that original righteousness would have been sexually transmitted "if the Parents had not sin'd and lost it."[42] And Thomas Traherne makes the remarkable statement that "by his commanding them to be fruitful, and to replenish the Earth, is intimated the Purity of the holy Ordinance in the State of Innocency, and that it was lawful and blessed to beget their Similitude; forasmuch as it was part of the divine Image conceded to them above the Angels."[43]

But Milton's is surely the fullest salute to "the sum of earthly bliss" (8.522). Because Augustine was concerned to separate prelapsarian, voluntary procreation from lust, the effect of sin, his version of nuptial rites is quite bloodless. If one looks at paintings of Adam's and Eve's exuberant passionate flesh with his and other patristic commentaries in mind, passion appears suspect. Milton's version, on the contrary, amply admits passion and pleasure to Paradise, even the "commotion strange" which transports Adam and which he understands must not "subject" him (8.531, 607).[44] The Fall, subjecting just perceptions to ambition and appetency, does not institute passionate love but cankers it, and with it the harmony of creatures that the harmony of Adam and Eve keeps tuned.

Unlike Augustine, Milton affirms that Adam and Eve enjoyed actual sexual union in paradise, without conception taking place there. Nevertheless, wedded love is the "true source / Of human offspring," a "Perpetual Fountain of Domestic sweets" in that way as well as in the multifloriate pleasures of erotic mutuality, and in his apostrophe to it, Milton with his celestial spear dispels the vain imaginings of prurient hypocrisy. His description of connubial love as the "sole propriety, / In Paradise of all things common else" (4.751-52) annoys readers who believe that "bourgeois marriage" is a patriarchal power-game and the "sun-clad power" of chastity a repressive concept in fancy dress. Maureen Quilligan thinks the phrase means "property rights."[45] Rather, it echoes Tertullian, who, Elaine Pagels points out, distinguished Christians from Romans in this way: " 'We hold everything in common but our spouses,' exactly reversing the practice in outside society, where, he said sardonically, most people voluntarily share nothing else!"[46] Sexual self-government, with all things common else, Pagels argues, liberated Christians from their own passions and the most vulnerable members of society—women, children, and slaves—from sexual exploitation.

Milton's line alludes also to Plato's idea, in *The Republic*, of the community of women: that is, that among the Guardians "wives are to be held in common by all; so too are the children, and no parent is to know his own child, nor any child his parent."[47] Donne parodies the concept in "Communitie" by a legalistic reductio ad absurdum; its result is that "chang'd loves are but chang'd sorts of meat, / And when hee hath the kernell eate, / Who doth not fling away the shell?" Ordinarily in this metaphor the shell is the body and the kernel is the soul. Here, both are anatomical; the implication is that holding women in common depends on the premise that women do not have souls.[48] No serious commentator on Scripture committed such a heresy. An orthodox statement in "The lyfe of Adam" from Voragine's thirteenth-century *Golden Legend*, printed by Wynkyn de Worde in 1527, shows how perverse wits might skew commentary to produce it: "Man was made to the ymage of god in his soule, here is to be noted that he made not onely the soule without the body, but he made bothe body and soule, as to the body he made male and female. . . . For yet he was not perfyte tyl the woman was made. And therfore it is redde, it is not good the man to be alone."[49] The message is that the division into sexes applies to bodies only, not to souls—not that females have only bodies. Both Donne in his poems about true love and Milton wherever he addresses marriage assume that women are spiritually complete, and that faithfulness in marriage goes hand in hand with faithfulness to God, with analogous amazing illuminations. "Sole propriety" is the opposite of "community of women."

By wedded love, "adulterous lust was driv'n from men," and "Relations dear, and all the Charities / Of Father, Son, and Brother first were known" (4.753-57). As Traherne expresses it, "*Adam* and *Eve* became the Parents of all the World, and we, by that, Brethren to one another."[50] "Relations dear" may imply not only matrimonial and familial ones, but the whole fabric of personal relations; friendship is protected by monogamy because loyal marriages make room for "Love unlibidinous" (5.449) and establish trust in other relationships. The patriarchal language of "Father, Son, and Brother" is part of Milton's defense of marriage, since without the union of man and woman those other relations, that some masculinists prized more highly, would not exist.

The passage suggests that a civilization that supports diverse arts and just relations depends on men's acknowledgment of, and responsibility for, the paternity of their children.[51] Responsible fatherhood as well as motherhood makes possible a community that can get beyond the basic economic essentials and create the arts, liturgy, just civil government, strong networks of friendship, and good care of the earth.[52] The feminist critique of patriarchal systems observes that in return for protecting women and children and establishing a complex social fabric founded on law, patriarchy demanded excessive power. Equally, matriarchy that denies fathers any rights of paternity demands excessive power. Rigidly patriarchal societies have not practiced mutuality of labor, as Milton's Adam and Eve do, and some have violated the body of earth, pulling Babels out of forests and mountainsides and Babylonian feasts out of the skies and seas, and reenacted the story of Cain and Abel all over the globe. Milton's epic opposes these abuses.

Although the Milton of the divorce tracts frequently speaks with the voice of patriarchal authority, he confirms women's spiritual capacities and represents marriage as a mutual, reciprocal, and spiritual relation. In *Of Reformation* Milton looks for the fulfillment in his own time of the scriptural prophecy of "an extraordinary effusion of God's Spirit upon every age and sex."[53] In *Paradise Lost*, he challenges all the misogynous assumptions of his predecessors. Rather than dividing reason and passion, or heaven and earth, by sexes, Milton draws both the heavenly and the earthly and the masculine and the feminine nearer together than perhaps any other poet; insofar as Adam and Eve both, in proportion, represent "contemplation" and "grace," he draws

heaven and earth together through man and woman. To think that
Eve's fall proclaims the rights of the flesh or the primacy of the visible
is to do women an injustice. Milton's Eve while unfallen, and again
when regenerate, incorporates the values of both flesh and spirit, the
visible and the divine. Fallen, she is temporarily debased and trivial-
ized in both body and soul.

## Two Great Sexes

Visual artists depicted Adam and Eve hand in hand or with their
arms around each other when God speaks to them at the Admonition
or they converse with each other (figs. 26, 48, 55, 56); and they participate in visual mutuality of stance and equality of dignity, or loss or
resumption of it, in many medieval and Reformation images of their
marriage, prayers, fall, and repentance. Milton invests their sexual,
emotional, and rational lives with dignity and mutuality and carries
them into ethical, artistic, and spiritual activities never before imagined. The nature of their relationship is imaged astronomically in the
world of light in whose depths they dwell, which is summed up in
them. Each world is the macrocosm of the other. Their relation to each
other and to the created universe depends on inward light, and everything they do before they fall manifests the golden links of heaven, the
heavens, and earth.

Eve and Adam naturally embody what people sometimes call "the
feminine" and "the masculine." But Milton is interested in the relation, rather than opposition, of these qualities, and that relation is part
of a profound cultural change that transforms the epic hero from an
ideal of humanity that overvalues physical prowess to one that values
self-restraint and mutual help. The progress of civilization from dominance by military power to an order based on conscience and reciprocal respect depends on its incorporation of qualities traditionally
thought masculine and heavenly, such as a dispassionate sense of justice and a piety (like that of Aeneas) that guides and tempers personal
inclination, with those traditionally thought feminine and earthly,
such as sympathetic intuition and concern for nurture. Milton incorporates these qualities in the union of Adam and Eve, but also pro-
portionally in each of them. He includes more of the earthly in Adam
and more of the heavenly in Eve than other writers had done. Adam is
"for God only" and Eve "for God in him" (4.299), yet at Adam's first
sight of her heaven was in her eye (8.488); they are types of Christ and
the Church but it is often Eve who anticipates Christ.[54]

Maureen Quilligan objects that the line "Hee for God only, shee for
God in him" deprives Eve of a direct relation to God.[55] But it has
more positive functions. Kathleen Swaim finds illumination in the

parallelism of "Hee for God only, shee for God in him" for the relation of faith and experience: "Eve is more closely tied to earth, the phenomenal. . . . Adam recognizes that intercourse with the heavenly is open-ended and freeing, that no satiety is possible with divine sweetness; Eve does not distance herself from the sweetness through intellection."[56] Yet theirs is not precisely a marriage of the masculine-heavenly and the feminine-earthly, since both contain and reciprocally share that fusion. Their thoughts are "more closely tied," his to the heavens and hers to growing things, but each is interested in both. Their marriage shows the process of integration of "divine and human things"[57] that is for Milton the work of poetry and of life.

The offensive line also parallels, and lets Adam and Eve personify, the summary of the Law. Adam "for God only" represents the commandment to "love the Lord thy God with all thy heart, and with all thy soul, and with all thy mind," and Eve "for God in him" represents the second that is like unto it, "Thou shalt love thy neighbor as thyself." These two tables of the Law are indivisible. Loving one's neighbors means loving first what is divine in them, the soul that connects each to God, and giving "meet help" to nurture that connection. Eve, while unfallen and again in her motion of reconciliation, especially personifies that kind of love. But so does Adam in his counsel after Eve's dream and after reconciliation has begun. Since Eve is both a delightful spouse and a type of the church, "those graceful acts, / Those thousand decencies that daily flow / From all her words and actions" (8.600-602) relate to Adam's contemplative mind in the way that good works relate to faith, which without them, like sun without earth, "barren shines" (8.94).

Variants of this interaction are apparent in their language. At first consciousness, Adam asks sun, earth, hills, dales, rivers, woods, plains, plants and animals (at which point empiricism fails) "how came I thus?" and goes straight to the first cause: "some great Maker. . . . Tell me how I may know him, how adore" (8.278-80). Eve also wonders "what I was, whence thither brought, and how" (4.452) and, rather than interrogating nature as Adam does, goes to a lake that "seem'd another Sky" where she finds "answering looks / Of sympathy and love." Since these turn out to be her own, she exchanges them (reluctantly at first) for Adam's. Both combine gestures of contemplation with seeking of society in their first hours, but while Eve's first move is from self-contemplation to sociability, Adam's is from investigation of phenomena to adoration of "Presence Divine" (8.314). The immediate result of Adam's study of nature and God, however, is his bold request for a proper mate.

Again, the fusion of the contemplative and the social, or the divine and human, in each, but in different proportions, occurs when they discuss the stars. As they walk hand in hand toward their "blissful Bower," Eve, admiring "this fair Moon, / And these the Gems of Heav'n, her starry train," asks Adam, "wherefore" and "for whom / This glorious sight, when sleep hath shut all eyes?" (4.648-49, 656-58). Male critics have thought this question a display of vanity, claiming that Eve herself wants to be admired and thinks existence worthless if no one is looking. I agree, rather, with Janet Knedlik[58] that her question is supremely important: one of those queries that opens up the cosmos. Later, Adam, rephrasing Eve's question to Raphael, asks the philosophic "how": "reasoning I oft admire, / How Nature wise and frugal could commit / Such disproportions" (8.25-27). Eve asks the ethical "for whom." If she is ethnocentric in thinking only of diurnal Eden-dwellers like herself and forgetting nocturnal creatures and watching angels, Adam promptly reminds her of the system of interstellar nurture of which they are a part (4.660-88). The stars, he points out, are already ordered to minister light to nations yet unborn; they foment and warm, temper and nourish "with kindly heat / Of various influence" and shed their "stellar virtue" on all things that grow, making them "apter to receive / Perfection from the Sun's more potent Ray." Even if there were no human beings, there would be plenty of spectators: "Millions of spiritual Creatures walk the Earth / Unseen," with "Celestial voices . . . Sole, or responsive each to other's note . . . With Heav'nly touch of instrumental sounds / In full harmonic number join'd" in an angelic Monteverdian multichoral psalm. Eve's question has elicited a cosmic philosophy and a defense of the arts, as is fitting for one who is linked to Milton's muse.

In this passage, Eve turns our attention to the immediate and the personal, Adam to the cosmic design. Adam and Eve, however, do not just embody this distinction; they are both learning to think both ways. Eve is interested in a matter of principle—the cosmic economy—and Adam in nurture. Eve activates the divine image in Adam by her question, and so is for God in him. But so is his answer for God in her: moon and stars minister light prepared for "all kinds that grow / On Earth," and angelic voices "lift our thoughts to Heaven." In the great synthesis of Milton's poem we see that everyone is both for God only and for God in everyone else—or else, as in Satan's case, for neither. When both Adam and Eve sever the ethical "for whom" from faith, both fall. Until then, they compose a "Harmony to behold in wedded pair" (8.605) that links them dynamically, interactively, and linguistically to the "fair musick" of all creation.

James Turner reopens the question of equality and subordination and finds that Milton's "vision of Eros based on his reading of Genesis ... stands out from all others because his imagination responds generously to both ... the ecstatic egalitarian love of 'one flesh' [and] the patriarchal love of superior and inferior; he has hatched the contradictions in the text and the tradition that elsewhere lie dormant." But Turner shies away from the scriptural "contradictions" Milton "hatches," remarking that "it is the conjunction of Eros and submission that seems to inspire the sharpest authorial excitement in *Paradise Lost*."[59] The "contradiction" between equality and hierarchy is hatched in Raphael's speech on the "two great sexes," where Adam learns that excellence resides in "solid good" (8.150, 93).

The problem of equality in *Paradise Lost* is a false dilemma, not because political and judicial parity is not necessary as the world now is, but because in paradise each person promotes the happiness of each other person—which is not self-sacrifice but mutual love—and each person's luster and talents are distinct, like Dante's angels'.[60] Paradisal minds are naturally interested in the quality of soul—that is, of the whole person—of each being they meet. When they see splendors in others, they rejoice; and they see splendors in everyone, from angel to emmet. Satan, in contrast, feels himself impaired by others' excellence and grows increasingly less capable of being interested in anyone but himself. Political equality in itself accomplishes no bliss, but hedges in the greed and solipsism that Genesis calls the Fall in order to make possible the full and unidentical growth of each identity.[61]

If paradisal consciousness is not precisely egalitarian, but appreciates differences without pride or envy, neither is it in practice patriarchal. When Eve expresses gratitude for being given the superior mate, and calls him her author and disposer, one may say as Christine Froula does that Milton imposes a patriarchical mentality upon her. But Adam does not feel superior to Eve or limit her freedom: "Greatness of mind and nobleness thir seat / Build in her loveliest, and create an awe / About her, as a guard Angelic plac'd" (8.557-59). Adam's admiring speeches and Eve's grateful ones show their capacity to illustrate St. Paul's advice, "in lowliness of mind let each esteem other better than themselves" (Philip. 2:3). Lowliness is a compound of faith, gratitude, and perspective, and Milton does not limit these virtues to Eve.

In spite of his apparently satisfactory answer to Eve's question about the economy of light, Adam sees the opportunity, when a celestial traveler arrives, to learn more, and repeats her concern from an extraterrestrial perspective. "When I behold this goodly Frame," says Adam,

                                                            this World
Of Heav'n and Earth consisting, and compute
Thir magnitudes, this Earth a spot, a grain,
An Atom, with the Firmament compar'd
And all her number'd Stars, that seem to roll
Spaces incomprehensible (for such
Thir distance argues and thir swift return
Diurnal) merely to officiate light
Round this opacous Earth, this punctual spot,
One day and night; in all thir vast survey
Useless besides; reasoning I oft admire,
How Nature wise and frugal could commit
Such disproportions.

                                                            (8.15-27)

Then, a proto-Copernican, he wonders why the "sedentary Earth" does not fetch light for herself with far less effort than it takes the whole vast universe to circle around her.

At this point Eve goes off to take care of the "Fruits and Flow'rs" that "toucht by her fair tendance gladlier grew," not undelighted by nor incapable of "such discourse," but preferring her astronomy lessons mixed with loving looks and kisses; the narrator, far from finding this separation a breach, exclaims, "O when meet now / Such pairs, in Love and mutual Honor join'd?" (8.44-58). But we are not to suppose that her concerns are inferior to Adam's "thoughts abstruse" (40). In fact, the point that love and taking care of the earth are more important than intellectual speculation is exactly the lesson Raphael will ultimately draw from Adam's question: "joy thou / In what [God] gives to thee, this Paradise / And thy fair *Eve.*" After a hundred lines of astronomy, he tells Adam to do as Eve is already doing.

After Adam has asked his version of Eve's question, the genial archangel approves and then corrects him, in a perfect demonstration of "candor," as friend to friend. For Raphael, Adam's question is not just a scientific but an ethical one; science and ethics can not be separated in a paradisal consciousness, which is ecological and promptly sees the connections in things. "Ecology" means knowledge of the house, the habitat. Adam knows that our house is the cosmos, and Raphael calls God the "Architect" of the "Fabric of the Heav'ns."[62] Raphael first points out that the "Architect" of this wondrous "Fabric" conceals some mysteries in it. But the angel also perceives a moral flaw in Adam's question. (In Milton's paradise moral inadequacies can be corrected before they do any harm.) You, who are to lead your offspring,

Raphael says to him, suppose that "bodies bright and greater should not serve / The less not bright, nor Heav'n such journeys run, / Earth sitting still, when she alone receives the benefit." But that is a serious error.

> [C]onsider first, that Great
> Or Bright infers not Excellence: the Earth
> Though, in comparison of Heav'n, so small,
> Nor glistering, may of solid good contain
> More plenty than the Sun that barren shines,
> Whose virtue on itself works no effect,
> But in the fruitful Earth; there first receiv'd
> His beams, unactive else, thir vigour find.
>
> (8.90-97)

This observation contains a whole ethical system. At the political level, we see that we are not to judge of inward good by outward show, and that the duty of authorities, whose greatness does not prove excellence, is not to receive but to give, serve, and foment fruitfulness. Earth—the small, subordinate, and feminine planet—is the recipient of light and the producer of value. Even the sun, without which nothing can live, is barren without another to receive his beams.

But ultimately, even if the whole heavens do circle around the earth, all these lights are "officious" not to Earth but "to thee Earth's habitant." If to a twentieth-century thinker that statement lacks perspective, it seemed cause for grateful reflection to the psalmist (as in Psalm 8) and to Donne, for whom "It is too little to call man a little world; except God, man is a diminutive to nothing . . . for, as the whole world hath nothing, to which something in man doth not answer, so hath man many pieces of which the whole world hath no representation."[63] As Browne, also aware of this "punctual spot," says:

The earth is a point not onely in respect of the heavens above us, but of that heavenly and celestiall part within us: that masse of flesh that circumscribes me, limits not my mind: that surface that tells the heavens it hath an end, cannot perswade me that I have any; I take my circle to be above three hundred and sixty; though the number of the Arke do measure my body, it comprehendeth not my minde: whilst I study to finde how I am a Microcosme or little world, I finde my selfe something more than the great. There is surely a piece of Divinity in us, something that was before the Elements and owes no homage to the Sun. Nature tels me I am the Image of God as well as Scripture; he that understands not thus much, hath not his introduction and first lesson, and is yet to begin the Alphabet of man.[64]

And, Raphael continues—restoring any humility that his previous statement may have shrunk—the cosmic lights may also serve other worlds: the "Heav'ns wide Circuit" speaks of "The Maker's high magnificence . . . That Man may know he dwells not in his own"—that is, in his own house—but is rather in "An Edifice too large for him to fill, / Lodg'd in a small partition, and the rest / Ordain'd for uses to his Lord best known."

Raphael then switches astronomies.

> What if the sun
> Be Centre to the World, and other Stars
> By his attractive virtue and their own
> Incited, dance about him various rounds?
> (8.122-25)

Nor is earth's "Regent of Day" (7.371) necessarily the only one:

> other Suns perhaps
> With thir attendant Moons thou wilt descry
> Communicating Male and Female Light,
> Which two great Sexes animate the World,
> Stor'd in each Orb perhaps with some that live.
> (8.148-52)

"Male and Female Light" is a Pythagorean concept, but Milton declines the dichotomies that usually go with it. In some visual representations of the Creation in Milton's time, Day is personified as male, and Night as female. Night is "she" and sun is "he" in *Paradise Lost*, too; the convention is found in Hesiod and embedded in Greek and Latin myth and grammar. But whereas myths often align day and night with good and evil, Milton assures us that as parts of creation both are good. In heaven "ambrosial Night with Clouds exhal'd / From that high mount of God, whence light and shade / Spring both" changes "the face of brightest Heav'n . . . to grateful Twilight" and "Melodious Hymns about the sovran Throne / Alternate all night long" (5.642-44, 656-57). Raphael describes the division of lights as "Glad Ev'ning and glad Morn" (7.386), and Adam and Eve acknowledge in their prayer "Thou also mad'st the Night."[65] Similarly, sun is "he" and moon and earth are both "she." The moon borrows her light from the sun, "for other light she needed none" (7.378), but does not appear as a symbol of female mutability. One may, reading this passage, follow Traherne's advice: "Elevate thy Spirit, O my Soul, and contemplate the Moon as a Sign and Symbol of holy Souls, which Almighty God doth call beautiful as the Moon; which Beauty and Splendor consisteth in always beholding the infinite Sun of the Divinity, as in receiving from him the Splendour of divine Grace."⁶⁶ And one may remember the praise of moon and her changes, as well as the sun, in Ecclesiasticus, that powerful creation poem prescribed in the lectionary of the Book of Common Prayer: "He made the moon also to serve in her season for a declaration of times, and a sign of the world.... The month is called after her name, increasing wonderfully in her changing, being an instrument of the armies above, shining in the firmament of heaven; the beauty of heaven, the glory of the stars, an ornament giving light in the highest places of the Lord."⁶⁷

Earth and moon receive light from the sun, but in *Paradise Lost* "Male and Female Light" does not mean only direct and reflected beams. The moon may be inhabited and the sun is "barren" without the fruitful earth. Earth is created in Genesis before both sun and moon and is the reason for their existence. Moreover, not only the moon but also the sun receives the light it transmits. Light, created on the first day, is not lodged in the sun until "God made two great Lights, great for thir use / To Man," and transplanted light into the sun on the fourth day of creation, since when the sun comes forth as a bridegroom "jocund / to run his Longitude" (7.346-47, 372-73). The heavenly bodies are "Signs, / For Seasons, and for Days, and circling Years, / And let them be for Lights as I ordain / Thir Office in the Firmament of Heav'n / To give light on the Earth" (341-45). They are not to be worshiped (Deut. 4:19 and 17:3), but appreciated for their beauty and usefulness.

Milton is not always egalitarian, but he always questions stereotypes and false hierarchies. It does not matter "Whether the Sun predominant in Heav'n / Rise on the Earth, or Earth rise on the Sun" (8.160-61); what matters to Adam, Raphael says, is "this Paradise, / And thy fair *Eve*" (171-72). Raphael's speech asking Adam to "consider first, that Great / Or Bright infers not Excellence" pertains to every hierarchy of power. His discourse on the "new philosophy" throws in doubt ancient mythic sexual archetypes. The two sexes, both great, both in their natural innocence communicating light, animate the fabric of the universe and of the poem. And this astronomical amelioration of the feminine, this opening up of old myths and asking us to "consider," is typical of Milton's style. In his dramatization of the lives of Adam and Eve, Eve is not just reflected light. She has light of her own; she questions and sometimes leads; she gives Adam ideas and perplexities; she

receives, at the end of the poem, when she is supposed to be more subjected than before, direct light from God that allows her to prophesy:
"By mee the Promis'd Seed shall all restore" (12.623).

"Light," in Milton's invocation to Book 3, is holy, the "offspring of
Heav'n first-born," "since God is Light"[68] and dwells in the "Bright
effluence of bright essence increate" that existed "before the Sun,"

> and at the voice
> Of God, as with a Mantle didst invest
> The rising world of waters dark and deep,
> Won from the void and formless infinite.
> (3.1-12)

That effluence pours forth to fill the "Male and Female Light" of the
created world. Earth is within "the Precincts of light" (3.87). Light
irradiates the minds and shines in the "looks divine" of Adam and Eve.
All those who follow conscience will receive "Light after light" if that
light is "well us'd" (196). Everything in the scale of creation, from the
brightest angels to the lowliest stone, possesses some degree of glory.
Milton is remarkable in the lavishness with which he gives both Adam
and Eve, before their fall and after their regeneration, spiritual light.
Its shrine of flesh matters deeply to him. But to rob Eve of holy light,
and declare her the champion of flesh alone, is unjust to women, to
Milton, and to the world. The Garden of Earth needs masculine, feminine, religious, scientific, political, ethical, and artistic voices, and in
them the Light that Milton entreats: "Shine inward, and the mind
through all her powers / Irradiate, there plant eyes" (3.52-53). Eve and
Adam, engaged in love, the care of the earth and its creatures, and the
pursuit of temperate knowledge and complex moral understanding, ra-
diate both spiritual and intellectual light, which go, like them, hand in
hand.

## NOTES

1. Early in his poetic career, Milton began to eject dualistic phrasing,
scoring out, for example, the words "snatch us from earth a while / us of our
selves and home bred woes beguile" in the manuscript of "At a Solemn Musick" (Fletcher, *John Milton's Complete Poetical Works*, 1:391).

2. Swaim sums up distinctions in *Before and After the Fall*, chap. 5.

3. Davies, *Feminine Reclaimed*, 246-47.

4. Even pastoral poetry, Vergil's and Spenser's for example, has georgic
and political themes.

5. Hesiod, *Theogony*, in *Poems*, 64-65.

6. Traherne, "Adam," in *Thomas Traherne*, 2:91.

7. For exceptions see Lindenbaum, "Lovemaking in Milton's Paradise"; Turner, *One Flesh*, chap. 2; and Wehrman, "Midrash in *Paradise Lost*." Wehrman points out that some Jewish commentators envisioned both sex and work before the Fall.

8. Low, *Georgic Revolution*, 319. Cf. Otten, *Environ'd with Eternity*, chap. 2, "The Values of Terraculture."

9. William McClung discusses Edenic architecture in *The Architecture of Paradise* and reproduces the drawings in which "alone among the illustrators of *Paradise Lost*, William Blake expresses the living architecture of the bower, in walling, flooring, and furniture synthesizing nature and craft" (112-13).

10. An annotation to Psalm 150:4 in the Douai Bible (published for English-speaking Catholics in 1609) notes of postlapsarian musical instruments, "the Psalmist interposeth againe two especial things, which make perfect harmonie, without which no instrument is grateful to God: Vnitie amongst his seruants, signified by the Quire of consonant voices: and mortification of passions, signified by Stringes, which are made of dead beasts bowels" (*Holie Bible*, 2:266). Edenic and angelic instruments could not depend on death. If a new-cast snake skin (symbol of renewal) could be resilient enough to make a viol string, that would be a great improvement over the use Satan made of the whole snake.

11. Craig Harbison echoes a common misapprehension when he writes of "the amazing Christian aphorism that knowledge is sin and therefore brings on death," in *Symbols in Transformation*, 18. For interpretations of the name of the Tree of Knowledge see Chapter 3, n. 25 above. Caxton expresses a common understanding of prelapsarian knowledge: "Adam knewe all the seuen scyences lyberall entyerly, without fayllyng in a worde, as he that the creatour made and fourmed with his propre handes.... But syth they tasted of the fruyt whiche God deffended them, ... he felt hym so bare of his witte & entendement, strengthe & of his beaute, that hym semed he was al naked.... But notwythstondyng this, yet abode wyth hym more witte, strengthe and beaute than euer ony man had sythen" (*Mirrour*, 153-54).

12. One may compare both the popular idea that work is a curse (not shared by Protestant exegetes) and Freud's theory that civilization depends on male children's repressed incestuous desires.

13. Boyd M. Berry finds tension in Milton's poem between a paradise fully lost, therefore utopian, and one not entirely lost that is really about our condition, but still utopian because it "blunts the distinction between fictive and external reality while suggesting that the former should determine and shape the latter." This "tension between change and lack of change ... creates the distinctive veiling of utopian impulses in *Paradise Lost*" (*Process of Speech*, 244). These distinctions underrate Milton's hearty belief in regeneration and its effects on "external reality."

14. Virgil, *Georgics* 1.121-25 and 139.

15. Vergil, *Aeneid* Book 4.

16. McClung, *Architecture of Paradise,* 105.

17. McClung, *Architecture of Paradise,* 19.

18. Donne, *Essayes in Divinity,* 70.

19. Although many commentators denied "dominion" or government of the animals to Eve, the annotation to Genesis 1:26-28 in the *Testamenti Veteris Biblia Sacra* of Junius and Tremellius (a Latin translation from the Hebrew for Protestant readers) insists that "qui dominentur" includes the man and his wife and their posterity: "Vir & uxor cum posteris: nam in totam speciem beneficitum fuit." See also the use of the dual pronoun in the Anglo-Saxon *Genesis,* mentioned in Chapter 2 above.

20. MacCallum, *Milton and the Sons of God,* 122; Browne, *Religio Medici,* in *Works,* 2:72-73. Leonard emphasizes Adam's understanding of his own nature by comparison with the animals in *Naming in Paradise,* 25-32.

21. Schwartz, *Remembering and Repeating,* 41.

22. Halley, "Female Autonomy."

23. Haller and Haller, "Puritan Art of Love," and Summers, *Muse's Method,* chap. 4.

24. For bibliographical references see McColley, "Milton and the Sexes," 164-66.

25. For a variety of opinions see *Milton and the Idea of Woman.*

26. Le Comte, *Milton and Sex,* 4.

27. Davies, *Feminine Reclaimed;* Turner, *One Flesh,* 303.

28. Corcoran points out that in Thomas Scot's *Philomythie* (London, 1616), 68, the cormorant is "an unscrupulous bird symbolizing 'Law-State-Church Pyrats'" (*Milton's Paradise,* 37-38).

29. MacCallum raises this problem (*Milton and the Sons of God,* 140) and cites Rajan, *Lofty Rhyme,* 71. Swaim suggests that Adam "allays Eve's anxiety and clears her mind totally of the event. There is no residue of troublesome memory to burden her future or, as we see in retrospect, to aid her judgment in the moment of crisis" (*Before and After the Fall,* 229).

30. Lewalski, *"Paradise Lost" and the Rhetoric of Literary Forms,* 199-203.

31. Gilbert, "Patriarchal Poetry."

32. Woolf, *Diary,* 1:193.

33. Sara Van den Berg argues that since there is "no precedent in Genesis, biblical exegesis, or hexametrical poetry for this episode," beliefs associated with witchcraft "provide the only source," and that Milton uses this scene to free Eve from associations with witchcraft; he "undoes the equation" by which "the story of Eve, used so long to equate woman and evil, impinged fatally on those women who were branded witches—seductive, insatiable, and murderous" ("Eve, Sin, and Witchcraft," 358 and 365). Eve's response to her dream could hardly have been more different from what a witch-hunter might have expected.

34. Alter discusses this reversible figure in *The Art of Biblical Poetry,* chap. 8, "The Garden of Metaphor."

35. Le Comte observes that Milton does "no fussing" over this question in *Milton and Sex,* 4.

36. *Articles,* sig. B4r.

37. *De Doctrina Christiana* 1.11, in *SM,* 996-99.

38. Low demonstrates Milton's habit of transcending either-or dilemmas in *Blaze of Noon.*

39. *Tetrachordon,* in *SM,* 657-58.

40. Pagels gives a brief history of this affirmation in *Adam, Eve, and the Serpent,* chap. 1.

41. Augustine, *Of the Citie of God,* Book 14, ch. 18, pp. 521-25.

42. Baxter, *Two Disputations,* 67. Baxter's main point is that Adam "was commanded by supernatural revelation certain positive duties for the exercise and maintaining of [original righteousness], and for the attainment of salvation, which was its end. . . . And now we are deprived of it, we cannot expect its restoration but by means supernatural; even by Christ, and the Spirit, and supernatural revelations."

43. Traherne, *Meditations,* 73.

44. Although many writers thought "heavenly mindedness" required mortification of the flesh, Milton is not alone in believing that reason's dominion over the passions exalts them. Robert Crofts, in *Paradise Within Us,* writes, "If the Will doe chuse to obey reason rather than Passions, and so preferre Heaven before the Earth, the same doth make not onely itself but even those sensuall parts (which it then commandeth as a Mistresse) to become Divine and Celestiall, and the whole Mind to be filled with true joy and felicity" (21). Crofts's "before the Earth" and "as a Mistresse" display a dualism and sexism that Milton avoided.

45. Quilligan, *Milton's Spenser,* 236; Turner replies in *One Flesh,* 233.

46. Pagels, *Adam, Eve, and the Serpent,* 50.

47. Plato, *Republic,* 156.

48. Donne, "Communitie," in *Complete Poetry,* 119-20. Donne gives several cynical answers to the question "Why hath the Common Opinion afforded Women Soules?" in *Paradoxes and Problems,* 47-48.

49. Voragine, fol. ii. This statement is marred by its woodcut of Adam pointing to Eve while she takes a fruit from a woman-headed Serpent.

50. Traherne, *Meditations,* 74.

51. Cf. Stone, *When God Was a Woman,* 222 and 240-41.

52. Carol Gilligan's *In a Different Voice* contends that males, even as children, base their ethical choices on abstract principle, females on a desire to preserve human relationships. A society that can use both methods is clearly in a better position to practice equity, see alternative solutions to conflict, and avoid violent ones. Although we need not divide those virtues along gender

lines, respect for both fatherhood and motherhood seems likelier to promote them than either patriarchal or matriarchal autonomy.

53. *Of Reformation*, in *SM*, 453; Acts 2:17-18, 5:14, 8:12, 10:36-42. Wittreich appreciatively discusses Eve's final prophecy in *Feminist Milton*, 103-10. Biblical prophecy as the basis of a feminist hermeneutics is the subject of several essays in Russell, *Feminist Interpretation of the Bible*.

54. See Summers, *Muse's Method*, chap. 7, and McColley, *Milton's Eve*, 51-57. Some points in this section have been anticipated in McColley, "Milton and the Sexes."

55. Quilligan, *Milton's Spenser*, 225.

56. Swaim, "Hee for God Only, Shee for God in Him," 127-29.

57. Milton, *Of Education*, in *SM*, 729.

58. Knedlik, "Faith, Fancy, and Generative Mimesis," 36: Eve's query is "the hinge upon which the epic theodicy turns in Book 8 and the crux of the poem."

59. Turner, *One Flesh*, 232, 285, 235. Turner resorts to a reductive psychologizing out of keeping with his own thesis when he relates "Milton's trouble with subordination" to "the neurotic fear of sexual pollution . . . in the virginal philosophy" of the Mask (222) and calls Eve's "subjection" a "fetish" (272).

60. *Paradiso* 31.132-33. I would like to correct James Turner's impression that I think "sacrificial love" appropriate to Paradise before the Fall and also to disagree with his inference that "sacrificial love, supposing Adam had been told of it, would have encouraged his fall even more" (*One Flesh*, 276-77, n. 56). Adam could have practiced such love only by offering to share Eve's mortification without eating the fruit.

61. In a recent retort to William Shullenberger, Lawrence W. Hyman objects that, trying to take into account the complexities of *Paradise Lost*, Shullenberger "must arrive at a doctrine that is so complex as to be useless as a political program." If he wants to convince feminists that the poem is " 'a possible source of life, health, strength, and self-knowledge' " he must either become specific, and reduce the complexities of poetic experience to a political truth, or else refuse to do so and allow the " 'strength and self-knowledge' to be bound up with the particular arrangement of words and sounds that exist only within *Paradise Lost*." This seems to me a false dichotomy; a poem can activate our imaginations in ways that enrich us as ethical beings, without being reduced to political doctrines.

62. A "fabric" is (here) a structure or building.

63. Donne, *Devotions*, 23.

64. Browne, *Religio Medici*, in *Works*, 1:87.

65. I can see no suggestion that Milton, who did not think God the author of sin and writes his poem "nightly," allegorizes phenomenal night to emblematize evil. "Old Night," the principle of darkness, is kept at bay outside

the firmament by the stars, lest she take advantage of phenomenal Night to "regain / Her old possession" (4.665-66), but her namesake is within God's providence and displays the jewels that declare his glory (Ps. 19:1).

66. Traherne, *Meditations,* 48.

67. BCP, *Aprocrypha,* 216. Ecclesiasticus 43 was assigned in the BCP lectionary for November 16.

68. On Milton's "theophany of light" and its scriptural, classical, Hermetic, exegetical, and liturgical forerunners see Lieb, *Poetics of the Holy,* 185-211. "*Paradise Lost,*" Lieb wonderfully remarks, "embodies a series of hallelujahs to the Light" (188).

# Illustrations

Figs. 1-12. Genesis series, Jacob Floris van Langeren and William Slatyer, c. 1635. Reproduced by permission of the British Library.

fiat lux,

Principio Cælumq̃ suo, terramq̃ Creauit   בְּרֵאשִׁית בָּרָא אֱלֹ עֶלְיוֹן
Verbo Elohim Primo Luxq̃ oriunda Die.   אֵת כֹּל וַיְאוֹר בַּיּוֹם רִאשׁוֹן
ῼκυον ἐν ἀρχῇ κỳ φᾶ῍ος ἀνέϊορα τείϑας. In the beginninge God Created.
ϡυαλι φως πρώζω δϊὸν ἐκ͙ϛ ϑεος.,  Heauen & Earth. light first day related.,

Expansu esto inter aquas et Cælu vocetur

Æthera vt Expandit, Firmamentuq̃ Jehoua   בְּיוֹם שֵׁנִי רֹן בַּשָּׁמַיִם
inter aquas, et aquas Nata secunda Dies.   רָקִיעַ מַבְדִיל בֵּין מַיִם לְמָיִם
τὴν δὲ μέζαϑυ ὑδάτων σίζευμα τε καλωτ ἰδεαλς.The second day. shend Gloriously.
ἐκ̃Ζελαῖ ζηλ τηδὲ κỳ δελʒερ ῍ηνεγ ἕλω.,   Heauens Curteines & Braue Canopy

2

Tertia lux aridam ǫduxit, et ǽdita tellus.
éruta aquis, ǫfert Germinis omne genus:
τὸ τρίτον ἦμαρ ἐ̓ως πρῶ̓ϊζε͂ ἀπο γᾶ̓ια χαλωϕὸ̓η.
ϕίλα ϕἐρων ἐν̓δ᾽ρον. ϗ̓ πέρες ᾐ̓δὲ ϕυζῶ̓ν.

בְּיוֹם הַשְּׁלִישִׁי יְבַשֵּׁר
יֵרָאֶה וְכָל־עֵץ דֶּשֶׁא בָרָד

The third day sheŵd yᵉ dry-land where,
Grasse, herbs, trees, fruits & floŵˢappeare,

Quarta dies.sua signa perennia.lumina Cælo,
Temporibus metas.Nocte dieǫ, referͭ—
ηϳαζί ϟμιῶ̓ρεϗϕιο ϗ᾽ἀ̓ϳόϳηϛϕιλα ΣἐΙλυν.
νϗϳὲ̃ ἀναγϳα.ϰϰϑιes.αϊ̓ϳα χϳ ηϵλιεϳͭ—

רְבִיעִית שֵׁשׁ וּמְאוֹרוֹת
לְהַשֶׁל בִּיוֹם וְלַיְלָה.

The 4 day great and leſser light,
Made gouerne day and darkſome night,

3

Quinta dies. volucres Cæli. pisces q, y vndas
Æquoreos Ciueis. Aereos q, tulit

נֶפֶשׁ חַיָּה וְעוֹף שָׁמַיִם
בְּיוֹם הַחֲמִישִׁי שָׁרְצוּ מַיִם

The 5. day foules and fishes are,
Seene in seas, flouds, and liquid aire

Sexta dies Cpfert animalia Cætera. Terræ.
Incola Rexq, homo sit. Mundi. et Jmago dei

וַיֹּאמֶר אֱלֹהִים תּוֹצֵא
חַיָּה בְּיוֹם שֵׁשׁ אָדָם

The sixt day yeelds each livinge thinge
On land. & man yᵉ creatures Kinge.

4

Sanctius ecce animal,montisq,capacius altæ.
Natu.et scrutis subdita Cunsta suæ.,
τρις καλὸς ἐκ χθονὸς ὑδὲ θεεσῷ ἐτόλμησε coṁp. Clay-form'd man by Gods breath devinde
lividē πλεΚαν θεὸς, πεπλὲ ὑ πέτεͅ ὑ τῷ., All Creatures names,their Lerd designdē.,

Puluere Adam.Cofta formatur et illius Eua,
Cui datur auxilio dicta,Vira,indè Viro.
ἐκ χθονϑ ἀρθρο͂α, θεὶς, πι.εσνὶδ᾽ δεπι πεεαε γυναικα,That man liue not alone,was to man
ὑ μηζὴς ζὄρλαν πὸρ ερος ἀκγλις ελιˑ.,  A helper geuen,by him namdē woman.

Ponuntur in Eden

Septima Sabbata Sancta hominiq. deoq̃ ſalutis   יום השביעי הזה כלה  
   æterne ſignu, ſanctificata quies.,   לאל שבת תקדש אהל  
   ἑβδόμων ὅτε θεὸς δέδερ ἀνθρωσιν. ανεργον ἤμας  The Lord from worke y. 7. day Ceaſt  
   ἐgplums zẍbins Avrẍnde τω πῶϛ   And man muſt ſanctiſy y. reſt.

Pomo Cultores Paradiſi, Callidus, Euam   בגן עדן נחש השיא  
   Decipit ac ſerpens, decipit illa Virum.   אישה בחפוח, אישהתרי  
   Τῶ ſυzεψṽ μṉ̓dῳ παρρodευόὴ ἐιεῤὴ γuvaĩκἄ  Jn Paradice plac'te y.e Serpent Eue  
   ἡ πεπεπευεν ὅψις, φῃρίῷ, ἀνδρα γuvṅ.)   Doth tempt and by her man deceiue.

6

Adam ubi es

Conscia mens.Studio,fugit odit.et abdit manu נָא שַׁ֫בֶן שֶׁיתֵם

Se.vocat acre videns.nil fugit oræ Dei. וָאִירָא נָחֲבֵא מְפָּנֶיך אֱלֹהֵיהֶם

Ἀξ κήτω γεληνὶε xxxxi ορφε ἀ πείσρεπτω ἀείνδες Man guilty faine to hide and fly

χνηνε. Τῷὶ ἐφροϊοῦ παντῷε ϑεῷ οὖμμα θεός. God calls. none scape th'Almightyes ey

Cur ita fecistis.

Primoru ob facinus. maledicta vbi cuncta parentu אָרֶץ אָר֫וּד הַפְרוּ אֱלָֽיסֵן

Ficulnas vestes. Pelliceasq.gerunt. עֲלֵי הָאֵנָה עֹֽר יַלְבֵּשֵֽׁמ

ὁς θεὶς ἐῤρε πὶη πρίλαν τρέψ ἀλαιρϕα τεχήων Th'earth curst. God skin-coats the Guides

ριϊλλ. ἐϑνὶ. Ἀδαχὶ δεηυεΖω̃λῦuϊε⊖ερὶ. That fig-leaues fend. their shame to hide.

7

*Ceu Paradiſiacæ, pulcherrima Edenis ab horto*
*Pulſus Adam fuerat, Mors labor, horror adeſt.*
*& πϱοπαδεϳουκεϲϑ xǹ.π' Hɛ̃lω & ɛ̄ πɛϱϵϳϲ.* Man Expeld Paradice muſt be faine
*ρϵϑϵϵ' Adxu θκϱϲϵϑϵ παϰϳεϱϲ, ⁿⁱⁱⁱϲϵ πoῑϱϖϊ* To till yᵉ Earth, nᵗʰ toile and paine

שָׂמוֹ עֵדֶן בּוֹ
עֲדִי זָה עָדוּ בְיָדוֹ

*Seruat via arboris vitæ*

*Angelus en ſeruando via, arcet ab arbore vitæ*
*Et Gladio, flammæ more minatur eis.*
*Aϳϳϵ.ϑ' ϵϳϳϵϱ' ϵϳϵϊ' xϰϱϵ xϳ ϑϵϑ ϕϵxϑϵ zϵϊϊϲ.* The tree of lief, and Paradice hard
*ϵϲ ϑϵϑϵϲ ϵϳⁱ xⱼⁱ ϵⱼⁱ & Hϵϵlwϵϳϲ ϑϵϵϳ & ⱼ* Wᵗʰ flaminge ſword. & Angelis guard

מְלְאָךְ חֶרְבּוֹ אֵשׁ מַהֲהֲפְכָה
עֵץ חַיִּים גַּן עֵדֶן אוֹרְכָה

8

dant pænas

eua puerperus.varusq, doloribus ægra.
Dura.labore graui.terra colenda Viro.
ἔυᾶ τόκῳ, vilvoisle ἐκυeſιεκ, moivω xἰ ἐκμῷ Eue
πιχελῃ ἐν νιδιοις. ουῇ ὀλον. νὲε μελῃ. /

Child-bed paind spins. man in sweat
Of browes, his bread, must gett and Eat. /

בְּעִצָּבוֹן וְאֶל אֶל חֲמֵוּ
אִישׁ וּבְלֶחֶם תֵּלֶד אִשָּׁה

Sacrificant

Haud Cain.at munus respexit.Abelis.et ipsu
Numén.dlost.votis Cospitiuq, Suis.
ἔχι vῆ ὁ Καιν, ἀλλ᾿ ἐπειλέκεθεν ἰκαιε υέςει
τῷ ἔλῃ ἰν Θ.Ἀβέλ. ἵμαᾷ ἔγδε θεᾶ.

Cains churlish guifts though God despise
Respects meeke Abells Sacrifice. /

אֶל מִינְחָה הַבָּהָ שַׁעַר יָד
עַל קַן וּבְמִזָה לֹא חָיָה

9

occidit fratrem

Invidia accensus, fratrê Cain mactat Abelê            הרג לבן על אחיו
  Quom fugat, orbe Vagu, Vindicis Ira dei.            להרוג אחזו כי צדיק הוא
Ζηλ̣ῳ ὁ Καιν. εφηλ̣ ᾓ̓ ἀκλεβαν̣ ἀκλητ γολαθιυς Cain cause meeke Abell's just & good
εκ ιχορ, αρ ορθαιζας, δ᾽ λαδετ ομμα θετ̣     Embrewes his hands in's brothers bloud

Cain, ubi est frater tuus            יהוה

Vox tonat e Cœlo tenuis demissa per auras            בל לבן אה אחי
  Execrata Virum sanguinis atq. doli,            עו ונד חתי דמו עלך
ηαπλανε̣ς βοημ̣. ἐι̣ ασδερβ̓ ευδεα φερν̣     Ged calls for Abell. Cain replyes
εκλ̣ηφαλε̣ πελ̣λ.α. πι̣ωρλω ολε̣ γοωδ̣αρι̣ Se curst, a Vagabond liues & dyes

10

*Abel. Luctus.*

*Cain perit.*

Heu laceru᷈ Corpus miseri fleuére parentes
Monstru᷈,atat.horrendæ Cædis in orbe noua.

λυςιμερεῖς ῥίξοις πείζμον κλάϊβει ζοκνεs *Adam.alas, and wofull éue.*
πὶ συϊεορλε ρεῖρας.ψψιχλεῖ.ετερjυκελερὶ, *O're their sons dead corps, sadly greeue.*

Caini euo.Vltor adest,Iabel.Iubal.atꝗ Tubal-Cain
Lamech habet.bina ex Coniuge Zillā et Adā.

πὶ Καιντ᷈ saccor᷈ όονε᷈ ὸ xj ἀ᷈ρτ᷈λεωλ᷈ ὲοιο . *Cains offspringe bigamous Lamechi traine*
τνῆμα Λχϳέχ. διζΤω.ωλαιρερ᷈ωὶ᷈e ϳαινε᷈.Iuball.artiϳtᵉ. Iuball.Tubal = Cain.

Enoch Ciuitas.

Conditur Henocha vrbs prima, ac mænia surgunt, שֵׁם חֲנוֹךְ נִבְנְה עִיר רִאשׁוֹן
Plurimaq, artifici, tersa, polita manu. וְּמֶלֶאכוֹת רַבּוֹת נֵם צָאוּן
Καπνιαδιτ πρωτε πραλιτ ει αυ ραω ασυ θλωδει First City built on Earth, by Name
ιθνου εχαν, πργράν κι μαδα πολλα κχαυι. Enoch, where flourish, arts of fame.

Enoch rapitur

Seth oritur Soboles, Nomen, Numenq, vocan
Cæpit in orbe, dei, raptus Enochq, Deo
Enδι seuua, δθε δεn πθνου ιν ιιγε και θιδω
αν θεων θινιη δειι Θρανει ιει εταζ
הֹורִיד שֵׁת חֲנוֹךְ לָקַח יְהֹוָה
תוּחַל קָרָא בְּשֵׁם יְהֹוָה
Seth's offspringe, Enoch rapted, then
Gods name, gan bee invok't by men.

12

Figs. 13-14. Nicholaes de Bruÿn, after Maerten de Vos. The Creation of the Firmament and the Creation of Vegetation, from a Genesis series. Reproduced by permission of the Rijksmuseum-Stichting, Amsterdam.

CREDO IN DEVM PATREM OMNIPOTENTEM, CREATOREM CŒLI ET TERRÆ.

*M. de Vos inuent.*      *Adrian. Collaert excud.*

Figs. 15. Jan Collaert, after M. de Vos, published by Adrian Collaert. The Creation. Photo © Museum Plantin-Moretus and Print Room, Antwerp.

CREDO IN DEVM PATREM OMNIPOTENTEM, CREATOREM CŒLI ET TERRÆ.
M. de Vos inuent.                                    Visscher excud.

Fig. 16. Jan Collaert, after M. de Vos. Creation of Eve. Published by C. J.
Visscher. Photo © Museum Plantin-Moretus and Print Room, Antwerp.

Fig. 17. Jan Sadeler, after Crispijn van den Broeck. Adam in Paradise. Published by C. J. Visscher, 1643. Photo © Museum Plantin-Moretus and Print Room, Antwerp.

*Ecce nouo demptam tollit de corpore costam, Et capit hinc formæ facta puella decus. Genes. 2.*

Figs. 18-20. Jan Sadeler, after Crispijn van den Broeck. Creation of Eve, with Admonition; Shame and Clothing; The Family of Adam. Published by Gerard de Jode, 1585. Reproduced by permission of the Henry E. Huntington Library and Art Gallery, San Marino, Calif.

Ad patris irati uocem formidine capti, Aufugiunt Culpam, noscit utraq; suam. Genes. 3.

19

Cryspin · X.                                                          Theodor · f.

Lapsus · homo tolerat miseram cum coniuge · vitam ,    Cunctaq; tabescunt membra dolore graui · Genes · 5

20

Fig. 21. Jan Sadeler, after Michael de Coxcij. Mourning over Abel, 1576. Published by Gerard de Jode, 1585. Reproduced by permission of the Henry E. Huntington Library and Art Gallery, San Marino, Calif.

5

IOHAN · WIRICX · INV · ET · F · EXCV · CVM · PRI

*Inspirauit in faciem eius spira:
culam vitæ.*

Figs. 22-23. Jan Wierix. The Creation of Adam and The Judgment of
Adam and Eve. Photo © Museum Plantin-Moretus and Print Room,
Antwerp.

*Dixit Dominus: Quis enim indicauit tibi quod nudus esses.*

Fig. 24. The Marriage of Adam and Eve. French, c. 1410. MS. FR 6446, fol. 3v. Reproduced by permission of the Bibliothèque Nationale, Paris.

Figs 25-26. Frans Franchen II. Painted cabinet, c. 1650. Reproduced by permission of the Fotocommissie Rijksmuseum, Amsterdam.

26

Figs. 27-29. Basilica of San Marco, Venice. Mosaic Creation Dome, thirteenth century. Alinari/Art Resource, New York.

29

Fig. 30. Jacopo Tintoretto (Venetian, 1518-94). The Fall. Scuola di San Rocco, Venice. Alinari/Art Resource, New York.

Fig. 31. Paolo Veronese (Paolo Caliari, Venetian, c. 1528-88). Creation of Eve, oil on canvas, c. 1570, 81.5 x 103.8 cm, in the Charles H. and Mary F. S. Worcester Collection, 1930.286. Photo © the Art Institute of Chicago. All rights reserved.

Fig. 32. Chartres Cathedral. The Creation of Eve. Thirteenth-century sculpture, exterior, North Portal.

Fig. 33. The Windmill Psalter. Initial B from Psalm 1, *Beatus Vir*. M.102, fol. 1v. East Anglia or Canterbury, thirteenth century. Reproduced by permission of the Pierpont Morgan Library, New York.

Fig. 34. The Bohun Psalter and Hours. Creation series with Adam and Eve in Paradise. English, late fourteenth century. Bodleian MS. Auct.D.4.4., fol. 1r. Reproduced by permission of the Bodleian Library, Oxford.

Fig. 35. The Carrow Psalter and Hours. An angel gives tools to Adam and Eve. Eastern England, c. 1250. Reproduced by permission of the Walters Art Gallery, Baltimore.

Fig. 36. Trinity Psalter. The Harrowing of Hell. Trinity Ms. O.4.16, fol. 114. Reproduced by permission of the Master and Fellows of Trinity College, Cambridge.

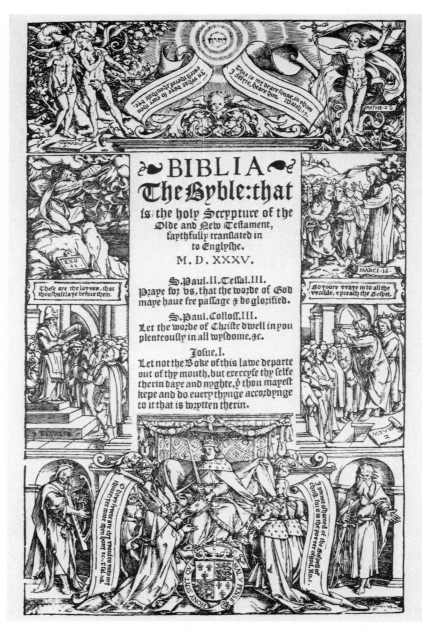

Fig. 37. Title page, Coverdale Bible, 1535. Reproduced by permission of the Department of Special Collections, Van Pelt Library, University of Pennsylvania.

Fig. 38. Headpiece to Genesis, Coverdale Bible, 1535. Reproduced by permission of the Department of Special Collections, Van Pelt Library, University of Pennsylvania.

Fig. 39. Title page, Matthew Bible, 1537. Reproduced by permission of the Department of Special Collections, Van Pelt Library, University of Pennsylvania.

Fig. 40. Frontispiece, Matthew Bible, 1537. Reproduced by permission of the Department of Special Collections, Van Pelt Library, University of Pennsylvania.

Fig. 41. Inset illustration to Genesis 3, Coverdale Bible. Reproduced by permission of the Department of Special Collections, Van Pelt Library, University of Pennsylvania.

Fig. 42. Inset illustration to Genesis 3, The Great Bible, 1541. Reproduced by permission of the Rare Book and Special Collections Library, University of Illinois Library, Urbana-Champaign.

Fig. 43. Frontispiece to Genesis, Geneva Bible, 1583. Reproduced by permission of the Department of Special Collections, Van Pelt Library, University of Pennsylvania.

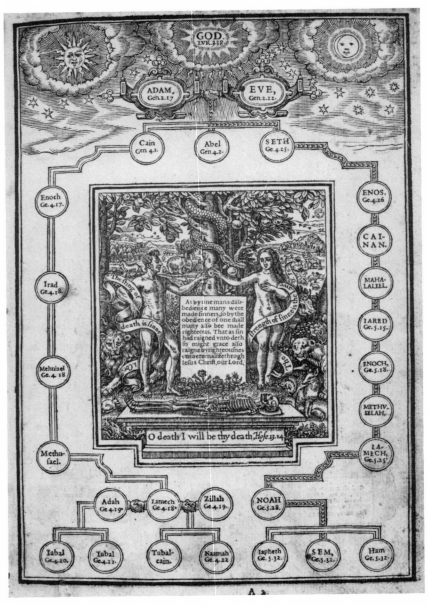

Fig. 44. John Speed, Genealogy (1610), inserted into Authorized Bible, 1612.
Reproduced by permission of the British Library.

Fig. 45. Frontispiece to Genesis, Authorized Bible, Edinburgh, 1637. Reproduced by permission of the British Library.

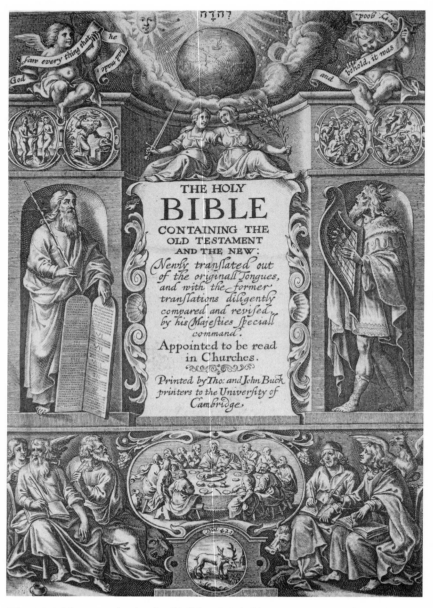

Fig. 46. Title page, Authorized Bible, Cambridge, 1630. Reproduced by permission of the Rare Book and Special Collections Library, University of Illinois Library, Urbana-Champaign.

Figs. 47-52. Jan Saenredam, after Abraham Bloemart. Genesis series, 1604.
Reproduced by permission of the Centraal Museum, Utrecht.

A. Bloemaert excu.
J. Saenredam sculp. 2.

Jusserat auricomo nemus omne grauescere foetu
Rerum opsfex, hominem silvas habitare beatas,

Et colere, et legem ruris servare fruendi
Posse datum; rapta est per devia prona voluntas.

G. breve.

48

A. Bloemaert. inue.
J. Saenredam sculp.
3

Ambitiosa fames, vetitique insana cupido,    Letharunt mortale genus; cum perfida pellex
Stultaq; credulitas stygio insinuata draconi    Aufa est fatales decerpere ab arbore fructus

49

A. Bloemaert inuen.
J. Saenredam sculp.

*Reddita lux oculis; pudor, et gravis ingruit horror*
*Attonitis: Cum torta tegens finuamina ferpens*
*Verrit humum: Superâ ruit aliger arce satelles,*
*Qui flammâ intactas defendat vindice filuas*

50

A. Bloemaert in.
J. Saenredam sculp.    5

Horrida iam dumis tellus, et decolor ætas    Suadebat, terramque rudi tentare ligone,
Stramineas habitare casas, et figere cervos    Longaque versa diffundere stamina fuso

51

A. Bloemaert inue.
J. Saenredam sculp.
6

Horna fruge Cain, sectoque aram imbuit agno     Sanguine fraterno terram incestavit avitam:  Herculius
Gratus Abel: Tum felle Cain accensus, et ira,     Heu lessum faciunt natorum in cæde parentes!

52

Fig. 53. Adrian Collaert, after Hans Bol. The Creation: God Speaking to Adam and Eve. Photo © Museum Plantin-Moretus and Print Room, Antwerp.

Jeﬀu le foum̃rai
comcncauc et
lumiere parfaitte.
en auoy touttes
choſes viſibles et
nuiſibles paſſees preſentes et ad
uemr maniſeſtemeir et aperte

moumement dair. Et ſachies q̃
Dieu eſt ſa parolle et ſa parolle eſt
Dieu. Et eſt ceſte parolle complie
et parfaite par m̃. ſouueraimes
Dictuttes ſaus leſquelles Dictuttes
la parolle dieu ceſt a dire ſa dette
ne puet eſtre acoplie ne parfaite

Fig. 54. Frontispiece, *The Seven Ages of the World.* Mons, c. 1460. MS. 9047, fol. 1v. Reproduced by permission of the Bibliothèque Royale Albert 1er, Brussels.

Fig. 55. Adam and Eve in Paradise, from Joseph Fletcher, *The Historie of the Perfect-Cursed-Blessed Man* (London, 1628). Reproduced by permission of the Rare Book and Special Collections Library, University of Illinois Library, Urbana-Champaign.

Fig. 56. Adriaen van de Venne, from Jacob Cats, *'sWerelts Begin, Midden, Eynde* (1643). Reproduced by permission of the Rare Book and Special Collections Library, University of Illinois Library, Urbana-Champaign.

Fig. 57. Johann Ulrich Kraus, after Georg-Christoph Eimmart. Adam and
Eve praying to God. From Christoph Weigel, *Biblia Ectypa* (Augsburg, 1695).
Photo © Museum Plantin-Moretus and Print Room, Antwerp.

Fig. 58. Gerard Vander Gucht, after Matthias Scheits. Adam and Eve in Paradise (The Kitto Bible, vol. 2, fol. 200, cat. 49000). Reproduced by permission of the Henry E. Huntington Library and Art Gallery, San Marino, Calif.

Fig. 59. Jan Swart van Groningen. The Temptation of Adam. Netherlandish, sixteenth century. Oil on panel, 198 x 166 cm. Reproduced by permission of the Minneapolis Institute of Arts: The William Hood Dunwoody Fund.

Fig. 60. Zacharias Dolendo, after Bartholomeus Spranger. The Fall, 1611.
Reproduced by permission of the Rijksmuseum-Stichting, Amsterdam.

# Bibliography

Aarsleff, Hans. *From Locke to Saussure: Essays on the Study of Language and Intellectual History.* Minneapolis: University of Minnesota Press, 1982.
——— . Seminar, "Linguistic Thought from the Renaissance to Romanticism," in the 1989-90 Program of the Folger Institute.
Addison, Joseph. *A Familiar Explanation of the Poetical Works of Milton. To which is prefixed Mr. Addison's Criticism on "Paradise Lost."* London, 1762.
Ainsworth, Henry. *Annotations vpon the five bookes of Moses.* London, 1627.
Alston, William P. *Divine Nature and Human Language: Essays in Philosophical Theology.* Ithaca: Cornell University Press, 1989.
——— . *Religious Belief and Philosophical Thought: Readings in the Philosophy of Religion.* New York: Harcourt Brace and World, 1963.
Alter, Robert. *The Art of Biblical Poetry.* New York: Basic Books, 1985.
Andreini, Giovanni Battista. *L'Adamo.* Milan, 1613 and 1617.
*Articles agreed upon by the archbishops and bishops of both prouinces, and the whole cleargie, in the conuocation holden at London in the yeere 1562.* London, 1629.
Asals, Heather A. R. *Equivocal Predication: George Herbert's Way to God.* Toronto: University of Toronto Press, 1981.
Augustine. *Confessions.* Trans. William Watts. London, 1631. Reprinted in *St. Augustine's Confessions.* Loeb Classical Library. 2 vols. Cambridge, Mass.: Harvard University Press, 1961.
——— . *Of the Citie of God, with the learned comments of Io. Vives.* Trans. John Healey. London, 1610.
——— . *On Christian Doctrine.* Trans. D. W. Robertson, Jr. Indianapolis: Bobbs-Merrill, 1958.
——— . *Sancti Aureli Augustini Opera: De Doctrina Christiana, Libri Quattuor.* Edited by William M. Green. *Corpus Scriptorum Ecclesiasticorum Latinorum,* 80. Vienna: Hoelder-Pichler-Temsky, 1963.
Austen, Ralph. *A Treatise of Fruit-Trees.* Oxford, 1653.
Ayerton, Michael. *The Rudiments of Paradise.* New York: Weybright and Talley, 1971.
Bacon, Francis. *The Complete Essays.* New York: Washington Square Press, 1963.

Bardi, E. G. Girolamo. *Della Cose Notabili Della Citta di Venetia, Libri II*. Venice, 1587.

Barker, Arthur E. "*Paradise Lost:* The Relevance of Regeneration." In *"Paradise Lost": A Tercentenary Tribute*, ed. Balachandra Rajan. Toronto: University of Toronto Press, 1969.

———. "Structural and Doctrinal Pattern in Milton's Later Poems." In *Essays in English Literature from the Renaissance to the Victorian Age Presented to A. S. P. Woodhouse*, ed. Millar MacLure and F. W. Watts. Toronto: University of Toronto Press, 1964.

Bartholomaeus Anglicus. *Batman vppon Bartholome his book De proprietatibus rerum Bartholomaeus*. London, 1582.

Bartsch, Adam von. *The Illustrated Bartsch*. General editor Walter L. Strauss. Vol. 26: *The Works of Marcantonio Raimondi and of His School*, ed. Konrad Oberhuber. New York: Abaris Books, 1978.

Batten, Adrian. "O Praise the Lord." Printed in John Barnard, *First Book of Selected Church Musick*. London, 1641. Edited by Anthony Greening in *The Oxford Book of Tudor Anthems*, comp. Christopher Morris. Oxford: Oxford University Press, 1978.

Baxter, Richard. *More Reasons For The Christian Religion*. London, 1672.

———. *Two Disputations on Original Sin*. London, 1675.

Benet, Diana Treviño. "Abdiel and the Son in the Separation Scene." *MS* 18 (1983): 129-43.

———. " 'No Outward Aid Require': A Note on Eve in Separation." *ANQ* 2 (1989): 90-94

Bénézit, Emmanuel. *Dictionnaire des Peintres, Sculpteurs, Dessinateurs, et Graveurs*. 10 vols. Reprint. Paris: Librairie Gründ, 1976.

Bennett, Joan S. " 'Go': Milton's Antinomianism and the Separation Scene in *Paradise Lost*, Book 9." *PMLA* 98 (1983): 388-404.

———. *Reviving Liberty: Radical Christian Humanism in Milton's Great Poems*. Cambridge, Mass.: Harvard University Press, 1989.

Berry, Boyd M. *Process of Speech: Puritan Religious Writing and "Paradise Lost."* Baltimore: The Johns Hopkins University Press, 1976.

Beza, Theodore. *Job expounded by Theodore Beza, partly in manner of a Commentary, partly in manner of a Paraphrase*. Faithfully translated out of Latine into English. Cambridge, 1589.

Blessington, Francis C. " 'That Undisturbed Song of Pure Concent': *Paradise Lost* and the Epic-Hymn." In *Renaissance Genres: Essays on Theory, History, and Interpretation*, ed. Barbara K. Lewalski. Cambridge, Mass.: Harvard University Press, 1986.

Blith, Walter. *The English Improver Improved*. London, 1653.

Bloom, Harold. *The Book of J*. Translated from the Hebrew by David Rosenberg, interpreted by Harold Bloom. New York: Grove Weidenfeld, 1990.

———. *Ruin the Sacred Truths: Poetry and Belief from the Bible to the Present*. Cambridge, Mass.: Harvard University Press, 1989.

Blunden, Edmund. "Some Seventeenth-Century Latin Poems by English Writers." *UTQ* 25 (1955): 10-22.

Boccaccio, Giovanni. *Decameron*. Edited by Charles S. Singleton. Baltimore: The Johns Hopkins University Press, 1974.

———. *The Modell of Wit, Mirth, Eloquence, and Conuersation* [*The Decameron*]. Trans. anon. London, 1625.

Bonnell, John K. "The Serpent with a Human Head in Art and in Mystery Play." *American Journal of Archaeology*, 2d series, 21 (1917).

Bowen, Elizabeth. *Collected Impressions*. London: Longmans Green, 1950.

Bradley, S. A. J. *Anglo-Saxon Poetry*. London: Dent, 1982.

Browne, Sir Thomas. *Works*. Edited by Geoffrey Keynes. 4 vols. Chicago: University of Chicago Press, 1964.

Bullough, Geoffrey. "Milton and Cats." In *Essays in English Literature from the Renaissance to the Victorian Age presented to A. S. P. Woodhouse*, ed. Millar MacLure and F. W. Watts. Toronto: University of Toronto Press, 1964.

Bulwer, John. *Chirologia: or the Natvrall Langvage of the Hand*. London, 1644.

Byard, Margaret Mather. "'Adventrous Song': Milton and the Music of Rome." In *Milton and Italy: Contexts, Images, Contradictions*, ed. Mario A. DiCesare. Binghamton: Medieval and Renaissance Texts and Studies, 1991.

Byrd, William. *The Great Service*. Edited by Craig Monson. Vol. 10 of *The Byrd Edition*, gen. ed. Philip Brett. London: Stainer and Bell, 1982.

*The Caedmon Manuscript of Anglo-Saxon Biblical Poetry*. Introduction by Israel Gollancz. London: Oxford University Press, 1927.

Calvin, John. *A commentarie vpon Genesis by John Calvin Englished by Thomas Thymme*. London, 1578.

*The Cambridge Companion to Milton*. Edited by Dennis Danielson. Cambridge: Cambridge University Press, 1989.

Castiglione. *Il Libro del Cortegiano del Conte Baldesar Castiglione*. Venice, 1528.

———. *The Courtyer of Count Baldessar Castiglio . . . done into English by Thomas Hoby*. London, 1577.

Cats, Jacob. *Alle de Wercken van der Heere Jacob Cats*. Amsterdam, 1712.

———. "Gront Houwelick." In *'s Werelts Begin, Midden, Eynde, Besloten in den Trou-Ringh*. Amsterdam, 1643.

Caviness, Madeline Harrison. *The Windows of Christ Church Cathedral, Canterbury*. In *Corpus Vitrearum Medii Aevi: Great Britain*, 2. London: Oxford University Press, 1981.

Caxton, William. *Mirrour of the World*. Edited by Oliver H. Prior. EETS, 101-2. London, 1913.

Charlesworth, James H., ed. *The Old Testament Pseudepigrapha*. 2 vols. Garden City: Doubleday, 1983.

Chaucer, Geoffrey. *The Poetical Works of Chaucer*. Edited by F. N. Robinson. Boston: Houghton Mifflin, 1933.

*The Christian World: A Social and Cultural History.* Edited by Geoffrey Barraclough. New York: Harry N. Abrams, 1981.

Christopher, Georgia. *Milton and the Science of the Saints.* Princeton: Princeton University Press, 1982.

Cinquemani, A. M. "Henry Reynold's *Mythomystes* and the Continuity of Ancient Modes of Allegoresis in Seventeenth-Century England." *PMLA* 85
(1970): 1041-49.

Cockerell, S. C. *A Book of Old Testament Illustrations.* Cambridge: Cambridge
University Press, 1927.

Cockerell, S. C., and M. R. James. *Two East Anglian Psalters at the Bodleian
Library, Oxford.* Oxford: Oxford University Press, 1926.

Cocklereas, Joanne Lewis. "Much Deceiv'd, Much Failing, Hapless Eve: Iconography and Eve in Milton's *Paradise Lost.*" Ph.D. dissertation, University
of New Mexico, 1973.

Corcoran, Sister Mary Irma. *Milton's Paradise with Reference to the Hexameral
Background.* Washington, D.C.: Catholic University of America Press,
1945.

Corum, Richard. "In White Ink: *Paradise Lost* and Milton's Ideas of Women."
In *Milton and the Idea of Woman,* ed. Julia Walker. Urbana: University of
Illinois Press, 1988.

Cowley, Abraham. *The Complete Works in Verse and Prose of Abraham Cowley,*
ed. Alexander B. Grosart. 2 vols. New York: AMS Press, 1967.

Crofts, Robert. *Paradise Within Us: or, the happie mind.* London, 1640.

Culler, Jonathan. "Comparative Literature and the Pieties." In Modern Language Association, *Profession* (1986), 30-32.

Cuzin, Jean-Pierre. *Raphael: His Life and Works.* Trans. Sarah Brown. Secau-
cus, N.J.: Chartwell Books, 1985.

Danielson, Dennis. *Milton's Good God: A Study in Literary Theodicy.* Cambridge: Cambridge University Press, 1982.

Dante Alighieri. *The Divine Comedy of Dante Alighieri.* Translation and comments by John D. Sinclair. 3 vols. New York: Oxford University Press,
1979.

Davies, J. G., ed. *A Dictionary of Liturgy and Worship.* London: SCM Press,
and New York: The Macmillan Company, 1972.

Davies, R. T., ed. *Medieval English Lyrics.* Evanston: Northwestern University
Press, 1964.

Davies, Stevie. *The Feminine Reclaimed: The Idea of Woman in Spenser,
Shakespeare and Milton.* Lexington: University Press of Kentucky, 1986.

Day, Malcolm M. *Thomas Traherne.* Boston: Twayne, 1982.

De' Bardi, "Discourse on Ancient Music and Good Singing" (c. 1580). In
Oliver Strunk, *Source Readings in Music History: The Renaissance.* New
York: W. W. Norton, 1965.

De Jode, Gerard. *Thesaurus Sacrorvm historiarum veteris testamenti.* . . . Antwerp, 1585.

Delaissé, L. M. J. *Miniatures médiévales de la Librairie de Bourgogne au Cabinet des Manuscrits de la Bibliothèque Royale de Belgique.* Brussels: Éditions de la Connaissance, 1959. Translated as *Mittelalterliche Miniaturen.* Cologne: M. Dumont Schauberg, 1959. *Medieval Miniatures.* New York: H. N. Abrams, 1965.

Demouay, Patrick. *Rheims Cathedral.* Translated by Monique Dumond. Paris: La Goélette, n.d.

Demus, Otto. *The Mosaics of San Marco in Venice.* Vol. 2: *The Thirteenth Century.* Chicago: University of Chicago Press, 1984.

De Seyn, Eug. M. H. *Dessinateurs, Graveurs, et Peintres des Anciens Pays-Bas: Écoles Flamande et Hollandaise.* Turnhout: Établissements Brepols S. A., n.d.

DeWald, E. T. *The Illustrations of the Utrecht Psalter.* Princeton: Princeton University Press, 1932.

De Witt, Antonio. *I Mosaici del Battistero di Firenze.* Vol. 4: *Le Storia della Genesi e di Giuseppe.* Florence: a cura della Cassa di Risparmio di Firenze, 1954.

Dieckmann, Liselotte. "Renaissance Hieroglyphics." *CL* 9 (1957): 308-21.

Di Salvo, Jacqueline. *War of Titans: Blake's Critique of Milton and the Politics of Religion.* Pittsburgh: University of Pittsburgh Press, 1983.

Doane, A. N. *Genesis A: A New Edition.* Madison: University of Wisconsin Press, 1978.

Dodwell, C. R. *The Canterbury School of Illumination.* Cambridge: Cambridge University Press, 1954.

Donne, John. *The Complete Poetry of John Donne.* Edited by John T. Shawcross. New York: Doubleday and Company, 1967.

———. *Devotions upon Emergent Occasions.* Reprint. Ann Arbor: University of Michigan Press, 1959.

———. *Paradoxes and Problemes.* Reprint. Soho: Nonesuch Press, 1923.

———. *The Sermons of John Donne.* Edited by George Potter and Evelyn M. Simpson. 10 vols. Berkeley: University of California Press, 1953-62.

Duncan, Joseph. *Milton's Earthly Paradise.* Minneapolis: University of Minnesota Press, 1972.

Dürer, Albrecht. *The Complete Woodcuts of Albrecht Dürer.* Edited by Willi Kurth. 1927. Reprint, New York: Dover Publications, 1963.

Du Rocher, Richard. *Milton and Ovid.* Ithaca: Cornell University Press, 1985.

Entzminger, Robert L. *Divine Word: Milton and the Redemption of Language.* Pittsburgh: Duquesne University Press, 1985.

*Essays in English Literature from the Renaissance to the Victorian Age Presented to A. S. P. Woodhouse.* Edited by Millar MacLure and F. W. Watts. Toronto: University of Toronto Press, 1964.

Evans, J. M. *"Paradise Lost" and the Genesis Tradition.* Oxford: At the Clarendon Press, 1968.

———. "Mortals' Chiefest Enemy." *MS* 20 (1984): 111-26.

Evelyn, John. *The Diary of John Evelyn.* Edited by William Bray. Washington, D.C.: M. Walter Dunne, 1901.

Ferry, Anne Davidson. "The Bird, the Blind Bard, and the Fortunate Fall." In *Reason and the Imagination: Studies in the History of Ideas, 1600-1800,* ed. J. A. Mazzeo. New York: Columbia University Press, 1962.

Ferguson, George. *Signs and Symbols in Christian Art.* Reprint. Oxford: Oxford University Press, 1976.

*A Fine Tuning: Studies of the Religious Poetry of Herbert and Milton.* Edited by Mary A. Maleski. Binghamton: Medieval and Renaissance Texts and Studies, 1989.

Fiore, Peter A. " 'Account Mee Man': The Incarnation of *Paradise Lost,*" *HLQ* 39 (1975): 51-56.

Fish, Stanley E. *Surprised by Sin: The Reader in "Paradise Lost."* Berkeley and Los Angeles: University of California Press, 1967, rpt. 1971.

Fletcher, Harris Francis, ed. *John Milton's Complete Poetical Works Reproduced in Photographic Facsimile.* 4 vols. Urbana: University of Illinois Press, 1943.

———. *Milton's Rabbinical Readings.* Urbana: University of Illinois Press, 1930.

Flinker, Noam. "Courting Urania: The Narrator of *Paradise Lost.*" In *Milton and the Idea of Woman,* ed. Julia Walker. Urbana: University of Illinois Press, 1988.

Flores, Nona. " '*Virgineum Vultum Habens*': The Woman-Headed Serpent in Art and Literature from 1300 to 1700." Ph.D. dissertation, University of Illinois, 1981.

Fraser, Russell. *The Language of Adam: On the Limits and Systems of Discourse.* New York: Columbia University Press, 1977.

French, J. Milton. *Life Records of John Milton.* 5 vols. New Brunswick: Rutgers University Press, 1949-58.

Froula, Christine. "Pechter's Specter: Milton's Bogey Writ Small." *Critical Inquiry* 11 (1984): 171-78.

———. "When Eve Reads Milton: Undoing the Canonical Economy," *Critical Inquiry* 10 (1983): 321-47.

Frye, Roland Mushat. *Milton's Imagery and the Visual Arts.* Princeton: Princeton University Press, 1978.

Gallagher, Philip J. *Milton, the Bible, and Misogyny.* Edited by Eugene R. Cunnar and Gail L. Mortimer. Columbia: University of Missouri Press, 1990.

Gerard, John. *The Herball or General Historie of Plantes.* 1597.

———. *Leaves from Gerard's Herball.* Edited by Marcus Woodward. New York: Dover Publications, 1969.

Gerhart, Mary, and Allan Melvin Russell. *Metaphoric Process: The Creation of Scientific and Religious Understanding.* Fort Worth: Texas Christian University Press, 1984.

Giamatti, A. Bartlett. *The Earthly Paradise and the Renaissance Epic.* Princeton: Princeton University Press, 1966.

Gilbert, Sandra. "Patriarchal Poetry and Women Readers: Reflections on Milton's Bogey." *PMLA* 93 (May, 1978): 368-82.

Gilligan, Carol. *In a Different Voice: Psychological Theory and Women's Development.* Cambridge, Mass.: Harvard University Press, 1982.

Gilman, Ernest. *Iconoclasm and Poetry in the English Reformation: Down Went Dagon.* Chicago: University of Chicago Press, 1986.

Goltzius, Hendrick. *Hendrik Goltzius, 1558-1617: The Complete Engravings, Etchings, and Woodcuts.* Edited by Walter L. Strauss. New York: Abaris Books, 1977.

Gombrich, E. H. " 'Icones Symbolicae': The Visual Image in Neoplatonic Thought." *JWCI* 11 (1948): 163-92.

Gordon, D. J. *The Renaissance Imagination.* Berkeley and Los Angeles: University of California Press, 1980.

Greene, Thomas. *The Descent from Heaven: A Study in Epic Continuity.* New Haven: Yale University Press, 1963.

Greenslade, S. L. "English Versions of the Bible, A.D. 1524-1611." In *The Cambridge History of the Bible: The West from the Reformation to the Present Day,* ed. S. L. Greenslade. Cambridge: Cambridge University Press, 1963-70.

Griffin, Dustin. *Regaining Paradise: Milton and the Eighteenth Century.* Cambridge: Cambridge University Press, 1986.

Guibbory, Achsah. *The Map of Time: Seventeenth-Century Literature and Ideas of Pattern in History.* Urbana: University of Illinois Press, 1986.

Guillory, John. *Poetic Authority: Spenser, Milton, and Literary History.* New York: Columbia University Press, 1983.

Hagstrum, Jean. *The Sister Arts.* Chicago: University of Chicago Press, 1958.

Haines, Victor Yelverton. *The Fortunate Fall of Sir Gawain.* Washington, D.C.: University Press of America, 1982.

Hall, James. *Dictionary of Subjects and Symbols in Art.* Introduction by Kenneth Clark. Rev. ed. New York: Harper and Row, 1974.

Haller, William, and Malleville Haller. "The Puritan Art of Love." *HLQ* 5 (1941-42): 235-72.

Halley, Janet E. "Female Autonomy in Milton's Sexual Poetics." In *Milton and the Idea of Woman,* ed. Julia Walker. Urbana: University of Illinois Press, 1988.

Harbison, Craig. Introduction to *Symbols in Transformation: Iconographic Themes at the Time of the Reformation. An Exhibition of Prints in Memory of Erwin Panofsky.* Princeton: Princeton University Press, 1969.

Hawkins, Henry. *Parthenia Sacra.* 1633.

Hayter, Mary. *The New Eve in Christ: The Use and Abuse of the Bible in the Debate about Women in the Church.* London: Society for the Preservation of Christian Knowledge, 1987.

Heninger, S. K., Jr. *Touches of Sweet Harmony: Pythagorean Cosmology and Renaissance Poetics.* San Marino, Calif.: Huntington Library, 1974.

Henry, Avril. *Biblia Pauperum: A Facsimile and Edition*. Ithaca: Cornell University Press, 1987.

Herbert, A. S. *Historical Catalogue of Printed Editions of the English Bible, 1525-1961*. London: British and Foreign Bible Society; New York: American Bible Society, 1968.

Herbert, George. *The Latin Poetry of George Herbert: A Bilingual Edition*. Translated by Mark McClosky and Paul R. Murphy. Athens: University of Ohio Press, 1965.

————. *The Works of George Herbert*. Edited with commentary by F. E. Hutchinson. Oxford: At the Clarendon Press, 1941.

Hesiod. *The Poems of Hesiod*. Translated by R. M. Frazer. Norman: University of Oklahoma Press, 1983.

*History of Adam and Eve*. 1753.

*The Holie Bible Faithfully Translated into English* . . . By the English College of Doway. 2 vols. Douai, 1609.

Hollstein, F. W. H. *Dutch and Flemish Etchings, Engravings, and Woodcuts, ca. 1450-1700*. 37 vols. Amsterdam: Menno Hertzberger, 1949–; Roosendahl: Koninklijk van Poll, 1991–.

Homer. *The Odyssey*. Translated by Robert Fitzgerald. Garden City: Doubleday, 1961.

Hopkins, G. M. *The Poems of Gerard Manley Hopkins*. Edited by W. H. Gardner and N. H. MacKenzie. Oxford: Oxford University Press, 1970.

Horus Apollo [Horapollo]. *Orus Apollo*. 1543.

————. *Hori Apollonis: Selecta hieroglyphica*. Rome, 1606.

————. *The Hieroglyphics of Horapollo*. Translated by George Boas. New York: Pantheon Books, 1950.

Houvet, Étienne. *Cathédrale de Chartres*. Vol. 2: *XIIIe Siècle*. Chelles, S.-et-M.: Hélio, A. Faucheux, 1919.

————. *Chartres Cathedral*. Rev. ed. Edited and translated by Malcome B. Miller. San-Dié: Hautes-Vosges Impressions, 1985.

Hyman, Lawrence W. "Must We Pin Milton's Shoulders to the Mat?" *MQ* 21 (1987): 122-23.

James, M. R. *The Bestiary, Being a Reproduction in Full of the Manuscript I i.4.26 in the University Library, Cambridge*. Oxford: Oxford University Press, 1928.

————. *The Bohun Manuscripts: A Group of Five Manuscripts Executed in England about 1370 for the Bohun Family*. Oxford: Oxford University Press, 1936.

————. *The Canterbury Psalter*. London: Humphries and Company, 1935.

————. Introduction to Sydney C. Cockerell, *A Book of Old Testament Illustrations*. Cambridge: Cambridge University Press, 1927.

Johnson, Lee M. "Milton's Epic Style: The Invocations in *Paradise Lost*." In *The Cambridge Companion to Milton*, ed. Dennis Danielson. Cambridge: Cambridge University Press, 1989.

Johnston, Carol Ann. "'Heavenly Perspective': Thomas Traherne and Seventeenth-Century Visual Traditions." Ph.D. dissertation, Harvard University, 1992.

Jonson, Ben. *The Complete Poetry*. Edited by William B. Hunter, Jr. New York: New York University Press, 1963.

Julian of Norwich. *Revelations of Divine Love*. Translated by Clifton Wolters. Baltimore: Penguin Books, 1966.

Katzenellenbogen, Adolph. *The Sculptural Programs of Chartres Cathedral*. Baltimore: The Johns Hopkins University Press, 1959.

Kaufmann, U. Milo. *Paradise in the Age of Milton*. ELS Monograph Series, 11. Victoria, B.C.: University of Victoria, 1978.

Keats, John. *The Letters of John Keats, 1814-1821*. Edited by Hyder Edward Rollins. 2 vols. Cambridge, Mass.: Harvard University Press, 1958.

Kerrigan, William. *The Prophetic Milton*. Charlottesville: University Press of Virginia, 1974.

Kerrigan, William, and Gordon Braden. *The Idea of the Renaissance*. Baltimore: The Johns Hopkins University Press, 1989.

———. "Milton's Coy Eve: *Paradise Lost* and Renaissance Love Poetry." *ELH* 53 (1986): 27-51.

Kirkconnell, Watson. *The Celestial Cycle*. Toronto: University of Toronto Press, 1952.

Kleine-Ehrminger, Madeleine. *Our Lady of Strasbourg Cathedral-Church*. Lyon: Lescuyer, 1986.

Knedlik, Janet. "Fancy, Faith, and Generative Mimesis in Paradise Lost." *MLQ* 47 (1986): 19-47.

Knox, Ronald, trans. *The Holy Bible: A Translation from the Latin Vulgate in the Light of the Hebrew and Greek Originals*. New York: Sheed and Ward, 1954. Reprint. London: Burns and Oates, 1961.

Komroff, Manuel, ed. *The Apocrapha or Non-Canonical Books of the Bible: The King James Version*. New York: Tudor Publishing Company, 1936.

Kurmann, Peter. *La Façade de la Cathédrale de Reims*. 2 vols. Lausanne: Éditions Payot, 1987.

Labriola, Albert C. "'Thy Humiliation Shall Exalt': The Christology of *Paradise Lost*." *MS* 15 (1981): 29-42

Labriola, Albert C., and Edward Sichi, Jr., eds. *Milton's Legacy in the Arts*. University Park: Pennsylvania State University Press, 1988.

Lambotte, Paul. *Flemish Painting before the Eighteenth Century*. Translated by Herbert B. Grimsditch. London: The Studio, 1927.

Lancetta, Triolo. *Scena Tragica d'Adamo e d'Eua*. Venice, 1644.

Lane, Barbara G. "The Genesis Woodcuts of a Dutch Adaptation of the *Vita Christi*." In *The Early Illustrated Book: Essays in Honor of Lessing J. Rosenwald*, ed. Sandra Hindman. Washington, D.C.: Library of Congress, 1982.

Largent, Regina M. "A Multilevel Celebration: Milton's Morning Hymn." *MQ* 22 (1988): 63-66.

Lawes, William, and Henry Lawes. *Choice Psalmes put into Musick, For Three Voices.* London, 1648.

Le Comte, Edward. *Milton and Sex.* New York: Columbia University Press, 1978.

Legg, J. Wickham. *The Sarum Missal, Edited from Three Early Manuscripts.* Oxford: At the Clarendon Press, 1916.

Leonard, John. *Naming in Paradise: Milton and the Language of Adam and Eve.* Oxford: At the Clarendon Press, 1990.

Levi D'Ancona, Mirella. *The Garden of the Renaissance: Botanical Symbolism in Italian Painting.* Florence: Olschki, 1977.

Lewalski, Barbara Kiefer. *Milton's Brief Epic.* Providence: Brown University Press, 1966.

———. *"Paradise Lost" and the Rhetoric of Literary Forms.* Princeton: Princeton University Press, 1985.

———. *Protestant Poetics and the Seventeenth Century Religious Lyric.* Princeton: Princeton University Press, 1979.

Lieb, Michael. *The Dialectics of Creation: Patterns of Birth and Regeneration in "Paradise Lost."* Amherst: University of Massachusetts Press, 1970.

———. *Poetics of the Holy: A Reading of "Paradise Lost."* Chapel Hill: University of North Carolina Press, 1981.

Lindenbaum, Peter. "Lovemaking in Milton's Paradise." *MS* 6 (1974): 277-306.

Lindner, Kurt. *Queen Mary's Psalter.* Hamburg: Parey, 1966.

Loredano, Giovanni Francesco. *The Life of Adam: A Facsimile Reproduction of the English Translation of 1659.* Introduction by Roy C. Flannagan with John Arthos. Gainesville: Scholars' Facsimile Reprints, 1967.

Lovejoy, A. O. "Milton and the Paradox of the Fortunate Fall." *ELH* 4 (1937): 161-79.

Low, Anthony. *Blaze of Noon.* New York: Columbia University Press, 1974.

———. *The Georgic Revolution.* Princeton: Princeton University Press, 1985.

———. "Idolatry, Iconoclasm, and Beauty of Form." *Christianity and Literature* 38 (1989): 5-12.

MacCallum, Hugh. *Milton and the Sons of God: The Divine Image in Milton's Epic Poetry.* Toronto: University of Toronto Press, 1986.

McClung, William. *The Architecture of Paradise: Survivals of Eden and Jerusalem.* Berkeley and Los Angeles: University of California Press, 1983.

McColley, Diane K. "Free Will and Obedience in the Separation Scene of *Paradise Lost.*" *SEL* 12 (1972): 103-20.

———. "Herbert's Hierophons: Musical Configurations in George Herbert's 'The Church.'" In *A Fine Tuning: Studies of the Religious Poetry of Herbert and Milton, Festschrift for Joseph H. Summers,* ed. Mary Maleski. Binghamton: Medieval and Renaissance Texts and Studies, 1989.

———. "Milton and the Sexes." In *The Cambridge Companion to Milton,* ed. Dennis Danielson. Cambridge: Cambridge University Press, 1989.

―――. *Milton's Eve*. Urbana: University of Illinois Press, 1983.

McKerrow, R. B., and F. S. Ferguson. *Title-Page Borders Used in England and Scotland, 1485-1640*. London: Bibliographical Society, 1932.

McMullin, B. J. "The 1629 Cambridge Bible." In *Transactions of the Cambridge Bibliographical Society 8*, part 4.

Mahood, M. M. "Something Understood: The Nature of Herbert's Wit." In *Metaphysical Poetry*, ed. Malcolm Bradbury and David Palmer. Stratford-upon-Avon Studies, 11. New York: St. Martin's Press, 1970.

Mâle, Emile. *Chartres*. New York: Harper and Row, 1983.

Mander, M. N. K. "The Music of *L'Allegro* and *Il Penseroso*." In *Milton in Italy: Contexts, Images, Contradictions*, ed. Mario A. Di Cesare. Binghamton: Medieval and Renaissance Texts and Studies, 1991.

Marchant, John, ed. *Milton's "Paradise Lost." A Poem, in twelve books*. With notes, etymological, critical, classical, and explanatory. Collected from Dr. Bentley; Dr. Pearce, the present Bishop of Bangor; Addison; Paterson; Newton; and other Authors. . . . London, 1751.

Martz, Louis L. *The Paradise Within: Studies in Vaughan, Traherne, and Milton*. New Haven: Yale University Press, 1964.

Marvell, Andrew. *Andrew Marvell: The Complete Poems*. Edited by Elizabeth Story Donno. Harmondsworth: Penguin Books Ltd., 1972, rpt. 1978.

Masson, David. *The Life of John Milton*. 7 vols. London: Macmillan, 1877-96.

Matternes, Jay H. "4,000,000 Years of Bipedalism." *National Geographic* 168 (Nov., 1985): 574-77.

Mazzoni, Jacopo. *On the Defense of the Comedy of Dante*. Translated by Robert L. Montgomery. Tallahassee: University Presses of Florida, 1983.

*Milton and the Idea of Woman*. Edited by Julia M. Walker. Urbana: University of Illinois Press, 1988.

*Milton in Italy: Contexts, Images, Contradictions*. Edited by Mario A. Di Cesare. Binghamton: Medieval and Renaissance Texts and Studies, 1991.

Miner, Earl. "Felix Culpa and the Redemptive Order of *Paradise Lost*." *PQ* 47 (1968): 43-54.

Mitchell, Stephen. *The Book of Job*. San Francisco: North Point Press, 1987.

Molière. *The Misanthrope*. Translated by Richard Wilbur. New York: Harcourt Brace Jovanovich, 1965.

Mollenkott, Virginia. "Milton's Rejection of the Fortunate Fall." *MQ* 6 (1972): 1-5.

Monteverdi, Claudio. *Selva Morale e Spirituale*. Venice, 1640.

Moore, Marianne. *The Complete Poems of Marianne Moore*. New York: Macmillan, Viking Press, 1967.

Morceau-Nélaton, Étienne. *La Cathédrale de Reims*. Paris, 1915.

Morgan, N. J. *The Medieval Painted Glass of Lincoln Cathedral*. Corpus Vitrearum Medii Aevi, Occasional Paper 3. London: Oxford University Press, 1983.

Morris, Christopher, comp. *The Oxford Book of Tudor Anthems*. London: Oxford University Press, 1978.

Nasr, Seyyed Hossein. "A Muslim Reflection on Religion and Theology." In *Consensus in Theology?* ed. Hans Küng. Philadelphia: Westminster Press, 1980.

Otten, Charlotte. *Environ'd with Eternity: God, Poems, and Plants in Sixteenth and Seventeenth Century England*. Lawrence: Coronado Press, 1985.

Otto, Rudolph. *The Idea of the Holy: An Inquiry into the Non-Rational Factor in the Idea of the Divine and Its Relation to the Rational*. Translated by John W. Harvey. London: Oxford University Press, 1923. 2d ed. 1958; rpt. 1979.

Pagels, Elaine. *Adam, Eve, and the Serpent*. New York: Random House, 1988.

————. *The Gnostic Gospels*. New York: Random House, 1979.

Palestrina, Giovanni Pierluigi da Palestrina (1526-94). *Le Opere Complete*. Edited by Raffaele Casimiri. Rome, 1941.

————. *Sicut Cervus*. Performance edition by Robert Hufstader. Bryn Mawr, 1946.

Parker, William Riley. *Milton: A Biography*. Oxford: At the Clarendon Press, 1968.

Parkinson, John. *Paradisi in Sole Paradisus: A Garden of all sorts of pleasant Flowers which our English ayre will permitt to be noursed vp*. London, 1648.

Patrides, C. A., ed. *The English Poems of George Herbert*. London: J. M. Dent and Sons, 1974.

Pecheux, Mother Mary Christopher. "The Concept of the Second Eve in *Paradise Lost*." *PMLA* 75 (1960): 359-66.

————. "The Second Adam and the Church in *Paradise Lost*." *ELH* 34 (1967): 173-87.

Pechter, Edward. "When Pechter Reads Froula Pretending She's Eve Reading Milton; or, New Feminist Is But Old Priest Writ Large." *Critical Inquiry* 11 (1984): 163-70.

Pecorino, Jessica Printz. "Eve Unparadised: Milton's Expulsion and Iconographic Tradition." *MQ* 15 (1981): 1-16.

Peczenic, Fannie. "Milton on the Creation of Eve: Adam's Dream and the Hieroglyphic of the Rib." In *A Fine Tuning: Studies of the Religious Poetry of Herbert and Milton,* ed. Mary A. Maleski. Binghamton: Medieval and Renaissance Texts and Studies, 1989.

Perkins, William. *Workes*. Cambridge, 1618.

Phillips, John A. *Eve: The History of an Idea*. San Francisco: Harper and Row, 1984.

*Physiologus*. Translated by Francis J. Carmody. San Francisco: Book Club of California, 1953.

Plato. *The Republic of Plato*. Translated by Francis MacDonald Cornford. London: Oxford University Press, 1945.

Pointon, Marcia. *Milton and English Art*. Manchester: Manchester University Press; Toronto, University of Toronto Press, 1970.

Pollard, A. W., and G. R. Redgrave. *A Short-Title Catalogue of Books Printed in England, Scotland, and Ireland and of English Books Printed Abroad, 1475-1640*. London: Bibliographical Society, 1926.

Praetorius, Michael. "Canticum trium puerorum." *Gesamtausgabe der Musikalischen Werke von Michael Praetorius,* ed. Friedrich Blume with Arnold Mendelssohn and Wilibald Gurlitt. Vol. 10: *Musarum Sioniarum Motectae et Psalmi Latini (1607),* pp. 150-71, arr. Rudolph Gerber. Wolfenbüttel: Georg Kallmeyer Verlag, 1931.

Purchas, Samuel. *Purchas his Pilgrimage*. London, 1613.

Puttenham, George. *The Art of English Poesie*. London, 1589.

Quilligan, Maureen. *Milton's Spenser: The Politics of Reading*. Ithaca: Cornell University Press, 1983.

Radzinowicz, Mary Ann. *Milton's Epics and the Book of Psalms*. Princeton: Princeton University Press, 1989.

Rajan, Balachandra. *The Lofty Rhyme*. Coral Gables: University of Miami Press, 1970.

Ralegh, Walter. *The History of the World*. 1614.

Ravenhall, Mary D. "Francis Atterbury and the First Illustrated Edition of Paradise Lost." *MQ* 16 (1982): 29-36.

———. "Francis Hayman and the Dramatic Interpretation of *Paradise Lost.*" *MS* 20 (1984): 87-109.

———. "Sources and Meaning in Dr. Aldrich's 1688 Illustrations of *Paradise Lost.*" *ELN* 19 (1982): 208-18.

Ray, Robert H. *The Herbert Allusion Book: Allusions to George Herbert in the Seventeenth Century. Studies in Philology* 83: Texts and Studies, 1986. Chapel Hill: University of North Carolina Press, 1986.

Réau, Louis. *Iconographie de L'Art Chrétien*. Vol. 1. Paris: Presses Universitaires de France, 1955.

Reinhardt, Hans. *La Cathédrale de Reims*. Paris: Presses Universitaires de France, 1963.

Revard, Stella. "*L'Allegro and Il Penseroso:* Classical Tradition and Renaissance Mythography." *PMLA* 101 (1986): 338-50.

Reynolds, Henry. *Mythomystes*. London, 1632.

Ricoeur, Paul. *Essays on Biblical Interpretation*. Edited by Lewis S. Mudge. Philadelphia: Fortress Press, 1980.

Ripa, Cesare. *Iconologia o vero descrittione dell' imagini vniversali*. Rome, 1593.

———. *Nova iconologia di Cesare Ripa Pervgino*. Padua, 1618.

———. *Iconologie . . . grauées . . . par Iacques de Bie, et moralement expliquées par I. Bavdoin . . . tirées des Recherches & des Figures de Cesar Ripa*. Paris, 1636.

Robbins, Frank Eggleston. *The Hexameral Literature: A Study of the Greek and Latin Commentaries on Genesis*. Chicago: University of Chicago Press, 1912.

Robels, Hella. *Niederlandische Zeichenungen vom 15. bis 19. Jahrhundert im Wallraf-Richartz-Museum Köln*. Cologne: Wallraf-Richarts-Museum, 1983.

Roston, Murray. *Milton and the Baroque*. London: Macmillan Press, 1980.

Russell, Letty M., ed. *Feminist Interpretation of the Bible*. Philadelphia: Westminster Press, 1985.

Salandra, Serafino della. *Adamo Caduto*. Edited by Flavio Giacomantonio. Cosenza: Effesette, 1987.

Samuel, Irene. "*Paradise Lost*." In *Critical Approaches to Six Major English Works: "Beowulf" through "Paradise Lost*," ed. R. M. Lumiansky and Herschel Baker. Philadelphia: University of Pennsylvania Press, 1968.

Sandler, Lucy Freeman. *Gothic Manuscripts, 1285-1385*. 2 vols. A Survey of Manuscripts Illuminated in the British Isles, 5. London: Harvey Miller, 1986.

Sandys, George, and Henry Lawes. *Paraphrase vpon the Psalmes of David. And vpon the Hymnes Dispersed throughout the Old and New Testaments*. 1638.

Sansovino, Francesco. *Venetia Citta Nobilissima et singolare, Descritta in XIIII. Libri*. Venice, 1581.

Schleiner, Louise. *The Living Lyre in English Verse from Elizabeth through the Restoration*. Columbia: University of Missouri Press, 1984.

Schorsch, Anita, and Martin Greif. *The Morning Stars Sang: The Bible in Popular and Folk Art*. New York: Universe Books, 1978.

Schwartz, Regina. *Remembering and Repeating: Biblical Creation in "Paradise Lost*." Cambridge: Cambridge University Press, 1988.

Seznec, Jean. *The Survival of the Pagan Gods*. Trans. Barbara F. Sessions. New York: Pantheon Books, 1953.

Shakespeare, William. *The Complete Works*. Edited by G. B. Harrison. New York: Harcourt Brace and Company, 1952.

Shoaf, Richard. *Milton, Poet of Duality: A Study of Semiosis in the Poetry and the Prose*. New Haven: Yale University Press, 1985.

Shuger, Debora Kuller. *Habits of Thought in the English Renaissance: Religion, Politics, and the Dominant Culture*. Berkeley and Los Angeles: University of California Press, 1990.

Shullenberger, William. "Wrestling with the Angel: *Paradise Lost* and Feminist Criticism." *MQ* 20 (1986): 69-85.

Sidney, Philip. *An Apology for Poetry*. Edited by Forrest G. Robinson. Indianapolis: Bobbs-Merrill, 1970.

Smart, Christopher. *Jubilate Agno*. Edited by W. H. Bond. London: R. Hart-Davis, 1954.

Smith, Huston. *Beyond the Post-Modern Mind*. Wheaton: Theosophical Publishing House, 1984.

Snyder, James. "The Bellaert Master and *De Proprietatibus Rerum.*" In *Text and Image in Fifteenth-Century Illustrated Dutch Bibles,* ed. Sandra Hindman. Leiden: Brill, 1977.

Steiner, George. *Real Presences.* Chicago: University of Chicago Press, 1989.

Stevens, Wallace. *The Palm at the End of the Mind.* Edited by Holly Stevens. New York: Alfred A. Knopf, 1971.

Stone, Merlin. *When God Was a Woman.* New York: Dial Press, 1976.

Strachan, James. *Early Bible Illustrations.* Cambridge: Cambridge University Press, 1957.

Stroup, Thomas B. *Religious Rite and Ceremony in Milton's Poetry.* Lexington: University of Kentucky Press, 1968.

Strunk, Oliver. *Source Readings in Music History: The Renaissance.* New York: W. W. Norton, 1965.

Summers, Joseph H. *George Herbert: His Religion and Art.* Cambridge, Mass.: Harvard University Press, 1954.

——. *The Muse's Method.* London: Chatto and Windus, 1962.

Swaim, Kathleen. *Before and After the Fall: Contrasting Modes in "Paradise Lost."* Amherst: University of Massachusetts Press, 1986.

——. " 'Hee for God Only, Shee for God in Him': Structural Parallelism in *Paradise Lost.*" *MS* 9 (1976): 121-49.

——. "The Morning Hymn of Praise in Book 5 of *Paradise Lost.*" *MQ* 22 (1988): 7-16.

Temperley, Nicholas. *Music of the English Parish Church.* Cambridge: Cambridge University Press, 1979.

Tennyson, Alfred. *The Poetical Works of Alfred Tennyson.* Chicago, 1889.

Terrien, Samuel. *Till the Heart Sings: A Biblical Theory of Manhood and Womanhood.* Philadelphia: Fortress Press, 1985.

Tertullian. "On Fasting." In *The Ante-Nicene Fathers,* ed. Alexander Roberts and James Donaldson, 4:104. Grand Rapids: W. B. Eerdmans, 1968.

*Testamenti Veteris Biblia Sacra.* Translated and annotated by Immanuel Tremellius and Francis Junius. London, 1580.

*Text and Image in Fifteenth-Century Illustrated Dutch Bibles.* Edited by Sandra Hindman. Leiden: Brill, 1977.

Thieme, Ulrich, Felix Becker, Fred C. Willis, and Hans Vollmer, eds. *Allgemeines Lexikon der Bildenden Künstler.* 37 vols. Leipzig: Verlag von Wilhelm Engelman, 1907-10; Verlag von E. A. Seemann, 1911-50.

Thomas, Lewis. Elihu Root lectures for the Council on Foreign Relations (Nov., 1983), in *Foreign Affairs* 62 (1984): 966-94; excerpted in *Harpers Magazine* 269 (July, 1984): 27.

Thompson, Craig R. *The Bible in English, 1525-1611.* A Folger Booklet. Charlottesville: University Press of Virginia, 1958.

Todd, Henry J. *Some Account of the Life and Writings of John Milton.* London, 1826.

Todd, Richard. *The Opacity of Signs: Acts of Interpretation in George Herbert's "The Temple."* Columbia: University of Missouri Press, 1986.

Traherne, Thomas. *Meditations on the Six Days of Creation.* London, 1717. Reprinted with introduction by George Herbert Guffey. Los Angeles: William Andrews Clark Memorial Library, 1966.

———. *Thomas Traherne: Centuries, Poems, and Thanksgivings.* Edited by H. M. Margoliouth. 2 vols. Oxford: At the Clarendon Press, 1958.

Trapp, J. B. "The Iconography of the Fall of Man." In *Approaches to Paradise Lost: The York Tercentenary Lectures,* ed. C. A. Patrides. Toronto: University of Toronto Press, 1968.

Treip, Mindele. " 'Celestial Patronage': *Paradise Lost* and Allegorical Ceiling Cycles of the 1630's in Italy and England." In *Milton in Italy: Contexts, Images, Contradictions,* ed. Mario A. Di Cesare. Binghamton: Medieval and Renaissance Texts and Studies, 1991.

———. *"Descend from Heav'n Urania": Milton's "Paradise Lost" and Raphael's Cycle in the Stanza della Segnatura.* ELS Monograph Series, 35. Victoria, B.C.: University of Victoria, 1985.

Trinkaus, Charles. *The Scope of Renaissance Humanism.* Ann Arbor: University of Michigan Press, 1983.

Turner, James Grantham. *One Flesh: Paradisal Marriage and Sexual Relations in the Age of Milton.* Oxford: At the Clarendon Press, 1987.

Tuve, Rosamund. *A Reading of George Herbert.* Chicago: University of Chicago Press, 1952.

Valerian [Joannis Pieri Valeriani Bellunensis]. *Hieroglyphica, sev de sacris Aegyptiorvm aliarvmque gentium literis commentarii.* Lyon, 1610.

———. *Les Hieroglyphiques de Ian-Pierre Valerian vulgairement nommé Piervs . . . Novvellement donnez avx François par I[ean] de Montlyart.* Lyon, 1615. Facsimile, *The Renaissance and the Gods.* Edited by Stephen Orgel, New York: Garland, 1976.

Van den Berg, Sara. "Eve, Sin, and Witchcraft in *Paradise Lost.*" *MLQ* 47 (1987): 347-65.

Vaughan, Henry. *The Works of Henry Vaughan.* Edited by L. C. Martin. Oxford: At the Clarendon Press, 1957.

Vendler, Helen. *The Poetry of George Herbert.* Cambridge, Mass.: Harvard University Press, 1975.

Virgil. *The Georgics.* Translated by L. P. Wilkinson. Harmondsworth: Penguin Books, 1984.

Vondel, Joost van den. *Adam in Exile (Adam in Ballingschap).* 1664. Translated by Watson Kirkconnell in *The Celestial Cycle.* Toronto: University of Toronto Press, 1952.

Voragine, Jacobus. *The legende named in Latyne Legenda aurea that is to saye in Englysshe the golden legend.* London, 1527.

Vos, Rik. *Lucas van Leyden.* Bentveld: Landshoff; Maarssen: G. Schwartz, 1978.

Wade, Gladys I. *The Poetical Works of Thomas Traherne.* New York: Cooper Square Publishers, 1965.

Walker, D. P. *Studies in Musical Science in the Late Renaissance.* Studies of the Warburg Institute, 37. London: Warburg Institute, University of London, 1978.

Warren, Frederick E., trans. *The Sarum Missal in English.* 2 vols. London: A. R. Mowbray; Milwaukee: Young Churchman, 1913.

Wehrman, Golda. "Midrash in *Paradise Lost:* Capitula Rabbi Elieser." *MS* 18 (1983): 145-71.

Weitzmann, Kurt. "The Genesis Mosaics of San Marco and the Cotton Genesis Miniatures." In Otto Demus, *The Mosaics of San Marco in Venice.* Vol. 2: *The Thirteenth Century.* Chicago: University of Chicago Press, 1984.

Wentersdorf, Karl P. "*Paradise Lost* IX: The Garden and the Flowered Couch." *MQ* 13 (1979): 134-41.

Whitney, Geffrey. *A Choice of Emblemes.* Leyden, 1586.

Willett, Andrew. *Limbo-mastix . . . shewing . . . invincible reasons . . . that Christ descended not in soule to hell to deliver the Fathers from thence.* London, 1604.

Williamson, George C., gen. ed. *Bryan's Dictionary of Painters and Engravers.* 5 vols. Rev. ed. London: George Bell and Sons, 1904-5.

Wither, George. *A Collection of Emblemes Ancient and Moderne (1635).* Introduction by Rosemary Freeman, bibliographical notes by Charles S. Hensley. Columbia, S.C.: University of South Carolina Press, 1975.

Wither, George, and Orlando Gibbons. *Hymns and Songs of the Church.* London, 1623.

Wittreich, Joseph. *Feminist Milton.* Ithaca: Cornell University Press, 1987.

Woolf, Virginia. *The Diary of Virginia Woolf.* Vol. 1. Edited by Anne Olivier Bell. New York: Harcourt Brace Jovanovich, 1977.

Wormald, Francis. *The Winchester Psalter.* Greenwich, Conn.: New York Graphic Society, 1973.

Wulstan, David. *Tudor Music.* Iowa City: University of Iowa Press, 1986.

# Index

111; Ps. 117, 73, 95, 99*n7*, 111, 135, 139–40, 150*n72*; Ps. 148, 52, 53, 138, 150*n72*; Ps. 150, 150*n72*, 214*n10*

Psalters: Coverdale's, 70*n113*. *See also* Manuscript illustrations

Puttenham, George, 127

Pythagorus, 4, 122, 211; "masculine" and "feminine" numbers, 150*n71*

Queboorn, C. van den, 104*n70*

Quilligan, Maureen, 203, 205

Radzinowicz, Mary Ann, 150*n72*

Raimondi, Marcantonio 99*n9*

Ralegh, Sir Walter, 116, 130

Ramus, Petrus, 146–47*n22*

Raphael, Archangel, 75–76, 108, 128, 133, 185, 197; mentioned passim

Raphael Sanzio, 27, 31–32, 64*n37*, 99*n9*, 159, 209–12

Réau, Louis, 103*n48*

Reformation: iconoclasm of, 19; iconography of, 28, 29, 30, 34, 35, 41, 38–39, 91; interpretation of the Fall, 158–60; music of, 112. *See also* Calvin

Religious discourse, philosophical validity of, 15–16*n31*

Rembrandt. *See* Rijn, Rembrandt van

Revelation, Book of, 86

Reynolds, Henry, 64–65*n40*

Rijn, Rembrandt van, 161, 162

Ripa, Cesare, 76, 83, 102*n35*

Rizzo, Antonio, 61*n10*

Roston, Murray, 61*n3*

Rubens, Peter Paul, 62*n20*, 91, 99, 102*n28*, 159

Sabbath, institution or sanctification of, 73–74, 136, 201

Sadeler, Jan, 23, 30, 71–72, 92, 200, *figs.* 17–21

Saenredam, Jan, 61*n10*, 75–77, 98, *figs.* 47–52

St. Cecilia, 147*n27*

St. George, 118, 147*n27*

Salandra, Serafino della, 181*n33*

Salisbury Cathedral, Chapter House, 24, 36

Samson, 28, 45, 46

San Marco, Basilica of, 34, 36–44, *figs.* 27–29

Sandler, Lucy Freeman, 68*n91*, 102*n29*

Sandys, George, 138

Santa Maria Novella, Florence, 52

Sarum Group, embroiderers, 104*n60*

Satan: in Anglo-Saxon *Genesis,* 49; as female figure, 61. *See also* Serpent

Satan in *Paradise Lost,* 106–7; abuse of language, 126, 134; failure of imagination, 129

Savery, Jacques, I, 103*n41*

Savery, Roelandt, 91, 200

Scheits, Matthias, 97, *fig.* 58

Schleiner, Louise, 142, 151*n81*

Schorsch, Anita, 61*n11*, 102*n34*

Schwartz, Regina, 16*n35*, 101*n24*, 150*n72*, 194

*Sept Ages du Monde, Les. See* Manuscript illustrations: *Seven Ages of the World*

Serpent, representations of, 20, 29, 58, 74

Seth, 25, 46, 74

Shakespeare, William: quoted, 5, 82–83, 107, 195; mentioned, 127; works mentioned, 178

Shoaf, Richard, 14*n18*

Sidney, Sir Philip, 127, 134, 135, 142

Signorelli, Luca, 26

Slatyer, William. *See* Langeren, Jacob Floris van

Smart, Christopher, 127

Snyder, James, 102*n29*

Solaro, 62*n19*

Solis, Virgil, 57

Son of God in *Paradise Lost:* begetting of, 174; language of, 120–21; presentation of repentant prayers of Adam and Eve, 174–77. *See also* Christ; Incarnation

Song of Solomon, 199–200

*Speculum Humanae Salvationis. See* Manuscript illustrations

Speed, John, Genealogies, 58, 66*n55*

Spenser, Edmund, 83, 95, 127, 213*n4*

Spranger, Bartholomeus, 82, 161, 162, *fig.* 60

Stone, Merlin, 6–7, 15*nn24, 26*

Stroup, Thomas B., 145*n14*

DIANE KELSEY MCCOLLEY (A.B., University of California, Berkeley; Ph.D., University of Illinois) is associate professor of English at Rutgers, the State University of New Jersey, Camden College of Arts and Sciences. She is the author of *Milton's Eve* (Urbana: University of Illinois Press, 1983) and numerous articles and essays, a past president of the Milton Society of America (1990), and a member of the editorial board of *Milton Studies* (1992).